A 6P 8. 00

D0036804

CHINESE
VILLAGE,
SOCIALIST
STATE

CHINESE VILLAGE, SOCIALIST STATE

Edward Friedman

Paul G. Pickowicz

Mark Selden

with Kay Ann Johnson

Yale University Press

New Haven & London

Published with assistance from China Publication Subventions.

Copyright © 1991 by Yale University.

All rights reserved.

This book may not be reproduced, in whole or in part, including illustrations, in any form (beyond that copying permitted Sections 107 and 108 of the U.S. Copyright Law and except by reviewers for the public press), without written permission from the publishers.

Designed by Sonia L. Scanlon.

Set in Galliard type be Keystone Typesetting, Inc., Orwigsburg, Pennsylvania.

Printed in the United States of America by BookCrafters, Inc., Chelsea, Michigan.

Library of Congress Cataloging–in–Publication Data

Friedman, Edward.

    Chinese village, socialist state/Edward Friedman, Paul G. Pickowicz, Mark Selden with Kay Ann Johnson.

      p. cm.

    Includes bibliographical references and index.

    ISBN 0-300-04655-3 (cloth)

    0-300-05428-9 (pbk.)

     1. China—Rural conditions. I. Pickowicz, Paul. II. Selden, Mark.

HN733.5.F75 1991   90-71877

307.72'0951'15—dc20   CIP

A catalogue record for this book is available from the British Library.

The paper in this book meets the guidelines for permanence and durability of the Committee on Production Guidelines for Book Longevity of the Council on Library Resources.

10   9   8   7   6   5   4   3

For Joanna, Ken, Lili,
Natasha, Ruth, and Yumi

CONCORDIA UNIVERSITY LIBRARY
PORTLAND. OR 97211

✵ CONTENTS

❖ ILLUSTRATIONS

Photographs follow pages 110 and 184

Maps

Figures

Tables

❦ ACKNOWLEDGMENTS

In the course of a decade we have accumulated debts to numerous colleagues, friends, family members, and associates. We particularly wish to thank the many professionals who worked through innumerable drafts of this book, particularly Kathy Kruger, Gail Newton, Mary Reardon, Lori Schlinkert, and Michelle Zweifel at the University of Wisconsin, Nancy Hall of the Department of Sociology and Gloria Gaumer, Lisa Fegley-Schmidt, and the members of the University Manuscript Center at the State University of New York at Binghamton, and Donna Andrews at the University of California, San Diego. Our manuscript editor, Cynthia Carter Ayres, and Laura Jones Dooley and Charles Grench of Yale University Press, ably guided the manuscript to publication.

For sharing their notes, numbers, and impressions of Wugong with us, we are most grateful to D. Gale Johnson, Theodore Schultz, Andrew Watson, Greg O'Leary, Peter Nolan, Keith Griffin, Neville Maxwell, Ashwani Saith, Eugene Dorris, and Louis Putterman.

We developed feelings of warmth and respect for the hundreds of villagers we met and came to know over the years, especially Wugong's deceased leader Geng Changsuo, as well as Yang Tong, Zhang Chaoke, Qiao Liguang, Li Shouzheng, Li Zhongxin, Xu Yizhou, Geng Lianmin, Li Maoxiu, Li Lu, Li Xiuying, Shi Guiying, Wang Pengju, Zhang Mandun, Zhou Yuanjiu, Geng Xiufeng, and Zou Liji.

Our respective universities provided support in the form of travel grants and leave time for research for which we are deeply grateful. Edward Friedman received University of Wisconsin grants as well as support from the American Council of Learned Societies, the Wang Foundation, and the American Philosophical Society. Paul Pickowicz received support from the National Academy of Sciences, Ambrica Productions, and the University of California, San Diego. Mark Selden received grants from the State University of New York at Binghamton, the American Council of Learned Societies, and a SUNY-Binghamton Dean's Research Semester leave for writing.

❦ INTRODUCTION

Chinese Village, Socialist State portrays society in the North China plain, highlighting how families, villagers, and local leaders grappled with an emerging socialism that shaped life chances. It focuses on how new state leaders introduced reforms that permitted a far more equitable society and reknit disintegrating families and communities during China's revolution.[1] It goes on to explore the factors that limited further achievements and even undermined or reversed early achievements as a new system was established. The book details the building and entrenchment of a system that strengthened some of the least humane aspects of the culture and failed to resolve historically rooted problems, leaving China's people trapped in painful and humiliating dilemmas. In describing shattering change in the rural hinterland, the book focuses on aspects of nationalism, peasantry, poverty, state, and socialism whose impact extends well beyond the almost one-quarter of humanity that is Chinese. It charts a long decline in the presocialist era that shredded social bonds, which was followed by a revolution that restored human ties in a joyous honeymoon era of unity and achievement, only to be succeeded by another unraveling as the state imposed communist fundamentals on villagers, leaving them bereft of the blessings of the modern world.

The data were gathered starting in May 1978 when good luck made us the first American social scientists to conduct systematic research in the countryside of the People's Republic. We asked to go where villagers spoke a standard Mandarin that would permit us to work without translators. We ruled out both suburban areas, where proximity to cities facilitated economic success, and heroic mountain villages long intertwined with the revolutionary army. To reduce contemporary reliance on politicized memories of the old days and to provide a benchmark for gauging change, we sought a North China plain area that social scientists had studied before 1949.

The Chinese authorities suggested Raoyang county, which had been the southeastern tip of Dingxian prefecture in central Hebei province. Sidney Gamble's classic volumes *Ting Hsien* (Dingxian) and *North China Villages* proved wonderful introductions to the regional economy and culture.[2] In May 1978, visiting the Zoucun village market in Raoyang, we found elderly men having their heads shaved precisely as pictured in Gamble's *Ting Hsien*. When asked why he had a barber shave his head, one customer replied, "So that my hair won't fall out." Even today young men shave their heads, believing it will stimulate hair growth and reverse receding hairlines. There was much to learn about persistent tradition. Culture, in all its evolving diversity, pervaded and infused meaning and purpose. This book attempts to understand the deeper continuities of culture in relation to rapid changes in other realms.

Cultural norms that suffuse peasant life—including governance—do not make villages idyllic and harmonious communities. Cultural presuppositions and culturally approved behavior incorporated much that was violent, cruel, and life negating. In fact, the Communist party's army rooted its state power in the cultural expressions of tough, parochial young males. While trying to liberate traditional villagers from life-negating superstitions, the new order actually strengthened some violent and repressive strands in the culture.

To check the authors' understanding of the culture, the manuscript was given for critical reading to two American graduate students, both former residents of the region. Each corrected factual errors, provided additional information, suggested changing a few readings each found too negative on village culture, and helped decipher underlying meanings. The authors acted on these readers' corrections and suggestions and are especially grateful for continuing assistance and insight to Cheng Tiejun, who grew up in a Raoyang village.

Raoyang, 120 miles south of Beijing, was named Rao in 239 B.C. during the Warring States period when the monarch of Zhao presented the territory as a gift to a loyal nobleman.[3] Zhao, with its capital at Handan, 120 miles southwest of Rao, was the birthplace of China's first unifier, Qin Shi Huangdi.[4] The area was renamed Raoyang in 206 B.C. during the reign of Han dynasty founder Emperor Gaodi. The town wall was completed in the Song dynasty (960–1279) and rebuilt on a larger scale in the last years of the Ming (1368–1644). In the early twentieth century, Raoyang was the poorest county in relatively prosperous Dingxian prefecture, but in 1962 it became part of Hengshui, then the poorest prefecture in all Hebei province. Even in the 1980s Raoyang remained remote from modern rail and water transport to the major cities of Beijing, Tianjin, Baoding, and Shijiazhuang.

On that first research trip, in addition to three Raoyang villages, we investigated villages in neighboring Anping and Shenxian counties. We found, as Gamble had a half-century earlier, diversity in income, in economic and cultural activity, in lineage relations, and in ties to the state. There was, and is, no typical village. This book presents a spectrum of villages with diverse resources and social and cultural traditions, which interacted with the state in different ways. Yet all Raoyang was poor. Capturing how bad soil, unreliable water supplies, and climatic scourges had long made life difficult for Raoyang villagers, was the old saying, "Barren in spring, flooded in summer, the cultivated land could hardly nurture seedlings; alkali was everywhere and no food grew."

Although the Communist party, in trying to improve life, both adapted to and transformed peasant values and social relations, Chinese villagers—including party members—kept to their own agenda. Even when the party brought economic gain and cultural healing, center and hinterland were frequently at odds. Over time personal networks grew, connecting the system in complex and contradictory ways. The structure was not merely top down. Villagers were not pawns permitting socialist kings to push them around. Local leaders tried to woo and win the resources controlled by higher-ups. Villagers and their allies and patrons among officials also tried, as they had for many generations under various regimes, to dodge, deflect, and blunt the impact of demands detrimental to local interests and values. Those negative impacts gradually eroded the new state's popular legitimacy.

To capture more of this rich reality, on leaving China we explored Asian and American research collections and archives. Useful sources included an eighteenth-century Raoyang gazetteer, government surveys of the region published in the early twentieth century, and a wealth of provincial newspapers, radio broadcasts, and Chinese-language books and articles. The Chinese periodicals published since 1949 and collected in the Union Research Institute in Hong Kong contained detailed material on Raoyang and central Hebei. These sources revealed that Wugong, the village among the five investigated that the authorities presented as exemplifying China's socialist success, in 1953 was regarded as one of several hundred models of building socialism in the countryside. It was presented to the populace as it was to us, a typical place embodying what socialism had won for the rural poor.[5]

The gap between documentary research and the tales recounted in rural China made it clear that interviewing in the People's Republic is very different from interviewing in Hong Kong. Works on rural China by Anita Chan, Richard Madsen, Jonathan Unger, Ezra Vogel, Jean Oi, Martin Whyte, William Parish, and Bernard Frolic, based on interviewing in Hong Kong, have the advantage of having been conducted in an atmosphere free of the presence of an intrusive state.[6] Interviewees in Raoyang hewed to the policy line of the moment. Indeed, villagers had been instructed to accentuate the accomplishments of the Cultural Revolution and warned to tell nothing of the hard times in the famine caused by the Great Leap Forward. Life itself had taught people to be cautious and correct in their public utterances.

Yet there were advantages to interviewing in the village and region. We observed our informants interact with villagers and officials. We won access to vital local records. Eventually we located losers in local policy and power struggles who were delighted to recount their side of stories. Over a decade, we met interviewees again and again as events unfolded, as policy lines shifted, and as our ability grew to use reliable data as a basis for more-informed probing. Most interesting, many local leaders in post-Mao Raoyang continued to defend the Cultural Revolution and the Great Leap and to resist post-Mao reforms. Officials did not race to embrace reform.

In thousands of hours of formal and informal interviewing and discussion, we developed leads which, when added to documentary material, directed us to suppressed truths. To get beyond the official story, we interviewed all households on lanes chosen at random, gossiped at the barber shop and noodle stands, and found ways to meet outside the region both with local people and with outsiders who had worked in the county. When this method permitted us to unravel the twists and turns in a 1953 power struggle, a county official commented, "Congratulations! You figured it out." But it was not his job to help outsiders penetrate hidden realities.

A portion of the holdings in the Raoyang County Archive, which held classified inner-party reports to higher authorities, was photographed. We gained access to village clipping files and runs of the prefectural newspaper, which are restricted inside China to those registered as residents of the prefecture. The village accountant of more than thirty years handed over his record books covering the years from 1944 forward and responded in detail to questions based on other documents about the content and lacunae of the records. In 1978, in 1984, and in 1987, household surveys were conducted on the changing demographic, economic, income, educational, and political patterns of the previous half-century. Some of this material is summarized in tables throughout the book and in the appendix.

Librarians and archivists in Beijing and in the Hebei provincial capital, Shijiazhuang, made available uncataloged books and articles. We were also able to locate key figures in particular historical events who had since moved elsewhere. Archives in Taiwan contain valuable materials on the anti-Japanese resistance and land-reform periods in central Hebei that were captured from the Communist side during China's civil war. Journalists, artists, writers, local historians, and researchers from Beijing, Tianjin, Shijiazhuang, and Hengshui offered their experiences and insights. Other students of rural China who visited Wugong generously shared their numbers, notes, and impressions.[7] In addition, we took to the village agricultural specialists who could see much that we could not. Particularly helpful were D. Gale Johnson, a specialist on Soviet-type rural economies, and Theodore Schultz, a Nobel Prize–winning economist with great expertise in rural development. None of these helpful individuals is responsible for the general picture we paint.

This book recounts what could be pieced together by combining documentary and interview sources. Although we recorded the words of some informants, we did not attempt to present the content of interviews with several hundred villagers and officials. Documentary and archival data, which are noted, provided checks on the validity of interviews, and vice versa.

The research generated political, economic, social, cultural, and historical data on Wugong village, Raoyang county, and the North China hinterland as they established links to the upper reaches of the state. It is the state-society nexus, not the village, that is the focus of this book. Information on Raoyang county, Hebei province, and rural North China situates villagers historically and structurally within a dynamic and diverse state-society milieu. The data bring into focus informal networks of loyalty and mutual support that were formed before the conquest of national power. These networks channeled scarce resources—jobs, travel, medicine, investment, technicians, and so on— to favored communities, regions, and families. Villagers compelled to rely merely on their own production of grain fell behind.

Only a few favored places could enter the hierarchically privileged orbit of the new regime. The sad fate of excluded, forgotten, and sometimes devastated towns and villages, such as Yincun, Yanggezhuang, Gengkou, and Zoucun, a fate shared by most Raoyang communities, is an integral and complementary part of the story of their state-favored neighbor, Wugong. The pattern of the favored few and the excluded many has been played out with variations all across socialist China. Entrenched networks of privilege and power were decisive in shaping winners and losers. The book shows how a gap grew ever wider between the favored and the excluded.[8]

Viewing Raoyang as representative of significant aspects of China's vast rural hinterland at the periphery of foreign influence, major world markets, and modern industry, this book begins by exploring the failed reforms both of the imperial regime and of the early republic, and then sketches forces that generated peasant revolution and the rise of a socialist state. Focusing on the state-society nexus, we treat Wugong village as a node in the political networks that helped constitute the new system. The networks linking a favored village to officials at local, county, prefectural, and even provincial and national levels became ever more entrenched after the establishment of the People's Republic in 1949. This book chronicles that entrenchment, showing how it was shaped by forces at work prior to the arrival of the revolutionary army. The book is in harmony with historian Paul Cohen's admonition "to break through the '1949' barrier" and find continuity, not just rupture.[9]

Wugong was more than a node whose evolving ties and networks reveal the sinews in the anatomy of the socialist system. The village also helped pioneer culturally acceptable forms of cooperation in the 1940s, as well as Soviet collective institutions in the early 1950s, and more fundamentalist ones thereafter. Its history offers a contrast between an era of popular reforms and voluntary cooperatives and the far less happy results of taking the Soviet socialist road. In spite of the advantages of leadership, unity, and resources, not even a state favorite could race ahead in periods of fundamentalist policies that attempted rapidly to realize communist ideals. Destructive outcomes were probable in communities bereft of a favored village's special benefits.

The party-led effort at first inaugurated life-enhancing policies that met basic human needs and eliminated major forms of intravillage property-based inequality during the 1938 to 1952 era of popular reforms and silent revolution that began with the anti-Japanese resistance. But when the new rulers attempted to level all differences between poorer and more prosperous households, when they eliminated the mixed economy by curbing markets and imposing traditional Soviet collectivist socialism and enforced yet more fundamentalist policies, the effort boomeranged. The gap between better-off and destitute regions, communities, and families grew. Rather than propelling the economy forward, fundamentalist policies of extirpating everything private, customary, and market oriented, everything not in harmony with communist values, stalled the economy or even sent it into terrifying reverse. This book traces the origins and dynamics of that debilitating process. Not even its tragic consequences for the powerless rural poor during the Great Leap Forward could break or budge the networks that further institutionalized themselves in the post-Leap reforms with which this book concludes. A system called socialism had been entrenched.

Virtually none of the themes of historic continuity that this book details was highlighted by Chinese officials. Throughout, their concern was legitimating their policies by constructing a historical legend. Officials easily concealed essentials and misled short-term foreign researchers. Even the most decisive social relations can be invisible to outsiders.

Everyone in Wugong, even little children, knew that lineage conflict had, in the socialist era, excluded from power the once-dominant lineages residing in the village's center. We watched a father, walking with his son in the village center, point to a solid wooden gate and explain that the home had once belonged to a member of the old elite. Even in 1978 ordinary villagers could not afford such an expensive wooden gate. We could not ourselves readily distinguish among woods or experience what a local person felt on seeing a gate hewn of fine wood in this region where scarce and expensive timber is vital for home building, coffins, and show.

In fact, we were in the village twelve days before realizing that we had been introduced to no one from the village center, formerly the bastion of Li lineage power. Since the sixth century A.D. the Lis had been on top in Wugong. Every child knew it. Even old gates told the story. The Lis lost in the long twentieth-century revolution. Whereas lineage relations and residence propinquity defined winners and losers in the local power game, and although this history lived in anecdotes and artifacts reflecting centuries-old patterns of settlement, power, and land access, those relations were invisible to outsiders.

China's famous anthropologist Fei Xiaotong advised us to look for the invisible.[10] This book begins to fill in the picture obscured by official categories. The book moves up, down, and across a large canvas, up to prefecture, province, state center, and the international order, through party, state, and military networks. It moves down to villages, lineages, and households, and then across to try to paint in the culture, values, markets, and personal networks that helped connect Chinese society, shaping revolutionary prospects, socialist state building, and a repressive, dictatorial polity.

This study is different from the first-hand on-the spot accounts of land reform provided by C. K. Yang, William Hinton, and Isabel and David Crook, or by the novelist Yuan-tsung Chen.[11] These writers recount events they witnessed. In contrast, this story of the vicissitudes of state-society linkages begins centuries ago and ends seventeen years before the authors entered Raoyang county. Many people did reminisce, but too often their memories conflicted with the documentary record.[12] We dug to find data to verify interviews.

The prod to continuing research was the conflict between the official legend and documented history. The official story presented in 1978 ignored a shared culture and highlighted destructive class struggle. According to that story, a rich few once exploited the poor majority; the poor then rebelled and joined the revolutionary army; the party-state that army brought to power led people to a popular collective path that won prosperity, dignity, and security for the once poor and oppressed. In fact, the children of the old elite took leadership roles in the revolution. In fact, socialism did not bring prosperity to the poor.

A key to penetrating official legends was the opportunity to return eighteen times over a ten-year period to observe the continuity embedded in proclaimed changes and to follow up on data at odds with the official story. By 1984 it was clear that the recent campaign to bring new blood into the party, symbolized in Wugong village by making Zhang Mandun party secretary, changed little. True, young Mandun was the first person surnamed Zhang residing in the east village to hold village power. But his mother was the oldest child of the powerful local boss of almost four decades, Geng Changsuo. Geng's only adult grandson through a male line was a banker in urban Baoding. The party patriarch passed the torch of community power through the family line as best he could. Research had unearthed elements of the invisible, disclosing how deeply structured cultural forces shape state and society even in a socialist order.

In repeated conversations with villagers as well as with scores of national, provincial, prefectural, county, commune, village, and neighborhood officials, we explored the diverse accounts and the conflicting data revealed in documents and interviews. Gradually clues led to four larger patterns that the book describes: the dynamics of the party-state hierarchy, cultural continuities, a new nationalism, and the persistence of generations-old dilemmas and conflicts intensified by turmoil and war in the early decades of the twentieth century, and subsequently by policies of the socialist state.

During that initial month-long stay in North China when an official legend was first spun out, a request to interview the sole surviving landlord in the village, Li Maoxiu, was deflected. Local officials warned that the landlord might confuse us with lies and slanders. We persisted. County official Li Guanghui responded, "We'll arrange the interview." But, he added, "It will be necessary first to convene an all-village meeting to explain that you insist on talking with a class enemy. Villagers may be unwilling to speak to you after that is explained." That seemed too high a price.

Two years and four visits later, County Li[13] responded to a research agenda, "Fine, but don't you want to interview landlord Li Maoxiu?" Indeed we did. From 1980, conversation was possible with the rehabilitated Maoxiu, his wife Fan Shufang, and their entire family. Officials no longer tried to limit interviews to leaders, activists, models, heroic soldiers, the exploited of old, and the prosperous of today. As a result, this portrait of village life adds not only landlords, but also nuns, rapists, and wife beaters, Daoists and AWOL soldiers, the physically handicapped and young toughs, past leaders, fallen leaders, and the victims and adversaries of the powerful, the still poor and the once prosperous, propagandists, teachers, writers and artists, people who never participated in a political movement and those who suffered political opprobrium, including those dubbed class enemies and sent to prison labor camps, innocent victims turned into scapegoats, people like "landlord" Li Maoxiu and Shi Xishen, the tractor station chief who was punished for twenty-five years for refuting the economic irrationality of the Great Leap Forward.

A more complex and nuanced world emerged in the greater openness of the post-Mao era. The trips that permitted research to edge closer to core truths were made possible by the reform policy of opening to the world. Although there continued to be an official story, there also was easier access to villagers with diverse experiences and perspectives.[14] Raoyang officials, however, held to much of the prereform story.

To test the validity of our findings, an early draft of the manuscript was given to local officials. It was translated at the provincial level and read aloud to people mentioned in the text. This facilitated the correction of factual errors, including places, names, dates, offices, relations, and chronology. We are grateful for this help.

Local officials also argued against conclusions they found flawed, what they saw as bourgeois interpretations of events, and a slighting of class struggle and socialist achievement. Interpretive differences were discussed at length, at times with great emotion. Local officials did not want this book to include accounts of traditional cannibalism in time of famine, anti-American currents, local torture, official corruption, brutality, doctored statistics, and famine unto death in the Great Leap. All of these, however, are recorded in this book.

In the course of dialogue, of challenge and counterchallenge, people were interviewed again and again in efforts to probe further. Some individuals were approached dozens of times and at great length over a decade. This ability to discuss new and conflicting data with villagers and with writers, officials, researchers, and others was essential for getting beyond the legend.

For all the on-the-spot interviewing, this book largely remains a work of standard scholarship, utilizing archives, libraries, survey research, documents, and the achievements of numerous scholars. On so many topics, from a republican-era tax crisis to the tax reforms that helped legitimate Communist leaders,[15] to Frederick Teiwes's account of the class-struggle land reform of 1948,[16] to Chinese revelations in the 1980s of disputes between Deng Zihui and Mao Zedong in the 1950s,[17] to Jean-Luc Domenach's study of the big rural units (*da she*) of 1953 to 1958,[18] to Fei Xiaotong's analysis of collectiviz-ation in 1955–56,[19] to the politics and consequences of the famine of the Great Leap, ably described by Roderick MacFarquhar and by Thomas Berns-tein,[20] this work builds on or is at one with the impressive achievements of international scholarship.

Some scholars, such as Chalmers Johnson,[21] contend that peasant na-tionalism was the key to Communist victory, whereas others, such as Robert Marks and Mark Selden,[22] stress the importance of reforms in winning peasants to the revolutionary movement. This book finds merit in both explanations. It depicts how the patriotism of poor villagers combined with a commitment to social revolution and explores why many among the na-tionalistic elite promoted the socialist cause. If earlier debates in the profes-sion seem less divisive, there are new debates.

A number of recent scholarly works, including several analyses focused on the North China plain, highlight a long-term systemic crisis in Chinese economy and society. But they differ profoundly in assessing the character and cause of the forces holding back national development. Although the initial chapter of this book sketches features of that crisis, it does not introduce sufficient data to join the debate on decline in the late imperial era.[23] How-ever, our data suggest a long-term decline in the rural hinterland, as do Kang Chao and Philip Huang.[24]

Consistent with the findings of Japanese (Mantetsu) researchers and Ra-mon Myers on the strength of the traditional economy,[25] the book shows how rural markets historically permitted villagers to earn needed cash from peddling, trading, laboring, and selling household sideline products. By the twentieth century, however, this rural hinterland was in the throes of disin-tegration, threatening both the rural elite and the poor, who tilled the land or found their margin of survival in off-farm employment.[26]

Children of the old elite turned against the regime of their parents, whose incapacity to defend against Japanese invaders or succor China's people de-stroyed legitimacy. These radicalized, patriotic, elite youth enlisted villagers from all strata to join them in a Communist party led multiclass struggle.

People rallied to a program of resistance and reform. Centered on tax reform, the reforms brought a silent, liberating, and equalizing revolution to the North China rural base areas.

Successful resistance and reform created a honeymoon atmosphere of broad popular support for the rising socialist state, for building a rich, strong nation and developing an economy that would bring dignity and security for all, particularly for the poorest of villagers. The honeymoon atmosphere continued after the conquest of national power. As this book underscores, 1949 and the founding of the People's Republic cannot be conceived as a complete rupture with the past, the end of the old order and the beginning of the new.

Another long, strong continuity lay in the popular passions of patriotism. Nationalism had taken root among rural intellectuals before Communist party and Red Army organizers began recruiting in the villages. Patriotism was institutionalized during the anti-Japanese war as a powerful force. In addition, important elements of peasant political culture and values persisted and imposed their shaping force on the new state. This complex culture sometimes worked against and sometimes in harmony with socialist policies.[27] Increasingly, however, a foreign notion of socialism conflicted with customary ways of cooperation. The first conflicts were manifest by 1944.

The new system confronted deeply rooted, almost intractable problems: weakness, disunity, technological backwardness, and mass poverty. These had bedeviled Chinese rulers for centuries. Such problems would not be readily solved by the new rulers either. By focusing on deep continuities that transcend the founding of the People's Republic, we provide a basis for inquiring to what extent collectivist socialism was a solution, a hindrance, or even irrelevant to the problems of the countryside and of national development.

A negative continuity highlighted in this volume is market disruption. At one with the scholarship of Peter Perdue,[28] Kang Chao, and Loren Brandt, we find the market far more central to economic well-being in the traditional hinterland than did an earlier generation of researchers. So vital were market activities, even to poor tillers, that the market disruption and social disorder caused by war, political chaos, and foreign intervention ruined many villagers. The war on the market launched to build socialism continued to injure the poorest of the poor, locking them into their poverty.

When ruling groups abandoned reform policies rooted in broad-based alliances and compatible with popular consciousness and, instead, destroyed markets, traditional culture, and the household economy, they froze consumption at miserably low levels. The honeymoon ended when policies premised on Soviet prescriptions and communist fundamentalism were imposed. Ruling groups, in the name of preventing class polarization and the return of reactionary classes, splintered society, alienated people, and destroyed human relationships.[29] These delegitimating policies built on ideological and institutional tendencies that were already at work in the revolution before 1949, such as treating cross-class village unity and a flourishing peasant household economy as feudal and capitalist evils. Again, 1949 is not an absolute divide. Labeling villagers as members of good and evil classes, and using expropriation and violence against the supposedly evil classes long after the largest concentrations of private wealth had been eliminated through popular reforms, frightened many villagers even before 1949. People survived in part by learning to play the hypocrite, turning a false face to the powerful.

In this milieu of intimidation, some of the most vengeful village men moved to the fore in local politics. Nasty strains in the culture heightened the cruelty in irrational fundamentalist policies. In 1947, when cruelties in land reform shattered village unities, the competitive character of the civil war forced party leaders to back away from destructive and unpopular policies. Once they held a monopoly of power, however, some party leaders abandoned the popular reform approach. Even before 1949, party machines recruited on the basis of loyalty. These personal networks would adopt almost any policy from the center in order to retain power. Even before 1949, a pervasive police system modeled on Stalin's and a willingness to use force mercilessly silenced potential opponents and dissidents.

By 1953, in a little-known tragedy, villagers in poor Yanggezhuang already were devastated by socialism's war on rural commerce. The state seized monopoly control of the grain trade and imposed fixed low prices in order to channel the rural surplus to nation building, military expenses, and urban-based heavy industry. Villagers in Yanggezhuang, deprived of commercial and sideline income, declined economically. The war on the petty economy also wounded cherished cultural forms that had been restored and celebrated in the honeymoon era of revolutionary victory, peace, unity, and development. Market and culture were not hermetically sealed and separate realms. As the two were devastated together, the honeymoon atmosphere disappeared.

With the Great Leap Forward, the party treated popular mores and peasant norms as enemy forces. Even then, because revolution had built new networks of power and informed popular nationalistic identities, Mao Zedong and socialism remained legitimate in the rural hinterland. Loyal patriots blamed bad individuals, not Mao or the system. This book charts certain strands of violence-prone village culture working through militia, military, and a myth of Mao that bound tough village males to the socialist state.

This volume tries to illuminate the dynamics that pushed hopeful country people into the deadly Great Leap famine of 1959–61, in which millions perished. Leaders had to wonder what had happened to the high hopes for a modernizing socialist revolution.

Powerholders had much to rethink. In spite of everything, high ideals still motivated many people in state and village. Some among ruling groups would consider yet again whether popular reforms harking back to the achievements of the silent revolution of the 1940s and the honeymoon period of the early 1950s were needed to assure progress. Others committed to the dogmas of Leninist Marxism would consider whether the times demanded the traditional Stalin model or yet more rigorous imposition of the fundamentals of communism to carry forward revolution through class struggle. But the state of the revolution was no longer decided by this policy or that. Rather, there was an entrenched state of affairs that survived the trauma of famine intact and linked elements in village culture all too comfortably with a socialist state that seemed to operate along most traditional lines. The system blocked any easy opening to more liberating forms of modernity. This book details the creation and entrenchment of that system.

CHINESE
VILLAGE,
SOCIALIST
STATE

1 ⚬⚬⚬ THE COUNTY
DECLINES,
VILLAGES
DISINTEGRATE

In 1744, the ninth year of the Qianlong reign, a new magistrate, Shan Zuozhe, arrived in Raoyang. Much of what we know about economic, social, political, and cultural life in this small hinterland county in the years before it was affected by the revolutionary currents of the nineteenth and twentieth centuries is contained in a lengthy county gazetteer edited by Shan in 1749, in the wake of a state-sponsored campaign to spread Confucian ideology.[1] A glimpse of Raoyang at the height of the Qing dynasty offers a measure both of the decline that would follow and of continuities that not even revolution could transform.

Raoyang—seventeen miles from north to south and fifteen miles from east to west and one of the smallest counties in Zhili province—was located in Shenzhou prefecture, whose administrative center was twenty miles to the southwest. Because southern Zhili had suffered massive depopulation in the final chaotic years of the Yuan dynasty, it was regarded as a frontier region in the early Ming.[2] Waves of immigrants from neighboring Shanxi province, encouraged to resettle by the new state, flooded into the area. Between 1369 and 1404, there were 68 new villages founded in Raoyang alone. During the entire Qing period, by contrast, only 6 new villages were settled. Yet Raoyang's population continued to grow. In 1749 Raoyang had 175 villages, 23,753 households, and approximately 120,000 people.

The Political Economy of Raoyang

In 1749 Raoyang had 540,181 mu of farmland, averaging only 23 mu, or slightly fewer than four acres, per household. The principal crops, millet, corn, sorghum, and cotton, were sown in the spring

1

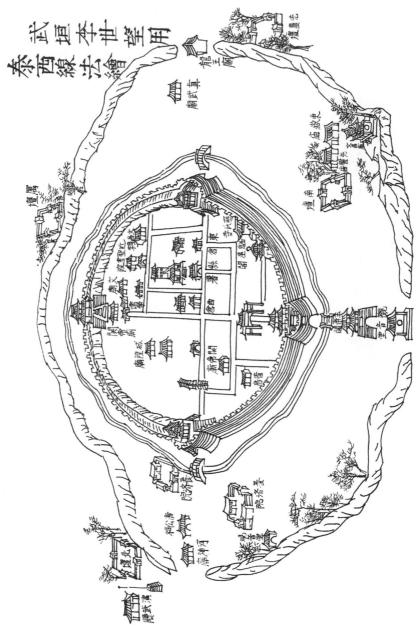

Figure 1 Raoyang Town, 1748. Illustration: Li Huai, 1990.

and reaped in the autumn. Some winter wheat was planted in the late fall and harvested in June. The smell of peppers, garlic, green onions, leeks, and yams permeated the mud-brick village homes. Horses, oxen, and donkeys were common beasts of burden; chickens, geese, ducks, sheep, and especially pigs provided sources of meat for rare splurges.

In this densely populated region, agriculture was the centerpiece of a more complex Raoyang economy. The most important sidelines were spinning cotton thread and weaving cotton cloth, tasks normally done by skilled women. Other enterprises included processing edible oils, distilling wine and vinegar, weaving reed baskets and mats, manufacturing soybean paste, and making rope, candles, salt, bricks, and fireworks. For many, selling agricultural and sideline products spelled the difference between subsistence and ruin; for a few, the market provided a route to relative prosperity and expanded landholdings. Cash was needed to purchase animals and tools and to pay the costs required for marriage, mourning, and festivals. To obtain cash, many looked to the market. Itinerant peddlers and such specialists as barbers, veterinarians, ropemakers, pig castraters, and coffinmakers followed the market from village to village. During the Song dynasty Raoyang had been known for making Rao silk headware for the emperor and high court officials. During the Qing it became known for a noodle soup delicacy, *zamian tang,* made with mung beans, wheat, and eggs. Raoyang pig castraters, some of whom matured into veterinarians, and barbers found work as far away as Mongolia; Raoyang fireworks—used even by the imperial household—were sold far and wide.

In 1749 Raoyang was laced with a bustling market network. Permanent daily markets operated within the walls of the town, as well as in Zhangpingpu (five miles west), Kongdian (seven miles north), Yanggezhuang (six miles southwest), and Xiaodi (ten miles southwest on the road to Shenzhou). Furthermore, periodic local markets were held at five-day intervals at twenty-two additional sites. In the south county, the focal point of this study, in addition to the daily markets in Yanggezhuang and Xiaodi, periodic markets were held in Zoucun on the first and sixth days of the ten-day marketing cycle, in Caozhuang on the second and seventh, in Hanhe on the third and eighth, in Xiaodi on the fourth and ninth, and in Zhangbao on the fifth and tenth. On any given day, most villagers were within a few miles of a market.

Government costs were paid for by a wide array of taxes. Agricultural taxes collected from landowners following the summer and autumn harvests were the most important. The common people also had to comply with corvée labor obligations, provide fodder for the magistrate's stable, pay levies on silk, black beans, and cotton, and pay special taxes on salt and alcohol.

In addition to the relatively new problem of "too many people and too little land," Raoyang peasants, like many of their neighbors on the North China plain, had been plagued for centuries by the twin curses of drought and flood. In 1737 the Hutuo River, which passed through the center of the county, flooded, inundating twenty-seven villages. In 1738 another flood engulfed forty-three villages. By 1742 corvée laborers finished digging seven drainage canals to prevent flooding. But in 1743, the year before Shan's arrival, a drought more destructive than the 1738 flood struck the entire region. The state sent substantial grain relief and silver to disaster districts. The grain was diverted westward from the Grand Canal, which ran through eastern Zhili. Raoyang's neighbors Hejian and Xianxian were among the counties classified as "total disasters" in 1744.[3] Between 1368 and 1749 natural catastrophes ravaged Raoyang an average of once every seven years.

The problems of drought and flood are related to special ecological conditions. Raoyang is in the middle of the 187,000 square mile North China plain. The Taihang Mountains rise 100 miles west of Raoyang, and the Pacific Ocean is 120 miles to the east.[4] In the clear and dry winter months stationary high-pressure cells over the central Asian steppes beyond the Taihang Mountains send cold southwesterly winds across the plain. By March, temperatures rise enough to permit spring plowing, but the weather remains dry. Some moisture is provided by patches of melted snow, but the short rainy season does not begin until midsummer, when the central Asian steppes heat up and a vast low-pressure system forms. Warm moist air is sucked in from the Pacific in a northwesterly direction across the plain. Annual precipitation in the Raoyang area averages only twenty inches, and as much as 70 percent of it may fall in July and August. By the middle of autumn the air is pleasantly cool and dry and the sky is clear.

Twenty inches per year is barely enough rain to support agriculture in localities like Raoyang that have few aboveground water sources. When spring and summer rains are light, the wind blows across the bone-dry plain, stirring clouds of fine dust and carrying away precious topsoil. If summer rains fail, there is little to harvest in the fall. Frequently the annual precipitation comes in a few localized thunderstorms so that drought-stricken areas adjoin clusters of villages that enjoy normal rainfall. In Shan's day the success of crops rested almost entirely on natural rainfall.

The problem of flooding is linked to the way rivers originating in the Taihang range flow down to the plain. In their upper reaches the rivers are narrow and move swiftly. But when rivers like the Hutuo, which cuts through Raoyang, reach the plain they slow down and spread out, depositing layer after layer of sediment. Gradually riverbeds rise. Consequently, heavy summer rains bring raging waters that spill over safety dikes. Low-lying areas are vulnerable to waterlogging from burst dikes and excessive rain. Crops rot when the water in the fields fails to penetrate the poor, claylike soil found throughout the region. Inadequate rainfall for most of the year means that contaminated saline soil cannot be leached naturally. Alkaline wasteland is covered by deposits of soda that resemble snow but are rock hard.[5]

In the mid-eighteenth century the Qing state, mainly through disaster relief, was able to provide some short-term security for the poor. In 1732, 1.4 million catties of surplus grain, or approximately 12 catties per person, were stored in Raoyang's central granary.[6] Another 1.6 million catties were added in 1738, and in 1744 an additional 1.4 million catties were stockpiled in satellite granaries in the east and west. The county also ran two charity centers just outside the town wall and budgeted 360 ounces of silver per month to feed one hundred orphans and poor people.

Magistrate Shan's pet project was the development of an additional network of public granaries supported by charitable contributions. Shortly after taking office, he appealed for contributions, recounting stories of civic generosity documented in Raoyang historical records and reminding people that things were so bad during a severe drought in 1641, when the Ming state was collapsing, that Raoyang people resorted to cannibalism.[7] Parents could not bring themselves to eat their own offspring. Instead, they traded away their own children for the children of others. It was said that people who ate human flesh felt fine for the first five days, but in the next five days became ill. By the eleventh day they began to show the symptoms of poisoning, and within twenty days they were dead.

Shan was determined to prevent such nightmares from happening in his Raoyang. By 1748 there were nine public granaries holding 387,500 catties. The magistrate erected a monument inscribed with the name of the worthies who had contributed more than 3,000 catties. In the spring, when food was in short supply, hungry tillers could borrow this grain. They returned it after the autumn harvest and paid 10 percent interest. But interest was waived if drought or flood brought a loss of 30 percent or more of the normal harvest.

Rituals of Authority

The longer-term efforts of the elite to preserve its privileged position and maintain social order stressed education and ritual. The Confucian temple was the center of higher learning in Raoyang. Its first rule was "Be loyal to the emperor and the empire." The more than twenty senior scholars who labored within its walls had passed the civil service examination given at the prefectural capital in Shenzhou and were preparing for the provincial examination, a major hurdle on the road to the wealth and power associated with official careers. Promising local scholars and aspiring officials usually received full financial support from the county. But in this rural backwater only twenty-eight Raoyang scholars passed the provincial exams and just two succeeded in the national competition for the jinshi degree in the first hundred years of Qing rule.

Much of the culture of the county town centered on its more than twenty shrines and temples. Magistrate Shan, a graduate of the elite palace examina-

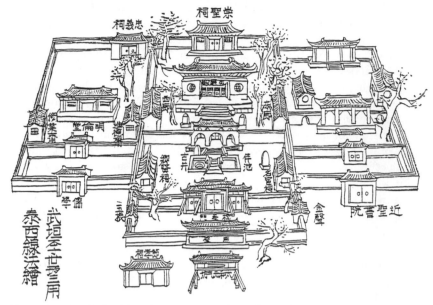

Figure 2   Confucian Temple, Raoyang, 1748. Illustration: Li Huai, 1985.

tion given in Beijing, scrupulously observed Confucian rituals, a moral cement meant to preserve the social order. Every spring and fall thanksgiving
prayers were offered to the gods of heaven, earth, wind, and rain at public
ceremonies held at four outdoor altars. And every spring and fall an ox, a
sheep, a pig, and containers of wine were sacrificed at the Confucian temple to
the spirits of Confucius, Mencius, and other sages.

Shan sought to shape public morality by honoring exemplars of moral
rectitude. Within the Confucian temple memorial pavilions were dedicated to
famous scholars, outstanding officials, and paragons of loyalty to the emperor.
Outside the main entrance to the temple was a shrine dedicated to filial sons
and virtuous wives. In 1748, during a state-sponsored campaign to instill
Confucian morality, Shan himself cited a sixty-three-year-old widow who, he
claimed, had honored her husband's memory by refusing to remarry in the
forty-four years after his death.[8]

Twice a year exemplary women were honored at the Temple of Chastity
and Filial Piety. For women, who were excluded from formal education,
official position, and property ownership, it was virtually the only path to
honor and official recognition. In the first hundred years of Qing rule, only
171 Raoyang women were cited as models of chastity, 2 for committing
suicide after being raped and 169 for abjuring marriage following the death of

a husband or fiancé.[9] In late imperial times, however, widows often did remarry. They were frequently forced into remarriage by relatives seeking to claim either a bride price or the patrimony of the deceased husband. Once remarried, such women were often regarded as morally inferior by their new neighbors.

Wives were the property of their husband's lineage. A married daughter was lost to her parents as a source of labor and support in old age. Women typically married out of their home village, and their loyalty passed to the husband's family. With the state presented as the family writ large, the absolute loyalty owed by wives to the husband's lineage was owed by all to the emperor and his official family, including Magistrate Shan.

The state did not monopolize all aspects of ritual culture in Raoyang, however. Over the years state-sponsored Confucian practices melded with Buddhist, Daoist, and a wide range of other popular beliefs. The county was an early center of Buddhist activity. In A.D. 541 a stone Buddha was erected in the north county at the site of a monastery that housed some two hundred monks. State practices reinforced and legitimated the norms of peasant household culture that dictated much of the conduct of life, from lineage rituals and life-cycle celebrations to authority relations and seasonal communal obligations.

Market and Culture

Within the town an array of popular gods and spirits received their due to ensure good weather and a bountiful harvest. The god of water was worshiped at the Dragon King Temple, and people sought to avoid locust infestations by praying at the King of Insects Temple. The Guandi Temple was dedicated to the god of war, while several temples honored Buddhist divinities, the most revered being Guan Yin, the goddess of mercy.

Marketplaces, such as Zoucun and Yanggezhuang in the south county, were also centers of a flourishing popular culture. The regular periodic markets brought together buyers and sellers, performers and spectators, worshipers and healers, people from all classes. The annual temple festivals and holiday markets attracted tens of thousands of buyers, sellers, and spectators from miles around. Farmers exchanged agricultural produce and the goods of cottage industries for draft animals, chickens, pigs, thread, yarn and cloth, furniture, baskets, seed, tools, and a variety of items for festivals, weddings, and funerals. Although there was scant written culture in hinterland Raoyang, the popular culture that enlivened market centers and remote villages alike was rich in lion dancing and stilt walking, dragon dances and boat races, *wushu* and other martial arts, music full of drums and trumpets, and traditional plays and operas.

Decline in the Early Twentieth Century

By the late eighteenth century, the Qing dynasty hurtled downward. The White Lotus Rebellion was followed by a wave of revolts in response to administrative breakdowns and by disruptions associated with imperialism. In the early nineteenth century foreign threats forced the Qing rulers to find more funds to update the military, build armament industries, and introduce modern technical education. A declining and overburdened traditional government could not meet new challenges and fell behind in maintaining the dikes, charities, and granaries that served as a minimal safety net for people threatened by economic catastrophes. If China could not revolutionize or modernize government and economy, expand wealth, and increase tax revenues needed for new public purposes, then more villagers in such counties as Raoyang would fall through gaping holes in a weakened safety net. The link between state and society was ever more one of life and death.

The mid-nineteenth-century Taiping Rebellion, inspired by messianic Christian and Chinese peasant values, swept north into Zhili promising land to the poor. At Zhengding the Taiping armies veered east, passing through Raoyang before imperial troops halted them near the port of Tianjin.[10]

At the end of the nineteenth century, a member of the Raoyang elite named Tiger Zhang, who is remembered in local folklore as having had three wives, four concubines, and three opera troupes, subsidized the county opera troupe. The Empress Dowager Ci Xi, China's de facto ruler in the final decades of the Qing reign, invited the Raoyang troupe to perform. That imperial performance became legend in Raoyang when Tiger Zhang fell while walking up the stairs. As he tumbled, local legend has it, the empress cried out, "My child!" Since the imperial word was fiat, Zhang was henceforth treated royally, almost as an adopted child. He was given a paraffin lantern symbolic of the palace. Soon thereafter, during a tour, the troupe ran into a local bully. On seeing the palace paraffin lamp, the bully dropped into a *ketou* and turned into a purring kitten. Raoyang people took pride in their opera, which, symbolized by the palace lamp, won fame for the county.

By the early twentieth century several Raoyang merchants had opened cloth shops and restaurants in Beijing. Raoyang merchants traveled to Ulan Bator in Mongolia and even to Czarist Russia to trade. They bought textiles, garments, and chinaware in Beijing, Baoding, and Tianjin and carried them to the northeastern provinces of Manchuria. They returned with herbal medicines that they sold in China's largest medicinal market, near Raoyang in Anguo county, or in large cities. Raoyang merchants sold silk and tea in Mongolia and returned with wool, hides, herbal medicine, horses, and cattle. Raoyang people believed that their pig castraters were the best in all China, being in demand as far away as Xinjiang, and that in North China only Baodi county turned out more skilled barbers.

In spite of increased taxes to pay for state strengthening, national humiliation and economic disruption intensified, giving birth to nationalistic politics that exploded in the antiforeign, anti-Christian Boxer Rebellion of 1900. The empress dowager fled south to escape punitive foreign armies. A saying spread that gave voice to the new nationalism: "The people fear officials; officials fear foreigners; foreigners fear the people." In 1902, with the foreign threat past, the empress called on the governor of Zhili, Yuan Shikai, to arrange her return to Beijing. At enormous expense Yuan prepared the 150-mile initial stage of the journey back to Zhengding, west of Raoyang.[11] Three months later southern Zhili erupted in rebellion against the conscription and new tax levies imposed on the region. The rebellion was crushed. But service in the expanding military became a lifesaver for the rural poor about to go under. People said,

> When the flag is hoisted
> Some come to eat grain,
> As long as troops are levied
> Some will sell their fate for grain.

Fragmentary evidence suggests that hinterland Raoyang, as did much of North China, suffered a prolonged decline after the Qianlong reign. The capacity to control flooding and provide disaster relief had shrunk, while landholdings declined, population increased, and agricultural technology stagnated. Handicrafts, commerce, and other off-farm work became more essential to survival, but the county marketing system shriveled.

A 1904 provincial report described Raoyang as a small struggling commercial center. "Although the land is barren, the people are hard working. Most of the men engage in small business activities, while the women weave." The leading Raoyang products were gunnysacks for transporting and storing goods and cotton leg wrappings.[12] Some merchants from the north county tied into dynamic regional and international markets centered on Tianjin. But North China's incorporation into world markets cost peripheral Raoyang its markets for traditional textiles. Raoyang laborers continued to go to Tianjin and Beijing each fall in search of work in trade, construction, and crafts. Repatriated earnings helped families back home fend off hunger and continue a moral life in keeping with customary rituals. A sorghum whiskey called Zhanggang spread in popularity.

Throughout the region the state imposed new levies directly on village communities to finance the modernization of schools, industry, military, and police and to pay indemnities to foreign powers. The new taxes quickly outstripped the land tax as the principal source of state revenues.

In the last days of the Qing, Raoyang implemented reforms in education and industry initiated throughout pacesetting Shenzhou prefecture. In 1907 Raoyang boasted, 2,494 students in modern schools and was selected by the Zhili Industrial Bureau as the site for a model textile factory.[13] The local elite, working with the county magistrate, supplied much of the capital. The factory provided scholarships for twenty young workers to study modern dyeing and weaving methods. But within a few years the factory closed its doors, and no other new industries gained a foothold.

The Qing dynasty collapsed in 1911, but no strong state emerged to impose a secure peace. North China was instead ruled and misruled by warlords. As the key to control of the capital and therefore international recognition (which carried the right to the nation's customs revenue), Zhili province became a battleground for competing warlords.

The 1920–21 North China drought and famine killed ten million people in a four-province area, leaving almost half of Zhili's eighteen million people destitute.[14] Wives and children were sold; millions fled to Manchuria; Raoyang was ravaged. In 1921 it received the second largest amount of grain provided by the United International Famine Relief Committee. Famine relief specialists considered the Raoyang region to be dangerously overpopulated; two surveyed villages averaged only 2.2 mu of land per person. High population density and vulnerability to flood and drought meant that disasters would reap a heavy toll.[15] In Raoyang, as in most of southern Zhili, very few had the capital to pay to drill deep wells to find sweet water. According to data compiled by John Buck, on the average 8.8 percent of the population of each generation died of famine in North China in the years 1850–1932, twice the national average. Deaths were concentrated in the poorest regions. Worsened by female infanticide, gender imbalances left one man in ten unmarried and therefore incapable of fulfilling the basic ethical dictate of continuing the family line.[16]

The Communist Party Fails at Revolution

In 1923 a reconstituted Nationalist party forged an alliance with the fledgling Communist party. Efforts to mobilize students, teachers, workers, and peasants, which began in South China, soon led to attempts to eliminate warlord power in North China. The Communist party first established a foothold in hinterland Raoyang. In 1925 a young intellectual named Wang Yaoyu was among the many activists sent by the party's North China Bureau in Beijing to the impoverished rural counties of southern Zhili to establish underground organizations. Taking a job as a teacher in the county town, Wang befriended students at the Raoyang Number One Senior Primary School and at the men's normal school.[17]

The Raoyang party branch consisted initially of a dozen students and rural intellectuals, including a returned student from Japan, Han Zimu, whose father's 200- to 300-mu farm was among the county's largest, and Wang Chunhai, a normal school graduate from Tunli, a market village in the south county. Schoolteachers such as Wang brought the party's message to villagers. These rural intellectuals were interested in what had aroused their urban counterparts during the tumultuous anti-imperialist, anti-Confucian May Fourth movement of 1919. These scions of the land-rich turned against the traditional order, seeking dignity for the nation and prosperity for the people through socialist revolution. They established a youth corps, read progressive journals, and struggled to transform traditional curricula. But with warlord Zhang Zuolin dominating the region, the party remained small and underground.

By 1926 rumblings were heard of a Northern Expedition to crush the warlords and unite the nation under the Nationalist party. Local authorities responded by elevating Raoyang to a rank two county, one with higher taxes (an additional eighty cents per mu), purportedly to field armies capable of halting the forces of the Northern Expedition. Anping and Wuqiang to the west and east were rank three counties, while Shenxian county, to the south, was rank one. The additional tax provoked riots, for which the nascent Communist party claimed credit, and in late 1926, it launched a campaign against the county tax collector. Small numbers of peasants and tenants, organized by the forty-member party in a new peasant association, sought to stymie tax collectors by reaping the crops at night. But the party and the youth corps were thrown into disarray in early 1927 when the warlord authorities arrested some leaders and forced others to flee the county.

In early 1928 the Northern Expedition reached the North China plain, ousting the warlord regime of Zhang Zuolin. Zhang's troops plundered Raoyang as they fled. The victorious Nationalists, with their capital in Nanjing, renamed Zhili province as Hebei. Hoping for peace and prosperity, in early 1929 Raoyang people formed a branch of the Nationalist party. Among the party's first moves were establishing a salt monopoly, so that the government could sell and tax all salt, and crushing the Communists, a policy the Nationalists had carried out elsewhere in China.

The Communist underground was still in disarray in 1930 when party officials called for armed uprisings. Led by a rural schoolteacher who was the son of a traditional medical practitioner, the tiny Raoyang party hoped to capitalize on strong antitax sentiments. People resented paying a tax on pigs slaughtered for home consumption, for which they earned no cash. They hated the tax collectors and thugs hired by those who had bid highest for the right to collect the tax. Because taxpayers were dunned by a contracted collector who hired local toughs to extract revenues, the funds actually received and recorded by the government as budget revenue grossly understated actual burdens on households. During a temple fair in Xiaodi, Communist party activists urged people to take up arms. Few responded. Although local security forces easily suppressed the rebellion, the local authority did abolish the hog-slaughter tax, recognizing that political legitimacy and stability were linked to the tax burden.

After the failure of the Xiaodi uprising, local Communists continued to organize secretly. A martial arts devotee, Hou Yutian, in 1931–32 organized a ten-member "salt militia," which smuggled in salt from south of Raoyang and made it available without the tax. The Communist party tried to organize and protect smugglers, seeking the popular acclaim that came from reducing the hated tax burden. The party members also worked with Raoyang students to persuade the government to legitimate non-Nationalist party student activities and to change antediluvian curricula. They were rebuffed. In 1933, when a member of the Communist party's Baoding Regional Special Committee defected, he supplied information that led to the destruction of underground Communist organizations in a six-county region that included Raoyang. The isolated party intellectuals who did not flee were arrested or killed.

The Nationalist Party Fails at Modernization

The Nationalists could not steady the shaky ship of state. In the first five years county magistrates averaged 298 days in office. Once again, the county suffered multiple natural disasters. In 1932 the rampaging Hutuo submerged one-third of the county, destroying crops. In waterlogged low-lying areas winter wheat could not be planted, so there was no June harvest in 1933. In contrast, the south county was bitterly dry. A summer 1933 flood drowned plow animals and left half the county's residents homeless.[18] Government investigators blamed the agricultural crisis on natural disaster.

A survey by Magistrate Yang Fengyu that summer found four fewer villages than had existed during the high Qing. The county reported collecting 181,747 yuan in taxes, of which 92,506 went for county use. Education took 40 percent of the county budget. In contrast to the 2,494 students of 1907, 452 teachers in 216 primary schools now taught 6,980 pupils. Public security took 30 percent of the budget, paying policemen 6 or 7 yuan a month. An attempt at modern police training had stalled.

Cottage industries included beekeeping, raising chickens, spinning thread, and weaving baskets from willow branches. County traders dispatched sesame oil, bean oil, burlap bags, grain, and homemade cloth. County investment in well drilling in 1932 was but 2,000 yuan. Civic organizations included a thirty-member chamber of commerce, a teacher's union, a women's association, and a peasant union. There were 610 temples (which owned 50,000 yuan in property), one bank, and ten cooperatives. The county town housed a charity welfare center and a medical clinic.

In 1935, when the Nationalists sent in another new magistrate, Wang

Wenbin, only seventeen inches of rain fell. Magistrate Wang warned that Raoyang was on the verge of becoming a wasteland. "The soil is bad, . . . there is not enough water," and the lives of the people are "dreadful to contemplate."[19] Magistrate Wang's data indicated that two hundred years later villagers were far more vulnerable and desperate than those of the 1740s. In 1748 there were 23,753 households and approximately 120,000 people in Raoyang. By 1935 the number of households had increased to 33,184, and the population had risen 60 percent to 192,819. Arable land decreased by 5 percent from 545,500 to 512,800 mu in 1933, according to Magistrate Wang's survey. Whereas in 1748 there had been an average of 22.7 mu of land per household, by 1935 there was only 15.4 mu, or two and a half acres, per household. With taxes rising, markets and sidelines contracting, and no significant improvement in technology, irrigation, soil, and grain yields, the margin of survival for villagers was shaved perilously thin.

When the Mongolian People's Republic was formed in 1921 as a Soviet client state and when Japan occupied Manchuria in 1931, the commercial decline intensified as Raoyang merchants and peddlers were cut off from two important markets. With the import of foreign yarn into North China in the early twentieth century, household cotton-spinning sidelines collapsed in Raoyang. Some strategically located counties along main avenues of transportation embarked on industrial development. But hinterland Raoyang, being far from a railroad and having no improved water access, no bus service, and no paved roads, could not so develop.

Local cotton production had fallen sharply. In 1936 less than 1 percent of Raoyang's arable land was planted in cotton.[20] The county, which had traditionally exported cotton textiles, by 1935 imported 20,000 catties of cotton and 9,000 rolls of cotton cloth from domestic sources, and an additional 4,000 rolls of cotton textiles and 3,000 cases of kerosene from abroad. The imports totaled 378,000 silver dollars. The value of exports, primarily peanuts, sacks, and leg wrappings, was just 100,000 silver dollars.[21]

Yincun, a market town in the north county, was the only Raoyang locality to forge commercial, craft, and industrial ties with modernizing sectors of the North China economy in the 1920s. A thermal plant in Yincun provided Raoyang's first electric power, and furniture, clothing, hardware, and even electrical machinery were sold there. But by 1937 half the merchants in Yincun were bankrupt, and its only modern factory, a textile mill built with Tianjin capital, moved to Baoding. Countywide commercial decline was reflected in the severe contraction of the local marketing system. In 1748 Raoyang was served by five daily markets and twenty-two periodic markets. In 1935 there was not a single daily market, and only eight periodic markets survived, which were limited to trade in grain, livestock, vegetables, and various items of daily use. In Zhanggang and Xiaodi only the alcohol shops remained in business.

In such hinterland counties as Raoyang, the whole society, including the elite, had long been sinking. At times the poor directed their rage at the relatively prosperous because the declining elite had reneged on their obligations to other villagers, but landlord exploitation was not the cause of decline. Landlords and managerial farmers owned only a small fraction of the land.[22] Owning 73 percent of the farmland, 80 percent of the county's farm households were owner-cultivators.

One important difference between Raoyang in 1744 and in 1935 was the state's capacity to respond to disaster. Whereas the Qianlong government had some resources to ease suffering, by the twentieth century the fragile Qing safety net had all but disappeared. Gone were the emergency granaries. The county budget was running a deficit: income was 65,838 silver dollars, whereas expenditures, largely for police work, amounted to 71,083 dollars. Only 100 dollars was set aside for feeding orphans and the poor. When flooding occurred in 1935, in contrast to the Qing, no central government help followed. Magistrate Wang requisitioned 130,000 catties of grain by requiring landowners in districts two and four, the only two that had surplus grain, to contribute 150 catties for every 100 mu of privately owned land. It was not enough.

Long-term economic and social decline disintegrated Raoyang cultural life. The Confucian academy had long since closed, seasonal thanksgiving rituals were no longer performed, and exemplars of moral rectitude were no longer honored at state-sponsored temples. Peasant values, many of which resonated with Confucian morality, however, were deeply ingrained in Raoyang. But the economic crisis of the early twentieth century denied many rural people the means to celebrate such key moments in the life cycle as marriage, birth, and death in time-honored ways. With temples devoted to the Buddhist goddess of mercy and other legendary deities in disrepair, popular religious life changed. Religious sects, secret societies, and self-help groups with such names as Dragon, Temporary Soldiers, and Poor People spread as villagers tried to defend themselves and compensate for the inability of the state and the declining traditional elite to lend a hand.

Culture became a contested arena. Although many villagers fled for work to Manchuria and the coastal cities, others put their faith in old and new gods. They prayed at the 610 Raoyang temples for rain and for protection from locusts, flood, sickness, and looting. Some sought salvation in Catholicism, which won 78,358 converts, a little more than 1 percent of the residents of southern Hebei.[23]

With life itself at stake, even religion could become a protection racket. In Yanggezhuang which traced its history back to the Western Han dynasty, Bai Qingcai, a Communist, who taught in the village school in the mid-1930s after fleeing Raoyang town, won almost two dozen students to front activity for the secret party. The Bai lineage predominated in Yanggezhuang, whose

Black Mountain Temple dated from the Yuan dynasty. The party group urged villagers to form a self-help group, the Society of Common People. When a prominent Yanggezhuang family member died, the society forced villagers to boycott the funeral so that there would not be enough pallbearers. After society members turned the coffin upside down, the mourning family had to pay villagers for assistance in the burial ceremony.

Modernizers also competed for cultural hegemony. Footbinding went out of fashion. Modern drama groups performed plays highlighting independent couples and marriages of love, while mocking traditional fathers and mothers-in-law. Yet, in spite of an infusion of modern and unorthodox views, popular dramas of the 1930s reflected the persistence of values subordinating women to men, particularly the taboo against women remarrying after the death of a husband.[24] Popular dramas performed in the marketplace, particularly at harvest time, at New Year's, and during the temple fairs, drew tens of thousands of spectators, providing momentary surcease from the worsening crises.

Magistrate Wang sought to put Raoyang back on its feet by a variety of modernizing reforms, with a stress on education. For centuries officials had sought to educate the talented who could bring China the benefits of science and technology. By 1935 there were 171 lower primary schools for boys and—quite new—35 for girls. The average was one school per village, providing three or four years of basic education for approximately 7,000 county youth. In addition there were four higher primary schools, including one for girls. At the highest level were the two teacher-training schools, one for men and one for women. In addition, "people's education centers," which offered young people and adults classes in reading, health, and recreation, were attached to 160 of the county's lower primary schools.

The county also initiated a heroin addiction program, which treated more than four hundred people between 1934 and 1935. Authorities estimated that there were an additional one thousand untreated addicts in the county. Narcotics smuggled into Tianjin by Japanese dealers reached Raoyang through local middlemen.[25] People cursed the Japanese whose drugs were destroying China's vitality. The county provided cash bounties for information about heroin dealers.

The state highlighted the modernizing achievements of four model villages, Wanggang, Nanhan, Xiliman, and Xiyanwan, which combined educational reform with the introduction of scientific farming. Each village had a boys' and girls' lower primary school, in addition to a tuition-free "common school" operated during the agricultural slack season. Local committees carried out experiments in public security, road improvement, tree planting, and well drilling. In the late 1920s and 1930s the county also helped set up fifty-one credit co-ops to aid farmers chronically short of capital. Three consumer co-ops and five co-ops that combined credit with transportation and marketing of goods were also established. The severe shortage of funds and an excessive tax burden restricted the new measures to a few experimental sites.

A search for water was central to modernizing agriculture. Even in prosperous Dingxian county, where sweet water was close to the surface, fewer than half of all farm households had access to wells.[26] But in hinterland Raoyang few could afford the capital, labor, and materials required to drill a basic fifteen-foot well. Although Raoyang was close to Dingxian, conditions in the two localities were a world apart. Rail and modern road networks linked Dingxian to Beijing, Baoding, and Tianjin. Modern ideas and thousands of new people invigorated the Baoding region. Isolated Raoyang, with its inferior soil and water, remained a poor outsider.

Facing a chronic budget deficit, Magistrate Wang had scant resources for modernization. With half the county's 33,000 households in trouble after the 1935 flood, the county tax base was further reduced. Wang's top priority remained police and public security. In 1935 there were 102 men in the public security force and 144 in militia units. Of the 71,083 silver dollars available for government spending in 1935, security accounted for 34,232, including 13,732 for operating five district public security offices and 16,314 to support local militia units. Without increasing the tax burden, which would have been intolerable, modernization was stymied. Yet patriotic anxieties intensified with the growth of the Japanese military threat to a disintegrating China.

A Hinterland Village Disintegrates

A closer look at one Raoyang village brings into clearer focus how the countywide crisis severed the ties binding community members. Villagers trace Wugong history to the sixth century A.D. when Raoyang native Li Delin became chief of the Imperial Secretariat at the court in the reign of Sui Emperor Wendi. Advised by a geomancer to construct a tomb for his deceased father near the county seat, Delin returned to Raoyang in 586. The site was said to be so auspicious that family members would be assured of holding office for five generations. Jingxin village became Wugong, meaning five dukes, or officials. If Delin and his father are counted as the first two imperial dukes of Anping, then Delin's great-grandson, Li Zongchen, was the fifth. In 684 he was implicated in an abortive insurrection against the Tang Empress Wu Zetian. She stripped the Lis of their title, ordered the family tomb destroyed, and barred Li family members from office. Legend confirmed the geomancer's prediction: there were five, and only five, consecutive generations of Li officeholders.

 Lineage residence and land access combined to define relations of power and prestige in Wugong village, nine miles southwest of Raoyang town and just west of a periodic market at Zoucun. The Lis dominated Wugong from the time of its settlement.[27] Latecomers, some of whom arrived in the early fifteenth century during the enormous wave of immigration from Hongdong county in neighboring Shanxi province, had to settle on the outskirts and till less-desirable land. Families surnamed Geng and Qiao settled in the east village, and Zhang, Yang, and Xu in the west village. There were a few scattered Ke, Wang, and Liu. East villagers specialized in ropemaking and candlemaking, those in the center grew and peddled vegetables, and west-end residents processed bean curd.

The twentieth-century crises that threatened so many households and so much of the cultural glue of village life forced a reorganization of traditional lineage relations. New bonds had to be forged to reknit the disintegrating society. Tensions associated with the declining Raoyang economy exacerbated rivalry between the northern and southern branches of the Li lineage. During the early nineteenth century, Wugong split into two villages, Big Wugong to the north and Small Wugong to the south, controlled by the Northern Li and Southern Li, respectively. In the 1870s the Northern Li was the more powerful, but by the end of the century it had declined, while landholdings of leading Southern Li households rose to 700–800 mu. After the fall of the Qing in 1911, Wugong's hundred-year-old division into two villages ended, with the Southern Li dominating the single village unit. As regional economic woes mounted, the Southern Li leaders formed a group known as the Eight Courtyards, which retained significant power into the 1930s. Two-thirds of all village households were Lis, half members of the Southern Li.[28]

Educational reform helped bring nationalism to village intellectuals who were excited by the prospect of the Northern Expedition throwing out warlords and foreign exploiters. By the 1920s, thirty to forty Wugong men had received five or six years of primary education in the privately run "new style" school that opened after the overthrow of the Qing dynasty. In the mid-1920s the school enrolled 70 students, who paid tuition of three dollars per year. By 1937 enrollment was 150 students. A few students continued their education after graduating from the Wugong primary school. Li Shude, the son of an Eight Courtyards leader, Li Chunrong, studied textile production in France in the early 1930s before settling in Tianjin. Teacher Geng Manliang, a Wugong east-end native who had been educated at the men's normal school in Raoyang, encouraged students to become proud patriots. In the 1930s, the three primary school teachers received their salaries from the county government. Although many villagers forgot politics after graduation, a number gathered in the two small village shops and exchanged news, rumors, and stories about political events. Communist party organizers active in southern Raoyang never approached the mobilizable rural intellectuals in Wugong.

In 1936, the village's 285 households and 1,390 people farmed 4,620 mu, about 770 acres. With the average farmstead 16 mu, there was slightly more than half an acre per person, about the county average. Only four Wugong households owned as much as 80 mu, with the largest holding 123 mu. None rented out more than 24 mu. All but one of the heads of these better-off households did field work. Only 80 mu of privately owned land, 2 percent of the total arable, was rented to tenants. Rent averaged three silver dollars a year per mu, worth about 75 catties of coarse grain in 1935.[29] The standard contract was for three years. Superior-quality irrigated land was occasionally rented out for vegetable growing under a ten-year contract, at an annual rental of eight to ten silver dollars.

Six households, five of them members of the Southern Li, one headed by east-ender Qiao Wanxiang, each hired one full-time farmhand. During the plowing and harvest seasons, these and a few other households hired short-term laborers. The few who rented out land or hired labor were small fry with modest incomes. Poverty was pervasive. Even better-off families ate fine grain only on festivals. The vast majority, as in most of the North China plain, were owner-cultivators. Two hundred Wugong households, 70 percent of the total, rented no land from others and hired no farmhands.

Wugong had more than seventy owner-tenant households who supplemented their meager holdings with rented plots. Most rented plots came from the village's 150 mu of lineage and temple land.[30] In 1936 owner-tenants rented an average of 3.2 mu per household. Some owner-tenant household members also worked as farmhands. A short-term laborer earned about one silver dollar for five days' work. Long-term hired hands earned forty to fifty dollars a year plus room and board.[31] During the busy seasons they worked nearly twelve hours a day, less in the slack season.

In 1936 just thirty-three villagers worked as long-term hired hands, all but five in neighboring communities. Ninety-five villagers, almost all of them from landowning families, hired out as short-term laborers. They went at dawn to the market at Zoucun, a walled village that traced its commercial origins to the Ming dynasty, and lined up before employers. One-third of Wugong households had members who worked part-time as hired laborers. At the bottom of the Wugong economic ladder, five landless households attempted to survive on insecure wage labor. The male offspring of barely subsisting landless households might be too poor to marry. Their family segments would die out, an ultimate act of immorality toward lineage ancestors.

An average household of five working 15 mu (2.5 acres) could, in a good year, expect to harvest 2,250 catties of grain. With individual subsistence requiring 300 catties, little was left for farm expenses, repairs, taxes, household goods, clothing, and emergencies, or to pay for weddings, holidays, and funerals.[32] In 1935 it cost 100 silver dollars to buy one mu of high-quality land, 150 to build a standard three-section brick house, 70 for a wedding, and 100 dollars for a funeral. A silver dollar was worth about 25 catties of coarse grain.

As elsewhere on the plain, in the 1930s the land-population ratio worsened and agriculture stagnated. The technology was primitive. Plows penetrated only a few inches into the hard soil, insecticides and chemical fertilizers were unknown, and tillers were short of draft animals and even rudimentary tools. Almost no one experimented with seed strains, interplanting, or new ways of rotating crops. Electricity and tractors were not yet even distant dreams.

Wugong's poverty also reflected its ecology. Located on a slight rise, outside the Hutuo flood belt, Wugong's main climatic problem was drought, not flooding. There was no aboveground water, and in 1936 there were only thirty wells, most on land belonging to members of the Li lineage. Even a mild drought significantly reduced grain yields. Serious drought meant hunger, the breakup of families, flight, and sometimes death.

Zhang Zhan, born in 1921, was twelve when his father died. An elder brother died at about the same time, following the deaths of two other brothers. That left Zhang Zhan, his mother, and a younger brother. When Zhang was eighteen the family sold its last two mu of land, surviving by renting two mu from the Zhang lineage and by earning income as seasonal laborers. The family had little hope that Zhang would ever marry and continue the eternal lineage.

In the 1930s more households careened toward disaster. West-ender Zhang Zhou's father died before she was born in 1905. As a child, to help the family survive, she learned to weave, manipulating the loom with bound feet. Schooling was unthinkable. After marriage to a Wugong pig castrater, she supported a daughter and son after her husband fled to Manchuria. No money or word came from the husband. Zhang Zhou wove and pulled a plow through the fields to till the family's four mu. She and her two children barely escaped starvation.

While life became more perilous, the state was less able to provide disaster relief. Theft worsened. Because of their location on the dirt road to the Zoucun market, Wugong villagers, hit less hard than neighbors by recent floods, felt themselves a target for thieves. A "shadow wall" at the entrance to courtyards, in addition to keeping out ghosts and evil spirits, kept strangers from seeing in when the gate was open. Insecurity grew and taxes rose. In 1936 national taxes were half a dollar for every ten mu owned. Local taxes were ten times higher, at just over half a dollar per mu. The increasing miscellaneous taxes weighed most heavily on beleaguered households, driving a wedge between villagers and the tax-taking state.

Although people sought to retain sacred ties to the soil in which ancestors were buried, survival required that families break apart and young men seek work elsewhere. Some found construction work, factory jobs, and commercial opportunities in Tianjin and Beijing, and even as far away as Shanghai and Fuzhou. Others labored as veterinarians and ropemakers in towns across North China. Wugong residents were among the close to eight million who migrated from North China to Manchuria in the first half of the twentieth century in search of land and factory jobs.[33]

Cultural Chaos

Economic and social disruption was accompanied by cultural turmoil. Tradition dictated cultural norms by gender, age, and family. Although boys were raised to be rambunctious, villagers feared they might get out of control and become immoral when forced to flee to survive. Elders therefore admonished that the young should not read "Monkey" because its hero Sun Wukong might set too mischievous a model. By the 1930s the village was having a difficult time holding to custom. Society seemed about to rip apart.

The two most popular temples in Wugong, both depending upon donations, the sale of incense, and rent on twenty mu of temple land, were crumbling from lack of funds for upkeep.[34] The Pusa Temple, also known as Venerable Mother Temple, a rundown Buddhist shrine honoring Guan Yin, the goddess of mercy, who brought good fortune to those suffering personal disasters, was the favorite of the poor. It was located at the west end of the dirt road that ran through the center of the village. The San Guan Temple, located on the eastern outskirts and devoted to the worship of the Three Rulers of Heaven, Earth, and Water, housed large images of the three principal deities. The temple featured the plump figure of the Laughing Buddha, a humble and unpretentious protector of the common people. The major occasions for worshiping at the San Guan Temple were at the New Year and after a birth, when parents carried newborns, particularly boys, to the temple to be blessed. Living in the San Guan Temple were forty-year-old monk Qiao Cengpiao and twenty-year-old nun Tian Changjin. Her parents had sold the child first as a servant and then to a neighboring village's Guan Yin Temple to become a nun. There an old nun scarred her face by burning incense sticks into her cheeks for errors made at prayer. In 1934 at age eighteen Tian was sold as a wife to Qiao Cengpiao at Wugong's San Guan Temple, which consisted of two courtyards, one for living and one for worship. As with ever more marriages in the region, it broke with sacred tradition, in this case the custom of men marrying slightly older women. People said, "A wife three years older is pure gold. A wife five years older looks older than your mother."

Wugong also contained three small unoccupied shrines. In a field in the northeastern outskirts, where a few wells had been successfully dug, a small temple honored the Dragon King, the god of water. The declining elite favored two small shrines, the Guandi Temple, located in the village center and devoted to the worship of the fierce, red-faced god of war, and the Tian Qi Temple in the east end, devoted to the worship of a deified public official of the Warring States period. The Nationalist government sanctioned temples dedicated to historical worthies but, in an effort to advance science and reduce superstition, frowned upon temples associated with purely legendary figures and discouraged incense burning.[35]

The three leading lineages, the Southern Li, Northern Li, and Zhang, helped villagers in difficulty by renting 150 mu of corporate land to poorer lineage members at one-third below prevailing rates and by allowing the homeless to live in their respective lineage temples.[36] The powerful Southern Li centered activities at its lineage temple. Inside, inscribed in black ink on white cloth were the names of all ancestors from the founder to the present. Only names in the male line were recorded.

The high point of lineage ceremonial activity was the Qingming festival, held in honor of clan ancestors on the third day of the third lunar month. At dawn on Qingming the lineage head led the males of each household to the clan graveyard, where each mound was swept, fresh earth added, and white paper and incense burned in memory of departed ancestors. A feast in the lineage temple followed. Diners, cooks, and all service personnel were male members of the lineage. After the meal, the men took home a few buns for the women. At Qingming the two rival branches of the Li lineage enacted a symbolic display of unity. Carrying food and wine, Northern Li males marched to the southern Li temple, bowed, and worshiped before a wooden tablet of the Southern Li founder. The dominant Southern Li then reciprocated, sending a delegation to worship at the Northern Li shrine and to present gifts of food.

Not even Qingming rivaled the importance of the New Year. On New Year's eve villagers often stayed up all night. Festivities continued for a fortnight, culminating in a fireworks display on the fifteenth day of the first month. During the holiday, villagers cleaned courtyards and homes, visited relatives, gambled, worshiped ancestors and local gods, and wore new clothes. They enjoyed relaxing, exploding firecrackers, drinking, and festival going as they anticipated gorging on delicious meat-filled wheat-flour dumplings dipped in vinegar.

To eat one's fill of pork dumplings was a good omen. To pass the New Year without meat dumplings was as inauspicious as having no New Year at all. Fate was sealed at New Year: "The year is set at the New Year, the day is set at dawn." But by the hard times of the twentieth century poorer villagers were resorting to fake dumplings, called red dumplings, to fool the gods. The poignance of the season was captured in a local lament:

New Year comes, New Year comes.
Young girl wants flowers, little boy wants firecrackers.
Old wife says I need three pecks of wheat, two pecks of millet.
And still need five *sheng* of sticky millet for New Year cakes.
Old man says the less money I have, the more you people prattle.

Villagers burned incense at the major temples on the last night of the year and again on the fifth day of the New Year to the beat of eighteen drums, the biggest of which were four feet wide. Mounted on a cart, each was played by four men. There were also smaller drums, as well as cymbals, gongs, and two lion dancers. Seventy-three-year-old Li Yufu beat out the cadences for us, describing ritual drumming in the 1930s as the happiest time of his life.

The Medicine King Temple festival, held at the end of the fourth lunar month in the Zoucun market, was the most exciting event in the region. The annual fair drew twenty thousand or more people, with merchants coming from Shandong, Henan, and Shanxi. During the temple fair hundreds of head of livestock were gathered to the north near a section filled with outdoor restaurants, and a bustling market for cloth and shoes stretched to the west. A large tent theater offered free traditional and contemporary dramas three times a day during the five-day fair. Itinerant storytellers and balladeers conveyed the action and intrigue of ancient tales and contemporary warlord struggles. Magic shows, opera singers, and by the 1930s, even a newfangled lantern shadow play delighted the crowds. Gamblers, too, were out in force. Villagers came to pray, watch the fun, peddle vegetables and sideline goods, and buy scarce specialties, such as ceremonial items for weddings and funerals. Attendance augured good health. Fairgoers burned incense and offered food to Guan Yin to cure the sick and to assure health and success in the new year. As temple bells rang, people bowed and tossed coins into a large contribution box.

Religious culture not only was incorporated in the market, but also suffused the critical moments of lineage life. Marriages and deaths were moments of supreme importance. It was demeaning and boded ill to celebrate them other than in the proper way. But the proper way was costly. High dowries were customary, but families increasingly could not afford them. Daughters were often forced to marry old men, alcoholics, opium addicts, or beaters. One such bride, Bian Qiao, married a man sixteen years older. She guffawed to us about life in the 1930s after marriage. "Nothing happened after I got married. He was too old to satisfy me." Ill-founded marriages brought disillusion and despair.

In 1935 an acceptable standard for a wedding was equal to 1,750 catties of coarse grain, the value of the annual grain harvest for many Wugong households.[37] A proper wedding began at dawn when four runners carrying the groom in a red sedan chair, accompanied by another four runners carrying a green chair for the bride, set off for the bride's house. The sedan chairs were usually rented, but in some cases they were provided as a service to poorer lineage members. At the bride's home the groom dismounted from his chair and bowed to the bride and her parents. Returning to the groom's home, the couple dismounted and bowed to the north, where the god Tian Di resides, then entered the courtyard to bow to the parents of the groom and other relatives. The couple then ate dumplings, symbolizing the joining of husband and wife. After the guests presented gifts of money, usually one or two dollars, all sat down to a feast of steamed buns, rice, and dried ginger. If the family had enough money, the couple wore special clothing, a hat and traditional long gown for the groom and a ceremonial headdress for the bride.

Ritual teasing followed the wedding. The bride was forced to her knees as a guest held out a tray of money. Each time the bride awkwardly tried to grab the money, the tray was snatched away. Teasing continued after the couple retired to their chamber as young people outside shouted jokes. Various ceremonial devices, such as placing food on the brick bed as an offering to the gods, were meant to assure a male heir. Marrying without a feast, guests, and musicians was like eating coarse porridge rather than meat dumplings at the New Year. Improper weddings, which increased in the 1930s, were considered to be illegitimate, even immoral, and bad omens for the lineage.

Funerals were even more costly than weddings. Failure to bury parents properly dishonored their memory, shamed the household, and condemned the departed to an eternity of disorder that would bring retribution against the immoral children. Of course, if death ended the lineage, ceremony was not needed. If a partner in an elderly couple without family died, the corpse was placed in a coffin in the courtyard. Bricks were piled around it with a hole left in which to burn incense. A grizzly stench spread, but coffin and odor remained until the survivor died. Then, saving the cost of separate funerals, the couple were buried together. Old timers in the 1950s recalled that in hard times in the Qing the expression "At sixty, go home" had horrifying implications. Some poverty-stricken families were said to have dug a grave for old people to live in until they died.

The biggest single expense in a funeral was the coffin. Trees and lumber were scarce and costly, but a wooden coffin was indispensable. Household survivors often went into debt to mount a decent funeral, including transportation, ceremonial expenses, the services of several monks, and a feast. Elders dreaded dying before a proper funeral could be arranged. Those who could purchased their own coffin. Decades later people still remembered that in the 1930s Liu Yuqiao's father-in-law was placed in the ground without a coffin. Neighbors donated two small boards to prevent the earth from settling directly on the corpse's face.[38]

A shared culture bound villagers to a common vision of a proper life. Among its most important elements were marrying in the time-honored way, having many children (including at least one son to stay home and continue the lineage), enjoying meat dumplings at the New Year, worshiping ancestors at Qingming, and being buried in a wooden coffin. A society that could not put these things within the reach of villagers lacked legitimacy. In the 1930s many people found these elements of a proper life beyond reach. Cultural underpinnings were collapsing.

New ways of survival in times of hardship threatened the moral bonds of society. Wives were left alone to care for home and children as men in search of work disappeared for years at a time. Families feared that village men who worked outside the region and lived among immoral strangers would forget their duties to the household. A father dying among strangers could not be buried in lineage soil. Since daughters could not inherit property, a family with no male heirs was considered fair game for neighbors who were eager to encroach on land, trees, and courtyard. A broken family could become carrion. As cultural bonds disintegrated, violence increased with the spread of banditry, theft, and kidnapping. "The fierce fear those who are bolder," people said, "and the bold fear those who act regardless of life."

The Anatomy of Conflict

The story of Li Mingde and his sons illustrates how decline and insecurity intensified conflict in the 1930s. Li Mingde, the head of the Southern Li lineage, was a broker in the late nineteenth century when the village was divided into two parts. Anxious to consolidate his position in the rivalry between the Southern and Northern Li, but having no sons to succeed him as lineage head, Mingde adopted a boy from nearby Shenxian county, naming him Li Huanan. Later, Mingde procreated two sons, of whom the older, Huaqi, was made heir and lineage head in the early years of the republic. Denied his presumptive rights as eldest son, the embittered Huanan turned to crime, leading a small group of toughs and running the village gambling den in the Southern Li temple.[39] Li's gang, like bands led by the infamous Xu the Number Two Black in neighboring Shenxian and others in nearby Wuqiang and Xianxian counties, lived by kidnapping, extortion, theft, and protection schemes. When the Nationalist party launched a province wide campaign to wipe out local bullies who deprived the state of tax revenues,[40] Li Huanan was hunted down and shot to death.

A threat to the dominant position of the Southern Li came in 1936 when a clash exposed raw social tensions. Customarily, before the harvest, poorer villagers were organized to watch the crops to prevent theft.[41] In fall 1936 Li Huaqi announced that seventy households, most belonging to his Southern Li lineage, would guard their own crops and no longer pay others for crop watching. Li Huaqi's tenant Xu Dun, a west-end resident, was soon charged with stealing Li's unharvested millet to compensate for the loss of his crop-watching income. Raoyang public security officers hauled Xu off to jail and handed the millet to Li Huaqi.[42] Friends and kin saw Xu Dun as an innocent victim of greed. No longer capable of feeding his children, they said, he had harvested his own unripe millet and was drying it in his courtyard.

The Xu Dun rift hastened the rending of the fabric of village life. After the arrest, the seventy households in the Li Huaqi group refused requests for donkeys, carts, and equipment for use in marriages and funerals. Feeling the economic squeeze, the declining elite withheld traditional services. A scuffle broke out when Qiao Laohui, from the east village, was denied use of a wagon to transport his father's body to the burial ground. Tempers flared. Before the incident could be controlled, knives flashed. Several people were wounded.

A 1935 spate of crimes by Southern Li powerbroker Li Yingzhou had already incited popular anger. Yingzhou had accused Li Tietou, who had just quit working for him, of chicken theft, and then nearly eliminated Tietou's entire family. The economic decline threatened family. Seven women died within a month of giving birth in 1936, and many newborns died in delivery or soon thereafter. Even marriage became problematic for the poor in decline. After the death in the early 1930s of the Second Master, a geomancer who lived in Wugong and presided at weddings and funerals, only more prosperous households could afford the services of a geomancer at a wedding ceremony or funeral.

Although the Li Huaqi faction included several prosperous households, it was composed primarily of Southern Li lineage members, most independent tillers. The prosperous households of Li Chunrong and Qiao Wanxiang did not side with Li Huaqi. The faction backing Xu Dun was also composed primarily of independent tillers. Whereas 100 households remained neutral, 110, led by Xu Dun's kinsman Xu Yizhou, organized against Li Huaqi's group.[43] The dispute pitted a landlord against an owner-tenant, yet the battle lines were shaped mainly by lineage, tradition, and residence. The Li Huaqi faction was principally based in the village center, while the Xu Yizhou faction brought together villagers from the east and west. Dissident leaders even included members of the declining Northern Li lineage. It was the first time outsiders who lived on the outskirts of the village, joined together. After the 1936 autumn harvest, Xu Dun's supporters met in the Pusa Temple in the west village, the Xu lineage end of the village. They bowed and burned incense before the goddess of mercy, vowing to band together to prevent injustices of the sort suffered by Xu Dun.

Xu Yizhou was a gaunt illiterate who spoke in a rhythmic cadence. His heart went out to his clansman Xu Dun and his desperate household. Xu Yizhou came from one of Wugong's poorest households, who owned three mu of land. His mother died in 1919 when Xu was twelve years old, his father was chronically ill, and his sisters, ages three and seven, were too young to work. When drought struck in 1921–22, one sister died. Unable to repay a loan, in 1922 the father fled to Manchuria, shortly to die. At age fifteen Xu Yizhou had to survive on his own. He placed his remaining sister with a maternal uncle and went to Fuzhou, two thousand miles away on the South China coast, where he worked as an apprentice in a handicraft shop. After five years Xu returned to farm scraps of family land and a vegetable plot rented with savings. Xu supplemented crop income by working as a short-term laborer. At age twenty-five, he at last married. It was a simple affair, but the bride brought a large beautiful wooden dresser.

Xu told the villagers in the Pusa Temple that by uniting they could avoid Xu Dun's fate. Speakers suggested banding together to form the Association. Fate was linked to moral faults in one's family, not to heaven's arbitrariness. When local people said, "Look in the market to see if there are no fish in the river," they meant that if you fail to catch fish (earn money, have a son, and so on), you have only yourself to blame since it is obvious from the fish selling in the market that fish are there to be caught. Throughout the region various semisecret self-help organizations, such as the Celestial Way, the Tea Leaf Society, and the Just Sect of the Central Gate, were already functioning. Westender Zhang Wenchen, an educated man of extremely modest means, who later briefly served as village chief, helped draft a protest statement. Under the eyes of the compassionate goddess of mercy, Association members swore an oath, shouting out each line in response to Association leaders:[44]

The suffering poor of Wugong
To survive
Join together
In unity
To share weal and woe.
If one has difficulty
All will help
Swearing to struggle
Against the money lords.

The Association fruitlessly sent representatives to accompany twenty of Xu Dun's kin to the district government in Xiaodi, and twice to Raoyang itself, where Xu remained behind bars. Finally Xu Yizhou asked the newly elected village chief, Li Chunrong, a member of the traditional elite not linked to the Li Huaqi faction, to travel with him to Raoyang to lend clout to the appeal. Li had the connections and Xu Dun was released. But there was still the matter of the seized grain. The Association was a force to reckon with, so Li Huaqi offered to return the grain to Xu Dun. Li then held a dinner in Xu Dun's honor to acknowledge publicly the wrong done Xu.[45] No real reconciliation occurred, however.

The village was in disarray. Few were willing to assume village leadership, which entailed collecting taxes, organizing labor conscripts, mediating disputes, and serving as liaison between villagers and the authorities in Raoyang. Zhang Yunshan, a respected west-end independent tiller who had been chosen by the lineage heads to serve as village chief in 1911, stepped down in early 1936, before the Xu Dun affair. His successor, well-to-do Li Chunrong, lasted barely a year.[46] In early 1937 a poor farmer named Li Zhenjia took over, but gave up after only a few months. The thankless job went in spring 1937 to Li Jianting, a prominent member of the floundering Eight Courtyards, which no longer could hold the village together.

The Burden of Resistance

In July 1937 Japanese forces, who six years earlier had conquered Manchuria, launched an all-out attack in North China. They first pacified core regions along the railroads and in the plains surrounding Beijing, Tianjin, Baoding, and Shijiazhuang. The first detachments of Japanese soldiers that passed through Raoyang merely visited a few villages, giving out candy, playing with children, antagonizing no one. They quickly moved on. That autumn the county government tried to organize villagers to prepare for a Japanese advance, ordering implementation of a system of collective responsibility. As in imperial times, groups of ten households were set up for tax collection and labor recruitment for public works. In addition, mutual surveillance by group members required reporting unusual developments. Failure brought punishment to all. The system exacerbated village divisions.

Nationalist party authorities in Raoyang ordered the Wugong village chief, Li Jianting, to recruit laborers to construct defenses in Nanhan village, five miles to the northwest. Li informed the recruits they would be paid sixty coppers a day, a bit more than the going rate for short-term agricultural laborers. Needy farmers volunteered for the winter slack-season work, returning after half a month, but Chief Li had not received funds to pay them. Anger exploded into protest. The split touched off by the Xu Dun conflict was fresh in people's minds, and Li Jianting was a prominent member of Li Huaqi's lineage. Jianting's father and Huaqi had the same paternal grandfather. The Association stepped forward to represent the unpaid, demanding that Li Jianting pay it all. After saying he was not responsible for the county government's failure to pay, Li proposed, to ease tension, that prosperous village households each contribute one dollar for every dollar that the Association contributed to the labor fund. The Association, which included a core of independent tillers who had savings, agreed. Each side contributed one hundred silver dollars. The Association then took care of its own, giving almost all two hundred dollars to laborers who were Association members.

Shortly thereafter two hundred dollars more was raised, three-quarters of which was also distributed to Association members. Finally, a third distribution of two hundred dollars was made, but some of the money owed to the laborers had still not been paid. The matter lapsed until the eve of the lunar New Year, the customary time for settling accounts. The Association approached Chief Li on behalf of the laborers who without full pay would be unable to celebrate in the time-honored way by eating tasty pork-filled dumplings, which helped guarantee an auspicious future.

It may be going too far to call the incident of New Year 1938 the Dumpling Revolt, but the main grievance addressed to Chief Li was that the more prosperous were eating meat dumplings that very evening, while too many other villagers had only a coarse porridge. Li Jianting knew the symbolic significance of dumplings. He agreed to hand over one thousand catties of tax grain to those who had still not received full wages. A few weeks later Li Jianting stepped down as village chief. Li Fuxiang, a poor tiller, would hold the job for two years. The old local elite could no longer provide much insurance against fate or secure help from higher levels.

The Nationalist party's modernization effort had brought a weak attack on bandits and a feeble war on the religions of the poor. It had failed to mobilize latent nationalism, address the key issue of spiraling taxes, or reverse economic decline. Households disintegrated and the traditional local elite no longer could keep the social fabric whole.

2 ❧ BONDS
OF
WAR

Japanese forces began encroaching on North China in the early
1930s, when people in Raoyang and other areas of central Hebei
were struggling with economic decline and political and social disintegration. In 1931 Japan seized China's northeastern provinces
and established the puppet state of Manchukuo. By 1935 Japanese
troops had probed south into northern Hebei, testing Chinese defenses. Student protesters demanded that the Nationalist government stop fighting Communists and mobilize the nation for war
with Japan. The kidnapping of Nationalist leader Jiang Jieshi in
December 1936 led to a second united front between Nationalists
and Communists. But in July 1937 the Japanese launched an all-out
invasion to integrate North China into an economic zone including
Manchuria, Korea, Taiwan, and a greater Japan that had annexed the
Ryukyu Islands and Hokkaido. Japanese forces were stretched thin,
occupying major cities, central markets, and vital railway lines. Initially, the invaders viewed peripheral places like Raoyang as inconse-
quential or left administration there to unreliable and politically
illegitimate Chinese collaborators.

Patriotic urban students fled to relatively uncontested rural areas
to work with Nationalist, Communist, and independent forces in
organizing resistance. These were liberated zones in which patriots
recruited in the absence of direct Japanese occupation.[1] The people
of counties like Raoyang were about to become important actors in
the history of twentieth-century China. The Communist party, to
build support, led wartime resistance and implemented popular, but
gradual, economic reforms. Its ability to influence and control economic, political, and social life in places like central Hebei would
contribute mightily to its postwar struggle to seize power.

Regional Resistance

Lu Zhengcao headed the central Hebei military resistance in the early stage of the war. Lu's career illustrates how some people with no previous links with the Communist party followed a patriotic path that advanced the Communist cause. A native of Manchuria, Lu, after graduating from primary school, rose rapidly in the warlord army of Zhang Zuolin. When the Japanese captured Manchuria in 1931, the Northeast Army retreated south into Hebei, where it was reorganized by the Nationalists. Lu was made a regimental commander in the new 53d Army. When the Japanese struck again in July 1937, Lu's unit retreated from the Hebei capital, Baoding, just ahead of enemy forces advancing south along the Beijing-Hankou railroad. Lu, now in contact with Communist party representatives in Shijiazhuang, initiated guerrilla operations two hundred miles south of Beijing and joined forces with other partisan groups in central Hebei and along the Shanxi-Hebei border.[2]

Communist guerrillas were linked to the 115th Division of the Eighth Route Army under the command of Lin Biao and his deputy Nie Rongzhen. In September 1937 the 115th Division cooperated with Nationalist units to defeat Japanese forces in a major battle in Shanxi province. Following the battle, a high point of the Communist-Nationalist united front, Nie led troops of the 115th Division into the Wutai Mountains on the Shanxi-Hebei border, where they eventually linked up with forces commanded by Lu Zhengcao and others. Nie Rongzhen, a worker-student in France in the early 1920s and then a student in Moscow, was the leading military figure in the region during the war. Peng Zhen, a member of the Communist party's North China Bureau, became the top party figure with the army. In November 1937 a Jinchaji (Shanxi-Chahaer-Hebei) Party Committee was established with headquarters in Fuping in the mountains west of Baoding near the Shanxi-Hebei-border.

In January 1938, the Jinchaji Border Region, the first of a series of united front bases that brought together Nationalist, Communist, and independent forces, was formally inaugurated. Its chairman, a non-Communist, was Song Shaowen, a former Hebei county magistrate under the Nationalists. Communists played an active role under the border region administration. In April 1938 the first Jinchaji Communist Party Congress was convened in Anping county, just west of Raoyang in the secure backwaters of central Hebei. That month resistance forces in an area including Raoyang linked up to form the Central Hebei Military Region as a subdivision of the Jinchaji Base.[3] Raoyang, Anping, and Shenxian counties formed the solid core of the central Hebei resistance.

The Central Hebei Military Region embraced thirty-eight counties in 1938. Japanese-controlled Beijing and Tianjin were its northernmost outposts, and it was bounded east and west by the enemy-occupied railroads

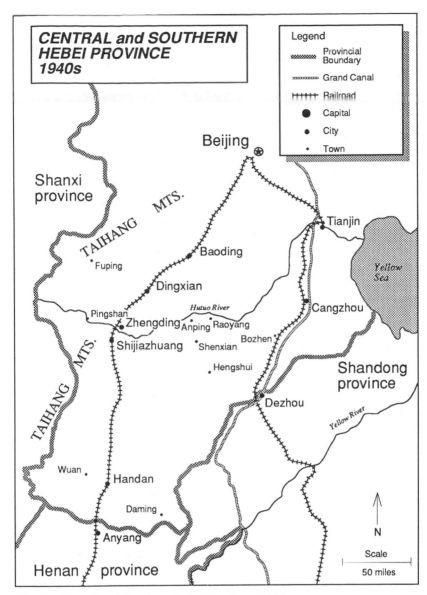

Inside the map:

CENTRAL and SOUTHERN HEBEI PROVINCE 1940s

Legend
- Provincial Boundary
- Grand Canal
- Railroad
- Capital
- City
- Town

Beijing

Shanxi province

TAIHANG MTS.

Fuping

Baoding

Dingxian

Tianjin

Yellow Sea

Pingshan

Zhengding

Hutuo River

Anping Raoyang

Cangzhou

Shijiazhuang

Shenxian

Bozhen

Hengshui

Shandong province

Dezhou

Yellow River

TAIHANG MTS.

Wuan

Handan

Daming

Anyang

Henan province

N

Scale
50 miles

Map 1   Central and Southern Hebei Province, 1940s

running south from those two cities. Unlike mountainous resistance bases, central Hebei, in the heart of a plain, provided partisans little cover. Japanese forces could occupy any part of the region. The guerrillas responded by constructing tunnels and ditches, honeycombing resistance villages and even connecting villages.[4]

The Central Hebei Military Region military commander was former warlord and Nationalist officer Lu Zhengcao. When a Central Hebei Resistance Government was organized in spring 1938, Lu became its chair and concurrently a member of the nine-member governing committee of the larger Jinchaji Base Area. In the early years of the war, the leading Communist party official in the Central Hebei Military Region was Party Secretary Huang Jing. In the early 1930s Huang was political mentor, lover, and husband of the Shandong-born actress who later, under the name Jiang Qing, became the wife of Mao Zedong.[5] A physics student at Shandong University, Huang was caught up in student politics in 1931 when Japan invaded Manchuria. In 1932 he joined the Communist party and led students in the anti-Japanese patriotic December Ninth movement of 1935. In mid-1938, shortly after the formation of the Central Hebei Resistance Government, the Nationalists dispatched a general to central Hebei to coordinate armed resistance. But within a year, cooperation turned to acrimony, and the general withdrew along with most Nationalist administrators. By mid-1939 Communists politically dominated the region. Individual Nationalists and independents continued to play important roles in military and political affairs in central Hebei, but the Nationalist army and civil administration never returned.[6]

County Resistance

Poor hinterland Raoyang, far from railroads, major commercial rivers, and central markets, became, in Japanese military parlance, an unpacified area. Its value to the resistance lay in mobilizing people for the army, providing such strategic resources as grain and cotton to support that army, and harassing Japanese forces in the plains. Many of the leading grass-roots organizers of popular resistance to Japan were the rural intellectuals (often linked to declining traditional elites) who had been active from 1925 in the small county Communist party until the crackdown of 1933.[7] Jiao Shoujian, a leader of the abortive Xiaodi uprising in 1930, helped rebuild the county party underground after Japanese forces began probing into northern Hebei in 1935. The new party organization, which consisted of such veterans as Wang Chunhai and Li Xuchu, who had strong ties to county education and medical elites, was supported by a secret party group at the men's normal school. By mid-1936 the underground party, now dedicated to promoting class unity and the patriotic cause, had seventy members.

As in 1925, the party placed a high priority on contacting county school-

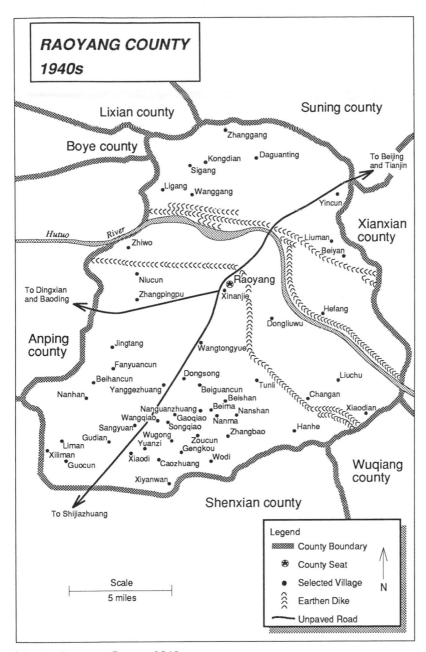

Map 2   Raoyang County, 1940s

teachers and other members of the educated elite like Yu Shiyu, who taught primary school in Beiguan village. Yu was educated in a Christian secondary school in his native Liaoning province. Following the Japanese occupation of the northeast in 1931, he joined Zhang Xueliang's Northeast Army retreating into Hebei. Dissatisfied with military life, Yu made contact with a former classmate who hailed from Raoyang and settled down in Beiguan village on the outskirts of the county seat to recruit patriotic county students. Like many of the local elite and teachers in resistance work, Yu joined the Communist party and rose high in the county administration.[8]

In late 1936, the revitalized Raoyang Communist party quickly expanded. Students and teachers who had been activated after 1935, in the first round of nationalistic resistance mobilization, headed off to outlying areas. By the end of 1937, only months after the all-out Japanese invasion, the Communists had established organizations in forty-three Raoyang villages and claimed 592 members. The Raoyang Anti-Japanese Resistance Government was established in winter 1937 with the support of some former Nationalist authorities, the new Communist organization, and various independent groups.

Armed resistance in Raoyang was led by a coalition of larger landowners and merchants. In mid-1937 they deployed militia units, each with three hundred men, in the north county, in Raoyang town, and in the south. Following the arrival of Lu Zhengcao in the fall, the three units were reorganized as the Raoyang Self-defense Force, but unification sputtered. The third unit deteriorated into a band of thieves and rapists. In early 1938, when the Central Hebei Military Region was formed and Communist military power grew, Eighth Route Army forces killed the leader of the renegade band, reintegrating it in their county resistance force.

Another local bandit leader, Xu the Number Two Black, organized an anti-Communist army headquartered in Shenxian county. The Raoyang Self-Defense Force commanded by Tian Tongchun attacked and routed it, but Xu the Number Two Black escaped. His men disguised themselves as pallbearers and bore their leader to safety inside a coffin. However, in 1938 Xu's forces were again defeated, and Xu was executed. Another bandit leader who joined the Hebei resistance was Old Lady Jin. She inherited leadership after her husband, who had led the hundred-strong band, was killed. Following Japan's invasion, her forces were integrated into the Eighth Route Army.

Raoyang belonged to the Eighth Military Subdistrict of the Central Hebei Military Region, which, in turn, fell within the larger Jinchaji Base Area.[9] Raoyang villagers began to join the 16th, 23d, and 30th regiments of the Eighth Route Army's 102d Division in 1938. North and south of Raoyang in the counties of Xianxian and Hejian, Moslem cavalry units were formed whose feats were soon legendary. For the poorest villagers, the army continued to be a way out of a hopeless decline.

With Japanese troops paying little attention to Raoyang until 1939, the resistance was free to mobilize. In May 1938 the Central Hebei Tax Bureau was established; in August an anti-Japanese academy, headed by Yang Xiu-feng, opened in Shenxian offering a three-month training course for political cadres; and on September 10 the first issue of *Dao bao*, the central Hebei party committee's newspaper was published. County newspapers followed, including one in Raoyang. Song and dance troupes spread resistance propaganda. Calling their work "living newspaper plays," activists with painted faces and costumes performed to crowds at markets, satirizing Chinese collaborators and praising the resistance. Anti-Japanese national salvation organizations were formed to involve young people, teachers, workers, peasants, and women. New schools and literacy classes won popular support.[10]

During the resistance war in North China, party propagandists did more than stoke patriotic passions. The songs the propagandists taught villagers included lyrics that rang with hosannahs to the Soviet Union, praising not only its Red Army fighters, but also its collective farms. These educated propagandists also tried to undercut what they regarded as backward ideas that perpetuated the inhuman evils of feudal despotism. They vouched instead for new forms of authority based on elections and constitutions, and new lives liberated from exploitative landlords and usurers. These modern-minded intellectuals saw the old culture as cannibalistic, the murderous residue of a slave society. The propagandists therefore spoke against religion, promoting atheistic materialism as enhancing life. At party-sponsored rallies, propagandists urged villagers to destroy superstition in order to advance a new democratic revolution. Villagers were urged to simplify customs, reduce expenses on funerals, and eventually eliminate all feudal superstition.

By early 1938 Raoyang was regarded by the central Hebei authorities as a model resistance county. It was so secure that for brief periods in 1938 important regional resistance organizations, including the central Hebei Communist party committee, field hospital, arsenal, and bookstore, were based near the county town. The appointment of Communist party member Du Qingzhe as Raoyang county magistrate in October was indicative of a political shift.[11] United front was praised, but the once-outlawed Communist party now dominated the resistance coalition. Remnants of the old Nationalist county administration and the various nonaligned groups that did not flee south were absorbed by the Communist-led administration.

Building Village Resistance

Compared to its neighbors, Wugong village's resistance to Japan got off to a slow start. In patriotic Zoucun, villagers tore down ancient town walls so the Japanese could not make Zoucun an armed stronghold. Unlike its neighbor Yanggezhuang, an important market village in the south county during the Qing dynasty, Wugong village had not been involved in the revolution in the late 1920s and early 1930s. It had no Communist party branch and no connections with the patriotic movement based in the county seat. In contrast, Yanggezhuang had several dozen young people ready to join armed units in late 1937.

Not until late spring 1938 did a Communist organizer, one Jin Qinglian, walk into Wugong. He was the party secretary of Raoyang's fourth district. Having married the older sister of Qiao Wanxiang, a prosperous east-end farmer, Jin Qinglian was family. Jin stayed in the home of Prosperous Qiao, as we called him, and learned about the Xu Dun affair, which led to the creation of the Association, and about the recent dumpling rebellion, which pitted the Association against Li Jianting, the former village chief. Prosperous Qiao himself had stood aloof from these disputes.

Jin acted on the party's united front policy, which stressed class unity to resist Japan. This strategy reflected the interests of independent tillers, who constituted 70 percent of Wugong households. Initially, Jin did not even contact the Association. Like party organizers elsewhere, he helped establish a mobilization committee. It included among its leaders representatives of all village sectors, the Southern Li lineage and the Association, people from the east, west, and central village, the elite, and the once excluded. By contrast, in Raoyang villages where the most powerful lineages were excluded from resistance organizations, a basis was laid for vengeful rule by the heretofore powerless.

Stories of Japanese soldiers raping any woman they could grab were told by pregnant women who fled occupied Shijiazhuang, the railway junction southwest of Raoyang.[12] Tales circulated about a notorious Japanese rapist, an officer called Big Gold Tooth, who was stationed in the Hutuo River town of Luhan. His troops, it was said, rounded up young girls and forced them into prostitution. Parents tried to protect their daughters by covering them with dirt and rags so they would seem sick, ugly, and old.

Villagers prepared to defend themselves against invaders and atrocities. The mobilization committee set up a Peasant Anti-Japanese Patriotic League, a Worker Anti-Japanese Patriotic League, and similar groups for women, youths, and children. Chosen to lead the Peasant Anti-Japanese Patriotic League was west-end independent tiller Xu Shengfa.[13] He was linked with Li Huaqi's faction, not the faction led by Xu Yizhou, during the Xu Dun affair. As a Xu lineage member tied to Li's group, Xu Shengfa could perhaps bond what had been broken. In this way, first steps were taken to reunite the community.

Jin Qinglian successfully approached members of the traditional elite headed by Li Huaqi with a proposal to form a Communist party branch. Only then, on July 5, 1938, did Jin create a second party organization centered in the Association and inaugurated by Li Wenkao, west-ender Xu Yizhou, and east-ender Geng Wenduo. Each party branch represented a power center in the village; each contributed to the resistance.

Neither group was supposed to know of the other, but information about Li Huaqi's branch leaked to Xu Yizhou. He asked Jin Qinglian if the rumors were true. Jin told Xu he did not need to know. Keeping secrets, Jin said, was for the good of the village and the resistance. Members were warned not to discuss membership or party work even with blood relations. The two Wugong party branches acted separately and secretly. For security reasons the branches held no group meetings. Party members knew only their recruiter. Jin Qinglian alone knew the names of all party members. Jin sought to establish leadership over the patriotic associations by placing undercover party members in strategic positions. Villagers assumed that the united front resistance government was coordinating mobilization activities. Few knew that the district party was making appointments through Jin Qinglian.

The Li Huaqi party branch collapsed by the end of 1938, but prosperous and influential Wugong households, like their counterparts throughout central Hebei, continued to play active roles in the wartime resistance. Twenty-one-year-old Li Feng, the son of Li Jianting, joined the party and subsequently rose in the national Salvation Youth Corps in the Central Hebei Military Region. In 1946 Li Feng would enlist in the People's Liberation Army. Li Jianting's second son, thirteen-year-old Maoxiu, in 1939 began two years of anti-Japanese propaganda work among children in Raoyang's fourth district. Recruited by the director of youth work in the county, Maoxiu eventually took charge of children's work in the thirty villages of the fourth district. Among those under him was Zhang Duan, who headed children's work in Wugong, a relationship that many years later would be brutally reversed.

Li Fengxiang, a nephew of Li Jianting, joined the party in Wugong in 1938 at age twenty. He rose to direct resistance cultural work in Raoyang. His brother, Fengtai, also joined the party, making a career in the military. Li Yongkuan, a son of former village chief Li Chunrong, was twelve years old when the war began. He attended a resistance school in Shanxi in the mountains west of Wugong, a first step in a military career as an officer. Throughout Raoyang, educated nationalistic youth from prosperous and powerful households were among the first to respond to the appeals of the patriotic united front. Many assumed leadership positions in home villages, while some rose in the party and army in the region. Others established party and military careers that took them to distant reaches of China.

In late 1938, a thirteen-member guerrilla team was organized in Wugong, led by a reliable and respected west village independent farmer and Communist party member, Xu Mantang. The twenty-year-old Steady Xu, as we called him, lived with his mother and farmed five mu of land, supplementing this income by working as a short-term hired laborer and peddling vegetables. Armed with a few old pistols donated by prosperous households, the guerrillas guarded the village and provided intelligence. Drums were beaten to warn of approaching Japanese troops.

Geng Shupu, a teenage primary school graduate and east village rope spinner for whom Japanese invasion spelled the loss of markets, joined the party in 1938. His paternal uncle was a party member in Yanggezhuang village. Later that year Geng Shupu was sent for guerrilla training at 120th Division headquarters. The trainees doubled as bodyguards for Commander He Long, who sported a straw hat, shirt, and shorts. On returning to Raoyang, Shupu joined the county military force, a one-hundred-member unit armed with rifles, pistols, and submachine guns, wearing uniforms of locally woven cloth. Their job was to protect villages, catch spies, and eliminate traitors.

Geng Shupu worked in a propaganda unit seeking to conquer fears that prevented villagers from housing, hiding, and caring for troops. His unit swept courtyards, carried water, and did small chores for farm families. Always fearful of betrayal, members of Geng's unit approached only trusted people, such as family. Members hid in tunnels and homes by day, coming out only at night, and moved to other villages every second or third day. They abjured large meetings, worked one on one, and kept out of Raoyang town, whose strangers they could not trust. In October 1939 central Hebei established a secret police apparatus, already in place at the party center, which mirrored the one in Stalin's Soviet Union, with Li Zhiguang in charge of both its Social Affairs Bureau and its Public Security General Office.[14]

From 1939 to 1942 Geng Shupu headed the National Salvation Youth Corps in the third district of Raoyang in the north county. The corps drew on eighteen to twenty-five-year-olds and was essential for military recruitment. In 1940 Shupu married Li Xiurong of the west village, and they soon had two children. With older brother Geng Jian farming the family land and assisting his wife and children, Shupu was freed to work in the resistance, which was in large part a network of trusted family connections. After a small Japanese contingent occupied the county town in late January 1939, Raoyang guerrillas organized sabotage teams to disrupt transportation and communication lines. Teams of villagers dug trenches and holes in the roads to block Japanese vehicles. As part of the county effort, the Wugong team dug trenches as far to the southwest as the Shijiazhuang-Hangzhou highway, which ran from western Hebei to east-central China. In 1938 a paramilitary women's self-protection corps was organized in Wugong. Some Raoyang women joined the army and were sent out of the county. One, Xu Supo, eventually became party secretary in Baoding. In 1939 Wugong east-ender Qiao Wenzhi, who led the women's organization while still in her teens, became the first female party member in

Wugong. Most women participants toiled into the night making shoes, socks, and uniforms for combatants. Women also dug tunnels to hide troops and activists and served as messengers. Activists urged mothers to have their sons join the Eighth Route Army. Getting everyone organized on behalf of the resistance was seen by patriots as ending the weakness of being a loose sheet of sand. Organization meant national strength. Of course not all villages met their recruitment quotas. Eighth Route Army recruiters sometimes resorted to methods associated with the Nationalists. They captured young men, tied them up, and hauled them off. Many of these young men fled at the first opportunity.

One hundred Japanese and puppet troops were quartered in Raoyang town with headquarters in the commandeered home of Han Shufu, an uncle of Communist pioneer Han Zimu. The family courtyard of the Tians, another landed Raoyang family, served the Japanese as a prison. Left alone by Japanese soldiers from 1937 to 1939, Wugong was also spared the worst of wartime horrors from 1939 to 1941. Japanese control was heaviest in the more commercialized north county. The resistance, therefore, was strongest in the south county, where Wugong was located. Japanese forces first appeared near Wugong in spring 1939. Those who spotted the Japanese described them as short, wearing leather shoes and hats, and carrying helmets on their backs. Officers were identified by their horses, swords, and pistols. The Japanese rarely ventured outside of the walled county town, which was surrounded by several hundred guerrillas. The county puppet government was headed by an outsider, Dou Ruyu, who was killed by local partisans in 1940.

Until May 1942 the armed presence of the invaders and the puppet administration was so marginal that patriotic associations in Wugong operated openly. These organizations, known collectively as the Wugong Resistance League, were coordinated by Li Fengxiang, nephew of the Southern Li lineage leader.[15] The league, like the mobilization committee founded in 1938, brought together the factions of the prior intravillage conflict.

In the early 1940s, Xu Yizhou, once the spokesman of the Association and now the intelligence link between the village and the partisan network that extended throughout the thirty villages in the fourth district, was chosen to replace Li Wenkao as Wugong party secretary. Under the guidance of Xu, Old Militia, as villagers came to call him, the party secretly organized more than one hundred "security families" to hide resistance workers passing through Wugong and to care for wounded Eighth Route Army soldiers.[16] A top Red Army military leader, Yang Chengwu, in order to communicate with soldiers whose accents were incomprehensible to others, traveled with speakers from Tianjin, Baoding, and Raoyang. Hinterland villagers were painfully self-conscious about their back-county accents. When traveling, they were silenced or shamed by city people mocking their rounded way of pronouncing words.

The Japanese army distinguished between two kinds of villages, those to be left alone and those to be crushed. In the years 1939–41, Wugong paid what the Japanese demanded, while also quietly paying taxes to the resistance. Wugong was left alone. Because of its secure status some people fled other villages for the safety of Wugong. By contrast, in neighboring Gaoqiao, the invaders buried alive five people. In a gruesome torture, a long bamboo shaft was shoved down the throat of one of the buried victims. Slowly, the pipe to the air outside collapsed. Slowly, the victim gasped and suffocated. Soon traitors captured by all combatants were killed in this slow manner. Most villagers tried to get on with both sides. The alternative was to be a target of one or the other. The prosperous Dong family in Raoyang town, headed by Big Wagon Dong, ran the county's top restaurant and wooed all sides.

As the occupation continued, Japanese forces became more destructive and brutal. They desecrated the Xianxian Catholic church. Hidden mines that blew a friend to pieces made it difficult for surviving Japanese soldiers not to think of all Chinese strangers as possible enemies. Forced prostitution, monumental arrogance, corvée labor, grain levees, rape, and reprisals outraged villagers. Rural people increasingly hated the Japanese. They told tales about how the enemy forced people to bow and crawl in a degrading manner, how a Chinese was pushed to his death from the top of a fortification or shot for sport. Indignities and injustices were subjects of daily gossip and outrage.

In reality, of course, Japanese behavior was quite diverse. When Chinese puppet troops under Japanese command stormed Wugong in 1942, diminutive Zhang Zhou found herself trapped at home with her two-year-old daughter. She cowered in a small rear room while the troops pounded the front gate. When a Chinese soldier grabbed her, he smashed her across the back with his rifle. The Japanese commander called off the soldier, saying, "Don't beat her. The child will be frightened." Such instances of mercy were taken as exceptions to a cruel rule.

Villagers came to believe that people in occupied towns and surrounding hamlets who cooperated with the Japanese were traitors, or as it was translated in peasant political culture, people devoid of any sense of moral duty. It was said of these morally tainted villagers on the outskirts of Raoyang town, "In Shao, Xi, Cai, Bai, no one will bury you even if you die."

The Political Economy of Tax Reform

Whereas educated people and declining traditional elites in peripheral areas of central Hebei cooperated with the Communist party in building an organizational infrastructure to serve the resistance, Communist wartime strategists believed that households barely eking out a living would be especially receptive to patriotic appeals if things improved on the economic front. This meant devising ways to pump life into the economy. A stronger economy could also place more precious resources in the hands of the Communist-led resistance. Economic reconstruction and state building would move ahead simultaneously. But economic reform would backfire if it drove the more prosperous and the traditional elite out of the wartime coalition. The solution was gradual tax reform.

The reform began in Wugong in mid-1938, after the village party branch was organized, and well before Japanese troops appeared in the county. First, the "rational burden tax" was implemented in base areas across North China. Guidelines came down to Raoyang from the Central Hebei Military Region.[17] The tax reform was introduced in Wugong in the name of the fourth district people's government—a united front administration dominated by Communists. Under the rational burden tax, investigators graded all fields by fertility, irrigation, and estimated yield. A mu of land normally capable of producing one picul (150 catties) of coarse grain was defined as a standard mu, and each standard mu was classified as a "unit of wealth." The first 1.5 units of wealth per person were tax-exempt. A household of five, regardless of landholdings, enjoyed tax exemptions on the first 1,125 catties of grain. The poorest were thereby exempt from the tax. A flat-rate agricultural tax was levied above the exemption threshold.

The Wugong tax collector was a better-off east village farmer, Geng Lianmin, director of village financial affairs and a top aide of village chief Li Zihou. Jovial Geng won a reputation for scrupulous honesty. He noted that Communist party organizers blamed hated taxes on the Nationalist party. These organizers told villagers pressured to attend meetings that Communists could reduce taxes. Throughout the 1940s, as Communists explained their tax reforms at meeting after meeting, country people, who seldom thanked outsiders for help, mockingly responded, "Under the Nationalists, too many taxes; under the Communists, too many meetings."

The party's administrative arm, the Raoyang people's government, levied 100,000 catties of grain from Wugong. Chief Li Zihou calculated exemptions and then apportioned a tax obligation to each household. Estimating that Wugong's 4,470 mu could ordinarily produce 804,600 catties (180 catties per mu), the village chief first deducted personal exemptions of 312,750 catties. To collect the required 100,000 catties, just over 20 percent of the remaining 491,580 catties of taxable grain was levied. If yields were higher, the real rate would be lower, and vice versa. In an average year 100,000 catties of grain was just over 12 percent of gross production.

The total amount of land taxes collected in such a year did not differ much from tax levels imposed earlier by the Nationalist government. But the tax gougers were gone, and personal exemptions distributed the tax burden in favor of poorer households. Grain produced by tenants on rented land was included in the gross production of the tenants themselves, most of whom were tax-exempt. Production on land tilled by hired laborers was included in the landowner's responsibility. The rational burden tax replaced a system assigning obligations based on land acreage regardless of productivity. That system had favored wealthier landowners who had more-productive, better-irrigated land. Off-farm income remained untaxed.

The rational burden tax reform, which exempted the first 225 catties of grain per tiller, exempted some 40 percent of Wugong households, including virtually all owner-tenants and about 20 percent of independent tillers. Most independent farming households paid the people's government about the same amount or slightly less than they had paid the short-lived Nationalist administration. The tax reform helped the poor without jeopardizing the broad middle stratum of independent tillers. In fact, even those independent tillers who paid about the same amount under the new program as the old welcomed a system that was administered evenhandedly and squeezed the prosperous a little.

Twenty-five more-prosperous independent farming households, particularly five that hired long-term labor or rented out significant amounts of land, bore the burden of the reform. The gap decreased between them and the poorest households, yet the basic structure of an independent tiller economy remained intact. The more prosperous were still allowed to rent out modest amounts of land and hire farm help. Landlords collected three silver dollars per year per mu from tenants.

Flooding in 1939 was so timely that crops in 1940 were the best in living memory, but the same year a cholera epidemic took an estimated twenty thousand lives. Out-of-control natural forces still decided life and death.

In mid-1941, three years after the first tax reform, the resistance government instituted a second tax reform, the "unified progressive tax." The rational burden had taxed all income above individual exemptions at uniform rates regardless of the amount of land owned or the wealth of the household. The unified progressive tax imposed higher rates on higher-income earners. Households with one picul of taxable grain were taxed at the rate of 10 percent, two at 12 percent, three at 13 percent, and so on, up to a 40 percent maximum.[18] Under this more progressive tax, a better-off household producing 4,500 catties of taxable grain per capita would pay 1,800 catties, or 40 percent, compared with 900 catties under the rational burden system. The progressive tax eased the burden of some independent farmers and further shifted taxes to the few households that produced more than 1,500 catties of taxable grain per person. The gap between richer and poorer was closing.

A wartime survey of twenty-seven villages in nine central Hebei counties, including Raoyang, in summer 1941 showed that 36 percent of hired laborers had acquired sufficient land to become independent tillers, classified by the Communists as poor peasants. Another 20 percent had achieved what the party called middle-peasant status, and another 1.8 percent had become rich peasants. Among previously poor tillers, 28 percent had risen to middle-peasant status, 0.4 percent to rich peasant. The other side of this land-equalizing tax coin was that among rich peasants, 34.9 percent had declined to middle peasant, 8.1 percent to poor peasant. Wugong's five largest land-owning households faced substantial tax hikes. Assuming yields of 200 catties per mu on the 395 mu of better land they farmed themselves out of a total of 465 mu owned, after exemptions of 11,700 catties of grain, they paid taxes at the highest rate, 40 percent, on 67,300 catties. This was double the rational burden tax system's top rate.

The tax changes initiated a quiet revolution throughout the base area. The poor benefited most. Prosperous farmers like Li Duanfu, pinched by rising taxes, sold portions of land.[19] Those in the best position to buy land were the more affluent independent tillers who had some cash on hand. Few of them rushed to buy land sold at below market prices, though, because they feared entering a substantially higher tax bracket and a worse political bracket in the eyes of a party that favored the poor. Farmers who owned little land purchased most of the available plots. The reforms greatly enhanced intravillage economic equality. On December 24, 1940, Mao Zedong declared that only about 20 percent of households in base areas should be tax-exempt.[20] That fully 40 percent of Wugong households were tax-exempt in mid-1941 was indicative of the relative poverty of the village and of Raoyang.[21]

More-prosperous households sought loopholes in the tax reforms. Li Jianting tried to conceal production and to conceal ownership of land to evade taxes. Li Chunrong temporarily "transferred" land to the poorest members of his lineage. Since the poor were in a low tax bracket or exempt, taxes on crops grown on transferred land were much lower. The poor became partners in a tax scam. In effect, Li paid relatives to farm his land out of his tax savings so the land would remain his. When such arrangements were detected, the owner was pressed to sign away the land. Li Chunrong refused and paid the tax. The patrons of the traditional village elite no longer wielded overriding political power.

Others pawned their land in an attempt to skirt the new taxes. Those who tilled pawned land were responsible for the taxes. The emerging party-state required all who pawned their land to do so for a minimum of ten years.[22] Some poor villagers would remember this as a period in which the rich attempted to "give away" their land. As with political power, economic power was passing out of the hands of the vestiges of the traditional elite. The long-term downward trend, which by the 1930s had resulted in the loss of gleaning rights, a withdrawal of traditional services, and the dissolution of families, had been reversed. The tax reforms favored the large and expanding majority of independent cultivators and the very poor while preserving unity within the anti-Japanese resistance.

A Quiet Revolution

In 1940 Mao Zedong called for the reduction of land rents and interest on loans in the base areas. The maximum rent reduction stipulated was 25 percent.[23] In Wugong this would have reduced land rent from 3 to 2.25 silver dollars per mu, but in most of central Hebei little was done immediately to implement the "double reduction." A government work team from Raoyang's fourth district entered Wugong in early November 1941. The outsiders, Huang Baozhi and Tian Luanzi, promoted the double reduction for four months.[24] Tenancy, however, was not a burning issue in Wugong. In 1936 only 80 mu of private land, 3 percent of the total, was rented out to twenty-five households. By the early 1940s the amount of rented land had dropped. The goals of rent reduction, including reduction of inequality and elimination of tenancy, were quietly being achieved through tax reform. The direct rent reduction policy was not implemented.

Huang Baozhi and Tian Luanzi did slightly increase the salary paid to Wugong's thirty-three long-term agricultural workers above prevailing levels of fifty silver dollars per year. Short-term farmhands were not affected. An important gain for long-term laborers centered on symbolically important moments in the life cycle. On the three major festivals, lunar New Year, Dragon Boat Festival, and Mid-Autumn Festival, employers now had to give each hired hand three silver dollars as a "gratuity." In the past, the workers had received only one dollar on each holiday. In addition, the employer was now expected to make a gift to each hired hand of thirty feet of homespun cloth at year's end.

With so many men away in the army, Huang and Tian encouraged villagers to form small sideline cooperatives and pool their resources. Only Steady Xu Mantang, the independent farmer who led the Wugong guerrilla squad, responded. In late 1941, with the winter slack season approaching, Xu convinced several west-end neighbors to band together to press cotton seeds, manufacture peanut oil, and make bean curd.

The tax reform policies repaired much that seemed damaged without introducing new ruptures in the village. The revolution was also a restoration. The united front brought together diverse and sometimes fractious lineages and social groups to resist Japan. The party reforms of 1938 to 1942 revived the economy, healed societal divisions, and made the party the dynamic factor in village political life. By early March 1942, when Huang Baozhi and Tian Luanzi left, Raoyang braced for Japanese attack.

War

In spring 1942 the Japanese threw fifty thousand troops into an assault on central Hebei, part of an offensive against North China bases. The troops encircled, blockaded, and squeezed the region. Communist military leaders asserted that the central Hebei resistance was a dagger pointed at Japan's soft underbelly. The Japanese needed Chinese grain to support their Pacific war against the allies led by the United States. The Eighth Route Army also needed the grain. The struggle grew murderously intense as drought—and a deadly flu epidemic—spread across North China. With Japanese soldiers seizing grain, some villagers were stripping leaves and tree bark for sustenance to stave off famine.[25]

In the first week of May, using search and destroy tactics and supported by Chinese quisling forces, the Japanese invaders swept across Raoyang to where they believed Eighth Route Army soldiers were hiding. Many central Hebei leaders, ill prepared for the attack, hid in Zoucun, a headquarters of sub-district government.[26] Japanese intelligence operatives had done their work; the offensive trapped important leaders. Wugong people hurriedly hid their grain in containers that were placed in the fields and covered with dirt to look like burial mounds. But not even foreign soldiers were fooled by this ploy.

To escape the Japanese encirclement, party leaders sought safety in places like Wugong, a reliable village remote from the county seat. Those who hid in the tunnel network laboriously constructed under the village included Eighth Military Subdistrict Party Secretary Jin Cheng, who stayed with east-end party stalwart Geng Shupu, and Luo Yizhuan, who hid with twenty-four-year-old Li Wanyi, the head of the village Cultural Corps. Jin would eventually become China's minister of water conservancy and Luo would serve as minister of agriculture.

In June, much of the regional leadership fled central Hebei.[27] Later in the war, regional party leaders used Wugong as a temporary base on numerous occasions. In late 1942, a woman code-named Han Qimin, who was in charge of mobilizing women in the Central Hebei Military Region, visited Wugong. She hid in the home of Qiao Yong, a virtually adopted younger brother of Communist Qiao Hengtai. Known as Big Han, she eventually rose to head the Hebei Health Bureau. Another official who passed through Wugong code-named Little Han, was the early party activist and salt smuggler Zhang Shuguang, who eventually rose in Hu Yaobang's youth league to become Hebei governor. Old friends would prove to be good and powerful friends.

The party lacked the capacity to keep Japanese troops from plunder and murder. In summer 1942, following a skirmish with a small Eighth Route Army unit passing through western Wugong, the foreign force decided to make an example of the village. Within hours, the troops set ablaze 110 Wugong homes, apprehended twenty young men, killed several people, and seized livestock, grain, and furniture.[28] Neighboring villages suffered even heavier losses.

One mile north of Wugong, thirty Japanese soldiers surprised Yangge-zhuang's three hundred households early one morning. The villagers were forced to the threshing ground and ordered to hand over all the clothes and weapons they had prepared for the Eighth Route Army. No one moved. Five people, including three of the oldest men, were placed in a pigsty and threatened with death. Young women were forced to strip and to parade naked. No one was allowed to eat. Midday passed and still no one talked. The five people in the pigsty were bound, set aflame, and burned to death. Late in the afternoon everyone was locked inside buildings and threatened. There were three traitors in the village, but they dared not speak openly. They had reason to be afraid; in 1943 Eighth Route Army soldiers executed the trio.

During the Japanese spring offensive 550 Raoyang partisans were killed. Furthermore, nearly 500 troops commanded by Lu Zhengcao, leader of the Central Hebei Resistance Government, were surprised and wiped out north of the Hutuo River in the largest battle in Raoyang. At great cost, villagers fed and fought for the resistance. The Wugong party branch, with forty-three members in 1939, had expanded to sixty-three, including thirteen women, by the end of 1942. The village also sent seventy young men to join the Eighth Route Army.[29] One of them Li Wanyi.

Li returned to Wugong from a Shanxi base area where he had been trained as a propaganda specialist. He was taught to tell people that victory and justice would be theirs, that the struggle was part of a global effort led by their elder brother, the Soviet Union, that the Soviets would no more surrender to the Nazis than happily slice off their own ears. The goal of China's Communist party, Li proclaimed, was to take the socialist road already pioneered by Stalin.

In spite of these reassurances, the 1942 Japanese offensive not only exacted a heavy toll in life and property but also in many localities temporarily broke the back of the resistance. The Japanese deployed planes, tanks, artillery, cavalry, and bicycle-mounted troops. Chinese military historians report that one thousand people were killed by poison gas in Dingxian, northwest of Raoyang.[30] The central Hebei base area, which before the offensive had grown to include portions of fifty counties and nearly ten million people was reduced by two-thirds. By the time the fighting ended, fifty thousand casualties were suffered.[31]

Yet in Raoyang and other bastions of the North China resistance, tough traditional villagers held and contributed to the growing strength of the Communist party and its army. Young men slept in the corn fields to avoid capture. Guerrillas operated at night. Old Militia Xu Yizhou ran the Wugong party from a makeshift hideout under a pile of cornstalks, not returning home to sleep for months at a time.

These northern peasants believed that they were more concerned with righteousness than people from less traditional parts of China. It seemed right to them that they be the heartbeat of China's patriotic cause. Zealous participation had its humorous side, too. Villagers soon were telling funny stories about children, whose job it had become to report on suspicious strangers, misidentifying party outsiders as traitors to the Han people. In truth, outsiders generally did seem suspicious to parochial villagers. One outsider in Raoyang, about whom positive stories spread, was a white foreigner performing surgery in Yincun, the Canadian doctor Norman Bethune. After his death he was eulogized by Mao Zedong as a revolutionary martyr.

Facing Two Ways

Shortly before the arrival of Japanese forces in Wugong, the organizations under the resistance league went underground. When Japanese soldiers entered Wugong they met the seemingly pliant independent farmer Li Zihou, who took over as village chief in 1941 in the first formal election held in Wugong. Li and other village representatives of a "Peace Preservation Committee," which served as a liaison group, handled all village interaction with the Japanese. Ten men, including five Communist party members, made up the committee. The Communists included Li Zihou and Zhang Yunshan. Zhang, having served for decades as village chief, seemed a pillar of village conservatism. The majority of committee members were independent farmers. Party committee members knew the real function of this ostensibly collaborative body. But most villagers, including non-party members of the committee, knew little about the Communist role in shaping the group. The committee complied with Japanese requests for information and labor; it also transmitted information about Japanese plans and activities to the guerrillas.

The Peace Preservation Committee also collected Japanese-imposed taxes. They took 25 catties of grain for every 200 catties produced, plus cash and material contributions equal to the value of another 75 catties of grain for every 200 catties produced.[32] But Japanese taxes were collected irregularly. When Japanese forces wanted supplies, they simply ordered the Peace Preservation Committee to collect them. The committee concealed as best it could village production to keep the occupiers' expectations low, but it had to collect and forward revenues on demand.[33]

Obedience to the Japanese saved lives and protected property.[34] After the retreat of Japanese forces in early 1944, no committee member was ever charged with collaboration. Chief Li Zihou retained his post until 1951. By contrast, in nearby Gengkou village, four men in the puppet administration were dragged before a mass meeting after the war, accused of collaboration, and promptly executed. The same fate awaited a collaborator in neighboring Songqiao. In other parts of central Hebei, such as Baoding and Anguo, where Japanese economic interests and military presence were much greater than in Raoyang, the local elite frequently collaborated with the invaders in peace preservation committees and puppet military units.[35] Poor villagers also enrolled in Japanese puppet forces. Chinese troops trained in Anguo county by the Japanese were sent into Raoyang. Although some locals mocked the Anguo uniform, this puppet unit killed a key Raoyang guerrilla leader named Zhai Jingwu, scion of the once-powerful Zhai landlords.

The strategy of using such Japanese organizational forms as the Peace Preservation Committee to deceive the invaders put Wugong's restored unity to the test. Wugong's declining elites, intertwined as they were with village, party, and resistance organizations, were in a position to betray the scheme to the Japanese. Yet the resistance and village unity held firm. Even members of the old elite like Li Huaqi and Li Jianting, who may have been disliked, feared, or envied by some for their land and power, were never accused of collaboration. Li Huaqi's younger brother, Li Huayou, was killed by the enemy. Only one person from Wugong was denounced as a traitor after he defected from the Eighth Route Army. Observed leading a Japanese plunder expedition, he was hunted down and shot by local partisans. Two other Wugong men, Li Yuntian and Li Nao, also joined the quisling army, but they were undercover agents following orders from Xu Yizhou. They provided intelligence and helped protect local people who were arrested.

After May 1942 villagers were press-ganged to dig trenches and construct fortifications for the fifteen hundred Japanese and puppet troops stationed in Raoyang. Hired laborer Zhang Zhan, who was still too poor to marry, was dragged away to dig trenches near the river. Marrying Zhang, as we called him, did not return for forty days. Wugong people helped construct more than forty three-story brick fortifications, each capable of containing up to fifty soldiers.

Six Japanese blockhouses went up within two miles of Wugong, in Beihan-cun to the northwest, in Yanggezhuang to the north, in Tunli to the northeast, in Wodi to the southeast, in Xiyanwan to the south, and in the market village of Xiaodi to the southwest. These forts served as observation posts and launching pads for sudden assaults on guerrilla enclaves.

With so many young men away doing construction work for the Japanese or resistance work for the Eighth Route Army, villages experienced a severe labor shortage. Local party members were instructed to mobilize households to exchange labor on an equal basis. Party leaders also hoped that cooperation would show villagers that a socialist organization of labor was morally and economically superior to households going it alone.

In spite of the Japanese military, Raoyang villagers protected members of the resistance. Two young Hebei women party members, for example, who had gone to the mountains to study at Resistance University at the party center, Yan'an, took cover in Wugong for ten days in 1942. Local people worried that if the Japanese came through, they would be able to tell, as any villager could, that the young women were outsiders. The one from neighboring Shenxian might pass, but if the woman from Dingxian spoke, her accent would be a dead giveaway. That seemed obvious to villagers who were self-conscious about their own back-country accents. Cultural status was revealed in speech. The solution was to dub the Shenxian woman a daughter and her comrade a daughter-in-law.

The resistance infiltrated every Japanese blockhouse and every puppet military unit in the county. Central Hebei resistance leaders designated Rao-yang as a model county for its success in providing grain to feed their troops. Given the famine that struck the North China plain in 1942, providing such food represented a true commitment.

On several occasions Japanese forces gathered Wugong's entire population in the courtyard of the Southern Li lineage temple to compel people to identify resistance activists and Communists. Bayonets flashed, interrogators raved, villagers were bullied and beaten, and homes were set ablaze. Anyone failing to attend such meetings could be shot on sight. One Japanese patrol fired on villagers hiding in graveyards in the west village, killing three and wounding ten.[36] Occupying soldiers also regularly demanded that the Peace Preservation Committee supply them with women.

When Eighth Route Army leaders returned to central Hebei in 1944, they experienced a heightened debt of gratitude to these tough traditional villagers. Some men had kept silent while being tortured to death rather than disclose where guerrillas were hiding. A woman hiding in a tunnel had suffocated her own crying baby to keep the enemy from discovering guerrillas hiding there. Military leader Yang Chengwu concluded that only the Long March was a more memorable event than the sacrifice of central Hebei villagers.

Legends of resistance heroes grew to mythic proportions as the struggles of peasant patriots reshaped commitments and identities. Resistance members shared pride in relaying news of the killing of the notorious rapist, Big Gold Tooth. Although legends expressing loyalty to the emerging state came to shape new identities, in truth many people had acted narrowly, foolishly, treacherously, or selfishly during the war. Facts regarding the quisling troops of Anguo county, villages that handed over women to the Japanese, leaders who dragooned recalcitrant villagers for the Eighth Route Army, traitors in Yanggezhuang and elsewhere, those who made bumbling attempts to hide grain, and the successful pro-Japanese spies, all pieces of a complex reality, had no part in the heroic mythology.

Participants and survivors proudly recounted larger-than-life tales of heroes and martyrs in their households and villages. In 1940, it was said, the leadership assigned Li Jian, a member of the Wugong guerrilla unit, to make mines. The resistance encouraged villagers to make the explosive ingredient for land mines. *Xiao,* a by-product of the saltmaking process long used in homemade fireworks, was the yellow powder that rose to the top of the boiling cauldron. Although the Japanese tried to end the manufacture of xiao, it was impossible to eliminate it altogether. Everyone could be a hero.

Li Jian was trapped in a Japanese sweep in spring 1943. He jumped in a well to commit suicide, but was dragged out, tortured, and questioned. Villagers learned to tell a dramatic tale of Li Jian's martyrdom. "Where are the guerrillas?" "Who's in the Party?" Silence. The Japanese soldiers tied Li to a tree and put firewood around him. They lit a torch and asked again, saying it was for the last time. Li kept still. The torch was touched to the wood. When villagers extinguished the flames, Li was dead.

Perhaps Li Jian lived and died precisely as the villagers recounted. We were skeptical of the quality of such exaggerated accounts. There seemed no end to the telling of such tales of anti-Japanese resistance, patriotism, and pure heroism. It was said that when the Japanese burned Wugong party member Li Erpiao to death, he bravely shouted, as the flames engulfed him, "Never surrender to Japan!"

Another Wugong guerrilla fighter, Geng Tiexiang, it was said, led a forty-member commando squad based in Raoyang's fourth district. Its greatest success, people boasted, was picking off the battalion commander of quisling forces based in the fort outside Xiaodi. These—and there were many more—were the myths that gave life and promise to a newly emerging nation.

Party member Qiao Hengtai headed the Worker Anti-Japanese Patriotic League in Wugong. His house was used for strategy sessions by Central Hebei Military Region representatives. One night in early 1944 Qiao sought to slow the movement of an enemy squad headed in the direction of a meeting at his home. He was shot and died soon after. Like the bomber Li Jian, Qiao is held in high esteem for refusing to provide information when subjected to repeated torture. Villagers who gave their lives for the resistance became heroes.

These idealized reconstructions of resistance history, linked, as they were, to the hard realities of sacrifice and suffering, gave new meaning to the lives of survivors and their heirs. Secret operatives, who appeared to cooperate with the Japanese but actually were acting on party orders, had to be saved from angry people. In Wugong all who contributed to the resistance, however humbly, attained a measure of prestige. Some built political and military careers on grand wartime exploits. The party pledged to provide for the households of army recruits and of martyrs, those killed in the resistance. The double-support movement of 1943 urged villagers to give preferential treatment to army and martyr households, while the army, in turn, pledged to cherish the people.[37] Wugong had fifteen martyr households that had lost one or more members. Most Raoyang villages contained families of martyrs, assistance to whom took the form of free field labor and relief grain. Wugong leaders claimed that they brought martyr families up to an average living standard. Those who were active in the party and the resistance found themselves part of potent networks of shared experiences, organizations, and trust.

Their wartime service, the risk of their lives for the benefit of a new nation, facilitated and legitimated their rise into an emerging state structure.

The men and women who took the lead in the Wugong resistance included the sixty-three people who joined the Communist party during the war, seventy men in the Eighth Route Army, and twenty local guerrillas. Perhaps thirty other non-party people were active in various organizations under the resistance league or served on the Peace Preservation Committee. Altogether some 150 Wugong people dedicated themselves to the resistance. For a village with fewer than three hundred households, in a region bypassed by the main revolutionary currents that had swept over China during the preceding half-century, the wartime mobilization was a resounding success. In village and county new leaders identified emotionally and organizationally with one another. Many became Communists. They often married and became family. Raoyang was haven and home for the Eighth Route Army.

The party had established a base of popular support in large peripheral zones like central Hebei by healing village splits, fostering cross-class unity, leading the armed resistance, and introducing economic and social reforms, especially tax reform. It was developing an organizational infrastructure, a military and state apparatus that gave the party substantial control over economic and political life. The party had won many friends during the war and was increasingly able to impose its will.

All strata contributed to the resistance. Independent tillers, owner-tenants, and those who sold their labor on a part-time basis were represented among the partisan rank and file and the leadership. But a striking number of leaders came from more-prosperous households with links to the declining traditional elite. They were better educated than the majority, had been exposed earlier to nationalist ideas, were actively courted by the fourth district and county people's government, and moved easily into leadership positions. They served the resistance loyally, and many of them and their children became party members and joined the army. In Wugong and throughout Raoyang human bonds were reknit and unity was held. The countryside was pregnant with a new nation and a vigorous nationalism.

3 ❀ STRAINS OF
SOCIALISM

Millions died across North China in 1943 when drought followed the plunder of grain by Japanese troops.[1] Whereas the need to deal with the American offensive in the Asian-Pacific theater led Japan to reduce its military pressure in central Hebei, the murderous North China drought continued unabated. A rural intellectual from the east end of Wugong, Geng Xiufeng, set up a cooperative to beat the drought, save lives, and build socialism. As the country boys fighting for the resistance made the hinterland politically central to the emerging state, so the co-op brought Wugong to the attention of Communist party leaders. But when party authorities directed early forms of socialism to fit those of the Soviet Union, they strained the ties of Chinese villagers to socialist cooperation.

the co-op

The arable land in Wugong fell in 1943 to 3,892 mu, compared with 4,470 mu in 1936. Population dropped from 1,390 to 1,347 people. But the tax reforms, which had reduced the land owned by the five most prosperous households from 465 mu to 279, increased chances of survival. This silent revolution across North China kept countless villagers from dying in the 1943–44 disaster.

In Wugong the 1943 harvest amounted to almost nothing. Between May 1942, when Japan's offensive began, and spring 1944, when the drought ended, 101 of the 320 Wugong households sold land and tools to survive. In addition, 29 households sold children, 25 others went begging, and 21 households fled. Two-thirds of the ninety head of livestock were sold. Fifteen people starved to death.[2]

Elsewhere the situation was worse. Just north of Wugong, death stalked the sandy and alkaline fields of Yanggezhuang. Without water the land was white and rock hard. Scores of Yanggezhuang's people fled. Twenty-seven households sold children, and more than thirty people died of hunger.

Survivors found it hard to mark life's momentous changes in morally proper ways. Li Duolin, known locally as the Iron Man, was thirty-seven when the two horrendous years began. He loved guns, and as a member of Steady Xu Mantang's guerrilla band, he always carried his rifle. At night he went out on sabotage raids. By day he hid and made ropes for the market. Dirt poor, Duolin could not afford a wife. One day his friends spotted a beggar woman passing through Wugong. Li permitted his friends to speak on his behalf. The beggar agreed, and the couple began to live as man and wife without benefit of a marriage ceremony. Their property consisted of his rifle, her begging bowl, a stick for beating away the dogs, and a few tattered pieces of bedding and clothing. The next day, and every day until the spring of 1944, she went out to beg and he went out to kill.[3]

The Idea Man

Before Japan's occupation of Hebei, one-third of Wugong households engaged in labor exchanges with kin and neighbors. Nationalist officials in their short tenure in Raoyang county had set up fifty credit co-ops, three consumer co-ops, and five co-ops that combined credit services with the transportation and marketing of goods. Fierce peasant attachment to lineage land did not block popular and economically rational cooperation. Rural intellectual Geng Xiufeng believed that socialist cooperation could save lives and improve life.

Geng was born in 1913 into a well-educated extended household. He entered the small old-style village primary school at age seven, but dropped out after two years. He returned at ten when his patriotic elder brother, Manliang, a recent graduate of the men's normal school in Raoyang, came home to teach in the new-style primary school that opened in the early 1920s. Xiufeng stayed in school for five years, receiving a nationalistic education. He learned how foreign powers tried to divide and control the nation. A poster hailing victories of the Northern Expedition of 1926 introduced him to the word *communism*. The Communists were in a coalition with the Nationalist party to defeat the evil turtles and crabs, that is, the warlords and imperialists who were devouring China.

When Xiufeng was born his household had 30 mu of land. When he finished school, it had more than 50 mu, three times the average for a household of five. The household consisted of his parents, brother, and sister-in-law, and Xiufeng. The family owned a donkey and raised peanuts, sorghum, and winter wheat. In busy seasons they hired temporary labor. Geng, fifteen years old in 1928, placed fourth in the entrance examination to the county senior primary school, but never attended because his parents deemed excessive the monthly tuition of five silver dollars. In 1930, when he was seventeen, Geng's parents arranged his marriage.

Pondering the role of patriotic intellectuals, Geng considered the idea of saving China through education. Subsequently, thinking China might be strengthened if peasants did well at farming, he became enthusiastic about agriculture. Geng made a habit of spending time around Wang Yuzhang's general store and tea shop in the north village and Li Kuanyu's traditional medicine dispensary in the south. Li was the father of Li Zihou, who would serve as village chief during the war of resistance.

Listening to travelers, Xiufeng became depressed about China's prospects. They said that heroin smuggled into Tianjin by Japanese dealers was destroying China. Some county officials and Wugong villagers were heroin addicts and pushers. Small robber bands sometimes preyed upon Wugong. Occasionally bandits kidnapped a villager for ransom. If local security forces were called in to help, their fee could run as high as twenty to thirty silver dollars.

When Japan invaded China in 1937, twenty-four-year-old Geng immediately joined the patriotic resistance. Geng was put in charge of the village primary school, soon heading the resistance league's committee on education and culture. His work attracted the attention of county education director Yu Shiyu. In 1941 Yu assigned Geng to teach first in Xiyanwan, which had been an experimental model village under the Nationalists, and then in Beiguan village.

In early 1942, on returning to Wugong, Geng Xiufeng led two lives, as did other members of the county resistance. The education department of the Raoyang puppet government had asked the Wugong Peace Preservation Committee to select a teacher to work under its direction in the village. They chose Geng, who secretly carried on anti-Japanese educational work. Before long the tall, confident, articulate Xiufeng was principal of an underground school district of five village schools.

Beginning in fall 1942, and throughout most of the murderous drought year of 1943, Geng was in charge of publishing for the resistance government under Li Fengxiang, a more prosperous member of Wugong's secret Communist party branch. The group reprinted *Victory*, a bulletin edited by the fourth district underground. Xiufeng's underground work put him in contact with key party people. Although not yet a party member, Geng became the villager with the outside contacts.

The Land-Pooling Group

Geng searched for a way to beat the famine. He had heard about land pooling and collective agriculture at Wang Yuzhang's store before the war. An independent farmer, Li Hengtong, remarked that Russia had become a communal paradise after its revolution. The cooperative ideal as a principle for organizing life excited Geng, but other Wugong households thought it a joke. In 1940 Geng read a pamphlet prepared by the underground government of the Central Hebei Military Region entitled *The Soviet Collective Economy*. When villagers gathered in midsummer to select a representative to Raoyang's fourth district underground government, Geng told them about collective agriculture in the Soviet Union, startling people with stories of machines crisscrossing fields to bring in bumper harvests. Working outside Wugong in the drought summer of 1943, Geng pondered a survival strategy of cooperative farming. He discussed it with his supervisor, Li Fengxiang. Dubious, Li asked how households with different surnames could pool land when people in the same household constantly divided land.

In the autumn Geng was reassigned to the Raoyang county seat to carry on engraving and printing activities. His boss, He Feng, also a primary-school teacher and a graduate of Raoyang Normal School where Xiufeng's brother taught, headed the county underground government. Remembering ancient stories about intellectuals who put aside their pens and acted to save the country, Geng Xiufeng walked off the job and returned to Wugong. He began discussing his socialistic ideas with trusted friends. One day while digging yams, Geng met three labor-poor east-village neighbors, Qiao Wanxiang, Li Yutian, and Lu Molin. He wondered if they might be receptive to cooperation.[4]

The life of thirty-year-old Qiao Wanxiang, a once-land-rich farmer, was made precarious in 1943 by the drought. Prosperous Qiao still owned 18 mu of land and two draft animals, but he had four children and a wife to feed. When his father died in 1942, the funeral left Qiao 100 yuan in debt. He began to sell furniture. Recruited by his brother-in-law, Jin Qinglian, Prosperous Qiao was among the first to join the secret Wugong Communist party. He had a few years of primary education and had learned the ropemaking trade from his father. Easygoing, if not indecisive, Qiao did not run his farm well.[5]

Thirty-five-year-old Li Yutian had a violent temper. When he was angry he sometimes pulled a dagger and threatened others. Villagers dealt with his rages by saying, "You'll be doing me a favor by slitting my throat. I don't want to live anyway." Then Li would back off. As a result of the recent reforms, in 1942 Li owned 11 mu of land, farmed an additional 6 mu pawned by others, and had a one-third interest in an ox. His large household consisted of three adolescent sons, an eight-year-old daughter, a baby girl, his wife, and a sickly father. Li's father had scrimped and saved to buy land. The tightfisted old man had raised wheat but, like so many peasants, refused to let anyone in the family eat fine grain. Instead he exchanged wheat for cheaper sorghum, pocketing the difference. Pressed under by the drought, Li would not sell his land. He invested everything to drill for water, but came up dry. Bankrupt, in the summer of 1943 he took his youngest son to the Wodi market and sold ten-year-old Hundui for 30 catties of sorghum.[6]

Lu Molin, short and dark skinned, was known as "The Black One." At fifty-eight he had a reputation for being irascible and argumentative. He and his daughter-in-law, Guifang, were always at each other's throats. Lu's wife dropped dead on her way to other fields to glean. His two sons joined the Eighth Route Army. Like Qiao Wanxiang, Lu knew how to make rope. After his corn crop failed, Lu, who had a bad arm, moaned that he did not know who would die next.[7]

After listening to the men lament their woes, Geng Xiufeng proposed a survival strategy. Why not pool land, resources, tools, and animals for joint farming and open a ropemaking sideline? The three agreed to consider the idea. Qiao Wanxiang suspected that his neighbor and friend Li Yantian might be interested. Li, who once had owned good land, was addicted to gambling. He whiled away time in the gambling house in the Southern Li lineage temple drinking and carousing, which poisoned his relationship with his wife. When the drought left Li Yantian broke, he sold his best land and was on the verge of selling his house to pay gambling debts. The weeds in his remaining fields seemed taller than the crops. Li was stiff and withdrawn, but he listened carefully to Qiao Wanxiang.[8] The four agreed that cooperation made sense, but they were dubious about Geng Xiufeng's proposal to pool land and farm it as a single enterprise. Who had ever attempted such a thing? Exchanging labor, on the other hand, was a common practice. They agreed only to set up a rope cooperative during the winter, a far less risky venture. But at the last minute, Geng Xiufeng, the man with all the ideas, pulled out. His father refused to allow him to commit the family donkey and other resources to the cooperative venture. Male elders held the purse strings. The other four households nevertheless went to work together making ropes.

Before long, the head of the underground county government, He Feng, visited Wugong. Geng Xiufeng told his former supervisor that his work in Wugong was more important than the printing. He Feng responded that he had heard that collectivization in the socialist Soviet Union had not gone smoothly, that it made for famine. He hoped China could find a better approach. At that time the Raoyang resistance authorities, responding to the drought, summed up current priorities in the slogan "Organize, Produce, Overcome the Drought."[9] He Feng agreed to relieve Geng of printing duties to organize cooperatives. If Geng had difficulties, He Feng would help. He cautioned Geng to explain ideas carefully to the farmers, to work closely with village leaders, and to base everything on personal ownership and willing participation. That would create an embryo for socialism. Above all, he emphasized private ownership and voluntary participation.

The four-household rope group had no one to keep records. Since 70 percent of village men were totally illiterate, keeping accounts was a scarce skill. Cooperative members tried to persuade their friend Geng Wensheng to join and do the bookkeeping. He declined, but agreed to teach Qiao Wanxiang. The co-op's biggest problem was a cash shortage. Geng Xiufeng suggested selling 15 catties of grain to buy hemp for ropemaking. But Lu Molin, the Black One, said he was too poor and too old to take on a new business. Lu was afraid to risk the little he had. He also worried that his inability to contribute financially would make the others suspect he was taking advantage of them.

Cooperation became attractive when Geng, who had the outside contacts, pried a loan of 200 catties of sorghum from the underground county government. There was one catch. Group members had to go secretly to nearby Xiyanwan, a Japanese stronghold, to pick it up. Lu Molin was terrified, but the three younger men decided to gamble. After their safe return to Wugong, half of the grain was distributed as food to tide member households through the winter.[10] The other half, combined with their own meager resources, served to finance the rope sideline born in winter 1943. Financial support from the emerging socialist state helped get the co-op off the ground. Since at least 1940 party members in the Jinchaji Base had fostered co-ops.

Support for the fledgling co-op was provided by Liu Fuzhai, head of Raoyang's underground Department of Industry and Commerce. Liu arrived in Wugong in late fall 1943 with instructions to promote a "hidden economy group" during the winter slack season. Its goal was to organize cooperative sidelines and deny the Japanese access to the output. Liu had 2,000 catties of county grain to loan to groups willing to launch co-op enterprises.[11]

In winter 1943–44 Wugong's hidden economy group, initiated by Geng Xiufeng with county support, included eight sideline groups. Apart from the ropemakers, others spun thread, wove cloth, ginned cotton, ground wheat flour, manufactured peanut oil, produced bean curd, and milled lumber.[12] Some who joined had been involved in the now defunct co-ops launched in 1941 by Huang Baozhi and Tian Luanzi. It was not easy to make a go of cooperation. The eight new groups were organized as "mutual-aid," or labor-sharing, teams. Members generated enough income to help their forty-nine households survive intact the disastrous winter.[13]

Although Geng Xiufeng was an innovator with good outside contacts, he was a failure as an administrator. The eight groups he helped organize were structurally weak. By spring 1944, when the drought ended, seven of the eight groups promptly disbanded. Yet that spring had an auspicious feel. The drought ended, and American naval advances in the Pacific led Japan to pull three thousand troops out of central Hebei. Members of the United States Air Force passed through with Chinese Communist guides to see what more could be done to save downed American fliers. Although Japan's puppet forces still occupied Raoyang town and periodically raided rural areas, the war had turned against them. They could not even hold the fortifications at Xiyanwan, Wodi, Yanggezhuang, and Xiaodi. Yanggezhuang celebrated the razing of its fort. Party organizers operated more openly.

Geng Xiufeng, with the support of Raoyang's Liu Fuzhai, encouraged the four ropemakers who had stayed together to go further and form a land-pooling group. If they could work together making rope, Geng argued, it made sense to cooperate in farming, too. The four agreed to try. In early spring they spent three days hammering out co-op regulations.[14] Geng's father continued to forbid him to invest family resources or join the group. Still, Xiufeng drafted the co-op charter. Its guidelines were straightforward.

After the autumn harvest, 10 percent of the total value of agricultural sales would be set aside to reinvest. The remainder would be divided, half based on the amount and quality of land investment, and half based on labor days contributed, ensuring that neither households with abundant land nor those with ample labor would feel cheated and quit. The rope sideline set aside 10 percent of gross income and distributed the remainder based on 60 percent for labor contributed and 40 percent as return on investment.[15] In accord with He Feng's directive, the land, tools, draft animals, capital, and equipment that members invested remained private property and would be returned if a household withdrew. The charter of the four-household group respected customary rights of ownership.

But in other ways the land-pooling group departed from village farming practice. The novelty lay in attempting year-round coordination of the resources and labor of several households. Something permanent and all-encompassing was established. Decisions about what to grow, how to grow it, how to market it, and how to distribute income passed from the household to the self-governing group. A simple banking system was set up. Members deposited cash with bookkeeper Qiao Wanxiang. When members needed funds for emergencies, they borrowed from the co-op.

The charter introduced a rudimentary work-point system of bookkeeping designed to record labor contributions in both agricultural and sideline work. An able-bodied man received one work point for a full day's work; a woman got .6 work points for a day's work. The work of children was calculated on a case-by-case basis. The system did not distinguish the skilled from the unskilled, the strong from the weak, the diligent from the lazy. Gender and generation differentials aside, a leveling notion of distribution was adopted in the interest of simplicity.

In March 1944, as the founding members prepared to agree to the co-op charter by affixing fingerprints in red ink on it, hot-tempered Li Yutian panicked. A cousin told him, "You will suffer losses. You have more land. Others will take away half your grain." Qiao Wanxiang tried to work out a compromise, but as spring planting approached Li bolted so others could not take advantage of him.[16] Peasants dreaded being shown up as fools in public. To fill the gap left by Li Yutian's departure from the co-op, Prosperous Qiao suggested an east-end neighbor, Geng Changsuo.

The Ropemaker from the Market

By the time Geng Changsuo was born in April 1900, his father, Geng Jichuan, had pawned half his 10-mu farm and set out for Raoyang to work in the ropemaking shop of Big Wagon Dong. There he could earn enough in a day to buy a catty or more of coarse grain.[17] Making rope was a Wugong tradition. A Raoyang folk song describes Gengkou village as renowned for weaving, Wangliu for producing bean curd, and Wugong for making rope.[18]

During Geng Changsuo's childhood, the family owned 5 mu and rented an additional 5.2 mu, looked after by Geng's mother, older sister, and older brother. But in 1910 the sister married out of the village, and the brother left to seek work in Manchuria. A younger sister died of illness as an infant. There was no money for school. Nonetheless, one New Year, to assure the family the good fortune that came with eating real meat-filled dumplings, father Jichuan took out a loan with his body as collateral. When the father fell ill and returned to Wugong in 1915 unable to farm, fifteen-year-old Geng Changsuo became the breadwinner. In early 1918 he followed in his father's footsteps, going to Raoyang to learn ropemaking and the ways of the market.[19]

It was young Geng's first trip to Raoyang, a two- to three-hour walk from Wugong. At the south gate police searched him from head to foot. Along the unpaved streets he saw laborers and beggars. He also caught a glimpse of a few people with money and power. Town and country are the same, he thought. All crows are black. Geng found work, as had his father before him, in Big Wagon Dong's rope shop. Geng worked hard but disliked running errands for the boss and helping to harvest his wheat. After his apprenticeship, Geng quit and returned to Wugong, having mastered a craft and tasted life in the market. Short of land, cash, and labor power, Geng Changsuo barely supported his aging parents by farming and making and selling rope.

In 1922 arrangements were made for a wife. Geng's parents struck a deal with a west village Xu household that was poorer than the Gengs. Although the culture approved marriages where the bride was older than a teenage groom, twelve-year-old Xu Shukuan was sent to live as the twenty-two-year-old Changsuo's bride-to-be. Shukuan's mother had died bearing her fourth child in 1920, right after the famine of 1919. Her landless father eked out a living as a construction worker. The father traded his daughter as a servant betrothed to the Geng family to keep Shukuan alive. Her sister, Xu Qin, had been similarly dealt to a family in Beihancun, a few miles northwest of Wugong.[20] Many destitute North China families that took in child brides were socially stigmatized. Such marriages were suspect, and the bride was subjected to extreme ridicule and treated, often violently, as a semilegitimate member of the community.[21]

The Gengs expected Shukuan to work hard, despite her bound feet. She collected twigs and grass for the fire, learned to push the great stone roller that milled flour, and mastered ropemaking. In 1926, without much ceremony, Changsuo and Shukuan married. He was twenty-six and she was sixteen. Before long she gave birth to a daughter, Xueren, the first of seven children.[22]

For the next ten years Geng and Xu farmed 10.2 mu of privately owned and rented land and twisted ropes, which he sold in the market. With old people and children to support, the household remained poor. Geng had to become wise and wily in the ways of the market to survive. He went out for days at a time in search of raw materials, buyers, and profits, traveling on foot to Linxian in northern Henan province to buy hemp, which he sold in the Zoucun market, where pig castraters used Wugong ropes to tie down frantic animals. Geng and others carried rope to such distant places as the Shaowu temple fair, twenty miles away, in search of higher prices.

The Xu lineage had moved into the region centuries earlier in fleeing a famine in Shanxi province. The Geng lineage had migrated from Nanma village to the northeast. Living in the eastern outskirts, the Gengs had no important ties to the Southern Li power bloc in the center village. In 1936, when strife led to the formation of the Association, Geng Changsuo stood at the rear of the crowd. His closest links were with the Qiaos, especially his neighbor Prosperous Qiao Wanxiang.

When Japan invaded, Geng joined the Worker Anti-Japanese Patriotic League, headed by Qiao Hengtai.[23] Like his father, Geng was viewed as a ropemaker from the marketplace. By 1941 he was among the leaders of the workers' league of the party's village administration. Tax reform helped Geng save enough to buy a quarter interest in an ox. In 1942 his father was one of forty villagers shot by Japanese soldiers.[24] Changsuo's asthmatic mother died soon after. When drought intensified in 1943, Geng sold his share of the ox, his prized plow, and most household possessions.

Geng bought 10 catties of peanut shells, the cheapest nourishment available. After using the coarser part for fuel, Xu Shukuan ground up the rest, mixed it with water, and steamed it for food, a traditional famine-coping measure. Geng was still weak after eating the shells, which left him painfully constipated. Another staple to stave off death from famine was tree leaves boiled in water, which produced diarrhea. Weak and dizzy, suffering from either constipation or diarrhea, Changsuo frequently fainted. He had nightmares about selling his children. In the desperate spring of 1943 he sold their eldest daughter, Xueren, to a household in another village for 45 catties of sorghum, but several months later she returned home. Changsuo never had to repay the grain received in exchange for Xueren.[25] Children for sale huddled in markets with sale placards hung around their necks. Children sold in distant marketplaces were sometimes instructed by their parents to run away at an opportune moment.

In the autumn there was nothing to harvest. Geng sent his wife, with three-month-old daughter Huijuan on her back and thirteen-year-old son Delu, to beg for food in Raoyang.[26] Along with millions of others, the Geng family seemed fated to die out.

Geng Changsuo and the Land-Pooling Group

In March 1944, when Qiao Wanxiang, Lu Molin, and Li Yantian agreed to invite Geng Changsuo into the fledgling land-pooling group, Geng Xiufeng decided to pay a call on his older clansman, whom he called elder brother. Changsuo was away selling rope when Xiufeng arrived. Peasants hid plight or plenty to avoid losing face or becoming targets of the envious. Xiufeng wrongly thought Changsuo was doing relatively well. When Xu Shukuan, wearing patched clothes, opened the gate, she snapped at Xiufeng, "Say what you have to say and go." If she had been younger than he, tradition would have forbidden a conversation. He asked how they were doing. She pulled him into the one-and-a-half-room house to see. The rear wall was collapsing. The bedding was falling apart. All that was left to eat was a handful of dry leaves. Rural society was full of mistrust, fear of being taken advantage of, secrecy, and false fronts.

Xiufeng asked Xu Shukuan what her husband thought about the Qiao Wanxiang group. She responded that Changsuo thought it was fine. Changsuo often made rope with Qiao Wanxiang's younger brother Wanjiang and joined Lu Molin in marketing rope. These neighbors knew the ropemaker from the market as easy to work with, honest, a skilled craftsman, and a tough bargainer. When Xiufeng asked if Changsuo would join the land-pooling group, Xu Shukuan said she was certain he would.[27]

Xiufeng found that labor-poor households were the most willing to join a co-op. Thirty-year-old Li Yantian's only child had died as an infant. His wife was dying. Lu Molin, with two sons in the army, was short of hands. Qiao Wanxiang's indebted household had many small children to feed. Geng Changsuo, with five young children, was short of both land and labor power. Self-interest led poor, declining, and labor-poor households to band together.

Qiao Wanxiang and the others wanted Changsuo to lead. Resilient, confident, and traveled, he was not only adept at ropemaking and marketing, but he was also a skilled farmer known for his speed in harvesting wheat. The spring plowing and seeding of the pooled land had already been completed. Someone was needed who could manage the co-op and resolve problems of organization and personal relations. Without a capable leader the co-op was said to be like a dragon without eyes. Three days after Xiufeng's visit, Geng Changsuo returned home, joined the co-op, and agreed to lead it. In addition to the land he owned and rented, Geng invested 20 catties of hemp and rope.

The land-pooling co-op consisted of four households, twenty-two individuals, (nine male, thirteen female), and the equivalent of 6.5 full-time laborers (4 men and 2.5 women). The co-op group had 40 mu of land, an average of 1.8 mu per person, far less than the village average. The group had no draft animals. The combined farm tools amounted to a plow and a hoe.[28] Villagers scoffed at the idea that a few poor and weak households could hold together. The harmonious big family was a Chinese ideal; the ordinary reality was a lot of squabbling. Doubters called the co-op a rabbit's tail, that is, something that could never be long. It was popularly assumed that bickering would lead to the rapid dissolution of an impossible venture.

Thanks to the contacts of Geng Xiufeng, two leaders of the Raoyang underground, Wang Yonglai, the new head of the county government, and Li Taiguo, commented favorably to the party on the land-pooling group. For them, the most important features were private ownership, voluntary participation, and real benefits. Wang instructed the secret forty-six-member Wugong Communist party branch to support the land-pooling group. In June 1944, three months after joining the group, Geng Changsuo was recruited into the party by east enders, war hero Qiao Hengtai and clansman Geng Shupu.[29]

Changsuo threw himself into the co-op, hoping it could restore life to a dying household. His parents had both died in 1942. His wife no longer had a family. Her father had died of cholera in 1932. Her oldest brother had died soon after his wife gave birth, and the wife then returned to her native village. Shukuan's youngest brother, Xu Dong, whose birth killed their mother, was the last member of either household, Geng's or Xu's, in Wugong. He joined the Eighth Route Army. Geng took pride in his patriotic brother-in-law, who occasionally returned to share the meager food of Changsuo and Shukuan. This happiness ended when Xu Dong was killed while fighting with the 23d Regiment fifty miles east of Wugong. Events fused in Geng's mind. The family was dying, the family was sacrificing for the nation, party, and army, but the family was being reborn in the co-op.

The underground fourth district government soon provided tangible support for the fledgling co-op, investing five hundred dollars in border region currency. The district party committee sent its new secretary, Jin Shufang, to investigate. Impressed, Jin presented a copy of a speech entitled "Get Organized" given by Chairman Mao Zedong the previous fall in Yan'an. Literate Geng Xiufeng read it aloud to the illiterate co-op members. Mao had urged labor model Wu Manyu and other labor heroes to cooperate to overcome famine, develop the economy, and strengthen the resistance.[30] Mao insisted that joining co-ops must be voluntary (absolutely no coercion). But Mao also believed in the bigger, the better. The untested assumption was that villagers would voluntarily agree that bigger was better.

The land-pooling co-op accepted Mao's article and a gift of three hundred bricks provided by the Eighth Route Army when the bunker in Xiaodi was torn down after the Japanese evacuation. A county-level army unit let the four-household Wugong group use a donkey confiscated from the Japanese. Given the famine-induced loss of draft animals, the donkey was a treasure.

Using all their resources, co-op members worked day and night to improve family well-being. A brief published account of the group of four households appeared in the Central Hebei Military Region's newspaper, *Jizhong daobao*.[31]

Co-op members learned that it was advantageous to capture the attention of authorities in a position to help. This required contacts. Although not a co-op member, Geng Xiufeng had those contacts and the conviction that cooperation was the socialist way forward for villagers and nation. But support was a two-edged sword. As Chinese villagers understood, gifts are not free. Officials who aided the co-op would expect their notions to guide work. Those socialist notions could conflict with the villagers' idea of cooperation.

Party Reforms

County and district authorities urged Geng Xiufeng to form a "harvest committee" in the summer of 1944. Although Japanese troops had retreated from Raoyang, the crops ripening in the fields still seemed at risk. Villagers had a stake in harvesting and hiding the wheat before the Japanese could seize it. Geng Xiufeng organized twenty-two mutual-aid groups, averaging 11 households, to speed the harvest. Altogether 246 households (85 percent of the village) participated. Almost the entire summer wheat crop was harvested and hidden in seven days without machinery. Of the harvested grain, 90 percent was distributed according to the amount of land owned by the participants, and 10 percent was allotted on the basis of labor. These temporary labor-exchange groups disbanded after the harvest.[32]

Following the harvest the fourth district government held a meeting in Zoucun to honor labor models. Geng Xiufeng received a cloth banner that read, "Advanced Model Worker."[33] Soon after, Wugong Party Branch Secretary Li Yun, who had taken over from Old Militia Xu Yizhou in 1943, summoned Xiufeng to his home to meet a tall outsider interested in Geng's work. He was Jin Cheng, party secretary of the Eighth Military District, who had hidden from Japanese troops in Wugong two years earlier.[34] Geng's and Wugong's circle of contacts was widening. Li Yun eventually served on the county party committee.

The meeting of labor models in Zoucun, like that earlier gathering of Wu Manyu and other labor heroes that Mao Zedong addressed in Yan'an, dealt with agricultural cooperation. Mao had talked of cooperation and of mutual aid not only as emerging measures to improve the base area's economy but also as stages in socialist collectivization.[35] Central Hebei promoted co-ops after the summer harvest.[36] Although war work remained the top priority, the party also organized such short-term temporary co-ops as the hidden economy group and the harvest committee. But Wugong's four-household co-op went well beyond these simple forms of cooperation by pooling land and labor, and by integrating agricultural and sideline work on a long-term basis. Some higher party leaders considered that more socialist. Their goal was to make life more socialist.

In July 1944, with the retreat of Japanese forces, the Communist party again raised the issue of reduction of rent and interest in North China. A new party secretary, Lin Tie, took charge in central Hebei in September. Unable to ride a bicycle, he rode about on a donkey. In October the Raoyang party committee sponsored a meeting in Caozhuang, less than two miles south of Wugong, to form plans for "double reduction." By early November a work team from the Eighth Military District's Public Finance Section arrived in Wugong to pick up where the fourth district work team had left off in early 1942. The group was headed by Yang Zizhen, Li Manke, and Wang Ce, the central Hebei region representative. The teams designated Wugong an "experimental site" for the district movement to reduce rent and interest. Results in Wugong were to have larger significance. Peripheral Wugong was becoming more central in the emerging socialist order. As the new system rose, those tied to it rose, too.

Elements within traditional culture worked against some reforms. The double reduction work team set up literacy classes in Wugong during the 1944–45 winter slack season. To such modern outsiders as urban youths working for the party in the countryside, the classes inviting attendance by all illiterates seemed an obvious improvement. Just 3 percent of Wugong women had any formal schooling. But tradition could prove lethal. A twenty-one-year-old woman who had married into a household in the village center when her "groom" was nine years old, decided to attend night school classes organized by the work team. Her in-laws forbade it. She persisted. They beat her to death. Another young bride went to a meeting despite the stern warnings of her in-laws. Her husband's older sister beat her and dragged her home where others knocked her around until she died. The customary values that glued Chinese villages together were in part patriarchal, hierarchical, and violent. The idea of women learning to read or going out of the house to mix with male strangers was anathema to many conservative villagers.

The work team shifted the rental system from fixed rents to a percentage of the annual crop, a form favored by tenants, who would pay landlords 37.5 percent of gross production. Again, the reforms did not threaten the independent tiller majority. Moreover, landlords could still turn a modest profit on rented land. Private ownership and sale of land and farm tools continued. From one perspective, rent had not been significantly reduced. In the late 1930s three silver dollars for rent for each mu of land was about the same as 37.5 percent of gross production in normal years. What risk-averse tenants won in the double reduction movement was an insurance policy for bad times. No matter how far yields fell due to disaster, their maximum obligation was 37.5 percent of the harvest. In bumper years, however, the landlord would share in the bounty. The work team also reduced interest rates by 25 percent, from the customary 3 dollar interest on 10 dollars to 2.25 dollars.[37] Few Wugong households were affected by rent reduction.

Model Village, Model Worker

The success of the Geng Changsuo co-op rested in part on coordinating field work by day and ropemaking at night, when women and children contributed. The work was exhausting, but by the end of the farming year the group produced 9,240 catties of grain, not including sweet potatoes.[38] The co-op's 223 catties per mu was well above what poor villagers usually harvested on unirrigated land. In 1944 farming households had average yields of 170 catties per mu.[39]

The land-pooling group took an unorthodox step by stressing winter wheat followed by late corn. More than 50 percent of their land was devoted to these two crops. Fine grain like wheat could be sold at a high price, but was vulnerable to drought and flood. The group's gamble on wheat paid off handsomely. Little cash was earned, however, from economic crops or household sidelines. The land-pooling group planted just three mu in a cash crop, peanuts. The group's rope sideline produced gross income valued at only 398 catties of millet, just over 4 percent of total gross income of 9,638 catties.

After setting aside such production costs as seed and fertilizer, 4,400 catties of grain were distributed, an average of 200 catties per person.[40] Those like Qiao Wanxiang, who had invested more or better land but had little household labor power, received their major earnings as a return on their investment. Others, like the Black One, Lu Molin, and Geng Changsuo, with little land or capital, relied heavily on labor for their income. Xu Shukuan, who worked with amazing intensity, kept up the Geng Changsuo household income.

The land-pooling experiment had won grain yields approximating those of prosperous independent farmers with superior land and animals. By the spring plowing season in 1945, aided again by party authorities in obtaining another draft animal, the Geng co-op had one mule, two donkeys, and an ox.[41] There were many reasons why the co-op thrived. The weather was good, so wells were not vital. The group was small. Members were friends and neighbors. No one felt taken advantage of since all were short of labor. And per capita landholdings were relatively equal, with the exception of Geng Changsuo, who had less. The distribution system did not blatantly favor some over others. When decisions had to be made, the group could discuss matters on the spot. The down-to-earth, capable, and honest leadership of Geng Changsuo was also important. The district and county-level contacts of Geng Xiufeng produced loans, animals, supplies, and administrative support.

Although the economy revived in 1944 as both Japanese troops and drought receded and Wugong village paid the county tax collector 100,000 catties of millet, explosive Li Yutian, who had pulled out of the co-op, met disaster. Li used most of his income from the rope sideline to buy food for his large household. By the spring he had almost nothing left. His four children were hungry. His wife, still distraught by the sale of their ten-year-old son the previous autumn, fled Wugong with her youngest daughter rather than sell another child. Later Li heard that after begging along Hebei's southern border, she moved in with another man. By the end of the year Li sold three mu of land, a section of housing, the wheels from his farm wagon, and two parcels of threshing ground. His ailing father passed away, imposing funeral expenses on survivors. The situation improved slightly by the end of the year when his youngest son, Hundui, wandered home and the resistance government intervened to return Li's wife and daughter to him.[42]

The Wugong co-op, in contrast, expanded to become the pride of its central Hebei backers. After the encouraging autumn 1944 harvest, thirteen new households joined. Full-time laborers rose from 6.5 to 22, and land from 40 to 218 mu. New members invested two plows and three large wagons. Membership jumped to an extraordinary 107 people. In addition to a number of Li lineage people, new members included Geng Xiufeng, his older brother, the patriotic schoolteacher Geng Manliang, and kinsman Geng Shupu, a top party activist. The newcomers, all east village independent tillers, had almost twice as much land for every full-time worker as the original members.[43] Yet co-op members still owned just over 2 mu per person, significantly lower than the 1937 village average of 3.2 mu. The thirteen new member households, many of which were short of labor, saw economic opportunities in the co-op.

Disintegrating families brought their skills and problems with them into the co-op. Among the new members was sixty-three-year-old ropemaker Li Huiting. He could work through the night twisting ropes and had a shrewd knowledge of distant markets. He carried his rope 125 miles southwest to Shuangjin on the Henan provincial border and returned home with raw hemp. As a young man, Li Huiting had inherited just 1.2 mu of land. He tried to survive by peddling vegetables grown on a high-quality rented plot. Later he sent his oldest son to the northeast frontier to find work. Li responded to the tragic news that his beloved son had died in the "land of opportunity" by spoiling his remaining son, Zhanhu. Now advanced in years, Li sought desperately to provide financial security for his descendants. But Zhanhu was addicted to gambling. Li and his daughter-in-law often went to the gambling den to plead with Zhanhu, who turned a deaf ear. Li Huiting joined the co-op for more than economic reasons. He had heard how the co-op had cured his fellow clansman, Li Yantian, of his gambling mania. Perhaps it could save his ne'er-do-well son.[44]

Another newcomer, forty-five-year-old Zhang Jinren, was a lighthearted optimist who loved to make people laugh. From age twelve he had worked in the fields, first on his late father's scraps of land, afterward as a short-term hired hand. The co-op invited Zhang, a crack farmer, to head agricultural work. He had been active in the resistance, first as a member of the Worker Patriotic League, and later in gathering intelligence. In 1939 he joined the Communist party.[45]

The co-op also welcomed Zhang's brother-in-law, forty-five-year-old Wei Lianyu, a tall, thin man who would rise quickly in the co-op and village power structures[46] as a protégé of the village chief, Li Zihou, who tapped him as an intelligence operative in the county resistance. When the enemy retreated in 1944, Zhang Jinren convinced Wei to join the Geng co-op. Wei contributed only 2.3 mu of land, but he had four years of primary education and his father had owned a small ropemaking shop in Raoyang before the war. Wei had traveled widely, working in Henan province early in the war. He knew the rope business and the ways of the market. In late 1944 Li Zihou appointed Wei to mediate disputes for the village government.[47]

Meddlers

Before moving on in early February 1945, the final act of the Eighth Military District work team, which made Wugong an experimental site for rent reduction starting in November 1944, was to revise the Geng co-op charter. When the team showed up at an early winter meeting of the co-op leadership, no one dared question them. Awarding 50 percent of net income in agriculture to those who had invested land, tools, and animals was "exploitative," they announced. Co-ops were intended to end exploitation. They then demanded that the reform standard for landlord-tenant crop distribution should govern co-op distribution policy. At least 60 percent of farm income should be awarded on the basis of labor.

Geng Xiufeng was uneasy when he heard the word *exploitation*. In the co-op, landlords were not exploiting tenants. Rather, independent tiller households were voluntarily working out a mutually beneficial basis for cooperation. There were income differences among members, he reasoned, but the more prosperous members were not exploiters. Hot-tempered Li Yutian had quit because he thought 50 percent was too low a return to those who invested land. How would he have reacted to 40 percent? Land, animals, and tools seemed to independent tillers to be the fruit of long, hard labor. It would seem exploitative to tillers to underreward the fruits of previous labor.

Still, Xiufeng would not talk back to officials from the military district. He was also apprehensive that he might be criticized for feathering his own nest since Xiufeng's land-rich household would be hurt by the proposed change. Geng Xiufeng sat silent, as did all co-op members. The authority of the emerging state was respected. The charter was revised to distribute 60 percent of net income according to labor. Sideline distribution was also adjusted: 70 rather than 60 percent would go to labor, and 30 percent to those who invested capital.[48] The work team hailed the changes as steps on the socialist path.

The revised charter added a "public welfare" component guaranteeing, at least in word, medical expenses for anyone injured on the job, as well as providing income during recuperation. It even guaranteed burial expenses for anyone who died on the job, and regular income for the dependents of the deceased for three years. The guarantees touched a responsive chord among households so recently poised at the brink of death. A critical question, however, was whether co-op resources would be sufficient to deliver on these costly promises or whether some would see themselves as being exploited by others. However, given the crises caused by burial expenses in previous years, this welfare guarantee was generally most welcome.

The outsiders also introduced provisions of "democratic management." That is, such important issues as selecting leaders would be decided by ballot. Elections were scheduled three times a year at the traditional festivals: the lunar New Year, Dragon Boat Festival, and Mid-Autumn Festival. In the early years of the co-op a group dinner accompanied the election meeting. The largest decision-making body in the co-op was the newly created Household Representative Council, with one representative from each household. The whole co-op would meet once a year to review the council's work.[49] Those elected to office could receive reasonable compensation for time devoted to co-op business, but they were to participate in manual labor as well. Otherwise members would look upon leaders as freeloaders who drew income without dirtying their hands like everyone else. Management did not quite seem real work.

The first election, like the new charter, reflected the will of the outsiders from the Eighth Military District. They ousted Ropemaker Geng Changsuo and put in as director "model worker" Geng Xiufeng. Geng Changsuo was put in charge of his specialty, sideline production. Geng Shupu became the deputy leader of the co-op group. Crop expert Zhang Jinren headed agricultural work.[50] Xiufeng lacked the farming and other work skills that would permit him to lead by example. His innovative mind would not fix on the daily details that were crucial to the success of a cooperative enterprise. What he had was higher party ties and an ideological commitment to socialism.

In spite of the term democratic management, all five co-op leaders owed obedience to the top-down secret Communist party, which dominated regional politics. District, county, and military district party authorities monitored developments within the co-op and issued secret directives through co-op leaders who belonged to the party.

Negative consequences of work team meddling surfaced when Geng Xiufeng looked for a qualified accountant to handle the expanded organization. He first approached Li Hengtong, the prosperous independent farmer and early party member who was reputed to be something of a local sage. Some years earlier in a discussion in Wang Yuzhang's shop, Sage Li, as we called him, had relayed gossip about Soviet collectives to Xiufeng. Li Hengtong obtained some of the highest yields in the village on his 12 mu of land. He had also spoken favorably of the co-op. But learning that only 40 percent of net agricultural income was paid as land dividends, Sage Li balked. He could do better farming his own fertile land. The new proposal looked good, Li responded diplomatically when asked to do the accounting, but his old brain was simply not up to the task. Instead, he offered to help bookkeeper Qiao Wanxiang whenever he had questions.[51]

Many Co-ops

In late 1944 the Eighth Military District work team urged Geng Xiufeng to set up more co-ops modeled on the original land-pooling group. Xiufeng did not require much urging. He approached his wartime mentor, Communist party member Li Fengxiang, the nephew of landlord Li Jianting, whose once-powerful extended family had recently split into several separate households. Tax reforms had further shrunk Southern Li resources. Although skeptical the year before, Li Fengxiang agreed to form a co-op consisting of once relatively prosperous independent farming households in the central-west and west village, six Lis and three closely related members of the Zhang clan. Geng Xiufeng had learned that it made sense to organize people who were already linked as friends, neighbors, or relatives and shared similar economic backgrounds. Significant differentials in lineage or ownership in land, tools, and draft animals could spawn destructive disputes.

Hard-luck Li Yutian, who had dropped out of the original four-household co-op and was burned in the subsequent farming season, took charge of a co-op of eight households. It was dominated by middle-income farmers including Li's two brothers, although three poorer households also joined. All except Hou Zhitang were of the Li lineage. The third new co-op organized by Geng Xiufeng consisted exclusively of poorer households. Led by Li Yuzhu, all six member households were Lis.

Prodded by the production drive launched by Raoyang Party Secretary Li Tai in the fall of 1944, and encouraged by the work team from the Eighth Military District, Geng Xiufeng also organized nineteen temporary sideline groups, each with four or five households. These specialized in transport, cotton spinning, bean-curd production, leather processing, peanut-oil extraction, and the sale of steamed bread. Furthermore, fifteen women's shoemaking groups, involving 120 households, were organized for the slack season. In all, 50 percent of Wugong households joined some sort of mutual-aid, labor-exchange, or cooperative group in winter 1944–45.[52] Like the twenty-two labor-exchange groups Geng Xiufeng had organized to bring in the 1944 summer harvest, the new sideline groups were temporary. In spring 1945, their specific tasks completed, all disbanded. The forty households in the four co-ops, however, continued together.

Sideline activities headed by ropemaker Geng Changsuo expanded vigorously during the winter months. The rope sideline involved ten people. The co-op opened a carpentry shop on the north side of the village's main east-west path and a bean-curd and sesame-oil shop on the dirt road leading to the Zoucun market.[53] With relative peace and order, it was again possible to earn money in the market.

In contrast to 1944 total sideline income of 398 catties, the 1945 gross income of the rope operation alone was valued at 22,000 catties of millet; the carpentry shop brought in 20,000 catties; and the bean-curd and oil-press business another 5,300 catties. Whereas gross per capita sideline income was 18 catties in 1944, in 1945 Ropemaker Geng Changsuo's sideline groups earned 442 catties of millet per capita, 49 percent of gross co-op income.[54] The co-op invested a portion of the profits from its sidelines to purchase the mule, two donkeys, and ox, making the animals co-op property. Sideline profits made agriculture more productive, thus increasing the marketable food surplus. An elated Geng Xiufeng passed along the news of success to his contacts in the fourth district and the county.

Rumblings

In spring 1945 Geng Xiufeng's achievements in co-op work won him a promotion from Raoyang Party Secretary Li Tai to work in the fourth district supply and marketing co-op in Xiaodian, ten miles east of Wugong. His political star on the rise, Xiufeng joined the Communist party, sponsored by his mentor Li Fengxiang. Leadership of the original co-op reverted to Ropemaker Geng Changsuo who, with his wife, Xu Shukuan, were known to visiting party propagandists as very loud singers. Literate Wei Lianyu was selected to head the co-op general affairs office, thereby reducing the burden on illiterate Changsuo.

As soon as spring plowing began, however, discontent erupted over the new, less "exploitative," more socialist system. Those who had invested relatively more land or had fewer able-bodied workers felt cheated. The charter revisions meant that both land-rich and labor-poor households would earn substantially less than they could working by themselves.[55] The party's socialism privileged the land-poor and labor-rich. It was a disincentive to investment, an incentive to population growth.

In addition, some complained that labor contributions were assessed unfairly. The crucial dimensions of skill and hard work were ignored in a system whose characteristics were simplicity and leveling. A skilled woodworker in the carpentry group felt that he should receive higher pay than less-skilled coworkers. Calculations that emphasized equal reward for unequal products undercut the morale of skilled workers. Socialism favored the largest, poorest, most unskilled families.

Other problems demoralized the enlarged co-op. Some members left farm work to pursue private business ventures. Li Qingshen opened a small wineshop after joining, content to receive a share based on his investment while others farmed the land. Some saw the co-op's lucrative sidelines as a vehicle to earn quick cash to invest in their own land or in household sidelines.[56] Others pleaded illness, and then took part-time jobs elsewhere. One member was caught spreading cooperatively owned manure on his own land.[57] By increasing the fertility of his soil, he would be better off should the co-op collapse or should he decide to quit. Given the culturally based fear of being taken advantage of by others, these practices could unravel the ties of cooperation.

The issue of women working also produced division. Beginning in spring 1945 Ropemaker Geng Changsuo, responding to the county government's production drive, urged women to work in the fields.[58] This irked households who had invested more land and whose women rarely worked outside the home. They claimed there was not enough work even for the men. If poorer women such as Ropemaker Geng's bound-foot wife, Xu Shukuan, worked, then given increased distribution by labor time, there would be less pay for households where only the males labored for cash. Such traditional households preferred that women remain at home. Some men found it degrading to work alongside women in the fields.[59] Lu Molin protested that when his daughter-in-law worked in the fields she neglected housekeeping.[60] Geng Changsuo compromised. Women were restricted for the most part to agricultural tasks deemed suitable, such as planting and caring for cotton. Plowing and working with animals and carts remained male preserves.

Finally, the new distribution system failed to address the problem of appropriate compensation for labor-short military-dependent households. Lu Molin had two sons in the Eighth Route Army.[61] Should Lu be entitled to more income for his patriotic household's land invested in the co-op? Or should the village be responsible for Lu's welfare? If the co-op tried to help dependent households, less remained to distribute to others.

Co-op morale dropped as the farming season began. The households recruited in 1945 had brought in good land, resources, skills, and farm tools, but the imposed socialism that paid more to labor time undermined the economic interests of new members. As discontent mounted, the co-op leaders became scapegoats. Too many leaders, it was said, neglected field work while receiving work credit for attending meetings and shuffling papers.[62]

Unknown Visitors

In winter 1944–45 Beishan village, four miles northeast of Wugong, was the secret headquarters of Lin Tie. A native of Sichuan province, a worker-student in France during World War I, and a 1926 graduate of the Nationalist party's Peasant Movement Training Institute in Guangdong led by Mao Zedong, Lin was party secretary of the Central Hebei Military Region.[63] Hearing of the Wugong co-op, Lin, accompanied by aides, trudged into the village one May day, disguised in rough peasant garb with a white towel wrapped around his head. At the home of deputy co-op head, party veteran, and militia leader Geng Shupu, Lin listened to an upbeat account of the co-op's development by Shupu and Geng Xiufeng, who had returned for the occasion. Lin offered a brief encouraging response: "Your co-op is good. It combines agriculture and sidelines, and members can turn to the co-op for loans in time of need. It is a comprehensive co-op." Lin Tie invited the co-op leaders to contact him if they experienced difficulty or needed help. He then melded into the evening dusk, heading for another village. In the years ahead Lin Tie would be a powerful patron of Wugong.

On May 13, 1945, local militia surrounded Raoyang town on three sides. Japanese forces were long gone. The puppet army that still occupied the county seat fled out the one open side. Raoyang was liberated without bloodshed, and the underground resistance government surfaced. The Raoyang party asked Anguo comrades to capture and send to Raoyang the Anguo puppet troops who had marauded and murdered in Raoyang. They were returned and executed. On June 25, when Xianxian was liberated, an effort began to restore the Catholic church, which had been desecrated by the Japanese occupiers. The Catholic faithful were assured by the party that, in contrast to the foreigners, the new Chinese authorities would respect religion.[64] When the happy news of Japan's August surrender reached Wugong, thirty young people hiked to Raoyang to join victory celebrations. Some were making their first visit to the county seat. A makeshift parade wound its way through the narrow dirt streets of the ancient walled town. It was a joyous day, temporarily eclipsing memories of the war dead, of looting, rape, drought, and famine.

The party erected a memorial tablet in Zoucun honoring soldiers from Raoyang's fourth district who had fallen. Party and nonparty members were listed separately. Standing seven feet high, the tablet looked like those traditionally put up to eulogize models of Confucian virtue. A list of seven Wugong martyrs included party members Qiao Hengtai and Li Jianzhang and nonparty members Li Fukuan, Li Xiong, Li Qishan, Li Hekai, and Xu Dong, the brother of Xu Shukuan.[65]

With Japan's surrender, Nationalist troops drove to regain control of northern China. By October Jiang Jieshi's forces had reclaimed the major North China cities of Shijiazhuang, Baoding, Tianjin, and Beijing and controlled the main railway lines. But in Raoyang and other counties of the central Hebei plain, Eighth Route Army forces remained.

Co-op Crisis

The tensions in the more socialist co-op exploded prior to the 1945 autumn harvest. Eight households, including those of deputy co-op head Geng Shupu and Geng Manliang, announced they were withdrawing immediately. Co-op leader Geng Changsuo reported the matter to Wugong Party Secretary Xu Mantang. The other three Wugong co-ops, led by Li Fengxiang, Li Yutian (now a two-time loser), and Li Yuzhu, had just folded. It was no easy matter to make voluntary cooperation work. Leadership and distribution conflicts had undermined the co-ops.[66]

Geng Xiufeng returned from his county job in the fourth district. Changsuo briefed him on the collapse. Xiufeng had already gotten an earful from Geng Shupu. Worst of all, Xiufeng's mother crushed him when he returned home. Why had he foisted his harebrained scheme on brother Manliang? Shupu and Manliang had invested considerable land, and both were short of labor power. With just 40 percent return on land, both lost. They were better off on their own.

Xiufeng blamed himself for having docilely complied with the directives of the work team from the Eighth Military District. He knew the distribution formula was unworkable, but he wanted to demonstrate his party loyalty. The imposition of outsiders' notions of socialism chilled village enthusiasm for cooperation. An urgent meeting of party and co-op leaders was held in Geng Changsuo's ramshackle house. They endorsed the recommendation of Xu Mantang to persuade the quitters to stay until the fall harvest, and the seventeen-household co-op then continued to limp along.

Grain yields fell slightly in 1945 from 223 to 215 catties per mu, and no one could blame the weather. Gross per capita grain output dropped from 375 to 368 catties. The gross value of agricultural production was 49,317 catties of millet. It was the decision to double the area sown in peanuts to expand marketable cash crops that allowed a modest increase in gross per capita crop output, from 420 to 458. The co-op's major success was in sideline production. Geng Changsuo's specialty, which produced gross income valued at 47,328 catties of millet.[67] This made possible a significant rise in gross per capita earnings from 427 catties of millet equivalent in 1944 to 906 catties in 1945.

The difficulty in distributing a harvest on principles unacceptable to a significant group of member households was compounded by a rise in agricultural expenses. Of the 215 catties produced per mu, only 77 were actually distributed. Those with more and better land or less labor felt cheated. Immediately after the harvest, eight households quit. The co-op lost two draft animals, two carts, one hoe, and some of the most productive land, but only slightly more than one-fourth of its full-time laborers.

A ferocious fight ensued over disposal of the assets of sideline enterprises. The dropouts demanded all the hemp so they could continue earning money by making rope. Lu Molin, the Black One, who stuck with the co-op, was furious. The co-op would be left with nothing but eight coffins built by the carpentry team. These would be hard to sell at once, Lu fumed. Where would the co-op get the capital to run its rope sideline? The stubborn Black One demanded legal action against the quitters.

But co-op leader Geng Changsuo prevailed in allowing the dropouts to take the hemp. Committed to expanding the co-op, yet sensitive to the fears of the community, Changsuo wanted to send a reassuring message. If villagers concluded that the co-op took advantage of people, cooperation was doomed. The long-term interests of a growing co-op were best served, Geng argued, by accommodating those determined to quit.

The dropouts also demanded a share of accumulation funds, 10 percent of the gross production of 1945, or 9,665 catties of millet. Co-op members angrily pointed to the charter, which stated that those who withdrew were entitled neither to a portion of the fodder salvaged after the harvest, nor to a share of accumulation money. The fodder was used throughout the winter to feed livestock and for fuel. But Ropemaker Geng, bookkeeper Qiao Wanxiang, and Geng Xiufeng (back again briefly after the harvest) pleaded with those remaining in the co-op to agree to some distribution of these items to avoid hard feelings. Those who quit were decent people. What counted was to learn from the experience, admit mistakes, and run the co-op better in the future. After some finger pointing and backbiting, the remaining members agreed to share the accumulation fund, the wood, and the fodder.

After the property was taken by the eight departing households, Geng Changsuo and Lu Molin spent the night at the co-op's rope workshop. Geng cried and Lu smashed furniture.[68] The remaining nine households responded to the walkout in late 1945 by revising the charter to award only 40 percent of income for agricultural labor and a whopping 60 percent for land. Those who quit were belatedly vindicated. The new charter also reverted to the terms spelled out in the original charter for sideline distribution: 60 percent of income to labor, 40 percent as return on investment.[69] The changes bid to win those with more land and resources. But as a concession to households that depended more on labor for income, and in an effort to draw in more women, the value of a full day's work by women was upgraded from 60 to 80 percent of what men earned. It was also decided that officials like Geng Changsuo and Qiao Wanxiang, increasingly involved in village affairs, would receive no remuneration from the co-op for time spent in political work in the village.[70] That countered a feeling that leaders got paid without doing real work.

Partly Ripe Li Number Two

Several households that had joined the co-op in 1945 did not leave. Party member Zhang Jinwan and his well-traveled brother-in-law Wei Lianyu reaffirmed their commitments. So did old Li Huiting, consumed by his desire to provide a decent burial for himself and a nest egg for his descendants, and still agonizing over the gambling addiction of his spoiled son. As much as Ropemaker Geng Changsuo appreciated these people, he had a special affection for Li Dier, Li Number Two, a huge, slow-witted man. Li's family had disintegrated in the 1943 famine, forcing him to go begging.[71] He joined the co-op in late 1944 to survive. Thirty-two-year-old Li Dier was so strong he could pick up an iron-wheeled cart with one hand, but his mind was as slow as his hands were large. Villagers called him Partly Ripe Li because, they said, his brain was like a melon that had not grown to full sweetness. When Partly Ripe Li was frustrated or confused, he cried. When he was angry, he stomped around like a wild ox. On occasion he resorted to the use of threats and daggers.

Just after joining the co-op, Partly Ripe Li was walking home with a heavy load of firewood on his back when a man in an ox cart poked fun at him, saying Li's two feet were less useful than the four hooves of a big ox. From that moment on, Partly Ripe thought of little else than getting an animal to do an animal's work. He pleaded with Ropemaker Geng Changsuo, whom he called Uncle Suo, to buy some draft animals. One day, when Partly Ripe Li was carrying water home for his wife, he spotted a cart pulled by a powerful horse entering the village. Still lugging the water, he followed the horse for almost half a mile before his bewildered wife caught up with him. In spring 1945 the co-op purchased an especially large black mule and put Li in charge of the beast. All day long he doted over Big Black, feeding, brushing, and talking to him. With a beast of burden to care for, Partly Ripe Li felt more human.

Li was confused by the talk of quitting the co-op. Belonging to the co-op and taking care of Big Black made him feel important. Uncle Suo let him know that the co-op family needed his brawn. The money earned in the first year enabled Li to eat, drink, and reunite with his father during the Qingming and Mid-Autumn festivals. But six of the eight households that quit were from his lineage group. Should he not follow them? One day he was going to stay, and the next he was going to quit. Lineage ties were strong. Finally, Li went to see Uncle Suo, who never joked about Li's slow wits. The co-op leader persuaded the dark-faced giant to stick with the co-op.

The nine co-op households celebrated the 1946 lunar New Year together. As friends and neighbors gorged themselves on the traditional meat-filled dumplings, Partly Ripe Li lumbered out of the room to the stable. He fed dumplings to the big black mule. "You eat these dumplings," he said. "I want you to work hard for the co-op. Are you listening?"

Geng Changsuo increasingly thought of the co-op not only as an economic organization but also as a large family. Co-op leader Geng was patriarch, and those with a personal problem could turn to him for help. In return Geng demanded respect and, above all, loyalty. Old Li Huiting had joined the co-op, in part, to save his wayward son. Whatever the father earned Zhanhu lost in gambling. Geng Changsuo set about transforming Zhanhu into the son his father wanted. Boss Geng[72] dragged Zhanhu out of the gambling house, threatened him, shamed him in public, and encouraged him when he worked effectively in the co-op. Geng got the credit when the young man's habit was broken and the son's relationship with the grateful father was secured. It was Boss Geng's shrewd, self-effacing style to insist that it was the co-op that had saved Zhanhu.

Sometimes Geng and his wife, Xu Shukuan, did not wait to be asked before intervening in the personal affairs of co-op members. The relationship between sixty-year-old Lu Molin, the Black One, and his teenage daughter-in-law, Guifang, was explosive.[73] With Lu's wife dead and his two grown sons away in the army, he expected Guifang to manage the house and to care for him and his two younger children. When the co-op encouraged women to work in the fields, Guifang noticed that the clothes worn by the daughters-in-law of Li Yantian and Qiao Wanxiang were better than hers. She complained that Lu never spent a penny on her. The Black One, in turn, ranted and raved about how poorly the house was kept since Guifang began working in the fields.

Knowing that Lu could never be convinced to buy cloth for Guifang, and that she would continue to feel maligned, Boss Geng and Xu Shukuan arranged with accountant Qiao Wanxiang to take some money from Lu's co-op account to buy Guifang cloth. They told her it was a gift from her father-in-law. Family relations improved. Geng later apologized for spending the old man's money, saying that it was the only way to make everybody happy and keep the co-op running smoothly.

Co-op farming expanded in Wugong in winter 1945–46 when Steady Xu Mantang got ten other west-end households to pool 120 mu of land. All but one of the member households were surnamed Xu. The new co-op lacked the many draft animals that made the Geng co-op attractive and envied.

Skepticism

heroes

In early spring 1946 Geng Changsuo for the first time represented the co-op at a meeting of local "heroes of the people" in Raoyang. He recounted the two-year experience of the co-op. Li Guangrong, new head of the county government, commented favorably, but others were skeptical. They wondered aloud about organizations that frightened the sort of independent farmers who had fled the co-op in the fall.[74]

But Geng Changsuo and the co-op had friends in high places. Earlier in the year the co-op had received a visit from Zhang Kerang, head of agriculture in the central Hebei region under Lin Tie. Zhang had heard good reports about the co-op and came to see for himself. He left talks with Geng Changsuo, Qiao Wanxiang, and Lu Molin impressed by the co-op's efforts to overcome difficulties and to help the poorest to survive. He noted its success in expanding the profitable rope business and combining both agriculture and sidelines. He praised the co-op's division of labor, which made use of Qiao Wanxiang's accounting skills, Geng Xiufeng's ideas, Geng Changsuo's leadership by example and marketing know-how, and Zhang Jinren's crop expertise. Elsewhere, leaders concentrated power in their own hands. In contrast, Boss Geng delegated responsibility. Zhang Kerang offered to provide technical assistance to the Geng co-op.

A few weeks after Zhang Kerang's visit, Geng Xiufeng reported on agricultural cooperation in Raoyang to a meeting of county leaders of supply and marketing co-ops sponsored by the Enterprise Section of the Eighth Military District. This time the criticism of the Geng Changsuo co-op was more forceful. Some condemned it as "petty bourgeois fanaticism," arguing that transferring property, wealth, and power from households to the group was premature. In 1946, with the Communists on the verge of engaging the Nationalists in civil war, it was vital that independent farmers not be frightened by alienating socialist experiments. The Nationalists had accused the Eighth Route Army of communizing women and other property. A man from the supply and marketing co-op in Bozhen, an industrial town fifty miles east of Raoyang, said that word had spread east of the Yellow River that a place called Wugong had in fact already been "communized." Xiufeng was pressured to dismantle the co-op, or at the very least to downgrade it to a mutual-aid team that merely exchanged labor and farm tools but did not pool land.[75] For Chinese villagers, household property was almost sacred.

When Xiufeng returned to Wugong, he reported the bad news to Geng Changsuo. Having recently been burned when they followed orders to make the co-op less exploitative, they decided on passive resistance. They neither reported to higher-ups their decision to continue a semisocialist co-op nor informed co-op members that the party had ordered them to disband. The co-op set about consolidating its gains. Thanks to the efforts of Geng Xiufeng, the co-op retained the support of county chief Li Guangrong. The co-op had other friends in Raoyang as well, including former Wugong party secretary and militia leader Xu Mantang, who had been transferred to the Public Security Bureau there in late 1945, right after starting a new co-op. Nothing undercut the words of encouragement and promises of further material support given by central Hebei party chief Lin Tie's aide Zhang Kerang.

Weathering the Storm

In 1946 the Geng Changsuo co-op contained nine households with forty-one people, including sixteen full-time workers, and 104 mu. Some of the most fertile land had been lost. But because the dropouts had large households, the per capita cultivated area of the nine remaining households actually increased from 2 mu in 1945 to 2.5 mu in 1946.[76] When Raoyang county was hit by a drought in the spring, the Geng co-op proved its worth. Zhang Jinren decided not even to seed the 10 mu of land with the least access to water.[77] Instead, the co-op concentrated labor on potentially more productive plots. Such a crisis response could not be made by individual households who worked alone. The co-op also substantially reduced the acreage devoted to coarse grains (corn, millet, and sorghum) and again increased the land devoted to peanuts, a commercial crop requiring less water. Peanut acreage and production levels were more than eight times those achieved in 1944. The co-op sought higher cash income in the market.

The co-op applied more natural fertilizer to the fields, approximately 1,000 catties per mu. Almost none of the co-op land was irrigated, and the co-op lacked the one hundred dollars it cost to dig a shallow well. In any case, it was risky to dig a well on the land of a member who might withdraw from the co-op. As the drought worsened through spring and early summer, co-op members carried water by shoulder pole the long distance to the parched fields.[78]

Carrying water paid off. Light late-summer rains permitted modest increases in millet, sorghum, wheat, late corn, and peanut yields. The average grain yield of 285 catties per mu represented an increase of 32 percent over the previous yield. Gross per capita grain output soared to 549 catties, and per capita gross income totaled 1,488 catties of millet equivalent.[79] For the second consecutive year sideline earnings approximately equaled agricultural earnings. The profits distributed trumpeted news of success. In a dry year, the co-op had raised yields and income for all members through commercial expansion, intensive and diversified cultivation, labor mobilization, and a division of labor and a remuneration system that had broad appeal.

The decision to focus sideline work entirely on rope paid dividends. In spite of fewer hands, the co-op produced rope valued at 30,104 catties of millet, up 37 percent from the previous year. The new party-led county government with which Wugong was now so entwined responded by placing a large rope order, the first institutionalized, profit-guaranteeing link between the co-op and the rising state.[80] One indication that things were going well for the Geng co-op was that yields on the land contributed by poorer households were higher than those of independent middle-income farmers. Since taxes were assessed on the basis of gross production on individually owned plots, some poor people in the co-op lost their tax-exempt status.

Talk from higher levels about forcing the co-op to disband was no longer heard. In mid-1946 Boss Geng, an increasingly effective folk politician, was appointed secretary of Wugong's sixty-four-member Communist party branch, tying more tightly the knots that bound the co-op and the Wugong party branch to higher party organizations. Boss Geng brought people loyal to him into the party's inner circle, starting with his wife, Xu Shukuan. She was introduced into the party in 1946 by the mother of Geng Shupu, who himself had introduced Changsuo into the party. Fast-rising Wei Lianyu joined the party after Geng Changsuo took over as secretary. Wei was the heir apparent to village chief Li Zihou, who promoted Wei's election as assistant village chief in late 1946.

However much the success of the Geng co-op and its increased contribution to tax coffers may have been appreciated by the emerging socialist state, within the village the prospering co-op, with its many party members, draft animals, and rope contract began to look to envious villagers like a specially favored group. The more the emerging government pushed villagers to arrange their lives in ways the party considered socialist, as it had in 1944, the greater the potential conflict with the cultural values and economic rationality of peasant households. A gap could grow between those favored by the socialist state and all others, and between a foreign vision of socialism and the indigenous roots of village cooperation.

4 ❖ SILENT
REVOLUTION,
SOUND
OF TERROR

With Japan defeated and civil war imminent, the Communist party leadership began to turn away from multiclass, nationalistic cooperation and from the gradualism characteristic of tax reform and of rent and interest reduction. On May 4, 1946, a Central Committee "Directive on the Land Question" called for land to the tiller.[1] The May Fourth Directive reflected an attempt to woo the poorest of the poor without alienating the independent tiller majority. Following Japan's defeat, some poorer peasants and local activists in various North China localities had seized and redistributed land. The directive endorsed such land seizures, noting approvingly that some communities had divided the land equally to achieve a distribution of three mu of land per person.[2] But it did not propose to universalize equal distribution. Rather, it established guidelines to ensure that land transfers would not infringe on the interests of independent tillers and even called for restoration of land confiscated from them.

The directive pinpointed the principal targets of a land to the tiller movement as big landlords, "evil tyrants," and those who had collaborated with the Japanese. It called for negotiation with small and medium landlords, especially those who had supported the patriotic resistance. Commerce and industry in the hands of landlords would be protected for the good of the local economy. The directive sanctioned execution and extreme physical violence only in cases of "extremely wicked traitors and public enemies."[3] In spite of these qualifications, for the first time since the mid-1930s, the party called for confiscatory means to transfer land to the poorest.[4] In July, as details of the May Fourth Directive were filtering down to villages in central Hebei, civil war erupted across North China. The directive would squeeze the old elite a bit more, but with victory in the civil war its first priority, the party leadership held back from all-out struggles that might splinter and paralyze villages. Independent tillers were the vast majority in Wugong and most of North China.

Land to the Tiller

After the 1946 autumn harvest, Raoyang county and fourth district officials instructed local leaders to implement land to the tiller. The basis for redistribution would be how much land each household owned in 1936, prior to wartime economic reforms. The leaders would assign each villager a class category based on the household's position a decade earlier.[5] In spite of patriotic service and the loss of land from tax reform, previously more prosperous villagers could suddenly be labeled enemies of the people.

The party defined "landlords" as the largest landowners, who rented out a significant portion of their land and may also have hired laborers to work the fields. "Rich peasants" normally had less land per capita than landlords, worked part of it themselves, and relied more heavily on hired labor than on tenants. Landlords and rich peasants were defined as exploiting classes whose ill-begotten wealth was taken from the labor of tenants and hired laborers. "Middle peasants" were independent cultivators who owned and worked the land themselves. "Poor peasants" included those who owned and cultivated very small holdings as well as tenant farmers and part tenants. "Hired laborers" were dubbed a rural proletariat. The poor peasants and hired laborers were classified as the poor and exploited. The May Fourth Directive instructed local leaders to mobilize the poor and exploited as the driving force for a redistributive land reform.

It was difficult for Wugong's leaders to comprehend the village in terms of the new and antagonistic categories of exploiter and exploited. Villagers knew that in 1936 there were powerful and influential people, though in the main they worked the land themselves with the assistance of a few hired laborers. Everyone knew that in 1936 there were people who went to bed hungry and people too poor to marry. But the notion that class exploitation based on landlord-tenant relations was primarily responsible for the plight of the poor distorted reality. Tenancy and hired labor accounted for a minute fraction of the cultivated area and labor power in the prewar village. By the 1930s all social groups were experiencing vulnerability to general decline related to disorder, market disruption, war, famine, and the worsening land-population ratio. Since Qing times Chinese leaders had fruitlessly grappled with these structured difficulties.

Rural dwellers experienced themselves in terms of community and consanguinity as members of lineages, neighborhoods, and villages, not as members of exploited or exploiting classes. Throughout the twentieth century the Southern Li lineage held sway in Wugong. The numerically and politically dominant Lis were concentrated about the village center. The smaller Geng and Qiao lineages in the east and the Zhangs and Xus, mainly in the west, were also organized. With the rise of the resistance after 1937, leaders named Geng, Qiao, Zhang, and Xu challenged Li supremacy.

Wugong was divided into four incest-taboo neighborhoods, one in the east, one in the center, and two in the west separated by a north-south lane. Villagers also knew that the east end was a center of ropemaking, that those in the vegetable-growing center had the best irrigated land, and that west villagers went in for peddling of all kinds.

Class categories, emphasizing polarization, exploitation, and social conflict, were difficult to square with Wugong's recent experience: the unity that carried the village through the resistance; the overwhelming independent cultivator character of society, which had been reinforced by a silent revolution initiated by tax reform; the prior long-term decline that affected the prosperous as well as the poor; the limited scope of tenancy and hired labor; the fact that renting land was by no means restricted to the poor and that even prosperous households farmed most of their own land. During the war people from all neighborhoods, lineages, and economic strata had united in the patriotic resistance and joined the underground Communist party and Eighth Route Army. Suddenly unity was to yield to something called class struggle.

The sixty-four-member secret Communist party branch made the final decisions regarding Wugong's class composition in consultation with fourth district officials. Ordinary villagers in the newly organized peasant association were not deeply involved. The leadership had difficulty finding anyone who fit squarely into the landlord category, even taking preform 1936 as the benchmark. In those days, Wugong's few tenants and part tenants had farmed less than 2 percent of the private arable land. Whatever the reality, loyalty to the party dictated that local leaders identify some villagers as exploiters and, therefore, targets for class struggle.

The alliance of outside lineages classified five households, all surnamed Li, as class enemies. The landlord label was pinned on households headed by former village chief Li Jianting and Li Huaqi, who had tangled with Xu Dun and the Association in 1936. These better-off farmers rented out a small portion of their land, both had one full-time farmhand, and both hired part-time laborers during the busy season for an average of one hundred days each (see table 1).

Three households were labeled rich peasants. Li Yingzhou and Li Duanfu had as much land as the landlords. All three also hired a year-round farmhand, and one rented out nearly as much land as the landlords. In 1936 the three rich peasant households hired part-time laborers at an average of ninety-three days each. Households classified as rich peasants were larger than those labeled landlord and, therefore, had slightly smaller per capita holdings. In reality, all five households classified as exploiters fit the party's formal defini-

Table 1   1936 Statistics for Households
Classified as Landlord or Rich Peasant in 1946

Class	Name of Household	Mu Owned	Mu Rented Out	Full-Time Farmhands
Landlord	Li Huaqi	123	24	1
Landlord	Li Jianting	80	20	1
Rich peasant	Li Yingzhou	122	8	1
Rich peasant	Li Duanfu	85	18	1
Rich peasant	Li Chunrong	55	0	1
		465	70	5

Note: Li Jianting and Li Duanfu were brothers; Li Huaqi and Li Yingzhou were paternal
cousins.

tion of rich peasants. A search for exploiters as the source of poverty caused
two of the five to be classified as landlords. All were labeled as class enemies of
the poor. The five "exploiting" households, all power brokers in the Southern
Li lineage, were residents of the village center or central west end. All had
supported the resistance. Two, Li Jianting and Li Duanfu, had sons in the
party risking their lives in the Eighth Route Army.

Party leaders, in consultation with poorer households, reconstructed from
memory 1936 village land tenure. The leaders classified more than 60 percent
of Wugong's 285 households as middle peasants. Borderline cases could go
either way. Qiao Wanxiang, a member of the Geng co-op and the party, had
hired short-term and long-term labor in 1936, and Li Laoshang had rented
out 10 mu of land. They were classified as middle peasants supposedly because
their per capita landholdings were not too large. Some villagers muttered that
Prosperous Qiao's ties to the east-end powerholders won his household a
nonexploitative classification. In 1936, 15 independent tiller households had
supplemented their income by hiring out members as short-term laborers.
Several independents had rented land from others, but their own landholdings kept them in the middle-peasant category.

The poor-peasant category consisted of 103 households. In 1936 only 25
of these had been part tenants; 28 had members who worked as long-term
laborers, mostly outside Wugong; 79 had members who worked at short-
term labor. Every one of those classified as poor peasants, including party
chief Geng Changsuo, whose fortunes had risen lately through the co-op,
owned some land. But with 1936 average per capita holdings of less than 1
mu, poor peasants fell far below the village average of 3.3 mu, just half an acre
per person. Five households were landless in 1936. Li Guanglin, Li Ertu, and
the others hired themselves out as long-term laborers. Because male members

Table 2   Wugong Landownership in 1936

	Household			People per Household	Land		Mu per Household	Mu per Capita
Class	No.	%	People		Mu	%		
Landlord	2	.7	19	9.5	203	4.5	101.5	10.6
Rich peasant	3	1.1	33	11.0	262	5.9	87.3	7.9
Middle peasant	172	60.4	808	4.7	3,534	79.1	20.5	4.3
Poor peasant	103	36.1	520	5.0	471	10.5	4.5	.9
Hired laborer	5	1.7	10	2.0	0	0.0	0.0	0.0
Village	285	100.0	1,390	4.8	4,620[a]	100.0	16.2	3.3

[a]Includes 150 mu of temple and lineage land.

of these households had great difficulty finding brides their family line could die out. They were the most vulnerable of the poor (see table 2).

These class categorizations obscured as much as they revealed. The survey ignored sideline and commercial income crucial to survival in central Hebei. The dividing line between categories, and even between exploiter and exploited, was frequently arbitrary. The classification was based on conditions that had long since changed and for which records frequently did not exist.

A decade of reform in a silent revolution had hastened the decline of the traditional elite and helped the poor. The holdings of the two landlord households had dropped during the 1936 to 1946 decade from 203 to just 76 mu; rich-peasant landholdings fell from 262 to 180 mu. During the wartime decade these five households had net land sales of 209 mu, close to half their land. By 1946 the landholdings of those classified as landlords and rich peasants were only marginally larger in per capita terms than those of middle peasants one decade earlier, 5.8 versus 4.3 mu. The middle peasants of 1936, especially those who owned a little more land, also lost ground during the war. Their total holdings dropped 26 percent from 3,534 to 2,600 mu.

The main beneficiaries of the silent revolution were the poor. Before the war, the 103 poorest landowning households had 471 mu. Ten years later, before land reform, they owned 1,425 mu, a 300 percent increase. By 1946, 58 of these households, who were classified as poor peasants, had acquired enough land to qualify as middle peasants according to the standard set for 1936. Per capita landownership of those classified as poor peasants soared from .87 in 1936 to 2.2 mu in 1946.

The gap between the most prosperous and the poorest had narrowed substantially. In 1936 per capita landlord holdings were twelve times those of poor peasants. By 1946, before the land to the tiller program, they were less than three times those of poor peasants. Middle-peasant holdings, 4.9 times the size of poor-peasant holdings in 1936, shrank to just 41 percent greater in 1946 through gradual reform. Landlords and rich peasants then each averaged 5.8 mu per person, middle peasants 3.1 mu, and poor peasants 2.2 mu. By the end of the war, tenancy and the hiring of labor had virtually disappeared as the poor obtained land and the prosperous were forced to mortgage or sell portions of their land. This stunning silent revolution, an achievement of gradual reforms in the service of the poorest households, has been largely ignored by analysts, as it was by party leaders whose goal was not property equity but an alliance with the poor against others (see table 3).

In spite of the war dead, including seventeen Eighth Route Army soldiers and dozens of villagers killed in Japanese raids, and in spite of the 1943 famine, Wugong's population increased by 130 during the ten-year span. The improvement in the economic well-being of poor-peasant and hired-labor males made it possible for most to attract wives. As the size and income of poor-peasant households increased over the decade, the traditional practice of "splitting" had occurred; couples built new mud-brick homes, farmed their own scraps of land, and set up autonomous households. Many of those classified as poor peasants on the basis of 1936 data had by 1946 entered the mainstream of village life during the silent revolution. As peasants experienced it, life was again being made whole and moral.

The large number classified as poor peasants could make it appear, on paper, that class antagonisms were rife. In reality, in 1946 the vast majority of villagers, including those labeled poor peasants, were independent tillers. If the class composition of Wugong had been based on 1946 tenurial relations, almost every household would have been designated middle peasant by the criteria that had been used to analyze 1936 conditions.

A real crisis, however, was confronting Wugong. That decade of reform had exacerbated the phenomenon of ever more people farming ever less land. The conditions that brought a measure of stability to the poor, which countered famine deaths and permitted the poor to marry, fueled population growth. Between 1936 and 1946 per capita landholding in Wugong dropped from 3.3 to 2.8 mu per person, and accelerated population growth lay ahead.

The decade of gradual change constituted a land revolution before the 1946 land to the tiller program. The holdings of the most prosperous in Wugong had been reduced by 1,143 mu in a peaceful way that preserved intravillage unity during stressful years of anti-Japanese resistance. The combined holdings of Li Huaqi and Li Jianting had shrunk from 203 to 76 mu. But in 1946 party leaders insisted that all emulate the most "advanced"

Table 3 Wugong Landownership in 1946

| Class | Household | | | People per | Land | | Mu per | Mu per |
	No.	%	People	Household	Mu	%	Household	Capita
Landlord	2	.5	13	6.5	76	1.7	38.0	5.8
Rich
peasant	3	.7	31	10.3	180	4.2	60.0	5.8
Middle
peasant	172	44.4	840	4.8	2,600	60.7	15.1	3.1
Poor
peasant	210	54.2	636	2.9	1,425	33.2	6.7	2.2
Village	387	99.8	1,520	3.9	4,431[a]	99.8	11.0	2.8

[a]Includes 150 mu of lineage and temple land.

Note: Percentages do not add up to 100 due to rounding.

achievements in class struggle and leveling redistribution. That could not be done without terrorizing respected villagers and shredding village unity.

As in most of central Hebei, there were no big landlords in Wugong, neither in 1936 nor in 1946. The directive distinguished between large and small landlords, and urged villagers to assess the service of landlord households to the patriotic resistance. If the village focused on a lack of large landlords and the existence of broad patriotic unity, then divisive struggle and violent clashes might be avoided. While the land to the tiller movement took on a nasty tone in some parts of North China, Wugong leaders emphasized the moderate thrust of the May Fourth Directive, which kept the village united.

A Quiet Revolution

Wugong village chief Li Zihou and Party Secretary Geng Changsuo found some land to redistribute by stressing the literal meaning of the slogan "land to the tiller." In order to reduce their own tax burden, the five landlord and rich-peasant households had mortgaged rather than sold parcels of land to poorer lineage members. Small tracts of land owned by temples and lineages were also farmed at favorable rents by the poor. Wugong transferred these plots to their tillers. In addition, although landlords and rich peasants would be allowed to retain enough land to support their dependents, any additional land would be distributed to the poorest.

The Geng leadership dispatched a small delegation to visit the five "class enemies" to negotiate a quiet transfer of land and such property as livestock, tools, and sections of housing. The youngest son of the deceased landlord Li Jianting, nineteen-year-old Li Maoxiu, was at home to meet the peasant association representatives. The son of a former respected village head and the brother of a Communist and Eighth Route Army fighter, Maoxiu had been active in the resistance. Nonetheless, with tales of violent struggles circulating, precautions seemed in order. Maoxiu's wife, twenty-three-year-old Fan Shufang, was sent to her natal village with babe in arms to be out of harm's way. Shufang, a native of Fanyuancun village, where her father's holdings had recently dwindled from 55 mu to almost nothing, and whose younger brother had been killed fighting in the ranks of the Eighth Route Army, married Maoxiu in 1945. He was seventeen and she twenty-one. Their son, Li Wei, was born in 1946. In Wugong, Fan Shufang was designated a class enemy, a member of a landlord household. Back home in Fanyuancun, however, she was a member of a martyr's household deserving party support. Her elder brother worked for the party in Raoyang's second district. For a woman, community and consanguinity codetermined class.

Maoxiu's father, Li Jianting, had died a few months earlier, and brother Li Feng was at the front with the Eighth Route Army. Maoxiu waited in the household courtyard for the delegation, which included two farmhands hired by the Lis. Treating teenager Maoxiu as household head, the delegates declared that compensation was required to settle accounts for past "exploitation." He listened to the demands and accepted them. There was no violence. The festive delegates left accompanied by clanging gongs and booming drums.

A few days after family labels were decided on in Wugong, a confiscation committee completed the transfer. The Lis were left 21 mu of land for the seven household members, an amount equal to per capita holdings of middle peasant households in 1946. They continued to live in one corner of the ample Li family courtyard, now shared with several poorer households. At a meeting following the confiscation, Li Maoxiu was praised for his cooperative attitude.

After the other four targeted households were visited, land available for redistribution totaled just 145 mu, 3 percent of the village's arable land. More land was sought. All 150 mu of temple and lineage land was confiscated. Five prosperous middle peasants eventually were pressured to give up 30 mu of land. In all, during the 1946–47 winter 325 mu of land, 9 percent of the village total, was distributed to poorer households. Just ten households had lost land in the quiet reform led by Geng Changsuo. Geng reported to higher authorities the successful completion of the land to the tiller program. Minor inequities existed in land, still more in ownership of draft animals and wells, but further leveling by confiscatory methods would have targeted the independent tiller majority.

One casualty of the land to the tiller campaign was the popular San Guan Temple in the east village, the only temple in Wugong that owned significant land. The May Fourth Directive labeled organizations that rented out land as exploiters. Throughout the war, the party-army had campaigned against superstition. Villagers were urged not to rebuild crumbling temples. The large River Spirit Temple in east Raoyang, reportedly constructed in the Song dynasty, was allowed to decay. Temples lost all their land. Razing temples was part of a party effort to destroy local religious shrines. Village leaders understood that to be in the good graces of the state required opposing religion.

The land was confiscated and the San Guan Temple was razed. No one consulted the faithful. Party leaders said that the bricks were needed to build a school. Believers carried home some of the small sacred images. Tian Changjin, the resident nun, stood by helplessly as the temple was desecrated and destroyed. Eventually she sold the remaining large images for a paltry sum at a local market. Young Zhang Chaoke, who would shortly join the Communist party, sacrilegiously lugged home the decapitated head of one of the large images. His incensed mother had him return it immediately.

In late 1946 the Communists controlled 88 percent of the 3,553 villages in the Eighth Military District. Yet a classified survey of the district prepared for the central Hebei party committee concluded that only 43 percent of the 3,136 party-controlled villages carried out the land to the tiller movement "thoroughly," 38 percent partially implemented the directive, and 19 percent did nothing.[6] Wugong shared much with villages that thoroughly implemented the directive. The 325 mu distributed to tillers in Wugong amounted to slightly less than the average in the Eighth Military District and was almost identical with the average in central Hebei (see table 4).

In the Raoyang village of Xi'nanjie, too, tenancy had disappeared by 1946. A total of 482 mu of the 2,711 available in Xi'nanjie was not cultivated by owners. No landlords were identified during the classification, but four rich peasants who owned a total of 295 mu, or 5.9 mu per capita, were targeted. They tilled 199 mu themselves and had pawned almost all the rest to avoid taxes. Lineage and temple land and plots that had been pawned by more prosperous farmers were redistributed. After the land to the tiller movement, the four victims were left at a middle peasant level with 121 mu, or 2.5 mu per capita.

Internal reports revealed that "struggle objects" were identified in 2,229 of the 3,136 Communist-controlled villages of the Eighth Military District. Yanggezhuang targeted two, Tian Han, the widow of a landlord, and Bai Jiluan, a political target labelled a rich peasant. Altogether 7,357 district households, an average of 3.3 per village, were designated as class enemies, of whom 68 percent were classified as landlords or rich peasants. Others were given such labels as traitor, local despot, and warlord. In most villages there was no violence. In the Eighth Military District the 1946 land to the tiller

Table 4   Land Transfers in Central Hebei, October–December 1946

District	Villages with Land Transfers	Total Mu Transferred	Average Transfer per Village (mu)
Eighth	1,440	538,302	374
Ninth	1,443	428,655	297
Tenth	716	287,740	401
Eleventh	699	150,740	215
	4,298	1,405,437	327

program seemed an extension of the quiet revolution that had unfolded during the reform decade.

In many villages in this independent tiller region, however, the movement to redistribute land never got off the ground. Of 8,567 villages in central Hebei targeted for land reform only 4,298 transferred land. Many local officials only went through the motions of implementing the directive. Investigators estimated that an additional 650,000 mu remained to be redistributed.

War Casualties

By late 1946 news filtered into Wugong of bloody battles. A Nationalist offensive launched in July compelled Communist forces to retreat. The Nationalists, backed by the United States took over the major cities of the northeast, began recapturing county seats in northern and central China, and cleared communication lines north of the Yangzi River. Fighting was fierce in the Shanxi-Hebei-Shandong-Henan border region south of Wugong. Between September 1946 and January 1947 the Communist side lost twenty-four of thirty-five county towns, including Handan, the capital of the region at the southern tip of Hebei. In March the Nationalists captured Yan'an, the wartime headquarters of Mao Zedong and the Central Committee. The Nationalist offensive advanced across North China.

The Nationalists, like the Japanese, concentrated their fire on major cities and more-prosperous counties to the west, east, and south along important railway lines. The fighting never reached Raoyang, but the civil war was as much a battle for resources as for territory and population. With no access to international supply sources, the Red Army required domestic grain, salt, cotton, shoes, and other essentials. As in the anti-Japanese war, Raoyang loyally provided supplies and recruits for the front.

The role of village party organization was intertwined with the mission of the armies at the front. Zhou Yuanjiu was a member of a poor and patriotic family in the west village. His eldest brother, Zhou He, a party member, had died in 1939 in distant Xinjiang province fighting with the 120th Division. His youngest brother, at the end of the 1943 famine when food became available, gorged himself and died. It was a common fate. Another younger brother, Zhou Fuhai, also a party member, died fighting in 1945, thus leaving the parents alone in the village. Zhou Yuanjiu, who had served as a radio operator in Shanxi, was in a field hospital recovering from wounds incurred in the battle for Datong when news reached him that his only surviving brother had died fighting. Zhou rushed home to care for his parents.

The party could not accept that. It had devised a set of privileged guarantees for the family members of its soldiers so that they would fight without anxiety about conditions back home. Burials were guaranteed, as was at least an average level of income. At the New Year, soldier families were to receive meat for dumplings. Village leaders were to see that those short of labor received assistance in the busy season. Such families sometimes received extra land during the reform, even when short of labor to till it. Soldiers' wives could not divorce them.

Yuanjiu arrived home to find that his family had received fourteen mu of good land. But the party treated his return as a shameful breach of trust that challenged the village-party-army tie. Zhou was declared AWOL. Despite all the blood shed by his family and his own service, he was barred from the party. In like manner, a Raoyang party secretary, who was an only child, refused to march south with the army and abandon his elderly parents. Villagers respected the filial action, but the party expelled him. Whereas some suffered for giving priority to familial traditions over party norms, Fan Shufang, the wife of landlord Li Maoxiu, as a result of patriarchal Confucian exogamy, could suffer in Wugong as a landlord's wife or be privileged in Fanyuancun as a martyr's sister. Life was better where a tie to the military won one rewards. During the campaign to redistribute land, she stayed in Fanyuancun.

Three new households joined the Geng Changsuo co-op in fall 1946, bringing the number to twelve. With her husband serving in the Eighth Route Army, Liu Shufang, a middle peasant, invested her household's land in the co-op. Because she was a military dependent, the village government was responsible for her welfare. Martyr and military-dependent households were supposed to receive 30 catties of grain from village leaders each month.[7] Families of fighters were guaranteed special treatment.

Twenty-five-year-old Zhang Zhan joined the co-op to find a bride. During the war his family scratched out a living by renting two mu of land from the lineage organization. In the early war years, Zhang also labored as a hired hand for Qiao Wanxiang, the most prosperous of the founders of the Geng co-op. In late 1946 Wei Lianyu, the number two man in the Geng co-op, urged Zhang Zhan to join. Wei, with no son, showered fatherly affection on young Zhang, who turned to Wei when he needed money or advice. Zhang's economic straits left him little chance of finding a wife. With no education, no skills, no land, and no savings how could he approach a matchmaker in search of a bride? The co-op, Wei advised, was Marrying Zhang Zhan's only way out.

As civil war intensified, the Eighth Route Army was renamed the People's Liberation Army. Raoyang county launched a recruiting drive, which enrolled seven hundred. Just after the 1947 lunar New Year the call went out to village leaders to transport grain west to war zones at the base of the Taihang Mountains. Able-bodied men between the ages of sixteen and fifty-five were conscripted for transport work. The Geng co-op contributed one of its two large wooden carts, its mule, Big Black, and the services of Partly Ripe Li, who was promised that if he died while transporting grain his survivors would be treated as a martyr household.[8]

As the column of grain bearers approached the front, Nationalist aircraft attacked. The teamsters abandoned their grain and fled, but Partly Ripe Li removed the mule to safety. He did not understand politics, but this episode roused a passionate hatred for the enemy. How dare they try to kill Big Black! When Partly Ripe returned to Wugong, he testified, "This mule is actually a god sent down to earth from heaven. As soon as he saw the enemy plane, he moved to one side. The bullets were afraid to come near him!" Four Wugong caravans delivered 80,000 catties of grain to the front, almost the village tax obligation for a full year.[9]

In the autumn, as casualties mounted, two veteran members of Ropemaker Geng's co-op, Qiao Wanxiang and the former gambling addict Li Yantian, volunteered as stretcher-bearers in a battle fought north of the Daqing River along the Beijing—Wuhan railway line. The Geng co-op also assisted non–co-op households whose sons were bearing stretchers for the wounded at the front.[10] Qiao Wenzhi, the young woman activist in the east village, organized small groups of village women to sew cotton shoes for the militia and for army regulars.

Geng Xiufeng, working in the supply and marketing section of the Raoyang government, continued to publicize Wugong. In July Xiufeng had been invited by Zhang Kerang, the head of the agricultural department of the Central Hebei Military Region, to a meeting on agrarian policy sponsored by the Jinchaji Border Region government, which included central Hebei Zhang, who had visited Wugong in 1946 and become its supporter, asked Geng Xiufeng to report on co-op history. Also attending that meeting and expressing interest in the Geng co-op was Nie Rongzhen, the top military leader in the Jinchaji Base Area.[11] Word came back to Wugong from Xiufeng that Mao Zedong himself was impressed that a co-op could grow even during the war.

The disruptions of civil war, however, took a toll on the Geng co-op. In 1947 grain yields fell 18 percent, to 234 catties per mu. The co-op planted three mu of cotton, a crop urgently needed by the army, but the cotton yield was a mere 25 catties per mu.[12] The gross per capita grain output of 382 catties was the lowest since 1944. And gross sideline income dropped 17 percent despite income generated by a new oil press.

Nevertheless, the Geng co-op was doing far better than many. Xu Yizhou, the pioneer guerrilla leader, organized a new co-op in winter 1946–47. His group of seven west village households owned more than 50 mu of land, but morale was low from the outset. People were skeptical that the new arrangement could work, and leadership was ineffective. The co-op ran a small cotton-spinning sideline. It stayed together long enough to do the spring plowing and planting, but collapsed before the wheat harvest in June 1947. Each family then harvested what was on its own land. In contrast, despite economic decline, the Geng co-op held together. Old Militia Xu ascribed the difference to Geng's able leadership.

Class Struggle to Wipe Out Exploiters

In the second half of 1947 the Communist party intensified land reform. Some leaders felt that land to the tiller had stalled or failed. Stories spread of rampant corruption of rural party branches. Giving a reverse twist to the heretofore successful united front that had won more-prosperous villagers to the party, it was now claimed that the party had been infiltrated by landlord elements. On July 7, the East China Bureau charged that because local leaders in Shandong had been too lenient in dealing with landlords and rich peasants, the demands of the poor for land remained unfulfilled, army recruitment lagged, and the party's war mobilization strategy was jeopardized.[13] Promises made to soldiers' and martyrs' families had not been kept.

Even before the fall of the Communist capital at Yan'an in March and the division of the Central Committee into two groups, with Liu Shaoqi leading one to a headquarters in the Jinchaji Border Region, the leadership jointly agreed that to liberate the masses required a thorough leveling of landowner-ship. Therefore, under a slogan of power to a peasant association of the landless and of those with little land, the earlier successful united front policy of village cooperation across divisions of wealth would be treated as feudal unity, a rightist error, a plot of the rich within the party.[14] From July 17 to September 19, the Central Committee convened a national land conference, bringing delegates to Xibaipo village in Hebei's Pingshan county to review the land question and map strategy. Liu Shaoqi chaired the conference.[15]

A key conference participant was Kang Sheng,[16] a public security specialist trained in the Soviet Union during Stalin's Great Purge. Kang arrived at the conference accompanied by Mao Anping, a son of Mao Zedong. Mao had placed Kang in charge of the political education of his son. Dong Biwu, one of the top five party leaders at Xibaipo who lived in a large house, made way for the Kang entourage. Appearing as Mao Zedong's trusted confident, Kang sat at the head table of the conference. He introduced his experience in Linxian county in Shanxi province of using fierce means to ferret out buried landlord treasures. It was an invitation for the conference to support terror.

The 107 delegates endorsed Liu Shaoqi's call for a class-struggle land reform to liberate poor villagers from exploitation and oppression. In Xibaipo itself, the last major landlord, Qi Shaoshan, had given away his land a decade earlier "so the Japanese dwarfs could not steal it," winning himself renown as a patriot and an enlightened member of the gentry. Few large landlords were left in the base areas. Nonetheless, on October 10 the Central Committee issued the Chinese Agrarian Reform Law as the basic directive in the land reform movement, which held that "China's agrarian system is unjust in the extreme." Landlords and rich peasants, "less than 10 percent of the rural population," the directive asserted, "held approximately 70 to 80 percent of the land, cruelly exploiting the peasantry." The peasants were said to be demanding eradication of that unjust agrarian system and the expropriation of land for equalized distribution to the poor.[17]

The directive raised thorny problems in provinces with historically low tenancy rates and particularly in base areas where reforms had eroded landlord power. Before 1937 Hebei and Shandong had the lowest tenancy rates in all China, just 10–11 percent.[18] It was a land of small and declining owner-cultivators with few tenants and hired laborers. Wugong and many other villages in central Hebei had long since eliminated remnant patterns of landlord power. Many communities, moreover, had no more land to distribute after the 1946 land to the tiller campaign. Yet article six of the new directive demanded the confiscation by the village peasant association of the property of landlords, rich peasants, and all public land, which then "together with all other village land" would be "equally distributed."[19] It called for a leveling redistribution, even when that meant taking land from the independent cultivator majority labeled by the party as middle peasants.

In October the Jinchaji Border Region convened a month-long meeting attended by a thousand officials. Nie Rongzhen, the top border region military leader, enthusiastically endorsed the new policy of equalizing landholdings.[20] The delegates were warned that many village officials had committed "rightist errors" in implementing the May Fourth Directive on land to the tiller. Many class enemies, it was said, retained power, while the exploited poor had been unable to throw off the feudal yoke. The directive found in residual exploitation the major reason for insufficient peasant responsiveness to military recruitment campaigns and military support work.[21]

But theory often obscured reality as it had in discrediting Wu Manyu, the most famous peasant model of the wartime movement. In the early 1940s Wu had won praise from Mao as he rose from poverty to modest prosperity. When Mao fled Yan'an in 1947, Wu stayed behind and offered his services to the Nationalists. That political betrayal was twisted by the party, which focused on economic classes as the source of evil and therefore attacked Wu as a rich peasant.[22] In the view of party fundamentalists, prosperity itself was suspect.

Echoing the call to smash exploiters, Party Secretary Lin Tie angrily charged that party organizations were in serious disarray in many parts of central Hebei. Corruption and outright sabotage had undermined the land to the tiller program. On the front page of *Work Communications*, a classified journal of the central Hebei party committee, Lin asserted that "in order to implement the Party's policy of equalization of land holdings, it is absolutely essential to rectify the Party."[23] Similar movements concurrent with the 1947 land reform were launched across North China.[24]

Internal reports claimed that landlords and rich peasants controlled 248 of the 636 party branches in Wuqiang and Shenxian counties, both of which bordered southern Raoyang. Only 24 percent of the party branches in these two counties were characterized as "good and basically good."[25] In Xianxian, on the eastern border of Raoyang, many local party leaders stole public funds and took the lion's share of plots distributed in the land to the tiller movement. Peasants asked to sacrifice their sons were outraged by wartime profiteers. In twenty-three villages in Xianxian, investigators reported, the peasants despised the local party leadership, and in twelve of these villages the people expressed a strong desire to "struggle" against corrupt officials. Elsewhere peasants complained that promises of financial support for the households of military martyrs were not being honored.[26] Mystifying the emerging political order, the real problems caused by unaccountable party political power were treated as a consequence of property inequality. The party therefore would destroy the economic elite, thereby intensifying the corrupt system of unaccountable power. Party leaders could not see that it was their political system that caused the problems they claimed to want to solve. Ideological blinders and self-interest left the beneficiaries of the emerging socialist system incapable of seeing how its state structures permitted party powerholders to act corruptly in their own interest.

In compliance with strongly worded instructions from above, Raoyang set up work teams to investigate party organizations, review the first land reform, and thoroughly implement the expropriating and leveling Agrarian Reform Law. Yu Guangyuan, a party theorist who led a land reform team in Genggezhuang in Raoyang, found no big landlords in the region. Nonetheless, the search for exploiters continued, splintering villages.

In November Raoyang authorities appointed Zhang Yukun to head the investigation in Wugong and rectify errors labeled rightist. Zhang's first act on arriving was to strip all power from Geng Changsuo and other leaders pending an investigation. The work team took control of the village and proclaimed that power now lay with the newly formed Poor Peasant Association.[27] At this time, nine years after its 1938 founding, the membership of the Wugong Communist party was made public. Party members were sought as targets by the work team. All across North China local party leaders were attacked for corruption, cronyism, and rightism, said to have sabotaged the 1946 land reform and military recruitment.[28]

During the previous year's land reform the Wugong party, forced to act on the basis of a decade-old situation, had disregarded the economic role of sideline production and had practiced a bit of political favoritism by classifying allies in low-class categories. Consequently, village discontent was mobilizable against the Geng Changsuo leadership. Zhang Yukun ordered "sealed" the doors of all who might be considered prosperous. Sealed doors identified prospective targets for reclassification as exploiters, enemies whose land would be confiscated and redistributed. Zhang urged the poorest of the poor to form a picket line in front of the homes of potential targets for expropriation to prevent the removal of personal property and to demonstrate militance. But almost no one responded.

There were tricks and techniques that could magically manufacture zeal and class enemies. Zhang announced that anyone joining the picket line would be entitled to keep any property that had been secretly moved or concealed by the suspected household. That raised the stakes. Former hired laborer Li Guanglin, who was without family and too poor to marry, and Zhang Duan, at age twenty-one a thin, fierce party veteran of seven years from the west village, volunteered to guard the homes of the new targets. Zhang Duan had headed the Wugong children's corps under landlord Li Maoxiu in the early years of the war against Japan and, following his father, joined the party in 1940 at the age of fourteen. Starting school late, towering over his classmates, Zhang made a mark for himself as a disciplinarian. People came to see him as "fierce and conservative." He rose in the militia. In the late 1946 land reform, Fierce Zhang Duan was classified as a middle peasant.[29]

In some villages this class-struggle movement carried to leadership positions those who most militantly opposed formerly prestigious figures. Many of these new local powerholders were young, uprooted, virtually illiterate toughs. Some used the campaign to seize power, settle grudges, rape, steal, and entrench themselves and their cronies, presenting themselves as superloyal practitioners of class struggle.

Others besides Fierce Zhang gradually came forward in Wugong. Prominent among them was Old Militia Xu Yizhou, the west village guerrilla leader who had served as party secretary but was shunted aside with the rise of a group from the east village led by Geng Xiufeng, Geng Changsuo, Geng Shupu, Qiao Hengtai, and Qiao Wanxiang. There was discontent in the west village about the east-village leadership. When the number of guards reached fifty, the work team proclaimed the formation of the Wugong Poor Peasant Association. Li Guanglin, a political outsider with impeccable class credentials as a former hired laborer, was its head.

Zhang Yukun's investigation of local party members and officials relied on the testimony of Li Guanglin's Poor Peasant Association. Old Militia Xu Yizhou and Fierce Zhang Duan passed the investigation with flying colors. However, Geng Changsuo, who classified himself as a poor peasant in the peaceful 1946 land reform, was identified by the work team with a middle-peasant cabal said to be holding back land reform. Boss Geng, they charged in the campaign's jargon, was a huge stone holding down and crushing the energies of revolution. The campaign scriptwriters would have lower-level people lift the stone and liberate the class energies of the exploited poor.

The harshest criticism was reserved for two veteran Communists, Li Zihou, who had served as village chief since 1941, and Li Zhengbang, one of his chief lieutenants. Both were classified as middle peasants in the 1946 reform. As village chief, Li Zihou had been responsible for collecting taxes both during and after the war. Li was also expected to fulfill wartime demands for corvée labor. Peasants received no pay for their work from the Japanese army, the Eighth Route Army, or its successor, the People's Liberation Army. In 1947 a chorus of invective rained down on Li's administration during the resistance war and postwar periods. In some Raoyang villages, officials were terrorized and beaten, sometimes alienating large sections of the community who perceived scapegoating as unjust. Others fled to the district, township, or county seat to escape the terror. Following its investigation, the Zhang Yukun work team, in cooperation with the Poor Peasant Association, prepared to reclassify households and redistribute property. Villagers looked on anxiously as neighbors were targeted for confiscation and humiliation. The work team posted lists at three places in the village with the class designation of each household.

With 387 village households watching, 71 rich peasant doors were sealed, including that of Geng Xiufeng, the originator of the Wugong co-op. Throughout North China, members of targeted households were forced out of their homes. In Wugong some unfortunates camped out in the dirt lanes during the month-long ordeal. Some set up temporary living quarters in the fifteen rooms and two courtyards of the now empty home of landlord Li Huaqi, who had fled Wugong. Others had their doors sealed but were permitted to live in their courtyards. The land, livestock, and implements of targeted households were recorded in preparation for a final settlement. Movable property in the homes of the 71 households was carted off to the Poor Peasant Association headquarters for cataloging. Redistribution awaited formal reclassification.

But how was the work team to classify members of the Geng Changsuo co-op? Cooperative efforts had boosted the incomes of all its members. Such people as Partly Ripe Li, Marrying Zhang Zhan, the Black One Lu Molin, Crop Expert Zhang Jinren, and Old Li Huiting had been poor all their lives and were still short of land, even after earlier reforms. But the virtue that had brought the co-op to public attention—its success in improving the lives of its members—now merited public denunciation and expropriation according to fundamentalist standards. Class struggle required evidence of wealth as proof of class exploitation. By the end of 1947 the Geng co-op owned a horse, three mules, two carts, and two plows; it also ran two profitable sideline businesses, ropemaking and peanut-oil processing. Envious villagers grumbled that the prospering co-op should pay higher taxes. Zhang Yukun's work team and the Poor Peasant Association labeled the Geng co-op a rich peasant organization.

Geng Changsuo was staggered. The co-op had loyally followed party directives, had channeled its slender resources to support the war effort, and had helped army households and the needy. Singled out as a model of cooperative development just one year earlier, it was now targeted for class struggle. For the second time Geng and the co-op were subjected to the imposition from outside of policies based on class notions of exploitation as sources of ill-gotten wealth. The first instance was in winter 1944, when outsiders imposed changes in the co-op charter to reduce supposed exploitation of labor. The result then was the loss of half the members of the co-op and the dissatisfaction of many others. Now representatives of the emerging socialist state, demanding confiscatory measures to level rich and poor, were placing the co-op in a position reserved for class enemies and traitors. Believing that treating wealth as a fruit of exploitation was ridiculous, Geng raced to Raoyang to ask justice from county Party Secretary Li Tai. But Li sent Geng home, saying that the work team would do justice. At the same time, patrons Zhang Kerang and Lin Tie at central Hebei regional party headquarters not far from Raoyang kept an eye on how Geng was faring.

The work team tried loyally and literally to apply the 1947 agrarian law, which called for expropriation and redistribution of the 70 to 80 percent of land held by the rich. But what if there were no rich? What if the once prosperous owned only a minute fraction of the land, as in Wugong, central Hebei, and much of North China in 1947? The party's reform measures of the preceding decade had so reduced the power of already declining landlords that the political economy of the base areas had become a party-led society of small tillers. Yet the operative categories imposed by the party insisted that the source of political and economic problems was the exploitation of the many poor by the few rich. The party, with its single truth and single career ladder, forced such local officials as Zhang Yukun to run roughshod over local notions of justice in the name of class struggle. To do otherwise might arouse the fury of higher levels and raise questions about one's loyalty to the party and its leadership. To act on local reality could ruin a career by exposing one to charges of rightism, the principal target of attack in the campaign. Under heavy pressure from their superiors to produce results, few officials were prepared to take such risks.

One poor northern Raoyang village loyally labeled five landlords and ten rich peasants. In a movement called pulling the landlords, which spread across the county at this time, they were dragged before public meetings and forced to confess where they had hidden their gold and money. When they were not forthcoming, ropes tied to their arms and legs were pulled until they confessed. In one village, two landlords were pulled to their death. In another, a landlord and two rich peasants committed suicide. Other reports told of people buried alive. Terror spread.

Orphans

In late December, six weeks after the tumultuous visit of Zhang Yukun's work team began, an acquaintance from a nearby village showed up at the doorstep of the besieged Geng Changsuo with two Wugong children. Moaning and weeping, she said the twelve-year-old girl, Li Zhuan, and her six-year-old brother, Li Tan, were homeless orphans. Their father, who owned thirteen mu of land, had worked as a teamster in Manchuria. In 1946 both parents died. The woman, their aunt, had no means of caring for the orphans. The co-op, she pleaded, was better positioned than any single household to look after the children and manage the land they inherited but were too young to work. Was it not true, she asked, that Geng's co-op operated much like a big family enterprise? Geng rejected her proposal. The 1947 harvest had been disappointing. The co-op, now labeled a "rich peasant organization," had problems of its own. The children were her relatives and she should care for them. But the aunt walked away, saying the problem was in Geng's hands.[30]

Geng convened the twelve member households to discuss the orphans. Most wanted nothing to do with the children. True, the children had thirteen mu of land, but they could not work and they would have to be fed, clothed, and looked after for years. The co-op was not an orphanage. But Geng and Xu Shukuan contended that the children should not be allowed to become beggars. Others angrily responded that if the children were taken into the co-op, soon everyone would be reduced to beggary. Moreover, villagers would gossip that the rich peasant co-op was exploiting the children. Xu Shukuan, the bound-foot mother of six who had once been forced to sell her own child, responded that if the co-op would pay for food not covered by the orphans' land dividends, she would clothe and care for them and proper accounts would be kept. In the end Geng and Xu brushed aside member objections and made the children co-op members.[31]

Five weeks later, just after the 1948 lunar New Year celebration, an eighty-year-old Wugong man walked into Geng's courtyard with two of his grandchildren, ten-year-old Li Xiuying and her six-year-old brother, Li Mengjie. The children were dressed in white mourning clothes. During the war their father had gone to Fujian province in South China to work in a textile mill. He was never heard from again. When the youngsters' mother died, the new

Poor Peasant Association donated a coffin and burial clothes. The revolution restored some rites of passage that economic decline had ruptured, but there was no one to care for the children. The old man begged Geng to take them into the co-op. They were homeless and heirs to only five mu of poor-quality land.

Some co-op members objected that the embattled group was carrying quite enough burdens with one set of orphans, the past year having seen declining incomes and political setbacks. But Xu Shukuan and her husband declared they wanted the children in the co-op whether the others agreed or not. They could live with the first pair of orphans and be looked after by Shukuan. Xu and Geng again prevailed.

With the revolution experienced in part as making families secure, even abandoned Japanese children were cared for. Party leaders became known for helping to raise orphans. Karl Marx's biography was reshaped by Chinese cultural preoccupations to stress that four of Marx's children died in infancy or early childhood and that Marx could not afford a small coffin for one daughter. By taking responsibility for poverty-stricken youngsters of the Li lineage whom no one in Wugong wanted, the Geng co-op seemed less like a selfish rich peasant organization. The co-op kept careful records of funds spent for the welfare of the orphans to show skeptics that, far from cheating or exploiting them, it looked after their interests.[32] When income from their land invested in the co-op did not cover living expenses, the co-op loaned the orphans money. The orphans accumulated a considerable debt. Some members resented the way Xu Shukuan, who was herself an orphan, represented the orphans' interests at members' expense. She diverted money to feed them from funds set aside for sideline production. When Zhuan and Tan needed a cotton quilt, old Xu took one owned by the co-op. When the orphans' roof needed repair, she told Partly Ripe Li to use two woven mats to repair the hole. When he refused on the grounds that the mats were co-op property, a shouting match ensued. Old Xu then walked to the supply room and took the mats.[33]

Mischievous, perhaps psychologically scarred, Li Tan was constantly getting into trouble. He skipped school, pissed in the wells, and shat on the ground and even on the grinding stone where people milled their grain. No one forgave him for that. Li Tan loved to fight. When he was losing, his gangly older sister joined in to protect the boy. Once when he beat up Geng Xu, the grandfather of the bloodied boy dashed after Li Tan. Xu Shukuan headed off the old man and gave him a tongue-lashing. Villagers were in for trouble if they tangled with Xu on any issue related to the orphans.

National Unity

By winter 1947–48 the party center had received numerous reports on popular reaction against the leveling and terroristic land reform. Many counties reported that the attack on local officials demoralized veteran leaders, fractured unity, and set back the civil war effort. Shredding Chinese society would not hasten the rise of a socialist state. Politburo member Ren Bishi was among the first to call for reining in the mounting violence of the 1947 land reform. The civil war was at a delicate stage. By early summer the Nationalist offensive had begun to stall. In November four hundred thousand troops of the People's Liberation Army fought a nine-day battle to capture Shijia-zhuang, a key railroad junction west of Raoyang. The victory in the first major city to be taken south of the Great Wall permitted a military linkup of base areas in Shanxi, Hebei, and Shandong.[34] Soon the Nationalists would have to redeploy troops from northeastern China to North China, leaving their armies vulnerable in both regions. Liberation Army troops raised in North China advanced into the northeast. People's Liberation Army victories in North China spelled the beginning of the end for Nationalist power on the China mainland.

In January Joseph Stalin's personal emissary, Anastas Mikoyan, arrived in Xibaipo to meet with Mao, Zhou Enlai, Ren Bishi, Liu Shaoqi, and Zhu De. Mikoyan passed on Stalin's request that the People's Liberation Army not fight for total power but seek an accommodation with the Nationalists. Stalin worried that a continuing war would lead American troops to intervene in China and threaten the Soviet Union's southern flank. As soon as Mikoyan left Xibaipo, however, Mao proudly declared that China's revolutionary ar-mies would proceed to liberate all of China and insist on Soviet recognition.

Communist leaders remained deeply divided over land reform priorities. A December 1947 report by Mao Zedong, while calling for the protection of middle-peasant interests, stressed that "the demands of the poor and farm laborers must be satisfied" above all. He warned that "many landlords, rich peasants, and riff-raff had sneaked into the Party."[35] Nevertheless, over the winter the party modified its position on land reform. Pointing to a North China village where 10 percent of households had wrongly been designated landlord or rich peasant, Ren Bishi in January argued that because so many soldiers were from independent-cultivator households, the policy of leveling landholdings, which hurt middle peasants, would cause defeat in war. On February 22, 1948, "The Central Committee Directive on Land Reform and Party Rectification in Old and Semi-Old Liberated Areas" proclaimed that land reform should be considered complete in villages where middle peasants, including new middle peasants who had acquired land during the wartime period, accounted for 50 to 80 percent of the households, and where poor peasants made up from 10 to 40 percent of the population.[36] The party drew back from leveling redistribution, which splintered rural communities and undermined the interests of large numbers of independent cultivators.

All across North China the political winds shifted. New work teams were supposed to correct the class-struggle errors of the previous work team. The party secretary of poor Gengkou waited for a work team that never came. He knew that it was wrong to have labeled twenty-three households in that small village as exploiters. Meanwhile, the poorest, who had seized the dwellings of those households, demanded permanent deeds. The party secretary temporized, finding excuses to delay making injustice permanent. The village stayed split and anxious. Vengeful feelings intensified. In Gengkou cooperation became impossible.

In March Zhang Yukun's work team was recalled from Wugong and replaced by a second land reform team, which entered Wugong to act on Ren Bishi's speech and the February 22 party directive. The team consisted of a husband and wife, Wang Fulu and Gao Zixia, and a young writer named Wang Lin, who was beginning a long involvement with Wugong. All villages that became leadership models had writers assigned to them. The work team reported directly to Lin Tie, party secretary of the Central Hebei Military Region.

The new work team, instructed not to damage middle-peasant interests, immediately dismissed Li Guanglin as leader of the Poor Peasant Association. It then reviewed and endorsed the original classifications made in late 1946 by Geng Changsuo.[37] The number classified as landlords and rich peasants was again reduced to five. For the rest of their lives individuals would bear the class labels fixed at this time, labels based on politicized assessments of one's household position in 1936.[38] The labels, which had profound political and social content, were passed on to wives and progeny through the male line. The children and grandchildren of those labeled landlord and rich peasant would face harassment and scapegoating. The more humble the class label (poor peasant, hired laborer), the higher one's new political and social standing. The new work team favored fifty-eight households classified by the first team as "new middle peasants" by returning them to the poor-peasant category. The majority, those classified as middle peasants, floated in a political limbo, sometimes linked to class enemies, sometimes located in the ranks of the good people. The supposedly scientific analysis of class was actually fraught with the subjective and the political.

By freezing life in a single frame, fate was sealed in perpetuity. A castelike system, not liberating equality, resulted from class-struggle land reform. Resistance activist and early Wugong party member Li Fengxiang was a member of a land reform team in Raoyang. Li's household in Wugong bore the label rich peasant. Such a class label could end a political career. However, some whose careers took them away from home or high enough on a career ladder replaced a damning label with such a shining one as "revolutionary official." Like thousands of other Raoyang recruits in the revolutionary army, Li Fengxiang was able to rise. So, too, was Li Maoxiu's brother Li Feng. But the patriotic younger brother, Maoxiu, who had the misfortune to be home in Wugong during land reform, fell heir to the father's pariah status of landlord.

When the work team affirmed that the only rich-peasant households were the three so classified in 1946, a great burden was lifted from the seventy-one households whose homes had been sealed and whose property had been confiscated and stored at the Poor Peasant Association headquarters. They were free to reclaim their property. No similar liberation from the splintering class struggle came to Gengkou.

Although the new Wugong work team endorsed the classifications made in late 1946 and confirmed that only 325 mu of land was available for redistribution, it rejected the way in which the land had been allocated. The 1946 land reform had placed land that was worked by long-term hired laborers and land that was pawned, rented out, mortgaged, or "loaned" by the owner in the hands of those who actually farmed it, literally, land to the tiller. In early 1948 the work team nullified the 1946 distribution, took back the land, and reallocated it and other confiscated property to the most land-poor, regardless of whether they were already cultivating it. This time all the transfers of land and property, including ten head of livestock and thirty-two sections of housing, were recorded in official ownership deeds issued to heads of households by the fourth district government of Raoyang county.[39] In many villages the newly landed were informed that Mao Zedong was their benefactor.

Beneficiaries in Wugong included Li Guanglin, the former Poor Peasant Association head. Li, who owned no land, received 2 mu, one-fourth of a donkey, one-fourth of a cart, and five sections of housing. Old Militia Xu Yizhou, another early activist in the 1947 class-struggle land reform, received 5 mu to supplement the 5 mu his household of three already owned. He also received one-fourth of an ox. Xu Mantang, the former Wugong party secretary then working as a public security officer in Raoyang, received 9 mu, giving his household of four a total of 11.3 mu. And the buddy of Fierce Zhang Duan, militia Iron Man Li Duolin, who married the wandering beggar woman, supplemented his 2.5 mu with 2.9 more. He also received two sections of housing and one-fourth of an ox. The homeless few who lived in temples received rooms in landlord and rich-peasant courtyards. The village government confiscated a rich peasant home to use as its headquarters. Martyr and military families were especially favored with animals.

Political power was returned to the Geng Changsuo group. Geng became secretary of a reactivated Wugong Communist party branch with Li Zihou as village head. The Poor Peasant Association was stripped of much of its power and renamed the Poor People's Association, allowing middle peasants to join. Li Guanglin, whose policies as head of the Poor Peasant Association had been repudiated by the work team, temporarily headed the association. But Li soon left Wugong, going south with the army. He eventually returned to a state-payroll job in Raoyang as manager of a shop. He was rewarded for his loyal service in the class-struggle land reform. The party promoted the zealous.

Officials of the emerging government learned that zeal in attacking people who could be described as reactionary, capitalistic, and rightist was never punished, whereas a lack of such zeal could hurt one's career. However cruel, divisive, and self-defeating, class struggle was institutionalized in the party's career structure.

The Geng Changsuo co-op was vindicated. The label "rich peasant organization" was removed. County Party Secretary Li Tai, who had rebuffed Geng's complaint, went to Wugong to assure Geng of his support. Co-op members did well in the final distribution of land. In 1946 they had received none of the confiscated land, but in 1948 a total of twenty-six mu went to Boss Geng, the Black One Lu Molin, Miser Li Huiting, Marrying Zhang Zhan, and Crop Expert Zhang Jinren. Li Tai even offered to see that co-op members received conveniently located high-quality land. Sensitive to charges of favoritism, however, Geng declined the special dispensation.

Leaders zigged this way or zagged that way, but networks of loyalty and mutual support became entrenched. Li Tai offered to help Geng Changsuo with a personal problem. Twice in 1946 Geng's son, sixteen-year-old Delu, had tried to join the army. Because he was an only son and rather young, Delu was twice sent home. In the spring of 1948, however, eighteen-year-old Delu enlisted again and was mustered into the 7th Regiment in Hebei. His father and mother were crying when Li Tai appeared at the Geng home and said that he had the power to send their son home again. Geng and Xu Shukuan were in an awkward position. A recruiting drive was under way, and the Raoyang party had been instructed to find four thousand recruits for the army. To accept Li Tai's offer would be to invite more talk about special privileges.

Delu enlisted along with eleven others from Wugong.[40] Having a son, particularly an only son, serving in the People's Liberation Army, the most prestigious institution in Raoyang, heightened the luster of Boss Geng as a selfless and patriotic leader. Patriarchal lineage continuity was assured when Xu Shukuan gave birth to a second son, Zhuanluo, the last of seven children. In spite of Geng Changsuo's rejection of a favor, the emerging structure of power facilitated and fostered favoritism and privilege.

That structure was manifest in March 1948 in the meetings of the party's Central Committee at Xibaipo, its last rural headquarters. Whereas ordinary soldiers ate outdoors, the top leaders had a separate indoor mess hall and their own cook. The paramount leader, Mao, ate separately at the home he shared with Jiang Qing. In addition to a personal cook, Mao alone was provided with a bathtub, a king-size bed, and a swivel-seat leather desk chair on rollers. The key members of the entourages of top leaders lived indoors. The top five leaders had commodious dwellings.

When the Central Committee met, seating was arranged in precise pecking order. Mao sat on a high-backed rattan chair in front of portraits of himself and army commander Zhu De. Facing Mao in the first row were soft-cushioned sofas that had been lugged on dirt paths up the mountains from the city of Shijiazhuang in the valley. Top leaders sat there, going right to left in hierarchical standing. The second row of leaders sat on hard-cushioned sofas, which also had been transported up the mountains from Shijiazhuang. Even when others went up front to speak, Mao never abandoned center stage. While Mao's primacy was clear, each status in the new hierarchy carried its precise place, privileges, and perquisites.

Wugong was still under pressure to show that it had met the land reform goal of 2.7 mu of land for former poor peasants, a target widely adopted in North China base areas. A sleight of hand was adopted, which soon became a standard way to display loyalty to arbitrary and imposed targets. Eighteen relatively prosperous middle-peasant households, each of whom owned more than 2.7 mu per capita, were reclassified and transferred to the poor-peasant group for the final tabulation. Presto! The average per capita holdings of those categorized as poor peasants became 2.7 mu. This transfer, moreover, resulted in the reduction of average landholdings of the middle-peasant group as a whole to just 0.1 mu more than the poor-peasant average (see table 5). A rigid system necessitated legerdemain as one of the keys to local success. In order to protect the interests of independent tillers and foster village unity while satisfying the contrived demands of the party center, the politics of classification was manipulated to exaggerate polarization in the past and equality in the present. In fact, because independent tillers predominated in the region and because tax reform had already wrought its silent revolution, only 7.7 percent of the land in the 764 villages of Raoyang, Hejian, and Shenxian counties had been confiscated and redistributed in the 1947–48 land reform.[41]

Although the decade of reform that began with tax reform initiated a process of equalization of landholdings, Wugong people remained poor and vulnerable to a potentially deadly natural environment. As a result of redistribution, scattered individual plots were smaller than ever. Population was still increasing whereas land under cultivation was decreasing. In 1936 the 1,390 people of Wugong cultivated 4,620 mu, including temple and clan land. As the village population rose to 1,557 by 1948, the cultivated-land area decreased to 4,282 mu. With poor soil, only 700 mu of irrigated land, primitive technology, and vulnerability to the ravages of nature, Wugong and the entire Black Dragon Harbor region of southern Hebei would test the ability of the new government to improve the lives of the rural poor.

Village Socialism

The final act of the land reform work team in spring 1948 was to organize the first "struggle meeting" in Wugong history. Its purpose was to forge unity among poor and middle peasants by disgracing a handful of class enemies and forcefully demonstrating the power of the party and the once poor. Struggle

Table 5   Classification and Landownership in Wugong after Land Reform

Class	Household			People per Household	Land		Mu per Household	Mu per Capita
	No.	%	People		Mu	%		
Landlord	2	.5	9	4.5	24	.5	12.0	2.6
Rich peasant	3	.7	31	10.3	83	1.9	10.3	2.6
Middle peasant	154	39.7	693	4.5	1,950	45.5	12.6	2.8
Poor peasant	228	58.9	824	3.6	2,225	51.9	9.7	2.7
Village	387	100.0	1,557	4.0	4,282[a]	100.0	11.0	2.7

[a]This includes 150 mu formerly managed by temples and clan organizations.

meetings were often brutal. The party insisted that class enemies be smashed in every village.

A crude stage was built in the north end of Wugong, and the entire village was summoned. The work team and village leaders sought a political target, a living "exploiter" whose crimes could arouse people's passions. But who? Landlord and former village head Li Jianting had died in 1945. His older son, Li Feng, was a Communist and People's Liberation Army soldier. His younger son, the unfortunate Maoxiu, had worked for the resistance and never harmed anyone. Landlord Li Huaqi's daughter had married the son of the prominent Wugong Communist Geng Shupu.

Li Huaqi was rumored to have died the previous year. In fact, he had fled over the county border and was still alive in not-too-distant Xitou. In like manner Wugong was a sanctuary for a small landlord from another village. Quite a few landlords reported to have died were actually protected by villagers and kin networks outside the home village. Members of the Tian lineage, perhaps Raoyang's largest landowners, fled to safety, some to Beijing, some to Tianjin.

Of those labeled rich peasant in Wugong, Li Chunrong had served fairly as Wugong village chief early in the war. As for Li Duanfu, his oldest son, Li Fengxiang, was a party member and an army veteran active in the county land reform movement. His fourth son was in the People's Liberation Army. That left Li Yingzhou, but because he was dying armed militia members seized his only son, Li Dalin, and forced him to the meeting ground.[42]

Li Yingzhou was a reputed bully and whoremonger, feared and hated in Wugong. His crony and cousin was Li Huanan, the hoodlum who was hunted down and shot by the Nationalist authorities before the war. Together with Huanan, Yingzhou had operated the gambling den in the Southern Li temple. He was said to have abducted widows, raped young women, and pilfered property.[43] Many villagers held Li Yingzhou responsible for the death of his neighbor Li Tietou, whose father, Li Cunli, had worked for forty years as a short-term farmhand on Li Yingzhou's land. In 1935 Li Tietou, who had refused to work for Li Yingzhou, filed a complaint with the county police charging Yingzhou with stealing Tietou's chicken to feed friends in the gambling den. To intimidate Tietou and his parents, Li Yingzhou reportedly had Tietou's mother beaten and threatened Tietou with a gun. But instead of jailing his tormentor, county police arrested Tietou, beat him, and kept him in the county jail for three months, where he was said to have been tortured. Shortly after returning to Wugong, Tietou died. His bereaved father soon became ill and died. Tietou's distraught mother then publicly accused Yingzhou of responsibility for the deaths. Yingzhou had her beaten a second time. She, too, died.[44]

Li Yingzhou's young son Dalin was responsible for none of this, yet it was he who was dragged before the crowd. Li Rui, the older sister of Tietou, was carried up on the stage to denounce Li Dalin. People were silent as the woman poured out her grief. When she finished, the crowd engulfed the hapless Dalin and beat him for the sins of his father, for all the outrages of previous years. Bound and dragged through the lanes, Dalin was smashed, twisted, and bullied, crippling his back. He was forced to confess to his alleged crimes, then jailed in the headquarters of the Poor People's Association. No formal charges were ever filed against Li Yingzhou or Li Dalin.

Vigilante justice was familial and eternal. In this and subsequent struggles imposed from above, a Li Dalin or a Li Maoxiu, the relatives of alleged criminals, counterrevolutionaries, and class enemies of socialism, would repeatedly be targeted for abuse. To the north, in Yanggezhuang, where no landlords survived, a little orphan girl, Song Duo, was preemptively made a landlord because of the political pressure to struggle against class enemies. That is, the village leaders decided that when Song Duo grew up she would be formally labeled a landlord and for the rest of her life be treated as an enemy of the people.

It was not just in the rural hinterland that zealots targeted purported class enemies. The potential for destructive zealotry was institutionalized in the emerging state. In the last year of the revolutionary civil war the fires of a literary inquisition nearly flared. Taking off from a Soviet script called *Front Line,* which had a character named Ke Likong who made false reports, North China zealots denounced other writers as Chinese Ke Likongs. Poet Ai Qing was denounced for a poem praising Mao's once-favorite model peasant, Wu Manyu, now a traitor with Jiang Jieshi's retreating forces. Writer Wang Lin, who served on the Wugong land reform team and won fame for a story, "Heartland," about central Hebei popular resistance to the May 1942

Japanese onslaught, was attacked for a fabulous tale of a Chinese martial arts expert who wiped out traitors. Zealots insisted that traditional martial arts were not the Marxist-Leninist techniques that won the war. Sun Li, the writer of romantic novellas about the Hutuo River region, was similarly attacked for a lack of realism. The purists writing in *Xin wen bao* insisted that materialism and socialism should not be subverted by myth and romanticism. In this instance, those criticized did not become objects for political struggle.

In places close to Wugong, however, the search for struggle objects cost innocent lives. In spring 1948, after the terroristic class-struggle phase of land reform had been officially repudiated, a struggle meeting attacked Song Ruhai of Dongliuwu village, seven miles northeast of Wugong. Song was active in anti-Japanese youth work and at age seventeen joined the party. By 1946 he had become secretary of the village party branch, but during land reform Song was classified as a counterrevolutionary rich peasant and charged with having persecuted poor and middle peasants. The charges were fabricated by his rivals, but there was no independent judiciary to hear Song's pleas of innocence. Following a struggle meeting he was taken out to the fields and shot. He was twenty-six years old. For the next thirty years Song's relatives were harassed and humiliated as the ritual scapegoats for all political campaigns in Dongliuwu.[45] The paralyzing and poisonous consequences of imposing permanent categories of class struggle would frame in frozen status and color in blood the politics of Raoyang and all of China.

While innocents like Song Ruhai perished, local people told each other that some members of the traditional elite were protected by powerful relatives. Lin Tie, the party secretary of the Central Hebei Military Region, whose first wife died a martyr, later married Gong Tongxuan, the daughter of a wealthy landlord in Anping county. Lin did not oppose the confiscation of his father-in-law's considerable landholdings, but, people gossiped, he protected his wife's father and family members from becoming struggle targets. Whereas many big landlords in the region were beaten and killed, Lin Tie's relatives were perceived as coasting through the land reform. People began to see a polarity, not in the class-struggle categories manipulated by the party-state, but between the favored and the forgotten.

Political ties facilitated arbitrary power, which privileged the favorites of the new state and marginalized others. The Geng Changsuo co-op, seeking more draft animals, as were most villagers after the famine and Japanese marauding, seized the donkey of a disabled veteran and party member named Li whom Geng disliked. Because of his pension, Li was wrongly classified as a rich peasant in the class-struggle land reform. When Li demanded the return of his donkey after his label was lifted, Boss Geng struck back. He convinced a visiting district party work team to allow the co-op to keep the donkey and to expel Li from the Communist party.

Building the Party and Socialism

The Wugong branch of the Communist party was rebuilt in April 1948. In accord with the February 22 land reform directive, the work team was to lead the recently resuscitated local party group in yet another search for class enemies, this time defined as "leftists."[46] In Wugong the movement merely helped consolidate the power of the loyalists around Geng Changsuo. He sought to make Wugong and his co-op embodiments of loyalty, which would make it impossible for the state or local rivals to unseat him.

Geng used the rectification movement to build a more tightly and personally knit party organization. The party Central Committee wanted party membership in each village increased to 3 percent of the total population.[47] The spring drive in Wugong brought the total up to 4.7 percent. Although many were illiterate, party members were to engage in regular, directed group study of documents passed down by the district and county governments, including directives issued by the Central Committee.

Party building allowed Geng to bring reliable recruits into his political family. He handpicked ten new party members, which was the largest yearly increase since 1940. Embedded in party ties were powerful personal loyalties. The elder brother of Geng Shupu—who had introduced Boss Geng into the party—marched south with the People's Liberation Army, eventually to return to Raoyang as a member of the county party committee. Geng Changsuo's political family was increasingly central to politics in Raoyang.

Illiterate Ropemaker Geng Changsuo also looked for educated and politically reliable young people who could contribute to the development of the village. One of the new members of Geng's political machine was Qiao Liguang, a triangular-faced lad of eighteen. Ropemaker Geng's connections with the east-end Qiao clan of Qiao Wanxiang had always been good. Young Qiao, classified as a middle peasant, had a quiet, almost docile, personality. His sister Wenzhi, who headed women's work in Wugong, and his older brother had both joined the party during the war. In 1936, before the war, Qiao's household included his parents, an elder brother, three elder sisters, and Qiao himself. They owned eleven mu of land. When the war began, his older brother did resistance work near Raoyang. The Qiaos had a history of commercial and sideline enterprise. Qiao's father, like Geng's, had been a ropemaker, and his grandfather sold kerosene.

Qiao Liguang had studied for four years in Wugong, then two more years in Caozhuang, less than a mile to the southwest, to finish higher primary school. He left school at fifteen. Within two years his parents arranged a marriage, and he settled down in the east village, not far from Boss Geng's home. Qiao was first active in the local militia, a road to power for many young male villagers, and later specialized in youth work in the years before the Wugong branch of the Communist Youth League was founded. Bound by ties of neighborhood, politics, and lineage alliance, literate Qiao became illiterate Geng's administrative aide, his "good right hand," as local people preferred to say.

The new state set out to control the economy and promote recovery and expansion. Two key organizations, state trading companies and supply and marketing cooperatives, were established to revive and direct commercial life.[48] The state would supply inputs and purchase the product. County Party Secretary Li Tai funded the Raoyang Promotion Society, staffed by thirty-four officials assigned to allocate raw materials and loans. Cotton was supplied to spinners in Yincun, the market town in northeast Raoyang whose wheels had been silent for years. Tools and technical assistance helped stimulate salt production in Ligang village in the northwest. Within a matter of months the number of villages producing salt in Raoyang jumped from fifty-eight to seventy-five. Efforts were also made to breathe new life into the ancient burlap-bag industry. The *People's Daily,* in its first primitive issue published in Shijiazhuang, reported that 2,900 Raoyang households had been organized in early 1948 by the Promotion Society. The advantage of the supply and marketing co-op, it said, was that farmers did not have to worry about marketing their goods. They could sell them to the co-op and use cash to buy livestock.[49]

Boss Geng's co-op had been forging ties to the state-run marketing system since 1943. Co-op originator Geng Xiufeng had been working for state-run supply and marketing cooperatives in the fourth district and in Raoyang town itself since 1945. Although the gross value of sideline production in the co-op fell by 16 percent to 20,975 catties of millet equivalent in 1948, the group was still a leader in sidelines in Raoyang. Grain yields leaped ahead in 1948 by 24 percent to 291 catties per mu, the highest in co-op history. Zhang Kerang sent an expert to help co-op leader Geng Changsuo increase cotton yields.

The conspicuous success of the Geng co-op made it an attractive target for the tax collector, who had difficulty keeping track of individual private commercial activity. In late 1948 the county Commercial and Industrial Tax Bureau ordered the Geng co-op to pay taxes that would cover the estimated industrial and commercial tax obligations of the entire village. Geng and bookkeeper Qiao Wanxiang stormed off to Raoyang to protest. The Tax Bureau beat a hasty retreat. Lesser authorities did not dare tangle with those favored by higher echelons of the state. But higher authorities who could reward the favored with gifts could also force them into policies they did not want.

Reports from the battle front were reassuring to party loyalists. The civil war had turned in favor of the People's Liberation Army. In April and June its forces, moving south, occupied Luoyang and Kaifeng in neighboring Henan province. The Nationalist party and state were crumbling. On September 25, 1948, Jinan, the capital of Shandong province, was occupied by the People's Liberation Army. The People's Republic, inaugurated on October 1, 1949, guarded against last-ditch American intervention by stationing the Third Field Army in North China. Boss Geng and his co-op looked forward to a peaceful 1949 in a China ruled by their patrons.

A delegation from northwest China inspects Wugong's model cotton crop, June 16, 1954. Boss Geng Changsuo is on the right. Photo courtesy Geng Changsuo household.

Boss Geng Changsuo signing autographs in Moscow during his six-month visit to the Soviet Union in 1952 to inspect collective farms. Photo courtesy Geng Changsuo household.

Lu Molin, ropemaker Geng Changsuo, gambling addict Li Yantian, and prosperous Qiao Wanxiang formed a four-household land pooling and sidelines cooperative in Wugong in spring 1944. Photo: 1968, courtesy Geng Changsuo household.

Four orphans were adopted by the Geng Changsuo cooperative in early 1948 after the group had been labeled a rich peasant organization by a land reform work team. The orphans were named, from left to right, Li Zhuan, Li Tan, Li Xiuying, and Li Mengjie. Circa 1953, courtesy Wugong history exhibition. Photo: Mark Selden.

Collectomaniac Geng Xiufeng, a rural intellectual. This life-long devotee of large-scale collective farming organized the famous four-household rope-making cooperative in Wugong in late 1943 during a massive regional famine. Photo: autumn 1980, Paul G. Pickowicz.

Boss Geng Changsuo's marriage in 1926 to his Old Companion, boundfoot Xu Shukuan, a resident of the west end of Wugong, was symbolic of a web of relations that united the east and west sections of the village. Photo: 1968, courtesy Geng Changsuo household.

Landlord son and patriot Li Maoxiu served five years in a labor camp in Dingxian prefecture from 1953 to 1957. Photo: spring 1983, Paul G. Pickowicz.

Boss Geng Changsuo links arms with Chen Yonggui, the famous model peasant from Dazhai village in neighboring Shanxi province. Geng first met Chen in January 1961. Photo: Wugong, July 1975, courtesy Geng Changsuo household.

Beginning in 1953, Geng Lianmin, a close relative and confidant of Boss Geng Changsuo, served as the chief accountant of the large, village-wide cooperative in Wugong. Photo: spring 1983, Paul G. Pickowicz.

Even in prosperous Wugong, schools were forced to economize by lowering educational standards during the famine of the early 1960s. The caption on this photo says: "Farewell to the students of section eight of Wugong Junior High who are being graduated ahead of schedule." Photo: July 1, 1960, courtesy Geng Changsuo household.

Brains Zhang Chaoke was among the generation of better educated Wugong leaders who emerged in the 1950s as the state took command of the village economy. Photo: spring 1983, Paul G. Pickowicz.

In August 1958 Mao Zedong visited Hebei's Xushui Commune outside Baoding, on the main rail line south from Beijing, making it one of two national models for emulation in the Great Leap Forward. Photo: cover of *Zhongguo nong bao* 21 (1958).

In autumn 1963 Wugong's foremost patron, Hebei Party Secretary Lin Tie (left), arrived in the village to join Boss Geng Changsuo (right) in a gala celebration of the twentieth anniversary of cooperative farming in Wugong. Courtesy Wugong history exhibition. Photo: Mark Selden.

5 ✦ HONEYMOON

Was 1949 any sort of break from the past?

The cultural healing and economic recovery that began as the tax reforms took hold, drought ended, and Japanese troops withdrew continued in the early years of the People's Republic. For some villagers the honeymoon lasted longer than a decade. Chaos gave way to order and family life began afresh. New wonders and old joys were the norm for North China villagers as the People's Liberation Army swept to nationwide victory. Thousands of Hebei villagers marched south with the conquering armies and won careers in the new socialist state. A son of Wugong's "sage," Li Hengtong, became a division-level army officer in the southwest.

The life of another poor villager, Li Shulin, turned into an adventure. Li had fled Wugong in the 1930s, finding work in an oil shop in the Dashala merchant district of Beijing. After Japan's army marched into North China, a Raoyang shopkeeper recruited Li and other impoverished Raoyang bachelors into the Eighth Route Army. In the face of Japan's 1942 offensive, Li's unit fled, linking up with Lin Biao's Fourth Field Army, which subsequently fought Nationalist forces in northeast China and then marched south. In 1949 Li became deputy head of a military station on the Guangxi provincial border with Vietnam and welcomed Ho Chi Minh's Vietnamese troops for recuperation and training. Those troops were clothed in Chinese uniforms, were paid Chinese army wages, and were supplied with army trucks and other good military equipment captured during China's civil war. Twice Li helped facilitate the passage of Ho Chi Minh to Beijing for secret talks. In 1953, forty-eight-year-old Li Shulin married a vivacious Zhuang minority woman thirty years his junior. The army sent lucky Li to school to learn to manage a state trading company. Military careers were sources of prestige and advancement.

A contingent of soldiers, including the class-struggle land reform activist Fierce Zhang Duan, who fought with regional and regular forces in the civil war, returned to Wugong as heroes.[1] It was a time of reunions, marriages, and births, of the building of homes and the resurgence of markets. The restored market brought itinerant craftspeople. Some made coal balls and coal bricks for winter heating.

111

Others turned cotton into smooth, beautiful warm comforters. Yet many soldiers did not return. An estimated eleven million Chinese gave their lives. Twenty-four soldiers from Wugong died in the anti-Japanese resistance and civil war. In less-populated Yanggezhuang, thirty-one sacrificed their lives. Wangqiao and Gaoqiao lost twenty-four and forty-three, respectively; in Gengkou, thirty-two fell, and in Zoucun, twenty were martyred, in addition to the hundreds of civilian villagers who were killed.

Government was reorganized.[2] The national capital moved from Nanjing, in central China, to Beijing, the capital of the Qing dynasty, 120 miles north of Wugong. Raoyang contributed to the celebration of National Day, October 1, as it had to the Qing emperors. The Duan family, one mile south of the county seat, helped put together China's finest traditional fireworks display. The explosive residue of saltmaking, no longer needed for land mines, served happier purposes.

Baoding was designated Hebei provincial capital. Resistance and civil war administrative units, such as the Jinchaji Base, the Central Hebei Military Region, and the Eighth Military District, ceased to exist. Yang Xiufeng, who became governor of Hebei, was a former professor at the Beijing Normal University who joined the Communist party in 1939 and served as chairman of the Shanxi-Chahaer-Hebei Border Region throughout the war years.[3] The most powerful figure in Hebei was Party First Secretary Lin Tie, patron of the Geng co-op.

Hebei was divided into prefectures, with Raoyang at the southeastern tip of Dingxian prefecture. The administrative heart of the prefecture was located in Dingxian county, famous for James Yen's mass education and rural reconstruction efforts.[4] The Communist party had criticized Yen for believing that education, not revolution, would save the poor. Party activists immediately went into Dingxian to discredit Yen's work and attack and silence his followers.

Zhang Kerang, who had been monitoring and promoting Wugong since 1946, headed the provincial Bureau of Agriculture and Forestry. In spring 1949 Boss Geng was invited to address delegates to a production meeting held in Raoyang town.[5] Peripheral Wugong and Raoyang were closely tied to the new centers of power. But when the first national official drove into Wugong, villagers expressed traditional suspicion about the ability of urban outsiders to understand their needs. Displaying spotless white shoes, the official stepped from the car into the dirt and muck. Villagers, who wrapped shoes in white only when a father died, snickered that the official must be mourning for his father.

"Develop the Household Fortune"

With favorable weather and political tranquility, in 1949 the co-op led by Geng Changsuo celebrated its second consecutive bumper crop. Grain yields of 329 catties per mu set a record.[6] Confident of its ability to succeed, that spring the co-op bought two mules and a large wagon for sideline operations, which proved to be the year's big success. Peanut-oil gross income increased nearly fivefold to 34,009 catties of millet equivalent. The sideline bonanza was facilitated by the loan of a large oil press from the Raoyang County Supply and Marketing Cooperative.[7] With gross income of 50,000 catties of millet, sidelines again produced close to half of co-op income following a decline in 1948.[8] When news of the co-op's autumn harvest reached Baoding, provincial agriculture chief Zhang Kerang sent in reporters. The fame of the co-op spread.

Many of Wugong's 369 independent farming households did well in 1949. Their wheat yields averaged 120 catties per mu, only 20 catties lower than the Geng co-op. But some fell behind. Among the approximately 15 Wugong households who were forced to sell some land was Li Wenrui.[9] His household included his wife, his mother, and eight young children, none yet of much help in the fields. Also in decline was Li Xiang, who had worked as a long-term laborer prior to land reform. He had no experience managing a farm and lacked tools and draft animals. When his family had barely enough to eat, a local broker arranged for Li to sell 1.5 mu of land as well as his house. The state guaranteed the right to buy and sell land and property.

Zhang Qingzhou also sold land. When his son became seriously ill, Zhang sold three mu of land to a resident of nearby Yuanzi to pay for medical treatment. Other households borrowed money to celebrate funerals and weddings. Some who were short of cash just before the harvest sold rights to part of their crops or borrowed from those with cash to spare, offering land as collateral. While the party publicized the slogan "Develop the household fortune," a few households declined, even in these honeymoon years of peace and recovery. In early 1950 the government called on farmers to enrich themselves. Mao Zedong urged "preserving a rich peasant economy in order to further the early restoration of production in the rural areas."[10] Soviet-style collectivization of agriculture, Mao declared, "is still quite far off."[11]

Educated families from the Li lineage living in the Wugong village center took advantage of wider access to education. They sent a dozen of their sons and a few daughters to high schools in Shenxian and Baoding as well as to the famed Xinji High School near Shijiazhuang. Several went on to university in Beijing and Tianjin, steps toward careers on the state payroll and an urban life.

Many of the writers, artists, and performers who had served the party during the war as propagandists took jobs in branches of the government's cultural bureaus. Throughout Hebei they helped organize classes in painting, singing, dancing, and acting. The Raoyang county administration supported an amateur Hebei opera troupe headed by a woman. The government selected promising youngsters, mainly males, for professional training in the county seat, which reduced the number of girls raised to play the parts of men.

Such girls were traditionally brought up in families specializing in Hebei opera. Although that loss made the county opera troupe less appealing, in poor villages that previously had no performers many young girls happily volunteered for new amateur opera groups. The cultural workers took pride in declaring this government the first to subsidize China's popular culture.

Peasants across North China rejoiced in the recovery. South of Raoyang, the famous Hengshui Distillery, damaged during the resistance war, reopened. Production quickly surpassed the previous record year of 1927. Hard-working villagers celebrated the New Year and other festive occasions with 135-proof Hengshui Old White Lightning sorghum whiskey, famous in the region and beyond since the Ming dynasty. Demand quickly far exceeded supply. Some villagers continued to prefer homemade alcohol.

Cultural Restoration

Lineages again celebrated as tradition dictated. Led by the eldest male, on the eve of the lunar New Year all males in a lineage donned their finest clothes and visited the graves of ancestors, where they burned ritual paper, left offerings of food and clothing to ensure the welfare of the departed, and set off firecrackers. The ritual acts performed on the second day of the New Year symbolized proper relations within the eternal lineage. People bowed in the customary ketou, touching their head to the ground. The young ketoued to their elders; women ketoued to their elder in-laws. Young boys received small cash gifts for ketouing. The rituals excluded girls; they would be marrying out of the lineage.

After feasting on meat-filled dumplings on the third day, the next high point was the fifteenth, the day of the lantern festival, a day of special delight for children. Lanterns were hung on gates and paraded around. Children had their own little lanterns with special treats inside. It was the happiest day of the New Year for youngsters. At other times, children enjoyed visits by traveling entertainers displaying cavorting dogs and monkeys. Faces lit up when the "dong" "dong" of a bell announced the arrival of a show. Children stared in wonder at the shapes of candy made by a traveling candymaker.

Children had more time for games, including kite flying, martial arts, tugs-of-war, springboard jumping, and contests to swing the highest or to keep a small leather pouch in the air by kicking it with the back of a heel. Young girls favored a game of throwing and catching smooth stones and jumping rope. Boys played marbles. More mischievously, they killed birds and tied them to tree branches. In winter children sought out the areas around homes built on rises and rigged up ways to slide down icy slopes.

Marriages proliferated in the honeymoon years. Villagers revived time-honored customs, including the use of a sedan chair or horse-drawn cart to transport the bride to a wedding. However, the Raoyang authorities, were mainly successful in substituting animal-pulled carts for sedan chairs supported by people. The wedding feast began before noon and continued throughout the day. Each course was served in sets of four, six, or eight dishes. A few families in each village kept the special cooking utensils required to prepare banquet fare, making them available, sometimes at a price, on special occasions. After those days of festivities, the bride and groom, accompanied by a small party, usually including a boy of about ten, went by horse-drawn cart to the bride's home for a final round of feasting. A proper wedding was not only a joyous occasion, but also boded well for the future of the couple and the lineage. A few marriages, especially of such villagers close to party leaders as the west-end's Li Lu, omitted supposedly more-feudal ceremonies, like the ketou to every member of an older generation and an ornate costume for the bride. The marriage of Fierce Zhang Duan was uniquely austere.

One significant change in marital patterns in the honeymoon years was age of first marriage. Earlier, marriage ages ranged from fourteen through the early thirties, with a few child marriages and long-delayed marriages in the case of desperately poor males. Our household surveys reveal that from the late 1940s, almost everyone who married was between the ages of twenty and twenty-four (by Chinese count). The process of homogenization of land ownership that accompanied the silent revolution and land reform was paralleled in marital practice.

Funerals were celebrated as custom dictated. The village of Wugu in the north county kept an enormous palanquin for transporting the coffin. Made of fine wood, with landscapes and Buddhist paintings, it was carried by up to thirty mourners in funeral attire.

An Exceptional Co-op

The party encouraged villagers to form small temporary mutual-aid groups to exchange labor, draft animals, and tools during the busy seasons. The co-op led by Geng Changsuo was exceptional. In organizing farming and sideline activities on a year-round basis, and in distributing income on the basis of labor as well as investment, Boss Geng was running what the party center called a "semi-socialist cooperative." By 1950 only 60 of the nearly 7.5 million rural households in Hebei had joined such organizations.[12] Of those 60 households, 17 were in the Geng co-op. The state continued to support Boss Geng. In the spring, the provincial government delivered a seven-inch plow to replace the standard four-inch plow. However, the co-op's 179 mu of land was divided into seventy-eight small plots, so the state's big gift was of little use.[13] Co-op members grumbled that outsiders never understood the needs of villagers.

The Geng co-op did not disappoint its patrons. Although the weather was good and grain production only inched up, co-op members enjoyed rising incomes because of flourishing sideline production. Gross sideline income in 1950 increased to 60,000 catties of millet, thanks primarily to a 31 percent hike in peanut-oil income. For the second consecutive year sidelines generated a substantial 45 percent of co-op income. The superior capacity of the co-op to save and invest, and its ties to state-approved marketing outlets, spurred sideline growth. Sidelines were becoming main lines.

That year the co-op altered sideline distribution regulations by handing out 70 percent rather than 60 percent of net income to those who did the labor. With profits high, investors were not discouraged. Outsiders imposing a similar reform five years earlier had alienated villagers. Timing based on local conditions made all the difference. Forcing all villagers into one centrally designed straitjacket, however, constrained economic initiative. Led by Boss Geng, members invested 47,000 catties of peanuts in co-op sidelines.[14] Co-op profits gave Geng Changsuo enough cash to build a new house in 1951. He dismantled two rooms in the old house and invested the clay bricks and timber in constructing expanded facilities for the booming peanut-oil business.[15] Word spread in the market that "if you want to do business well, the only way is to set up a co-op like Changsuo."

Although the media more and more equated large size with socialism, some Hebei writers attached to villages without co-ops called the relatively large Geng co-op prematurely large, a leftist error. In August 1950 the Hebei Writers Association rejected the charge, claiming that local conditions required such cooperation.[16] Debates and struggles by distant strangers in no way accountable to villagers could decide their fate.

Noting the Geng co-op's three consecutive years of gains, provincial authorities designated Geng a provincial labor model and invited him to the First Congress of Hebei Labor Models held in November in Baoding. Geng spoke on co-op history.[17] Once-invisible Wugong was gaining a reputation. On November 28 a brief report on the Geng co-op appeared for the first time in the *Hebei Daily,* the new provincial newspaper published in Baoding. The second character in Geng's name was written incorrectly, but a small photograph of the fifty-year-old leader excited villagers. Geng was honored among leaders of fledgling cooperatives and mutual-aid teams who were designated provincial labor models.[18] He was pioneering a path to socialism.

The Hebei authorities presented co-ops like Geng's as better positioned than individual households to "develop the household fortune." Villagers should not fear such organizations. One was free to join, free to quit, and all the land, tools, and livestock invested by member households remained private property. By pooling resources, cooperative groups were better able to generate funds for investment in agriculture and sidelines. By 1950, it was reported, individual co-op members had even been able to purchase a total of 13 mu of land, which they invested in the co-op. The Geng co-op's 1950 grain yield was said to be 50 percent higher than yields achieved by independent tillers in Wugong. The Geng co-op was prospering, but insiders knew that the authorities inflated the numbers.

The press gave many reasons for the success of the Geng co-op. Labor was organized rationally, distribution was reasonable, women were encouraged to work, 2,500 catties of natural fertilizer were applied to an average mu of land, and the co-op experimented with new seed strains. Credit was showered on capable leaders, especially Geng Changsuo. For the first time, the press presented Boss Geng, the secretary of the Wugong party branch and leader of the co-op, as a folk hero. A biography of Boss Geng invited readers to emulate his way of embodying communist ideals. He was portrayed as a selfless worker, dedicated to the welfare of the group. He did not accept work points for attending meetings called by the government or party. And, unlike other co-op members, he did not frequent the local opera in Zoucun in his spare time. He and Xu Shukuan were in fact somewhat ascetic, but it was a partial hearing loss, not rising communist consciousness, that led Geng to stop attending the operas.

Not everyone in Wugong was delighted by the sudden fame of Boss Geng. Li Hengtong, one of Wugong's most successful private farmers, was a brilliant storyteller. Known as Demon Four, he would pull up his stool early in the evening at the major village crossroad and spin yarns of millenniums past, heroic tales of the fabled Warring States and the Three Kingdoms. People listened enraptured. The Demon's word carried weight. One evening, Geng hurried silently past on the way to a meeting. The Demon broke from his story to comment loudly on officials who were too busy or too proud to talk to ordinary folk. Geng learned he had to have a word for each villager, to smile and chat, care and inquire. He mastered the art of small talk. He became an astute local politician whose manner marked him as a friend of the folk. To achieve that goal and fulfill his leadership tasks, Geng also learned to organize his time efficiently and to walk very, very quickly indeed. The prosperity of his co-op depended on Boss Geng learning the political ropes.

In June 1950 village leaders estimated that there were 37 "prosperous" households in Wugong, 326 that had "enough to eat," and only 34 with insufficient food. In addition to the 146 households of "old middle peasants" (those who were middle peasants in 1936), they reckoned Wugong had another 239 households of "new middle peasants," who had achieved middle-peasant status by 1950, most through the silent revolution of tax reform. Using the standards of 1936, there were only 12 poor-peasant households.[19] Life in Wugong had improved for nearly everyone.

The honeymoon period was interrupted by China's entry into the Korean War in autumn 1950. Raoyang people continued to join the army. Li Da-zhuang from the west village was one of three Wugong youths sent to Korea, having enlisted during the early phase of land reform. In Korea, Li cared for animals that hauled artillery to the front. He returned home in 1953 suffering from shell shock. It was terrifying to live in dark tunnels anticipating the thunderous bombings of American B-29s. Memories of friends killed and maimed continued to haunt Li. Life in the tunnels spread disease and death as people were surrounded by bodily and food wastes. Geng Changsuo's son Delu was also in the army at this time, but he remained in the Hengshui area and was not sent to Korea. No Wugong villager died in Korea.

In October a mass meeting was called at Yincun, the thriving market village in northern Raoyang, to spur China's war effort. Thousands of villagers from northern and central areas of the county trekked into Yincun on market day, carrying lanterns with such slogans as "Resist America, Aid Korea." The meeting was lit up by the swaying lanterns—Raoyang had no electricity—as people shouted slogans of unity in support of Chinese soldiers and their Korean allies and roared with laughter at the antics of stilt dancers dressed up as Uncle Sam, Harry Truman, Syngman Rhee, and Jiang Jieshi. No Chinese were struggled against, humiliated, or beaten. It was a patriotic holiday, a happy time of unity. Patriotic Wugong village contributed to the national campaign to raise funds to help China's soldiers in Korea.

No Longer Blind

In early April 1951 a Beijing representative of the Ministry of Agriculture inspected the co-op and dubbed it the Geng Changsuo Agricultural Producers' Cooperative. Outstanding co-ops were renamed in accord with their leader's name. The Pauper's co-op in Zunhua county east of Beijing became the Wang Guofan Co-op. The new name, painted in ten-feet-high ideographs on Geng co-op headquarters, lent authority to the leader. The Agriculture Ministry representative gathered information on the Geng co-op to be circulated in the capital.[20] Boss Geng declared that the co-op had been "working blindly," that its members had no idea what was right. To ensure that what was done was right and to enhance patriotic spirit, the co-op began subscribing to provincial and national news dailies. Geng promised to help co-op members think of the nation first and the household second.

The representative's report concluded that Geng's group had the aura of a prosperous family epitomizing the slogan "develop the household fortune." Peanuts were piled high at headquarters, horses and mules were strong and tall, ropemaking and peanut-oil production went on all day. Co-op members, the report gushed, were preparing to repair old homes and build new ones. Many were looking forward to buying additional land. Some prospering individuals had already purchased land; the co-op had collectively bought three mu.

The official invited Boss Geng to return with him to attend the first North China Agricultural Cooperative and Mutual-Aid Conference, which convened on April 22. It was Geng's first visit to the fabled city of Beijing. But in the capital Geng heard notes of caution. The emphasis in rural work, it was said, should be on assuring and improving peasant livelihood while gradually consolidating and expanding small-scale mutual aid. Semisocialist cooperatives of the sort run by Boss Geng, the delegates were told, could be set up only with the approval of the provincial party committee. Never before had Geng been surrounded by such powerful men. The environment was intimidating. He was pleased, however, to meet other North China labor models, including Wang Guofan. Geng and Wang would develop close ties.

Geng was invited to stay on in Beijing to observe May Day festivities. He was dazzled by the spectacle. Almost everyone was decked out in new clothes, blue outfits for civilian officials and green for military personnel. Geng got his first look at Chairman Mao and listened to a speech delivered by Premier Zhou Enlai. But Geng was self-conscious as he stood at the far end of the large grandstand in front of the Gate of Heavenly Peace. His old clothes were soiled and tattered and his head was shaved bald in the style of central Hebei peasants.

In 1951 Geng's hearing difficulties intensified, and he started to suffer from headaches. These physical ailments made it more difficult for him to follow discussions at meetings. And suddenly there were so many meetings. Ironically, others took his silence as proof of wise humility. He became humble Geng, the modest one. Whereas others bragged about their village's accomplishments, Geng sat silent. When pressed to state Wugong's achievements, Boss Geng replied that the facts spoke for themselves. "Whatever a person says, still one is one, and two is two." The state assigned a secretary to accompany the illiterate Geng to important meetings, a sign of stature and ties to higher-ups.

Two more households joined the co-op, bringing membership to nineteen. Wei Shuwei, whose father died in 1937 when Shuwei was seven, joined and quickly found a bride. But landlord son Li Maoxiu's request to join was rejected. Those classified as enemies of the people were barred from the co-op. Li and his family were outcasts.

In that dry spring Geng Changsuo organized co-op members to carry water to the fields. Some complained that shoulder-poling water to distant fields was too arduous and probably unnecessary. Complaints turned to anger when, to complete the work, co-op members had to pass up the exciting five-day temple fair that took place each spring in Zoucun. To make things worse, when late-spring rains fell, others scoffed that co-op members had wasted their time. But in the scorching months of June and July, the eight thousand buckets of water carried to more than 80 mu of dry fields seemed to make a difference. Although all villages did well, co-op crops were far superior.[21] Grain yields jumped an incredible 42 percent to 478 catties of millet equivalent.[22]

Geng was responsive to state requests. Having allied themselves with powerful patrons, village leaders had to heed their patrons' advice. In 1951 the Beijing government sought more cotton for the state. Independent farmers in Wugong balked. The state's barter price for cotton, eight catties of millet for one of ginned cotton, was too low. One could do far better selling almost anything else in the market. Nonetheless, Boss Geng pressured his co-op to increase the area seeded in cotton in 1952 by 55 percent.[23] The decision was unpopular. Nocturnal destruction of cotton plants became a symbol of protest. Crop theft, crop damage, and arson increased. Enthusiasm had been dampened by state demands.

Change within Continuity

Still, the new state seemed the source of the continuing honeymoon of the early 1950s. Villagers delighted in a happy normalcy. Old Militia Xu Yizhou's and Boss Geng Changsuo's were among the seventeen Wugong households that built a total of fifty sections of housing in spring 1951. The Black One, Lu Molin, built a new courtyard.[24] Marrying Zhang Zhan prepared to build a two-room house.

As new houses were erected throughout the village, women were still barred from digging foundations and participating in the joyous drinking when the foundation was completed. The belief that women were dirty and therefore polluters went unchallenged.

Households felt more in control of their destiny. They owned the crops they grew and sold. There was more to buy in the hubbub of the Zoucun market. The "bare sticks" in the village, men who were too poor to marry, now had hopes of finding brides. Responsibilities to revered ancestors would not go unmet. The elderly could look forward to dignity and to a decent burial.

Even the Raoyang dead married. The corpses of bachelors who had never returned from work elsewhere were dug up and brought home. After soothsayers were consulted for propitiousness, the deceased single males were reburied with single female corpses in the male's lineage graveyard. The marriage would guarantee children in the hereafter, thus assuring unbroken lineage continuity.

Mourning ceremonies expanded again to fulfill customary expectations. The ceremonies could last three to nine days, but always an odd number. The pallbearers were always even in number. The more numerous the pallbearers, the more influential the household. A truly influential family could be rewarded at the mourning ceremonies with a top party person as speaker. The mourners wailed while marching four to five abreast to the graveside. Two kinds of firecrackers were used, both different from the firecrackers set off for the New Year. One type was said to "dong" and "pan" on exploding high in the air. The other type, sounding more like a bomb, was set off in a fifteen-pound iron pot. If done carelessly that explosion caused terrible injuries.

The honeymoon years witnessed a cultural rebirth. Amateur groups specializing in popular Hebei opera sprang up all over Raoyang. Women were particularly active as singers and actresses. Taking advantage of the slack agricultural season, villagers wrote and rehearsed plays, operas, and skits for one to two months before New Year, the high point of cultural activity. The amateur performances were free from the fifth to the twenty-fifth day of the new year. On the fifteenth day of the lunar new year, a fireworks display, funded by remittances from Raoyang merchants in Beijing and the northeast, lit up the sky all over the county.

Education expanded. More girls began to attend school, though in the early 1950s three-quarters did not. The county government staffed primary and junior high schools with teachers. Given continuing poverty, there were no pens or notebooks so students wrote with pencils on rock plates. Parents sold meat and eggs to secure cash for school tuition and books. The youth league began to run night schools with literacy classes for adults. Elders learned to sign their name, thus ending the indignity of having to make their mark with a fingerprint. The state opened classes to educate leaders at province, prefecture, county, and village levels.

Raoyang also constructed its first modern county health clinic. Drab, simple, and understaffed, with few diagnostic tools, it nevertheless introduced modern medical care to peripheral Raoyang. The clinic focused on preventing disease, promoting hygiene, and helping local communities set up health stations. Chinese factories began to manufacture basic drugs from aspirin to penicillin. The clinic and the increased availability of inoculations and basic medicine were life-enhancing steps in providing basic health care. Whatever changes followed, rural clinics and vitamin and antibiotic factories continued to contribute to a secular rise in life expectancy that would eventually raise China high among poor, densely populated third world nations. The gains institutionalized in the honeymoon period were deep, real, and long lasting. The decline in the incidence of death during birth for mothers and babies was most welcome. Most villagers still chose traditional Chinese medical practitioners over the unfamiliar new treatment. In Wugong, Li Kuanyu's pharmacy, stocked with an array of Chinese herbal medicines, was doing so well that Li turned a deaf ear to the urgings of his son, village chief Li Zihou, that he join a co-op.

Unlike other steps taken by the new state in the honeymoon years, the Marriage Law promulgated in 1950 failed to win meaningful support in Raoyang. There was an overwhelming popular desire to enjoy a return of normalcy, in this case patriarchal familial norms. To promote marriage by free choice, a first-rate Tianjin opera troupe toured Raoyang performing "Xiao nuxu." In the story a mother arranges a marriage for her seven-year-old boy to a teenage girl. The girl resists making the marriage real, preferring a strong, handsome poor peasant. Her divorce case pits her and the party against the malevolent mother-in-law, a stock villain of Chinese theater. In another opera, "Li Qiaoer," a young girl disobeys her parents, who want her to marry a rich peasant. But the girl has an ideal mate in mind. Villagers enjoyed the plays, but nothing blocked the continuation of arranged marriages. Some traditional marital practices were challenged. Divorces were imposed on richer peasants and merchants with more than one wife. If neither wife pressed for divorce, however, the ménage à trois remained intact.

Although young girls were drawn to a well-received literacy campaign, female enthusiasm and state concern for gender equality, like two shooting stars, soon plummeted in tandem and disappeared. When we asked Wugong women who had been married in the harshest times of the 1930s and 1940s whether the marriage law had improved their lives, one, with other widows smiling and nodding agreement, called attention to the change that mattered: "He's dead."

Men sought to reknit traditional families that had been ripped apart during the decades of decline, not to create families with gender equality. Though women were brought into the work force and the schools, and women's rights to property ownership and divorce were written into law, no practical challenge was mounted to the values, practices, and institutions of male supremacy.[25]

Distant Rumblings

In midsummer 1951 policy toward mutual aid and cooperation was debated in Beijing. On June 29, Bo Yibo, party first secretary of the North China Bureau, asserted that it was sheer "fantasy" to believe that the gradual development of mutual-aid and cooperative organizations could "shake, weaken, and eventually negate private property" and thus pave the way for the collectivization of agriculture. Such erroneous thinking was a manifestation of "utopian socialist" mentality. "There are 1,800,000 Party members in North China," Bo pointed out, "of whom 1,500,000 members are of peasant origin." Educating these rural leaders away from traditional peasant views was of crucial importance. Mutual-aid teams, Bo insisted, were put forward as a way of developing agricultural productivity in the recovery period. They were "designed to protect, not to weaken or negate, private property." He advocated the further development of mutual-aid teams "built on the foundation of individual economy and private property," not a misguided rush to cooperatives and collectives. He cautioned rural officials not to criticize "individual peasants" and "rich farmers"; "Compulsion and commandism must be opposed in developing mutual-aid teams." The time for collectivizing agriculture would eventually arrive, Bo concluded, but collectivization would have to be based on the development of a nationalized industrial infrastructure.[26] In July, President Liu Shaoqi similarly cautioned against prematurely establishing large numbers of mutual-aid and cooperative groups and criticized utopian conceptions of agrarian socialism, that is, the notion that socialism could be popular and productive in the countryside even without modern inputs.[27]

Hebei was a national leader in the mutual-aid movement. In 1951, 42 percent of Hebei's 3.2 million rural households participated in simple mutual-aid teams, most of which functioned on a part-time basis. Raoyang had 293 mutual-aid teams. Nationwide, 17.5 percent of households belonged to mutual-aid organizations.[28] To Liu Shaoqi, Bo Yibo, and most state leaders, these numbers indicated impressive progress.

In the second half of 1951 ruling groups met again and again to discuss how best to prod Chinese villagers toward Soviet-style collectives. They considered reports sent up from county leaders on co-op formation and performance. Most of the success stories were from old liberated areas in the north and northeast. County leaders tried to develop models of what they believed state leaders wanted. Raoyang county and Hebei provincial officials forwarded materials on the Geng co-op in Wugong. The village's fate became entwined with that of the officials promoting it. The officials dispatched writers to propagandize their model's experience. Hundreds of such favored nodes in the state's structure of power developed. The material on the Geng co-op was taken to show the centrality of a good leader in persuading peasant households of the advantages of larger agricultural units that transferred household power to the cooperative.[29]

In September Mao Zedong drafted a Central Committee resolution that instructed the party to step up the transition to socialist agriculture.[30] Mao rejected the notion that rapid development of mutual-aid and cooperative farming had to await the development of a modern nationalized industrial base. Mao was part of a leadership consensus that saw mutual aid and small-scale co-ops as stages on the road to collectivist socialism. What differentiated Mao from many others was his insistence that cooperatives were developing too slowly. In 1951 there were 24 cooperatives like Geng Changsuo's in Hebei, but only 129 in all China.[31]

Following the co-op's record-setting 1951 harvest, and given its prominence in debates among state leaders, Boss Geng was honored as a provincial labor model at the Second Congress of Labor Models of Industry and Agriculture, held in Baoding on October 10.[32] More than fifty Hebei labor models were told that the government would promote competition in moving away from household farming. Successful co-ops would be rewarded. The immediate provincial goals were one thousand model villages, ten thousand model mutual-aid teams, and one thousand model households. Geng responded by announcing startling 1952 co-op production targets and challenging others to beat them: 400 catties per mu in wheat, 500 in corn, 600 in millet, and 6,000 in sweet potatoes.[33]

In early November, Geng, Wang Guofan, and other agricultural labor models attended an elaborate exhibition in Tianjin on North China co-ops. Geng was accompanied by a staff member of the *Hebei Daily*. The party's North China Bureau, which supported expanding sidelines to enrich households, organized the event and chose the models of cooperation to be featured. A factory labor model Geng befriended in Tianjin, Wei Zhenhua, became a valuable future contact.

Geng was treated as a celebrity. He was given accommodations at the former home of a wealthy businessman. A space at the exhibition hall was devoted to the story of the Geng co-op, with a picture of Boss Geng prominently displayed. The leaders of the North China Bureau treated this unassuming hero of cooperation with more honor than he had ever received. They even poured his tea.

The spirit of the exhibition differed from the cautious tone of the conference on cooperation and mutual aid he attended in Beijing in April. Mao attended the Tianjin exhibition to promote extending mutual aid and cooperation throughout North China. Size, socialism, and Wugong were praised. Mao's views on speeding up the organization of larger-scale farm units would be implemented.

Party First Secretary Lin Tie presided over the speed up in co-op formation in Hebei. In December 1951 the provincial government proclaimed that it would have three thousand co-ops in operation within a year.[34] Cooperation was presented as the key to overcoming Hebei's chronic grain deficit. Wugong, with a successful co-op that had been launched as early as 1943, exemplified the right way to develop the countryside. Wugong was the largest continuous successful co-op in the Hebei plain.

In late 1951, heeding the advice of his contacts at the *Hebei Daily* in Baoding, Boss Geng revised the co-op charter. Baoding-area party officials took the lead in building socialist co-ops. The system of 60 percent return for land investment and 40 percent for labor, which had been adopted in 1946 following the decision of eight households to quit, was dropped. A more "socialist" distribution system of 50 percent for land and 50 percent for labor was adopted.[35]

In the spring Li Huiting had paid hapless Li Mainian 6,000 catties of wheat for 4.3 mu of good land and a well. As Huiting explained to Accountant Qiao Wanxiang, "Without land, where would we get our food? I have squeezed pennies and lived simply just so I could buy land." The old man dreamed of additional purchases of land to invest in the co-op following the bountiful autumn harvest.[36]

Boss Geng discovered, however, that land transactions suddenly seemed exploitative to higher-ups. Just one year earlier the *Hebei Daily* had reported as proof of the success of the co-op that members of the Geng co-op had purchased 13 mu of land.[37] The party now discouraged land purchases, warning that purchase and sale of land was the road to class polarization, a road to wealth for the few and impoverishment for the many.

Upon hearing that Li Huiting, Marrying Zhang Zhan, Partly Ripe Li, and Li Genli were all on the verge of buying land, Boss Geng briefed the fourth district party organization, called a meeting of the co-op party members, and finally, summoned all co-op members. Concerned that his prosperous co-op might again become a target of village resentment and of criticism from above for being out of step with changing policies, Boss Geng exploded at sixty-nine-year-old Li Huiting before the entire co-op membership. A co-op, Geng declared, could not prosper by taking advantage of the misfortunes of others. Neither Li nor any other co-op member would be allowed to buy land.

Li Huiting fought back. The old man insisted that the government guaranteed the right to buy and sell land. What he had done served the interests of the co-op since he had always invested good land in the co-op. But Boss Geng, with party backing, prevailed. As the co-op extended its reach, members lost control over their land and such legal rights as the purchase and sale of land. Li, feeling cheated and aggrieved, returned the land to Li Mainian.[38]

Rumors in Raoyang of impending collectivization sent tremors throughout the market. Land prices rose and plummeted with the latest news. Households seeking to buy or sell land quietly approached a local broker. Only when agreement was reached did the parties meet to finalize the sale. A dinner consummated the deal. The agent received a 2 to 3 percent commission from each of the contracting parties.

Peanut Scandal

On December 25, 1951, Boss Geng and his cooperative were mentioned for the first time in the *People's Daily*, the national newspaper published by the party Central Committee. The paper listed Geng first among more than fifty Hebei labor models who attended a Baoding conference to promote competition in forming cooperatives. Geng's challenge to reach high production targets was good publicity, but promoting promethean production targets could be risky. With state aid, the Geng co-op had set production records in 1951, 170 catties per mu in wheat, 245 in corn, 250 in sorghum, 220 in millet, and 2,200 in sweet potatoes. These improved harvests were far short of the unrealistic targets proclaimed by Geng and other model peasants in October and again in December after the first Hebei Provincial People's Congress.[39]

Socialism in the countryside required more than the abolition of buying and selling land, the organization of group farming, and the fulfillment of such state priorities as producing low-priced cotton. A debate at the state center had been won by advocates of greater state control of commerce. Private long-distance trade, an important component of economic recovery during the honeymoon years, greatly enhanced efficiency. It brought together different geographic regions so that each could most cheaply buy what the other lacked. The years of chaos that ruined markets had badly hurt the economy. But now intraregional commerce was redefined as criminal speculation, an extreme form of capitalist exploitation. The state moved to take control of long-distance trade and of trade in key commodities.

In late 1951 a campaign attacked the "Five Evils" of bribery, tax evasion, fraud, theft of government property, and stealing of state economic secrets. In theory the campaign was to focus on the activities of remnant urban capitalists. In reality it lashed out at commercial activity of all sorts, including private and cooperative trading in the countryside. The market that had allowed marginal farmers to survive was being squeezed. The straitjacket tightened.

Months before the campaign against the "Five Evils" began, a casual business acquaintance of cooperative member Li Genli arrived in Wugong with several friends.[40] Li Hengxin, who hailed from a village north of the Hutuo River, presented Boss Geng with a letter of introduction from the Revolutionary University, a newly organized Beijing training school for party officials headed by Liu Lantao, third secretary of the North China Bureau. Li explained that the school had designated him as its purchasing agent. With supplies scarce and sources unreliable, urban units sought to assure supplies and even supplement their revenue by engaging in small-scale commercial activities. Li Hengxin offered to set up a purchasing station in Wugong and to act as a middleman for the Geng co-op. He guaranteed a market at a good price for peanut oil, which in recent years had provided important growth for Wugong and the Geng cooperative. The co-op had only to convert peanuts to oil, and Li would arrange shipment to the nation's capital. The school would thus guarantee its cooking oil at a modest price and sell the surplus, and the co-op could count on a handsome assured income. Li stayed in Wugong for nearly a year, living with Accountant Qiao Wanxiang. Li also had frequent dealings with Geng Changsuo, the assistant head of the co-op, Wei Lianyu, and the manager of co-op sidelines, Li Genli.

In mid-1951 Li Hengxin proposed selling Wugong's best peanuts on the market in Tianjin, where prices were higher than in the local market and far higher than the price paid by the state. Wugong could still sell the remaining second-grade peanuts to the state. Li Genli liked the plan, which promised to boost income substantially, but Geng Changsuo expressed misgivings. With the co-op receiving increasing support from the state, the venture seemed a risky move into uncharted waters.

Li Hengxin had other plans. He proposed together with the co-op to buy forty barrels of peanut oil with 10,000 catties of grain in Shenxian county for marketing in Tianjin. The profits would permit the co-op to buy a strong mule. As in the past, sideline profits would foster agricultural development. Recalling the incident decades later, Boss Geng remembered that he vetoed the plan, overruling sideline manager Li Genli. Why, Li lamented, spit out a pork-filled dumpling when it was already in your mouth? But for one year Li Hengxin remained in Wugong, helping the co-op market its peanuts.

Sidelines were at the center of the co-op's economic successes in the late 1940s and early 1950s. The sideline and commercial enterprises proposed by Li Hengxin in 1951 were legal. The Geng co-op processed the peanuts, kept the husks for fertilizer, and received a commission on sales. Everyone stood to gain.

In late December 1951, after Geng returned from the Tianjin exhibition and began to recast his co-op in a more socialist mold, Li Hengxin moved on. Soon after, however, a group of investigators arrived looking for Li. They said he had borrowed 30,000 yuan in the Geng co-op's name from a Raoyang bank and had failed to account for funds entrusted to him by the Revolutionary University. He had also purchased on credit considerable sums of peanut oil from merchants in Anguo and Shulu counties. Accountant Qiao Wanxiang's signature and the Geng co-op's seal were affixed to the bills.

Suddenly the co-op was under a cloud. It had collaborated with a crook. The illiterate Li Genli had even gone to the bank with the wanted man, Li Hengxin, to borrow money. Li Hengxin had forged the accountant's signature and made unauthorized use of the co-op's official seal. Eventually an audit cleared the Geng co-op and its accountant of criminal complicity in Li's activities, all of which were viewed in a sinister light since the state extended its control over markets and branded intraregional trade as antisocialist. The scandal and the dangers of involvement in sideline and commercial activities were taken by Boss Geng as a further lesson of what might befall the cooperative if the party again changed the ground rules in a more socialist direction. In spring 1952 Li was caught and sentenced to fifteen years in prison. The Geng co-op kept its good name, but it was shaken. A false step, perhaps even an unsocialist step, could bring the political honeymoon to an end with a crash. Commerce itself began to seem suspect.

The imprisonment of the peanut peddler discredited those who criticized Boss Geng for passing up good chances for the co-op to earn money in the market. Politics, not economics, was in command. The Geng co-op turned its back on household sideline production and the market and attempted to build on the combination of cooperative agriculture and ties to the state.

With antimarket pressure mounting, Boss Geng accepted the center's notion that "an agricultural cooperative must take agriculture as its base." He stressed that cooperative manual labor was good, that it was socialist; henceforth, the market was suspect.[41] The Geng co-op's own route to success, linking agriculture and marketable sidelines, would be forgotten, concealed, and repressed. The price of strengthened ties to socialist-oriented leaders was an extraordinary drop in the co-op's capacity to earn income through sidelines. From 45 percent of co-op income generated in sidelines in 1949 and

1950, the figure dropped to 8 percent in 1952. As the state moved to control rural markets and to centralize its control over the marketing of major crops, the bottom fell out all over the Chinese countryside. The Geng co-op abandoned such profitable enterprises as the tainted oil press. Gross sideline income plummeted from 60,000 catties of millet equivalent in 1950 to just 7,000 in 1952 (see table 6).

Beginning in 1951, not only long-distance trade but also commerce and services of all kinds were squeezed out. The tea shop, where co-op originator Geng Xiufeng had gotten his first taste for national affairs and Soviet collectives, closed its doors. Services shriveled up or disappeared all over China as the state moved against the private sector. During the campaign against the Five Evils, more than 450,000 businesses were investigated in China's nine largest cities alone.[42] The untold story was the campaign's rupture of services, shops, and market networks in the countryside.[43] The networks of periodic rural markets built up over the centuries began to be curbed, controlled, and dismantled.

The loss of the ability to market led immediately to economic contractions all over Raoyang, injuring daily life. Traditional Zhanggang alcohol, considered by many as superior even to Hengshui White Lightning, lost its markets and began to disappear. Agriculturally weak Yanggezhuang village, whose fragile periodic market had declined to a mere remnant by the 1930s, reeled under the attack. People in a village with miserable soil could not prosper on farming alone. The Geng co-op, with its special ties to the state, could recoup part of the losses inflicted by antimarket policies. But for poor communities with wretched soil like Yanggezhuang, the attack on sidelines and legal markets initiated a disaster, although villagers built a black market.

The Geng co-op expanded again during winter 1951–52. Qiao Liguang, the rising young Geng protégé from the east village, finally persuaded his household to join. One new member, Li Jinzhua, a resident of the village center, angered other members when he sold his donkey for cash before entering the co-op. Adding six households and 66 mu of land enlarged the co-op to 112 people,[44] an extraordinary size. Responding to the state's notion of building socialism, the co-op agreed to stress grain over such cash crops as peanuts and invested its earnings in new agricultural technology rather than sideline development. The decision would strengthen cooperative-state relations. Officials from Beijing and Baoding urged the Geng co-op to use all of its public accumulation funds (5 percent of gross income) to purchase new equipment.[45]

In mid-January 1952, the *Hebei Daily* praised the co-op for exceeding by 12,000 catties its target of 300,000 catties of natural fertilizer collected in the slack season.[46] But with many people and little land, co-op members wondered whether higher yields could make up for losses in sideline income.

Geng's loyalty to the state was recognized in March when the *People's Daily*

Table 6   Geng Cooperative Income Earned in Sideline Activities (Percentages)

1945	49	1950	45
1946	50	1951	30
1947	47	1952	8
1948	26	1953	12
1949	45	1954	5

featured a long article on the co-op.[47] Since the state increasingly monopolized scarce resources, advantages flowed from association with the favored of the state. Fame was a virtual guarantor of fortune. The *People's Daily* article was an upbeat version of the report written by the representative of the Ministry of Agriculture who visited Wugong in April 1951. It presented the Wugong story in such a way as to promote policies momentarily dominating state politics. Such legends would be reworked as policy changed.

In the 1952 legend nothing was said about the role of Geng Xiufeng in the founding of the cooperative. The split in the co-op in 1944–45 after it was made more socialist went unmentioned. No reference was made to the attacks on the co-op during the terroristic late-1947 phase of land reform. There was little hint of state aid at any stage. The report downplayed the co-op's earlier achievements in sideline production and exaggerated its agricultural performance. The claims for 1951 grain and cotton production, said to have been 510 and 61 catties per mu, respectively, were inflated. Figures, like legends, were larger than life.

Hewing to the new line on agriculture and commerce, the report warned that basic crops, not commercial sidelines, should be the focus of the rural economy. The co-op was urged to invest more in collective property and to reduce the percentage of net agricultural income distributed to land investors. By the time the article appeared the Geng co-op had already made the recommended changes. Sideline investment had been cut more than 80 percent. Geng had learned the political ropes.

On March 27, 1952, prefectural and county leaders, to promote cooperative development, convened a festive meeting in Wugong and announced that the Ministry of Agriculture had selected the Geng co-op as a national model.[48] Meng Tong, the Raoyang county magistrate, Fan Wenyu, a Dingxian prefectural deputy party secretary, Zhang Pingke, chief of the prefectural Agriculture and Construction Department, and Wang Yonglai, the Raoyang party secretary, presided. More than a thousand people streamed in from villages across the fourth district. A certificate of merit signed by Minister of Agriculture Li Xucheng, a cash award, and a medal were presented to the cooperative. Standing in front of two red flags, Boss Geng received the awards with both hands and bowed low before a portrait of Chairman Mao.

Four months before, Geng had pledged to Hebei labor models gathered in Baoding that the co-op would produce 15 percent more grain than in 1951. In the euphoria of the celebration, Geng now guaranteed a staggering 33 percent increase to 637 catties per mu in 1952. The co-op would stress better seeds, irrigation, fertilizer application, and pest control, in short, scientific farming. The village chief of nearby Gengkou village pledged to learn from Geng.

As the meeting ended, prefectural Deputy Party Secretary Fan Wenyu placed Geng, covered with flowers, on a horse. Holding various awards, he was paraded through Wugong lane by lane. People stood on their rooftops and climbed trees along the parade route. It was the biggest celebration in memory in dusty Wugong. A few days after the celebration, to further the movement to promote mutual aid and cooperation in Dingxian prefecture, Geng spoke at a two-day meeting of five hundred fourth district officials and peasant representatives held in Caozhuang village.

Destination, the Ukraine

The Ministry of Agriculture and the North China Bureau of the party decided to send a delegation to inspect Soviet collectives. It was China's first major agricultural delegation sent to study the Soviet Union's mechanized collectives for clues to the socialist future of China's countryside. Hebei leaders Lin Tie, Zhang Kerang, and Yang Xiufeng recommended names. A few days after Geng Changsuo's selection as a national agricultural model, the North China Bureau designated him one of the six Hebei representatives to join the delegation of officials, peasant leaders, and agricultural specialists to tour Soviet collectives. In April 1952 Geng left Wugong for Baoding, where he met provincial Party Secretary Lin Tie for the first time. With U.S. films banned, the one modern cinema showed Soviet films. Private services were squeezed by socialist policies, leaving Baoding's major shopping street with but one popular eatery for ordinary people, a *hundun* restaurant.

By the end of April, Geng was in Beijing to receive pretrip briefings. He would not return to Wugong for five months. It was an extended honeymoon for socialist tourism. The government had Western-style clothes made for the delegates by Beijing tailors. Geng had never worn such outfits. Each member also received thirty rubles per month pocket money. Just before departing for the Soviet Union, Geng joined Li Shunda and six other prominent North China peasant leaders who would accompany him to the Soviet Union in issuing a public challenge. They called on all cooperatives and mutual-aid teams to double grain yields in order to support China's war in Korea.[49]

The delegation was headed by Vice Minister of Agriculture Zhang Lianshi. The deputy leader was Sun Changmu, a secretary of the North China Bureau. The Geng cooperative was increasingly intertwined with the leaders of the bureau, which ran party affairs for North China. The seventy delegates were accompanied by ten interpreters, mostly from Shanghai. The visitors arrived in Moscow on April 27 after ten days of rail travel.[50] When a man with a mustache came forward to greet them at the station, Geng's heart skipped a beat. He thought that Stalin himself had come to welcome their delegation. Nothing seemed impossible in the honeymoon atmosphere.

In Moscow the Chinese delegates were housed in a fifteen-story hotel serviced by elevators. Each room had running water, electric lights, toilet, telephone, radio, phonograph, intercom, and shower. None of this existed in Wugong. During a ten-day stay in Moscow, the group attended the May Day celebration in Red Square, caught a glimpse of Stalin, and observed a military parade complete with the new earsplitting noise of jet aircraft breaking the sound barrier. One event humiliated Geng Changsuo. Delegation members were supposed to sign in next to their name on the name list. Boss Geng could not even recognize his name on the list. He promised himself that when he returned to China he would learn to read.

At the end of the first week in May the delegates traveled by train to the Ukraine for a look at the October Victory Collective, which had been formed in 1922 and destroyed by German forces during World War II. One basic message was hammered at the Chinese: the power of the tractor. Without the tractor, prosperity and a modern way of life were impossible. With the tractor, the collectivized countryside could achieve a life of abundance and happiness. At the October Collective farm, Geng and the others were told that one "Stalin" tractor could plow 450 mu of land to a depth of nine inches in one day. In Wugong this task would require 150 people, 150 animals, 150 plowshares, and still reach only a depth of four inches. The tractor and the collective were the secrets to unimaginable riches.

Homes at this special model collective were large, painted white, and had glass windows draped with sparkling white curtains. The houses contained spring mattresses, beds, tables, chairs, benches, clocks, and carpets, along with phones, running water, electric lights, and radios. The Chinese visitors concluded that the gap between city and countryside was much narrower in the Soviet Union than in China. The kitchens of households on the Soviet showcase collective displayed to their awed visitors ample bread, milk, beef, pork, sausages, beer, wine, and soft drinks. Work clothes were made of good cotton and embroidered with floral patterns.

Some of the older people the delegation interviewed stated that they were living in paradise. They no longer had to worry about food, clothing, or natural disasters and they could have as many children as they wanted. Indeed, the nation, especially the Ukraine, whose population had been decimated not only during World War II, but also in an unmentioned famine that accompanied coerced collectivization, rewarded large families. Given Chinese cultural predilections and recent history, the village leaders noted particularly that the Soviet state paid a family one thousand rubles a month for the fifth child and an additional three hundred rubles per month for every child beyond the fifth. Women with six children were designated "Glorious Mother Grade 1." Mothers with ten children were called "Heroine Mothers" and given a bonus of three thousand rubles per year. To be sure, China suffered from too little arable land to support its many people, but given the disintegration of Chinese families over recent decades, the family policy on Soviet collectives seemed like paradise to visiting peasant leaders. The equation of a big family with prosperity resonated with traditional Chinese values. It also resonated with party policy at a time when contraception was discouraged even in the cities and abortion was illegal.[51]

Prosperity seemed the norm at the twenty-five collective farms, eleven state farms, six tractor stations, nine research institutes, and numerous power stations the Chinese delegates visited during three and a half months. After visiting the Ukraine, the group returned to Moscow for a rest and then divided into eight groups. Boss Geng's party took another extended train trip, this time to Soviet Kazakhistan to observe how Soviet-style prosperity could be achieved even under conditions of poor soil and hostile weather. One state farm displayed a movie theater, day-care center, and bathhouse. One collective farm they visited had only 589 households (2,296 people) farming 55,000 mu of land, eight times more land per person than in Wugong. The supposedly typical household they visited consisted of a husband and wife, both working full-time, two children, and a grandmother. The household owned a three-room house, a storeroom, a shed, a horse, ten sheep, and two milk cows and was allowed to till 5.6 mu of land privately. In 1951 they worked 1,130 days, for which the collective paid them 4,520 catties of grain, 3,616 rubles, and over two kilograms of sugar. The head of the household was planning to buy his son a camera as a graduation present. A Chinese visitor asked him what he would do if, after spending his money, the collective had a bad year. "We don't have bad years," he responded. The chronic problems and failures of Soviet agriculture were hidden from the Chinese visitors.

Boss Geng was impressed by much that was presented to him as socialist paradise. He wondered how Soviet practices could solve Wugong's problems, knowing he had to grapple with reality back home. The honeymoon would end as he returned home to an increasingly socialist China.

6 ❖ THE
GAMBLE

While the honeymoon continued for most Chinese villagers, model units became involved in a political drama over how to move toward socialist agriculture. The Geng Changsuo cooperative was one of several such units in the Baoding-Dingxian region. With Mao's script calling for a rapid advance to socialism, officials tried to direct Boss Geng's co-op into a leading role. Following Mao's call for speed on the road to socialism, Hebei Party Secretary Lin Tie in winter 1951–52 chose Wugong as a pacesetter. Geng Xiufeng, who had risen to deputy director of the cooperative section of the Hebei Bureau of Agriculture and Forestry, was sent back to Wugong in late spring 1952 to direct the production. He promoted an ever larger Geng Changsuo co-op, encouraged the formation of new co-ops, and then called for amalgamation into one villagewide unit. Xiufeng won the local sobriquet "collectomaniac."

The publicity generated by Boss Geng's co-op in late 1951 attracted thirty-seven-year-old screenwriter Hu Su. It was standard practice to assign writers to units that higher officials wished to promote. The Hebei Federation of Literature and Art assigned Zhang Qingtian to Lin Jinhe's co-op in Zhoujiazhuang, east of Shijiazhuang. Li Mantian went to Shuixiangdangliu village to write a book. Yuan Qianli was assigned to Manchengxian in the northwest suburbs of Baoding, and Ge Wen went to Xijianyang. With the party pushing larger units, all federation writers went to the countryside to make propaganda for socialism. No one remained to produce Hebei's elite literary journal, *Hebei wenyi,* so it ceased publishing.

Hu Su was a native of Zhejiang province. He traveled to Yan'an in 1937, joined the Communist party, and studied creative writing at the Lu Xun Academy of Art. In 1939 he was sent to the Jinchaji Base Area and wrote about western and central Hebei. With the establishment of the People's Republic, Hu chaired the Hebei Federation of Literature and Art and the arts section of the provincial party committee's Propaganda Bureau, forging cordial links with First Secretary Lin Tie. In 1951 Hu was transferred to the Beijing Screenwriters Institute.[1] In early 1952, when the institute sent writers to villages to get ideas for film scripts, Hu looked to the Geng co-op. He and his wife, Liu Xi, transferred to Xiaodi, where Hu served for two years as deputy party secretary of the fourth district of Raoyang. He began at once to question Geng Xiufeng about the Wugong co-op. The Collectomaniac loved to talk.

Baoding officials rewrote Wugong's history as an exemplar of Soviet-style socialism. On June 7, 1952, the *Hebei Daily* published the text of a revised co-op charter.[2] Written in part by Boss Geng's media contacts in Baoding in early 1952, it stressed concentrating, as the Geng co-op supposedly had, on basic agricultural production, that is, grain and cotton. Sideline activity was only to support agriculture. The new charter predicted that the nationwide cooperative drive would pave the way for collectivizing agriculture, thus assuring the "rational" use of land, labor, and capital and the rapid introduction of modern technology.

The newspaper stated that the co-op had surged ahead because the previous winter it cut sideline and commercial work and reduced the return on invested land and capital. The theme of "enriching the household" disappeared. "The most significant weak point of the old co-op charter," Boss Geng was quoted as saying, "was the lack of patriotic spirit." A model co-op was now one that served the nation's economic plan. Co-op members should think of the state first and their households later.[3] The *Hebei Daily* invited readers' inquiries, featuring them for four days in July.[4] One reader was said to ask why the charter prohibited members from investing outside the co-op or engaging in private work. The editors answered that labor and capital had to be managed in a "unified" way to assure the smooth and rapid development of a co-op. Without alluding to the Li Hengxin peanut-oil scandal of late 1951, the paper warned that a conflict of interest would arise if sideline manager Li Genli made co-op purchases while also engaging in private business.

Another reader inquired why the co-op had lowered land dividends to 50 percent of net agricultural income. Higher return on investments, the editors responded, wrongly encouraged co-op members to buy land, make money without working, and "exploit" households with more labor. The Geng co-op stopped this, the paper wrote, in early 1951 after Miser Li Huiting bought four mu of land. In the future the big co-op would offer no return for land investment. Socialism rewarded labor.

The legend of the Geng co-op obscured the actual sources of its success, policies now branded as antisocialist. Rural dwellers were urged to reorganize according to principles never proven in Wugong. If anything, Wugong's experience belied those principles. Some charter bylaws, when applied in the 1940s, had so split members and damaged production as almost to bring the curtain down on the saga of the Geng co-op. The state expected such advisers as Geng Xiufeng and Hu Su to ensure that the new script won applause.

Clouds of Dust and Red Spiders

On the eve of departing for Moscow, Geng Changsuo had optimistically predicted that in 1952 the co-op would produce 637 catties of grain per mu, even though signs of drought were evident. Little snow had fallen in Hebei in the winter of 1951–52. Spring showers never came. The sun roasted the land, and by May hot, dry winds stirred up clouds of fine dust.[5] The leaves of Wugong's sorghum, millet, and corn shriveled and turned yellow. Cotton and peanut plants were infested with red spiders. In late spring members of the Geng co-op were pictured in the provincial daily digging a new well "to combat drought."[6]

In May in a highly publicized call for friendly competition between Rao-yang and Daming, a pacesetting county at the southern tip of Hebei, the goal was to harvest only 185 catties per mu.[7] Daming's leaders had pressured villagers to enroll in ever larger units with far less substance or support than those in Raoyang.[8] As the drought deepened, Raoyang Party Secretary Wang Yonglai summoned 1,500 district and village officials to reconsider production plans. The best way to beat the drought and outproduce Daming, Wang urged, was to get organized. Each district was to have ten model villages and fifty model co-ops and mutual-aid teams. Fear of drought was used to drum up support for co-ops.[9] Given a history of decline and disaster, many villagers welcomed reducing risk, not noticing that the change might also reduce prospects for prosperity.

At the Geng co-op, Deputy Director Wei Lianyu and other leaders called a two-day meeting on the drought. Some members wondered whether fame had eroded vigilance. Co-op leaders criticized their failure to apply more fertilizer and sow more corn seeds before Boss Geng left for the Soviet Union. The Black One, Lu Molin, said that the co-op should depend on all its members. Comments about the lack of popular participation and on mistakes made prior to Geng's departure did not reflect favorably on Boss Geng. Crop Expert Zhang Jinren, Wei Lianyu's brother-in-law, stated that he had depended too much on the leader. Recalling a legendary statesman and military strategist, Zhang invoked the cliché, "Three ordinary people are better than one Zhuge Liang."[10] The members formed a "production committee" to deal with the drought. Li Yantian, a charter member of the co-op, headed it, with Wei Lianyu second in command. The committee coordinated teams assigned to cotton, corn, and other crops. The committee met nightly to discuss problems; the teams gathered every five days to review their work.

Simmering conflicts surfaced. Wei Lianyu was not alone in resenting Boss Geng for garnering all the credit for the group's success. Others had been overlooked, whereas only Boss Geng was designated a "labor model." Only Boss Geng was invited to Baoding and Beijing to attend high-level meetings. Only Boss Geng was paraded around on a horse. Only Boss Geng was sent to the Soviet Union. As the 1952 drought worsened, members found an enormous gap between what Boss Geng promised the state and what the co-op could deliver. It was possible to scapegoat Geng, but the real problem was that model status brought impossible expectations from ruling groups.

The Dragon Boat Election

A co-op election was due in June 1952 during Dragon Boat Festival.[11] Before leaving for the Soviet Union, Boss Geng had directed that elections proceed in his absence. After all the resentments were exposed, however, a few members wanted to delay elections until his return. But the majority, sensitive to the implication that they were incapable of making sound decisions without Geng, called for a vote. When Wei Lianyu argued that Geng was ineligible for office because he was not present, it became clear that the deputy director wanted to oust Geng. Wei had served the cooperative well, and his supporters argued that the more worldly and literate Wei could be a better leader. Screenwriter Hu Su, unhappy about Wei Lianyu's plans, sought to postpone the election until Geng's return. When that failed, Hu tried to break up the election-planning meeting, saying that Wei had not consulted with co-op party members. But the charter gave no role to party members in co-op decisions.

In the election, Boss Geng and Wei Lianyu competed for the directorship. Hu Su campaigned on Boss Geng's behalf, rallying such loyalists as Partly Ripe Li to impugn Wei Lianyu's motives. The majority backed Geng for director and reelected Wei deputy director. Nonetheless, screenwriter Hu Su saw Wei as an unscrupulous plotter in a Dragon Boat conspiracy. Hu and Geng Xiufeng would see that Boss Geng was persuaded to their view of Wei as evil.

Bigger Is Better

The Geng co-op continued to attract members in early 1952. Li Wenzhi joined, bringing three mu of excellent land. Working alone, Li had planted grain to feed his family. The co-op would turn his irrigated soil to vegetables, thereby quadrupling output value. Traditional pharmacologist Li Kuanyu joined, too, giving his reason as having been "educated by heaven." He reckoned co-op members would do better in combating drought than he could on his own.

Collectomaniac Geng Xiufeng's assignment was to promote co-ops. But Wugong's other co-ops were not doing well. One, now led by Xu Zhuang, had functioned off and on in the west village since 1946. Two co-ops in the village center, organized by Li Wenkao, a charter member of the Wugong party branch, and Li Wanyi, a party member since 1939, were launched in

1951. All three were in deep trouble. Li Wanyi had been taught at party school in Shanxi province during the war that large Soviet-style collectives were superior, but he could not make even a small co-op work well. Fights repeatedly erupted in poorly run co-ops. Labor-rich households in Li Wanyi's co-op felt cheated by land-rich households, which devoted more time to commerce, sidelines, and handicrafts, enjoying the benefits of work done on their land by others. The more the state promoted co-ops, the more time village leaders spent settling squabbles among members. The Geng Changsuo co-op seemed a world apart. In spite of the unsettling Dragon Boat election, the co-op was united, well led, well endowed, and capable of keeping records and organizing labor to expand irrigation. Crop specialist Zhang Jinren began saying that all villagers would be better off if they were in organizations like Geng's.

Although the June winter-wheat harvest was relatively unaffected by the spring drought, when life-giving midsummer rains did not materialize, the corn, millet, sorghum, and peanut crops began to die. The concerns of April were the impending disasters of July. Collectomaniac Geng Xiufeng, arguing that only expanded cooperation could prevent disaster, wanted to mobilize the entire village! With the crops in the ground beyond help, he proposed preparing for the autumn planting of winter wheat by initiating a villagewide well-digging campaign. Water was the answer and labor mobilization was the method. Geng Xiufeng proposed organizing the entire village into cooperatives of ten households each.

Many households balked, preferring to farm on their own. Local people knew that most co-ops were poorly led, dissension ridden, and short-lived. Yet the achievements of the Geng co-op facilitated a successful late-summer drive that organized sixteen new co-ops totaling 160 households. The four old co-ops had 50 households. An additional 72 households of modest means formed twelve mutual-aid teams to share labor, draft animals, and tools. Mutual-aid teams were smaller than co-ops, and they did not pool land. The two officials trying to make a go of cooperation, Geng Xiufeng and Hu Su, boasted to provincial authorities that Wugong was simultaneously combating drought and expanding co-ops.

But conflicts threatened the project. Many members felt they had been pressured to join. Poorly organized groups demanded better leaders. Many households complained that they had been assigned to groups with few resources. The drive for group farming produced an organizational nightmare. Discontent centered on the plan to drill twenty-three new wells before summer was out. People quarreled over the location. Villagers did not want their water stolen to profit others, and no one wanted to dig in vain. The result was a wasteful crowding of wells in a few promising areas. Resentment and anxiety grew when sections of the village did not benefit from the well drilling.

Confusion mounted as the drought threat worsened. In August some party members began to say that rational development required organizing all village resources from one center. Collectomaniac Geng Xiufeng seized the opportunity to promote what no village in China had attempted: the formation of a single production unit embracing an entire village. Wugong would overcome the fragmentation of land and eliminate tensions among groups and individuals. Only in this way, Xiufeng insisted, could the gap separating poorer from more prosperous households and groups be overcome. All would prosper. This dramatic step was the best way to fight the drought and overcome the recent failure to organize numerous small cooperatives. Bigger would be better.

Most of Wugong's ninety-three party members had misgivings about Xiufeng's plan. No one had ever heard of anything like it. A co-op with 1,650 members and 424 households seemed wildly impractical. Successful earlier co-ops had formed around small groups of friends, neighbors, and relatives, but even small groups experienced difficult administrative and personnel problems. Differences in endowments virtually guaranteed a feeling of exploitation, not cooperation. Most co-ops quickly collapsed. After nine years of painstaking growth facilitated by official support, even the Geng co-op had only 25 households.

Burly Zhang Zhensheng offered an alternative. He had worked his way up through the ranks of the Raoyang Public Security Office before returning to Wugong in 1952 to replace Party Secretary Geng Changsuo, who had so many other responsibilities. Zhang proposed forming four medium-sized co-ops in four regions of the village. Each would be divided into several work teams. If cooperation could work on this scale, the basis for a villagewide unit might then exist. The Collectomaniac's grandiose project, Zhang held, was premature.

Collectomaniac Geng Xiufeng countered that Zhang's scheme was even more impractical. Where would all the leaders come from to direct four large co-ops? Would not conflicts erupt among the four on questions such as equitable land division? With the Wugong party branch stalemated, Xiufeng, the man with the outside contacts, carried his case to Raoyang. The head of the county government, Li Guangyong, liked Xiufeng's idea of a villagewide unit and agreed to accompany him back to Wugong. Li reminded the Wugong party branch that it had long taken the lead in cooperation. All China was moving toward socialism. When had Wugong ever waited for others to act first? This time the party branch endorsed the proposal for a villagewide unit.

The Wugong party convened a meeting of the leaders of the twenty co-ops and twelve mutual-aid teams to win them to a large organization. Party Secretary Zhang spelled out the problems of existing arrangements and called for a single Wugong unit. The co-op leaders expressed reservations. Old Yang

Laiyi thought the risk was too high, involving the lives of more than a thousand people. Li Xiushao said that managing a small co-op was enough of a problem. Could they really manage such a big one? In the end, the leaders agreed to take up the matter with their members. Villagers met in small groups and discussed the issues in detail.

When it became clear that the discussion would be long and heated, Geng Xiufeng returned to Baoding to confer with his superior, Li Ziguang, head of the party's provincial Rural Work Department. The Collectomaniac's classified report was characteristically optimistic.[12] A single all-embracing village organization, he declared, would slice through the maze of conflicting interests and enable the village to realize the full benefits of cooperation. Wugong, with its model co-op, was ready to take the lead. Others would follow.

Xiufeng claimed that the remuneration system would reward the industrious while protecting the interests of labor-short households that depended on land investments. The four orphans in the Geng Changsuo co-op and some of the elderly, who were weak in labor power, survived on the dividends paid on the land they contributed to the co-op. The big unit would not end dividends on property. Geng Xiufeng proposed a graduated scale of distribution that would place a floor under all but would increase income for more-productive teams. Dropouts could not reclaim their original land, but would receive equivalent land elsewhere so that production would not be disrupted by land reclamation. The households of individuals labeled class enemies would still be excluded. The Hebei Rural Work Department accepted Geng Xiufeng's report and advised him to discuss his plan with Boss Geng on Changsuo's return from the Soviet Union.

Beardless Geng

Geng Changsuo's delegation returned to Beijing in mid-September 1952. Geng, his goatee and mustache shaved, was wearing urban-tailored clothes and leather shoes. The delegates were briefed on the roles they would play as emissaries of mechanized collective agriculture in their provinces and localities. One of the first to visit Geng in his Beijing hotel was his son Delu, who had recently been demobilized from the army for poor health.[13] Geng Changsuo was linking into personal networks that reached to the provincial and national capitals, networks that controlled such scarce resources as good jobs on the state payroll. A comfortable office job had been found for Delu at the Central Documentary Film Studio in Beijing. He was moving toward marriage with Liu Qingying, a party member from Anguo county whom Delu had met in the army.

On September 16, the Hebei delegates were greeted at the Baoding railway station as returning heroes in a gala reception organized by the Hebei government, the Agriculture Department, the Bureau of Agriculture and

Forestry, and the provincial branch of the Sino-Soviet Friendship Association. For the next five days the group moved from one meeting to another. Boss Geng did much of the speaking as the leading peasant member of the Hebei delegation. He developed into a wry and well-paced teller of tales. He also began to lose his voice. On the evening of September 17, Boss Geng and his fellow travelers were honored guests at a meeting of more than one thousand Hebei officials held in Baoding's New China Auditorium. Governor Yang Xiufeng and provincial Party Secretary Lin Tie presided.

Geng stressed the need to mechanize agriculture. He spoke glowingly of tractors. Mechanization would send production soaring and the state and people would prosper, just as the Soviet Union supposedly had. To be sure, that was not how Geng Changsuo's own co-op had prospered. Still, Geng argued that mechanization held the key to accelerating development during the upcoming Five Year Plan. All the difficulties Geng and others had experienced in trying to make voluntary cooperatives productive suddenly seemed to melt away as he proclaimed the merits of gigantic Soviet-style collectives.

The return of the delegation coincided with the peak of Chinese adulation of the Soviet Union and Stalin. That autumn full pages in the Chinese press were devoted to pictures of Stalin and Soviet tractors and collectives as well as to encomiums to "our big elder brother," the Soviet Union, for its support. In November Tianjin's *Progressive Daily* featured the complete text of Stalin's *Economic Problems of Socialism.*[14]

Geng recounted his Soviet experiences before seemingly endless numbers of Baoding organizations and schools. The *Hebei Daily* interviewed him for a three-day series of articles,[15] and he was invited to Radio Hebei to broadcast his views to the entire province. Wugong village, however, did not yet have a radio. "The Soviet Union's today is our tomorrow," Boss Geng repeated time and again. "The Soviet Union's good points are too numerous to mention. I saw collective farmers' prosperity, saw their labor, saw their support for the Chinese people and their hatred for American imperialism, all of which will help us immeasurably to increase our strength."[16] Given the American-led economic embargo of China, the tractors, technology, and technicians required to mechanize agriculture would have to come from the Soviet bloc.

There was, however, only one tractor factory in all Soviet-aid plans for China, and that would not produce its first tractor for several years more. Chinese scientists estimated that a fully mechanized collective agriculture required 1.5 million tractors.

Before Geng left Baoding for home, he charged in the *Hebei Daily* that the United States was using bacteriological weapons in Korea and northeast China. Given how much the new nation had done for him and Wugong, Geng was more than willing to lend his support to the war effort. After having "read" a report by an international commission of scientists, illiterate Geng concluded, "the facts show how detestable the American warmongers are, how American imperialism has violated international law, and that the American aggressors are the enemies of the peoples of China and Korea and the peoples of the whole world."[17] As soon as he got home, Geng Changsuo set to work ending his embarrassing illiteracy. With the help of his daughters, Sujuan and Huijuan, and their textbooks, he diligently began to learn to read.

Geng Xiufeng followed the public progress of the travelers home from the Soviet Union and waited to speak privately with Geng Changsuo. When the two met in Baoding, Xiufeng asked about Soviet collective farms. Changsuo was firmly committed to realizing the benefits of mechanization and large-scale organization. The Collectomaniac then briefed Changsuo on the situation in Wugong, presenting villagewide organization as the solution to the problems facing the village. He also told Boss Geng about Wei Lianyu and the contested Dragon Boat election.

The support of Geng Changsuo and Party Secretary Zhang Zhensheng was essential for the success of the Collectomaniac's plan. Geng's east village co-op had nine donkeys and mules, and Zhang's in the west had four. Once again, the outside lineages would have to join and lead. Formation of a single big unit, by including less-productive land and households with little to invest, would for some years reduce the income of members of more-prosperous small co-ops. One attraction of a big unit for the poor was that they would benefit from the distribution of the assets of richer co-ops. The Collectomaniac knew that unless Boss Geng and Zhang promoted a villagewide unit, resistance by members of their prospering co-ops could not be overcome. If the more productive viewed the formation of a large unit as theft, then initiative and growth could be thwarted.

Geng Changsuo moved cautiously. He learned that Li Ziguang, head of the Hebei Rural Work Department, and Li Guangyong, Raoyang county government chief, were boosters of the plan. Xiufeng had also enlisted the support of Zhang Kerang, director of the Hebei Bureau of Agriculture and Forestry, who told Xiufeng that provincial Party Secretary Lin Tie would provide an 80,000 yuan low-interest loan to the big unit. Geng Xiufeng lined up scarce material and organizational support from the county level up to the province, resources that would be unavailable to other villages asked to emulate the model.

On September 25, as he arrived in a horse-drawn cart, local people poured on to the dusty road to greet Boss Geng, almost carrying him into the village. The co-op courtyard had been swept clean. Red flags flew from the gate. Boss Geng presented the co-op with prized gifts from the Soviet Union, a camera and a phonograph. With money saved from his expense account, he had purchased candy, toys, and biscuits for co-op children as well as a pair of barber's shears with which parents could cut their children's hair. Small gifts, such as postcards, photographs, and travel souvenirs, were presented to each of the other co-ops.[18]

While singing the praise of Soviet collectives, Boss Geng privately entertained villagers with a tale of the parochial quality of Chinese officialdom. In Moscow, Geng said, the leader of the Chinese delegation searched everywhere for Chinese food. One day he told delegates they would dine at a new Chinese restaurant. Geng then described a useless trek to a place still not open for business. Villagers joined in laughing at urbanites whose pseudosophistication masked ignorance.

Geng was bombarded with questions about the Soviet Union. He reported first to his own co-op and then to the entire village on the second and third days of his return.[19] The key to Soviet prosperity, he said, following the party line, lay in the combination of mechanization and collectivization. It was all based on "tractors," a word with no intrinsic Chinese significance. Most villagers had never heard the word. No one had seen one. They called out for him to repeat the word *tuolaji* and explain. What it meant, Geng told them, was the future.

Higher-ups had assigned Geng the role of assuring villagers that large-scale organization would bring abundance. He said he had seen that giant Soviet collectives brought prosperity. The Hebei government knew that Chinese peasants had to be convinced that big farm units in which villagers no longer managed their own land, animals, and tools were practical and ethical, that they would enrich large households. Geng gave such assurances in talks all over the region.

Geng touted organizing labor into mobile work teams to transcend identification with a particular plot of land. The teams would tackle specialized tasks (animal husbandry, construction, and so on) with payment based on performance. By copying the Soviet Union, Geng promised, "we can advance to socialist society faster."[20] In 1952 Chinese newspapers hailed "the nurturing of our big elder brother." Deriding the "capitalist science" of the United States and Europe, the papers praised "Bolshevik science," including the theories of Trofim Lysenko, president of the Soviet Academy of Agricultural Sciences, who advanced the view that heritable changes can be brought about in plants by environmental influences. Powerful Lysenko advocates at Beijing Agricultural College and North China Agricultural University drove out scientific geneticists and so-called bourgeois idealists and promoted Lysenko's methods in waterlogged areas of the North China plain. Contrasting themselves to scientists who believed only the fittest survived competition within a species, the Lysenkoans claimed that was how imperialists justified rule by might. If survival were the criterion of fitness, then traitors to China who survived in Japanese-occupied areas would be superior to patriots who were martyred. Condemning the imperialist science of struggle within a species, the Lysenkoans promoted close planting. Officials responded by using deep-plowing and close-planting techniques and Soviet seeds to produce bumper harvests.[21]

Boss Geng and the press offered a lush vision of a bountiful future. The harsh reality in autumn 1952 was drought, the most severe in Raoyang since 1943. Even Boss Geng's better-irrigated co-op suffered. In mid-March, on the eve of his departure for the Soviet Union, Geng had promised yields of 637 catties per mu. But the harvest was only 237 catties per mu, half the 1951 crop yield, the worst co-op harvest since 1945. Only 52 catties of grain per mu were distributed per member, the lowest in co-op history.[22] And sideline production, the secret of co-op success in the honeymoon years, had been cut back, in line with the state's anticommercial policies, to the pitiful level of 7,000 catties of grain equivalent. With nothing to sell to compensate for the grain decline, villagers were turned into wards of the state. The state quietly stepped in with 20,000 catties of relief grain for Wugong.[23]

The Big Gamble

Following the meager fall harvest, Boss Geng assembled villagers to win them to a villagewide unit.[24] The drought, he argued, proved that all were vulnerable to the ravages of nature unless they organized. Many individual farmers had yields only half that of his small co-op. A big unit was the logical extension of his co-op's ten-year experience. Soviet collectives proved that large-scale organization was necessary to achieve higher yields and mechanized agriculture. Although Geng's plan excited some, many others, particularly members of failed co-ops, were apprehensive. With Xiufeng having gotten so much upper-level support, with Mao promoting large-scale farming, and with the knowledge that socialist experiments were rewarded, Wugong leaders tried to prove themselves more socialist. The system of rewarding those who went first and fastest where the center pointed promoted zeal, encouraging people to crawl out on limbs.

For forty days in October and November marathon meetings were held among and within the various co-ops and mutual-aid teams. Boss Geng and Party Secretary Zhang Zhensheng directed the discussions, while Collectomaniac Geng Xiufeng and the screenwriter Hu Su advised behind the scenes. The leadership brushed aside a suggestion to exchange land and eliminate scattered plots as an alternative to a big unit. They also dismissed the idea that the size be cut by excluding the Li lineage.

Zhang Zhensheng spoke again in favor of dividing the village into four sections of one hundred households, each, in turn, subdivided into four teams of approximately twenty-five households. One section would be the east village, Boss Geng's power base, and one would be the west village, dominated by households loyal to Zhang Zhensheng and Old Militia Xu Yizhou. The east and west ends were home to most of Wugong's ninety-six party members. The now powerless center and central west end, the home of most better-off households in the old days, would be divided into two sections, further weakening the Li lineage. Eventually the leaders won backing for a single large village unit.

Leaders would make the main economic decisions. Villagers weighing the proposal recognized that their livestock, tools, wells, and machinery would be controlled by a single village authority that would then allocate items to the smaller units. Each team, or subunit, would farm a unified parcel of land. Income would first be calculated according to the productive performance of each team, and then distributed to individuals based on labor and dividends on land shares.

Opponents of a single big economic unit doubted that the village economy could be efficiently managed as a whole. The problems experienced by the closely knit Geng co-op over a decade would be many times greater in a unit of four hundred households. Members of the original Geng co-op saw joining a villagewide organization as sacrificing the gains painfully won over the past decade. The productive small co-op, with its superior irrigation and improved soil, could approach yields of 500 catties per mu in a good year. Now hard-won resources would be partially reallocated. Miser Li Huiting lamented, "It wasn't easy for us to transform the sandy and salty soil and ditches, and to produce 480 catties per mu. Our three old picks have been turned into nine big mules and donkeys. We better not join up with them." Partly Ripe Li could not bear the thought of parting with Big Black and other mules on which he doted.[25]

Boss Geng conceded that incomes in his prospering co-op would at first decline, but in the long run all would get more than a small well-run co-op could ever provide. Only large-scale organization could produce the resources for mechanization. Still, Changsuo met anxious villagers part way. Residual sideline operations could remain with each of the sixteen or so new teams for the time being. The critics in the Geng co-op were silenced if not convinced. The majority agreed to support the Boss. His small co-op's willingness to sacrifice superior resources made a deep impression on opponents of a villagewide organization who would acquire a share of wealth they had not earned. As always, fixing the ratio between remuneration for land and labor produced bitter disagreement. Households with little labor power needled Boss Geng proposing a 70:30 land-labor split in agriculture and a 90:10 capital-labor split in sidelines. In the end, however, a 50:50 land-labor split prevailed, the formula adopted by Boss Geng's co-op in late 1951 and favored by Hebei officials.[26]

After weeks of wrangling, a preparatory committee was formed and households were invited to apply for membership in the big unit. Some two hundred households signed up, but Geng insisted that success hinged on greater participation. Success required unified planning and overall land use. Discussions continued. So did resistance. One old man complained that things were a mess and talked about moving to another village. With a pile of valuable manure in his courtyard, he was sure he would lose in the big unit. Many feared being forced to surrender valuable property. Rumors flew. In late October, Geng called another village meeting to stress that joining was voluntary. One man, saying he had worked hard to get what he owned, asked what guarantees there were that he could quit whenever he wanted and recover all his property. Geng reiterated that members were free to withdraw all their property after one year.

Geng Changsuo went house to house to press recalcitrants. The staunchest holdout in Geng's own co-op was Marrying Zhang Zhan, who that year had at last been able to build a two-room house. Economic origins and class labels were weak indicators of attitudes toward the big unit. Geng responded to fears of being taken advantage of by pointing out that he and other members of the richest team stood to lose most. If he believed in the long-term advantages of the big unit, how could others claim they would be fleeced?

Geng announced a second registration. This time about three hundred households signed up, including some responding to a rumor that this was their last chance. Geng remained dissatisfied. He reassured holdouts that they would be repaid within three years for livestock, tools, and other resources absorbed by the big unit. If necessary, the villagewide organization would borrow money from member households for this purpose.

Following the second registration, Boss Geng urged each of the more than twenty discussion groups to nominate candidates for leadership. A slate of eighty names was reduced to twenty. In the end, Wugong's top Communists were selected to lead. Boss Geng was director and Party Secretary Zhang Zhensheng deputy director. Wei Lianyu, formerly the number two man in Geng's old co-op, was designated financial affairs officer. Boss Geng's good right hand, young Qiao Liguang, was chosen deputy director for agricultural production. Leaders came from the east and west village. The center, the bastion of the once-powerful traditional elite and many other Li lineage households, was left without representation.

With higher-level endorsement, the villagewide Geng Changsuo co-op was formally inaugurated at a meeting on November 8, 1952, when 295 households, 93 percent of the village, joined as charter members. Only 29 Wugong households with 110 people remained outside. Some, like prosperous middle peasant Li Shengdang and poor peasants Li Zhouxiu and Li Zhongpo, feared they would be cheated in the big co-op. The isolated and stigmatized households of Li Maoxiu and others labeled landlord or rich peasant, as in Soviet collectivization, were again prohibited from joining.

Representatives from the province, prefecture, county, and district attended the inaugural meeting. They joined with labor models from other counties in extolling Geng Changsuo. Raoyang officials proposed moving the local periodic market, located for centuries in Zoucun, to Wugong. But Boss Geng declined, fearing such a shift would poison relations with the market center. Villages slighted by the state were not enamored of neighboring models.

Too Big, Too Fast

Only four days after the big unit's inauguration, higher authorities expressed second thoughts. Deng Zihui, director of the party's Rural Work Department, and others of his persuasion in Beijing prevailed, arguing that forcing villagers to emulate big units led to coerced enrollment in unpopular and alienating organizations. Such an "adventurous" policy had to be replaced by economic "readjustment," that is, harmonizing with popular preferences to keep agricultural production up so as not to undermine the industrialization drive. Confiscated animals were to be returned to original owners. The zeal of local leaders to be "advanced" had to be tempered, or else agriculture would suffer as work effort declined.

Li Ziguang, director of the Hebei party's Rural Work Department, reported that the 1952 drive for mutual-aid and co-op development had enrolled 4.7 million Hebei households (68 percent of the total), mostly in mutual-aid teams. The number of co-ops increased from 14 to 1,082. But, Li added, 494 of the 1,082 co-ops in Hebei were clustered in just three counties, Raoyang, Daming, and Ninghe. Little Raoyang had 137 co-ops. Twenty-four Hebei counties still did not have a single unit in which land and sidelines were pooled for common cultivation and use. Moreover, Li reported, many mutual-aid teams and co-ops contained very discontented members who had been pressured into joining by local leaders responding to the ballyhoo of a campaign. Many organizations existed only on paper. In pacesetting Sanhe county 148 of 305 mutual-aid teams did not function at all. Finally, Li observed, echoing the center's policy switch, some Hebei units were too large, making prospects of failure high. Co-ops, he advised, should involve between ten and thirty households. Any unit that proposed more than fifty households required authorization by the prefecture. "Big co-ops," Li concluded, "should be based on the foundation of a smaller co-op that had been run well. Where such conditions do not exist, early experiments should not be conducted."[27]

Following the 1953 lunar New Year, provincial Deputy Party Secretary Ma Guorui arrived in Wugong to inspect Hebei's most ambitious co-op. Ma was a lieutenant of Party Secretary Lin Tie. After three days in Wugong, Ma told Boss Geng he would recommend that the experiment continue. But he also pointed to problem areas, including paralyzed sidelines and a need for tighter financial controls.

By late February major drawbacks in the three "big co-ops" in Dingxian prefecture, including Wugong, were publicly detailed by five staff members of the prefectural party committee, who used pseudonyms to express their views.

They discovered that nagging problems plagued Wugong village during the winter. The work force had been organized before it was clear how it would be deployed. Some villagers had nothing to do and complained, "Give us work." Others resented the pressure to join the big unit. Morale was low. "Others had signed," Li Lianggui confessed, "so I grudgingly signed my name too." Some peasants sold livestock and cut down their trees, fearing confiscation of precious resources.

Many villagers neglected to plow the land and sow the winter-wheat crop because it was unclear how a big organization would pay for labor. Boss Geng resorted to threats: work points would be deducted for land that was idle. "When Geng Changsuo's big unit was being organized," the report stated, "people were afraid of five things: it would be poorly run, there would be no freedom, there would not be enough to eat, the work would be extremely hard, and there would be no cash for individual daily expenses." The report found that all sideline work had stopped.

According to the report, the experience of the three big units in Dingxian prefecture showed that such experiments should be carried out in high-yield areas, rather than in regions prone to famine. Because Wugong had been hit by a severe drought in 1952, Geng's big unit could raise only 25 percent of the funds necessary for production in 1953. Some households not only had nothing to invest, but they also required emergency relief. The report recommended limiting units to one hundred households. Others should not rashly rush into large-scale organizations.[28]

As opposition mounted, Wugong was rocked by a scandal. Three officials in one work team in the west end were charged with embezzling. Li Xiaozhan, Li Fuzheng, and Xu Shulin reported figures below actual yields. The unreported grain was distributed to team members, many of whom received nearly twice the grain that the official records indicated. The team leaders responded to low morale by distributing more grain to disgruntled peasants by delivering less to those who directed the large unit. When other villagers found out about the scheme, they reported it. The three were arrested by Raoyang public security officers. Team head Li Fuzheng and Xu Shulin got two years at hard labor in a Raoyang prison camp, but party member Li Xiaozhan escaped imprisonment.

In April a telegram from the North China Bureau arrived at the Hebei Rural Work Department that reflected the views of Deng Zihui: "The phenomenon of going too fast exists"; "Too big, too many"; "Geng Changsuo's is a bit too big." The telegram was signed by Liu Lantao, third secretary of the party's North China Bureau. Geng Xiufeng, who worked in the Rural Work Department, consulted Ma Guorui, just returned from Wugong, contending that while 395 households was by no means small, Wugong could manage the big unit. Ma commented that for people like the Collectomaniac nothing seemed too big. The next day Zhang Kerang, director of the provincial

Bureau of Agriculture and Forestry, informed Geng Xiufeng that Wugong's big unit had been discussed at a provincial-level meeting of party and government organs. Zhang's bureau had urged that the experiment continue, but the party's Rural Work Department had spoken otherwise. Zhang expressed his regrets.

The dispute in Baoding reflected struggles in Beijing. By the end of 1952 there were 1,082 co-ops in Hebei, and 3,634 co-ops in all of China.[29] Liu Shaoqi, China's head of state, found these results impressive. Mao Zedong did not. Mao and his closest advisers on rural policy, particularly Chen Boda, sought more and bigger units to pave the way for collective farming. But other national leaders, including Liu Shaoqi and Deng Zihui, prevailed, stressing that to force the pace would alienate the peasantry, produce economic chaos, and preclude a voluntary transition to collectives. In spring 1953 the Central Committee moved to "check impetuosity and rash advance" in the socialist transformation of agriculture.[30] The North China Bureau ordered Lin Tie's Hebei party committee to bring Wugong's big unit into line. The state believed in one correct path, and Wugong was going the wrong way.

On April 20 a twelve-member provincial work team arrived in Wugong to impose conformity with national policy.[31] Guo Fang, deputy director of the Hebei party Rural Work Department, led the team, which included the deputy director of the Dingxian Prefectural Party Propaganda Department and a section leader of the Hebei Bureau of Agriculture and Forestry who had traveled with Geng Changsuo to the Soviet Union. The team also included Collectomaniac Geng Xiufeng and Lu Guang, a deputy section head of the party's provincial Internal Affairs Department. Villagers immediately commented on Lu Guang's shortness. In the traditional culture, physical disability of any kind was a subject of public ridicule. Village youngsters with handicaps were kept at home and did not attend school, saving the family from public shame.

With Wugong so prominent a model of cooperation, if the big unit were poorly run, the work team argued, it would deter others from taking the socialist road. County leaders were split. The new Raoyang party secretary, Gao Jian, opposed reducing the size of the unit and said so. But Zhang Ping, a rising deputy secretary of the Raoyang party committee, agreed to cooperate with the work team. Guo Fang instructed Geng Changsuo to reduce the size of the unit. Geng declined, feeling he had no choice. To be seen as a place full of mistakes that required a precipitous retreat might end one's role as a model. It was not obvious to Geng this time that following orders was the best way to maintain the ties between village and state, especially ties to the network of county, prefectural, and provincial leaders who had helped the village. Either conceding or resisting seemed risky. Boss Geng gambled on the big unit and stood against the work team.

The work team then approached Party Secretary Zhang Zhensheng. But

Zhang, who had earlier expressed reservations about the large size, stood by Boss Geng. The work team convened the ninety-six-member Wugong party branch. Remarkably, not a single party member buckled under pressure. Finally, the visitors called a meeting of the entire membership. Work-team leader Guo declared that higher-ups were dissatisfied. He demanded reduction to a maximum of eighty households. Above that size, administrative problems were insoluble at current levels of technology. "To try to run so big a unit is wrong," Guo said. "If there is nothing to eat, who will be responsible? You entered freely, so you can leave freely. Small co-ops can be run, and households can also work on their own. That's legitimate." In the heated discussion that followed, Boss Geng sat silent.

Geng Changsuo knew that the work team was not united in its resolve to reduce the size of the unit. After all, the Collectomaniac was on the team. Xiufeng could say nothing publicly, but behind the scenes he worked to influence others. Screenwriter Hu Su was also a friend of the experiment. Geng Changsuo and Zhang Zhensheng, confident that the experiment had supporters in Baoding, Dingxian, and Raoyang, resisted Guo Fang's ultimatum. Boss Geng urged villagers to stand with him in the biggest gamble of his career.

The weeks wore on. Guo became irritated with the opposition of Boss Geng and Zhang Zhensheng. As villagers who love the image of outsiders fleeing in embarrassed confusion remember it, Guo, complaining of a toothache, announced he would go to Raoyang. Guo directed his deputy to head the work team for three days and then went to Raoyang, where he reported to his superiors on Geng's insubordination. Rumors flew in the Zoucun market that Wugong was a mess, that the big unit was a failure, and that the "freedom of individuals" was being violated. The word was abroad that unreliable elements controlled the Wugong party branch. Zhang Zhensheng, Geng Changsuo, and all ninety-six members of the Wugong branch, it was said, would be investigated.[32]

Work-team leader Guo returned to Wugong and announced instructions from Lin Tie to reduce the size of the unit. The village party branch was directed to order members to abandon the experiment. Refusal constituted violation of a directive from the highest party authority in the province. Party members who left, taking with them enough people to set up a small co-op, were promised livestock and farm tools from the unit's holdings. Villagers feared that the last to leave would lose the most.

This time the work team got results. Almost 80 households announced they would drop out. With a little more prodding, twenty party members, including such prominent west-end members as Xu Mantang, the former party secretary and militia leader, agreed to quit, taking with them members from their smaller co-ops. In all, 108 households left and 287 households stayed. Geng Changsuo's gamble was in doubt.

Old Militia Xu Yizhou, another former party secretary and guerrilla leader from the west village, left, taking his neighbors and several poor members of the Xu lineage with him. Xu also tried to bring others in the west village around to his view, including Party Secretary Zhang Zhensheng. Xu's experience, even with very small co-ops, had been bitter. He would adhere to party discipline as he had in 1947 when he stood with the leveling land-reform work team that temporarily toppled Boss Geng. A distraught Zhang Zhensheng insisted that Old Militia Xu Yizhou present his decision to a Wugong party branch meeting. Geng Changsuo and other leaders pressured Xu to reenter the big unit. If party people, who were supposed to take the boat to socialism, reversed course, how would nonparty villagers respond? Isolated, Xu gave in. "I was wrong. A Party member can only get on the boat. A Party member cannot get off."

Nonetheless, Xu felt railroaded. When he got back home and started talking with those who had left with him, he reversed himself yet again. He would not abandon neighbors and relatives or buck the party. He would leave the big unit. Party Secretary Zhang again came to plead with Old Militia. Both lived in the west end. Zhang won Xu to the cause of village unity, and Xu agreed to persuade his neighbors to return to the big unit with him. He succeeded with most. But the episode cost Xu what remained of his position in Boss Geng's political machine. Geng would not forget disloyalty. Xu Yizhou never again played the pivotal role he had during the war years when he helped build the party in Wugong.[33] But Boss Geng did not totally destroy Old Militia Xu. Geng had married a west-end Xu. His allies in the Qiao lineage included women's leader Qiao Wenzhi, who was married to the tough west-end leader Xu Lianzheng. Geng remained committed to unity based on alliance among the outer lineages.

A central economic difference between Geng loyalists and the households that resigned was size of landholdings. The average remaining member owned 2.5 mu of land, the average nonmember 3.8 mu.[34] As in 1945, when the co-op overvalued labor in comparison with other productive factors, many departing households realized that with more and better landholdings, they would do better in smaller co-ops or farming as households than in a unit that paid only 50 percent of net earnings on land and property dividends. Most of the small co-ops organized in Raoyang in 1952 distributed 60 percent of agricultural earnings to land investors.[35]

According to Geng loyalists, a battered Guo Fang slipped quietly out of the village in mid-May, licking his wounds. Villagers told a similar story about the departure of every meddler in local life. Following the departure of the work team, the 287 households remaining in Geng's organization set to work. For the next six months, as Hebei leaders focused on consolidating smaller cooperatives, the national and provincial press ignored Geng Changsuo and Wugong. Others were no longer encouraged to follow Wugong's lead. The Geng leadership group worried about its gamble of being on the losing side in elite political combat.

Nonetheless, another reality, the treatment of all within the state orbit as special and privileged, became ever more central to Chinese politics. The spigot of state-monopolized resources stayed on for those entwined with state power. Resources flowed. The administrative office of Dingxian prefecture joined with the Hebei Water Bureau to dispatch a team to Wugong to drill the village's first power-driven well using diesel motors.

Settling Scores

In late spring 1953, after the departure of the work team, Boss Geng disposed of his disgruntled rival, Wei Lianyu. Wei's position as financial officer was abolished, and he was held responsible for some of the chaos and mismanagement that had generated prefectural and provincial criticism of the big unit.[36] Wei resented the scapegoating and the loss of face. He became increasingly isolated. Given the state's expanded reach over so much of life, to lose power was to lose a great deal. When pathetic Wei openly complained about his treatment, vicious charges rained down on him. During the resistance war, it was now said, Wei had joined the Nationalist party in Henan province and served as a local police chief. As a co-op leader he had squandered funds and worked hand in glove with Li Hengxin, whose shady peanut deals had almost wounded Geng's co-op in late 1951. Wei even beat his adopted son, Zhang Zhan.

Wei Lianyu was made to look like a stock villain. Those labeled enemies of socialism were portrayed as traitors, spies, social scum, and people of dubious family origin. Wei was subjected to repeated criticism and struggle sessions in the party branch. Ousted and stigmatized, he grew despondent and his physical and mental health deteriorated. In winter 1956–57 he died of a stroke. Old Militia Xu Yizhou, who had also been pushed out of the Geng inner circle, said Wei Lianyu had been "criticized to death." Almost no one attended Wei's funeral. This Communist, resistance leader, and early pioneer of cooperative agriculture had become a bad person, a nonperson, a dead person.

Other scapegoating continued. Resistance activist Li Maoxiu with his label as landlord was still deprived of political rights. He worked under "supervision." Whenever a crime was committed, Maoxiu was a prime suspect. There were numerous arson cases in the early 1950s as Boss Geng pressed unpopular policies that curried favor with higher authorities: cultivating low-priced cotton, cutting sideline investment, abandoning marketing outlets. The local militia and the county Public Security Office hounded the "class enemy," ritual whipping boy Li Maoxiu. When cases of crop theft and malicious crop damage were reported, he was apprehended and interrogated. No evidence ever linked Li to a crime, but scapegoating continued.

By late 1952, twenty-six-year-old Li Maoxiu saw life in Wugong as permanent harassment. In desperation, Li forged a letter of introduction and stamped it with a replica of the fourth district seal that he carved out of a turnip. His goal was to secure a factory job in the northeast, but the Wugong authorities reported Li Maoxiu to public security officers, who tracked him down. Li was sentenced to five years at hard labor in one of Dingxian prefecture's many new labor camps.

Following Maoxiu's arrest, his wife, Fan Shufang, and son left for her natal village. But when Li Feng, Maoxiu's older brother who worked for the party in Shandong province, visited Wugong, Fan returned to honor him in proper patriarchal fashion. While Maoxiu was in prison, the state used his skills. Owing to a shortage of builders and architects, he was drafted to design and help construct government buildings in the county town of Fuping. Prisoners were repeatedly subjected to physical beatings.

The Geng Changsuo leadership sought to show that Wugong was zealously committed to socialism. Having destroyed the village's only surviving temple in 1949, Wugong's leaders threw themselves into a national campaign to root out "feudal" religious practices. One of their targets was thirty-eight-year-old Li Jinzhua, the tiller from the village center who had angered co-op leaders when he sold his donkey before entering the co-op. Like his father, Li was a member of the Hongyuanmen sect. In the early 1950s the state attacked religious sects as carriers of antisocialist consciousness and active opponents of the drive to restrict private commercial activity. In 1952, when Jinzhua's son became delirious, he believed the boy's soul had been stolen. Li prayed to Cao Wang Ye, a god in the large Daoist pantheon, for the use of someone else's soul for his son. The son recovered, but Jinzhua was in trouble.

Upon hearing of his praying, Wugong security officers subjected Jinzhua to public degradation at a mass meeting. Li was expelled from the co-op and labeled a black element, an enemy of the people. He believed it was an act of revenge to punish him for having sold the donkey. He became part of a group of pariahs that included other Daoists, suspected saboteurs of the collective economy, and people like Li Maoxiu who were branded class enemies. The attack on religion extended to a large Catholic church in Xianxian, east of Wugong. The church, whose members had been assured of its restoration as a place of worship once it was liberated from Japanese desecration, was turned into a hospital.

Another Wugong internal exile in 1953 was Xu Jichang, a party member and former official who had worked for the county government in Raoyang. Rumors circulated in Wugong that Xu had gotten into serious trouble in Raoyang, perhaps having committed rape, certainly sexual misconduct. Xu was fired, labeled a "bad element," and sent home to labor "under the supervision of the masses." An ordinary person accused of such crimes would have been prosecuted, perhaps executed. In Xu's case, no formal charges were filed, no trial was held, and Xu never got a chance to defend himself. Village leaders were never briefed on the case. They assumed the authorities had good reason to insist on Xu's disgrace and exile. Guilt was more a political verdict than a judicial one.

Throughout Raoyang suspects were terrorized by the now-entrenched Soviet-style security forces. Headlights flashing, motorcycle operatives raced to a victim's residence at night, broke down the door, beat the people inside, stripped them, forced the suspect to kneel, and then smashed the furniture in a supposed search for evidence. Raoyang people said, "Gong an ju, bu an-chuan" (where there is Public Security, no one is secure).

All over rural China, groups of black elements became a forced labor corps. They were compelled to start work earlier than others, sweeping the lanes. If it snowed, they removed the snow. They had to put in longer hours of field work. They were forbidden to talk to people who were in good standing with the state. Local people rarely spoke to them, since such an association could lead to trouble. The corps shuffled through its tasks, heads down, eyes averted. Black elements were assigned to the lowest-status and dirtiest jobs, such as cleaning out latrines. Their sentences had no time limit. There was no due process, just political verdicts, repression, personal vendettas, and permanent revenge.[37] Among those assigned to watch Wugong black elements was forty-eight-year-old Iron Man Li Duolin, the tough militia veteran who had married the wandering beggar during the resistance war. Li still carried his rifle with him as he poked around the village. He believed class enemies were like Japanese marauders and wily foxes that raided local chicken coops. They had to be hunted down and shot.[38]

The court in Zoucun closed in 1953. For the next thirty years Raoyang residents seeking legal recourse in personal disputes involving divorce, inheritance, and injury could in theory go to the county seat for help, but in practice they turned to village party officials. There was no law. With the enlarged reach of the unaccountable state, villagers were increasingly vulnerable to this arbitrary power.

Back in the Limelight

On July 27, 1953, an armistice was reached in the Korean War, and on October 1, China's National Day, the party promulgated a General Line for the Transition to Socialism. The peasantry had long sacrificed grain, in the fight against Japan, during the civil war, and following the brief honeymoon. Mao concluded that to build the heavy industry needed for a modern war machine to defend the gains of revolution, rural living standards would again have to be held down. This time, moreover, it would not do to patch over the period of sacrifice with market earnings. That would further entrench anti-socialist attitudes in the countryside. Mao termed policy differences manifestations of the struggle between antagonistic classes, the bourgeoisie and the proletariat.[39] Intellectual Liang Shuming was publicly disgraced for challenging Mao and championing peasant welfare. Mao branded enemy and traitor anyone who opposed his policies of investing primarily in heavy and military industries while ending private agriculture. Mao was particularly galled by Liang's claim to best represent peasant interests.[40] Some Chinese subsequently speculated that in the wake of Stalin's death earlier that year "Mao wanted to be the leader of the world communist movement so he attempted to leap to socialism."[41] Since archives remain closed and Mao's colleagues stay silent, it is impossible to be sure precisely why Mao suddenly opted to press Chinese villagers on to the socialist road.

Party powerholders once again began to emphasize that large-scale agricultural units and state control of the market were the keys to socialist transformation in the countryside.[42] To realize high industrial targets, the state further curbed private commerce and sought control of the agricultural surplus. When floods in the northeast reduced 1953 grain procurements far below planned goals, Chen Yun initiated a policy of state control of grain.[43] In November Premier Zhou Enlai signed an edict that required tillers to sell their grain to the state in quantities and at prices imposed by the state and that also set quotas for each household. Above-quota grain could still be legally marketed, but after fulfilling quotas, there usually was little grain left to market.

The imposition of grain-sale quotas was intimately related to the state's interest in promoting the formation of multi-household production units in agriculture. Such units, especially large ones, facilitated state grain control. It was far easier to set tax and sale quotas on units with account books than on 100 million secretive households. Most important, the state extracted its share of the harvest from such institutions *before* grain passed into the hands of households. Compulsory low-price grain purchases freed ruling groups from competition in the marketplace for an assured supply of grain to feed the cities, the armed forces, and a burgeoning state apparatus and to accelerate industrialization. The November edict was a critical step in eliminating private trade in grain. Over the next four years, grain and cotton, the two staples of the rural economy, would be barred completely from free markets. Cotton clothing became scarce. Cities benefited in the short run from low prices, but peasant incomes and the willingness of villagers to work hard suffered.

State control of the grain market created artificial shortages. Warehouses and transport were not ready to replace tens of thousands of grain merchants forced out of business. A mammoth inefficient bureaucracy was swiftly built. Not only was much grain wasted but also the state secured large grain inventories for animal feed and for urban and industrial uses; it built stocks for emergencies, disasters, and the military; and it took still more for export. Given low state-set prices, no price differentials moved grain from surplus to shortage areas. Instead, people in grain-deficit areas grew anxious and demand skyrocketed. In October, rejecting the view that the state price was too low, Chen Yun, architect of grain policy, had successfully insisted that the state requisition grain before it passed into the hands of consumers. Ruling groups blamed speculators for keeping grain from the market and villagers for consuming more and finer grain. Some did hoard grain, hedge against bad times, and hope for higher prices. But the heart of the problem was state policy. To facilitate state control of grain for socialist industrialization, the military, state employees, and urban dwellers, the state asked villagers to prove their patriotism by consuming less grain, especially less fine grain.[44] The honeymoon was ending for those lacking privileged ties to the state and its economic monopolies.

In October and November, in a move consistent with state control of grain and accelerated industrialization, Mao Zedong sought to speed a socialist transition in agriculture. This time Rural Work Department chief Deng Zihui and others favoring gradual rural transformation could not deflect Mao's determination to move more swiftly toward collectivization.[45] In a talk to leading members of the Central Committee's Rural Work Department, Mao urged every county to establish one or two successful co-ops. Each locality was to organize immediately a "medium-sized or big" unit. A unit "of one or two hundred households can be counted big," Mao observed, but an organization of "even three or four hundred households" is possible.[46] "It is not right," Mao went on, as if directly addressing Boss Geng, "to force the dissolution" of units that meet state requirements. That was wrong no matter what the circumstances. "If socialism does not occupy the rural positions," Mao insisted, "capitalism inevitably will."

Suddenly Wugong was again in step with national policy. Mao's remarks had an immediate impact on provincial, prefectural, and county authorities. Wugong was a socialist pacesetter. Boss Geng's gamble had paid off handsomely.

Wugong's large-scale production unit of 287 households no longer suffered as in the drought of 1952. Still, agricultural productivity and per capita distribution remained far below the peak level achieved by the small Geng coop in 1951. Likewise, per capita sideline income was a small fraction of that produced in 1950 (see table A3).[47]

In line with the center's policy, provincial authorities applauded Geng Changsuo's big unit as Hebei's—and perhaps all China's—preeminent embodiment of expanded cooperation. Guo Fang, leader of the work team that had pressured the village to reduce the organization's size, returned to mend fences. Short Lu Guang, a former member of the Guo Fang work team, was sent by the provincial party organization to live in Wugong in midautumn. His job was to advise Boss Geng and to coordinate the technical assistance the state was now openly eager to channel to Geng's big pacesetting unit.

A team of Hebei writers led by Wang Lin settled in to gather material for a book called "The First Flower of Socialism." According to writer Ge Wen, the team was so put off by Collectomaniac Geng Xiufeng, who requested that the chapter on him be titled "The One Who Grew the Flower," that they made "Comrade Geng Xiufeng" the shortest chapter in the volume. We wondered if the writers, trying to promote myths of great leaders, sought to present Boss Geng as the unique leader in a new legend of Wugong.

The writers were surprised by the amount of sandy soil. When the wind blew hard, dust piled inches high in courtyards and people could not open their eyes. It was Geng Changsuo's co-op, not the village, that seemed special. Compared to other rural leadership groups these writers had investigated, the Geng group seemed selfless. Even the leaders of its smaller teams seemed far better led than the norm. Most villages lacked a similar corps of able, unified, honest leaders. The writers thought the small village's processing plants impressive. The primary school, however, was a disaster. Geng did not highly value modern education.

In November the provincial leadership started planning a gala for Wugong to celebrate the tenth anniversary of the original four-household co-op. The celebration would symbolize the state's commitment to large economic organizations as the path to socialism. Boss Geng's Tianjin model factory-worker friend, Wei Zhenhua, led a delegation to Wugong that included a film projection team and an opera. A vindicated Geng announced that Wugong would sell 50,000 catties of grain to the state. This was almost unheard of in poor Hebei and generated headlines. Higher leaders were delighted.[48]

The tenth-anniversary celebration of the co-op was held in Wugong on December 27 and 28, 1953. Provincial party committee and government representatives arrived by car to praise the big unit and Geng Changsuo. Leaders of Hebei co-ops and more than four hundred labor heroes came on foot or by donkey. Congratulatory letters and telegrams hailed Wugong. The provincial authorities presented Geng with a large red-silk banner emblazoned in foot-high yellow characters that read, "The Flower of Socialism."[49]

On the opening day of the celebration, Geng Changsuo was the first speaker on a stage built in the east end, his end, of Wugong. He related the ten-year history of the co-op. Boss Geng alluded to Mao Zedong's talk "Get Organized" as if it had inspired the original co-op. Geng shrewdly asserted that everything he and other co-op members had been doing over the last ten years was following the lead of Chairman Mao. Geng declared that although there were 287 member households at the moment, the unit would soon embrace the entire village.[50]

Geng was especially proud of his group's record in caring for the helpless and destitute. Before any outside official spoke, elderly widow Wang Yin took the stage to tell how her life had been saved. In the past, she said, she could eat only once every two or three days. Now, thanks to the big co-op, she was

eating well. She thanked Geng. Party Secretary Zhang Zhensheng then explained how Wugong was trying to solve the organizational problems posed by so large a unit. The former guerrilla activist Geng Shupu, who had introduced Boss Geng into the party, presented 1954 production targets, recklessly asserting that agricultural yields would rise 50 percent above the good 1953 harvest.

A professional opera troupe arrived to perform Hebei opera, the most popular opera form in southern Hebei. Troupes ordinarily performed in Raoyang only for the lunar New Year and the temple festival in Zoucun. Wugong was now rivaling the fantastic Zoucun fair. It was like a miracle: villagers could attend high-sounding speeches at which they and their leaders were honored, be entertained for hours by an opera troupe performing free in a huge mat enclosure, and eat and drink to their heart's content.

Li Ziguang, head of the Hebei party's Rural Work Department, led off the second day. Li had been among the first to encourage formation of the big unit in 1952 when Collectomaniac Geng Xiufeng approached him with the idea. Provincial Party Secretary Lin Tie, who planned the gala, did not attend, but Zhang Kerang, his chief of the Bureau of Agriculture and Forestry, did. Zhang valued Geng Changsuo's willingness to speak his mind. With the state controlling more resources, local leaders tended to say what they thought higher-ups wanted to hear. Truth was becoming such a scarce commodity that Zhang seized opportunities to visit Geng and chat with a man he considered to be a straight talker.

The highlight of the second day of the Wugong gala was the stunning announcement that Wugong had been designated the site of the first state-run tractor station in China to be located outside a state farm. Zhang Kerang's organization had been searching for a spot to establish Hebei's first such tractor station. Most of the co-ops Zhang originally visited in 1947 had fallen apart, but Geng's persevered. Wugong, with its 287-household unit, seemed the best bet to make good use of a tractor station.

China's small fleet of imported tractors had been concentrated in a few state-run farms. The Wugong anniversary celebration became an occasion to demonstrate what tractors could do for villagers who pooled land and labor. Zhang Kerang sent Shi Xisheng, a tractor technician at the state farm in Handan in the southern tip of Hebei, to head the Wugong Tractor Station. Shi had studied in Beijing with instructors from the Soviet Union, Hungary, and Czechoslovakia for six months in 1951. His daughter, Shi Guiying, entertained the happy throng at the celebration with her lovely songs.

Wugong was a village without electricity or running water. No paved road, railroad, or canal connected it to centers of political and economic power. Yet peripheral Wugong had become a center and symbol of modern socialist agriculture, the union of large-scale farm units and tractors. On December 28, 1953, Wugong villagers and labor models from elsewhere saw their first tractor. More than ten thousand people, the largest group ever assembled in Wugong, came from thirty surrounding villages.[51] Some thirty tractors from 25 to 54 horsepower, manufactured in Czechoslovakia, Poland, and the Soviet Union, rolled into the village. Villagers gasped as the first machine ripped up the soil at an unimaginable speed. The future had arrived. A villager asked Partly Ripe Li to compare the Soviet tractor to his beloved mule, Big Black. "The tractor is good," Li conceded, "but it doesn't produce any shit."[52]

After the dramatic demonstration of machine power, the guests viewed an exhibition on the ten-year history of the co-op and a photo display on Soviet collective farms, and then toured sideline industries. Model peasants from other parts of Hebei hailed the Geng Changsuo co-op as the elder brother of cooperative farming in China.[53]

Representatives from Dingxian prefecture, where reporters had recently detailed the problems that beset large agricultural units, were not among those who congratulated Boss Geng. Political scandal had rocked the prefecture when investigators at both the national and the provincial level found First Secretary Wang Chunhai and Second Secretary Lin Dayu guilty of abuse of power. Wang's father-in-law, a once-wealthy landlord from Anping county, had been the victim of an intense "struggle meeting" during land reform. It was claimed that Wang sent Lin Dayu to Anping to arrest and jail the person responsible. Lin Tie, who was believed to have safeguarded his own father-in-law during land reform, received instructions from Beijing to discipline the offenders. Instead, it was rumored, Lin Tie protected Wang. But Lin was overruled. In late 1953 the Investigation Committee at the party center, after many delays, removed Wang Chunhai and Lin Dayu from office. Wang was sent to raise chickens on a state farm, and Lin became a high-school teacher in Handan. Wang's power network was so entrenched that to break it up the state center abolished Dingxian prefecture. In April 1954 the southern portion of the prefecture, which included Wugong, was reassigned to Shijiazhuang prefecture and the northern portion was incorporated into Baoding prefecture.

In the first week of January 1954 Wugong was featured in the national press. The glowing accounts falsely presented Boss Geng as a charter member of the original 1943 co-op.[54] Where earlier reportage carried the names of four founders, the 1954 pieces highlighted only Geng Changsuo and allowed others to slip into obscurity. The contributions of Collectomaniac Geng Xiufeng, who had the ideas and connections, likewise disappeared. The focus was on the great leader.

Boss Geng welcomed back all 108 households that had dropped out of the experiment. Six that had never belonged also requested entry, bringing member households to 401.[55] Only 23 households remained outside, including those with bad class labels and others working under "the supervision of the masses" as well as a few poor-peasant households that refused to join. Geng's prestige had never been higher.

The state's imposition of monopoly control of grain and pressures to organize large-scale collectives constituted a big gamble with the lives and aspirations of hundreds of millions of Chinese. In 1953 Geng Changsuo won his political gamble by betting on Mao, big units, and opposition to the market. But the larger issue remained. Where would Mao's big gamble take China's villagers?

In the aftermath of the anniversary celebration, Boss Geng moved to associate himself and the big Wugong unit with the great leader, Mao Zedong. On January 4, 1954, the *People's Daily* carried a letter to Mao signed by Geng Changsuo.[56] The letter began: "We have been following the 'Get Organized' path set down by you and the Party for ten years now." Geng credited Mao and the party for all the achievements of the co-op. "We know that everything we have achieved is the result of leadership provided by you, the Party and the people's government." Having visited the Soviet Union, the letter said, Geng was in an excellent position to introduce the Soviet way in the village and the province.

7 ON THE SOVIET SOCIALIST ROAD

China's state leaders treated pacesetters as one of Karl Marx's locomotives of history that would pull the train forward. While the locomotive would be the first to arrive at history's stations of progress, its efforts assured that the rest of the train would also advance to happier destinations. Hebei provincial leaders and their subordinates had singled out Wugong as one of the engines on the socialist road. Patrons of large units (*da she*) competed for Mao's blessing, urging their units to race ahead on the Soviet socialist road. In late 1953, Hebei Party Secretary Lin Tie and the head of the provincial Bureau of Agriculture and Forestry, Zhang Kerang, appointed the diminutive Lu Guang to fire up the Wugong locomotive.

Lu, who worked in the provincial party's Internal Affairs Department, had been a member of the group that slashed Geng's big co-op. He was a high-school student in Beijing when Japan marched into North China. With other patriotic youth, Lu ran to the countryside and joined the Eighth Route Army, linking into the network of Peng Zhen, a leading Communist in the North China resistance. Adviser Lu was the key link between Wugong and high levels of power. Lu's eight-member work team went to Wugong in late autumn, before the tenth-anniversary gala. He could obtain the resources to demonstrate what could be accomplished by combining large-scale organization with mechanization, scientific water management, and other modern inputs. With the state commanding the economy's scarce resources, the choice was to go where rulers led or be left behind. By fall 1954 all of Wugong's 426 households joined the big co-op, except for 20 that ranged from the banned enemies of the people to two poor-peasant households that declined to join.

The Big Family?

"Those who joined the small co-op first became one family," Boss Geng told orphan Li Xiuying, "and those who now enter the big unit will also be one family."[1] But is a large agricultural labor organization "family"? Would a unit embracing more than four hundred households alienate tillers and undermine incentives? Adviser Lu Guang addressed these questions in revealing classified handwritten reports submitted to higher authorities in late 1953 and early 1954.

Local leaders were overwhelmed by Lu Guang's quickness and intelligence. The facts were always at his fingertips. People marveled at his capacity, without notes, to give relevant, accurate, well-organized, and fact-filled talks. They also enjoyed poking fun at his diminutive stature. Six-foot-tall Zhang Kerang mocked Adviser Lu, whose legs did not reach the floor when he sat on a couch. When Lu became excited, he leaped to his feet. Zhang then ribbed Lu by standing and saying, "I want to see how high you can jump." Lu would jump, but he never reached Zhang's height.

Adviser Lu reported that the thirteen production teams of late 1953 would be consolidated into eleven in early 1954 and ten the following year. Each administered its own land, draft animals, and equipment on the basis of unified guidelines. After receiving roughly equal shares of land and labor, each team was responsible for building up income and accumulation. Member incomes were based on a complex calculation combining the income in the large unit, the performance of each team, and the contribution of individual members.[2] Lu Guang found to his sorrow, however, that no matter how leaders tinkered with income-distribution schemes that sought to reward the efforts of the individual, the small work team, and the large administrative organization, the link between individual effort and individual pay was weak. The 1953 concern that a unit could be too big had a basis in fact.

In 1954 teams consisted of about thirty to forty households with an average of forty to fifty-five workers. Each team had a leader and deputy leaders in charge of sidelines, welfare, and women, in addition to an accountant and a work-point recorder. Specialized subgroups took charge of such tasks as cotton production and cart driving.[3] Power and initiative were concentrated in leaders.

Lu Guang discovered that squabbles and organizational nightmares beset the big unit from its inception. Both before and after the tenth-anniversary gala, teams with difficulties complained that they had been allocated inferior land or weaker labor. The leadership of some teams proved ineffective. Those who fell behind lost the drive to produce and became passive, waiting for their leaders or the government to find solutions. For Lu the central problem was how to elicit and sustain the initiative and commitment of members of a large unfamiliar organization.

Earlier co-ops remained intact as subunits of the big unit. Team one was based on the original Geng co-op; it included fifteen activists and party members as well as three accountants. But teams new to large organized farming had no one to handle accounts and few experienced leaders. Some reorganization was attempted to even things out. But taking from one to help another—or, more precisely, from Geng and Qiao to help Li—left members of such productive units as team one discouraged and bitter. To make a go of cooperation, they had, for ten years, leveled, irrigated, and fertilized soil. Suddenly the fruit of that labor was lost. Many of their draft animals and much of their equipment were allocated to poorer teams. Incomes of the former Geng co-op members would fall far below what they earned after the 1951 bumper harvest once income was shared with all villagers. Many feared that, should they get ahead, the fruits of their labor could be seized. Still, Boss Geng promised future gains for all.

The income share based on labor was calculated in the form of work points. As before, a man who put in a full day's work received ten work points; women and old people normally received six to eight points. This system, which provided little incentive for outstanding workers, had produced tensions even in the original Geng co-op, where bonds were strong and the group small enough to settle problems of labor intensity and remuneration. The big organization was far less united. Lu secretly reported to higher authorities that some members said, "If you are a go-getter, you get no more; if you are lazy you get no less." Strong skilled workers felt cheated when even idlers and incompetents received the same ten points. A remuneration system that appeared to place too many free riders on the backs of the industrious failed to motivate the majority. Adviser Lu's internal report estimated that 20–30 percent of labor was wasted.[4] The relationship between individual labor and income in the big unit was too remote to tap labor enthusiasm. Fine tuning the payment formula to increase reward to labor from 40 to 50 percent of net income did not resolve the problem.

True, a few people went to work early and returned home late, but most arrived later and later. "At first, team leaders rang bells to call them," Adviser Lu lamented, "but after awhile this had no effect." One afternoon, Lu disclosed for the eyes of officials only, the leader of team seven rang the bell for over an hour. When nineteen people still did not show up, he had to go door to door. Villagers laughed: "First time beat the gong, second time shout. Only on the third try do people turn out." No one began work in the fields until the leader said, "let's go." Some people stopped to rest each time they reached the end of a row. Members waited for leaders to solve problems for them. Initiative was drained. Lu Guang discovered that a big unit fostered economic disincentives and inefficiencies. Creating stimuli to hard work in a large agricultural unit seemed almost impossible.

Quotas and Incentives

To deal with the loss of incentive, in early 1954 Lu Guang's work team devised a system of income distribution based on output quotas. The scheme was promoted by Deng Zihui, head of the party's Rural Work Department. The press headlined the plan, and local leaders were urged to study it. Pauper's co-op leader Wang Guofan, who had attended Wugong's tenth-anniversary celebration and whose co-op just south of the Great Wall was becoming a favorite of Mao's, adopted it. The quota system became the crux of a continuing controversy over how to abolish the household economy and the market while maintaining experientially fair remuneration.

The quota system established standards for hundreds of tasks, from plowing a mu of land to planting cotton and harvesting wheat. It was piecework, which would reward superior workers. Having rejected the market as a mechanism to decide income, a new bureaucracy had to set quotas for all major tasks, with adjustments for quality. Working out so many standards equitably was a formidable job. Bookkeeping was a nightmare. Each team set quotas for yet smaller work groups and even for individuals, specifying the quantity, quality, and speed for completion of specific tasks and fixing a work-point value to their accomplishment.[5] The substitute for the simple, leveling work-point system, which was a disincentive to hard work, was a quota system requiring close bureaucratic monitoring and detailed record keeping.[6] Individuals as well as work-team leaders reported to the accountant each night. But unpaid and barely literate accountants, who had worked all day in the field, were often too busy or too inexperienced to record everything precisely. Inevitably mistakes and squabbles left people feeling undervalued or alienated. This was the case even when accountants were scrupulously honest, and when lineage and other intravillage conflicts were minimal. The potential for conflict was vast.

Teams one and two in the east village, including the nucleus of the original Geng co-op, and team eleven in the west village at first rejected the quota system as too divisive. It did not feel like cooperation. These three teams hewed to the simpler and more egalitarian work-point arrangement of the original Geng co-op.[7] The price of wooing the vast majority to the big unit was impersonal administration that discouraged the small minority whose special history made them capable of effective voluntary cooperation.

Another problem of incentives and morale centered on leaders. Alienated villagers, Lu's reports revealed, resented crediting leaders with income for time at meetings, which was considered talking, not working. Yet a team leader complained bitterly to Lu Guang that he "worked days and nights for a year, but got less than the average field worker. It's unfair. If I just worked in the fields I would earn much more." In a classified report to the provincial

Rural Work Department, Collectomaniac Geng Xiufeng suggested that team leaders work in the fields a minimum of fifteen days a month and receive remuneration equal to that of the best-paid worker. But that would increase the need for more administrators. The problem of pay for administrators festered.[8]

Adviser Lu bared prickly problems concerning the small groups within the ten teams. Everyone sought to work with the strongest to ensure that quotas would be fulfilled or surpassed. The old, the weak, and the lazy tended to be thrust aside. To make impersonal administration fair required abandoning the cultural basis of authentic cooperation—neighbors and relatives. Adviser Lu's team established two principles. First, impersonal work groups would comprise both old and young, both strong and weak workers, and would not be organized on the previously successful basis of such affective bonds as friendship and family. Second, women and men would work in separate groups. Leaders set the composition of work groups. The separation of men and women reified traditional norms. Still, some tasks, such as weeding, remained open to women and men.

In 1954 the national co-op drive highlighted the mobilization of rural women.[9] At that time one-third of the 558 laborers in the Wugong work force were women, nearly all of whom worked in the fields.[10] The state takeover of the grain market and the fixing of purchasing prices well below market prices brought down the value of farm labor. Devalued people did devalued work. In Wugong, as would soon be the case in much of rural China, younger and older women were divided into two separate groups.

Men sought better-paying urban jobs. In 1954 a few villagers found work in construction, others as teamsters, peddlers, and factory workers. But with the government constricting markets, private sidelines, and handicraft work, with factory jobs increasingly reserved for urban youth, and with more than three million men demobilized from the army after the Korean War, off-farm jobs were scarce and most were allocated by administrative command based on political connections.

In winter 1953–54 Wugong created six rectangular fields ranging in size from 108 to 717 mu.[11] These replaced the patchwork quilt of more than 1,300 tiny household plots. The fields took on some of the look of a Soviet collective, although ancestral graves continued to dot many fields. County officials helped Wugong exchange 600 mu of land interspersed with neighboring villages, which facilitated tractor cultivation and villagewide well drilling. Through elimination of old pathways, the big unit also added 150 mu of cultivated land. With field reconstruction, the very identity of household plots blurred. Many villagers watched nervously.

Each team grew grain, vegetables, and other crops in approximately the same proportions according to plans formulated by the Lu Guang team. To compensate for leveling disincentives inherent in the work-point and contract systems, teams competed for bonuses awarded for exceeding quotas. Adviser Lu noted that the lazy and the weak were not enthusiastic about the quota and bonus system. Some feared it would "sow divisions" by widening income differentials between strong and weak workers. But the disincentives and inefficiencies of the big farm unit convinced Lu that only quotas and bonuses could spur most villagers to work hard and well; political exhortation and socialist education could not. The locomotives on the socialist road were searching for ways to make big units productive.

Whatever the problems, no one dared openly to challenge the superiority of big units and, ultimately Stalin-style collectives. Rulers considered themselves socialists. Central to their notion of socialism was the superiority of large-scale collective agriculture over household cultivation and democratic small-scale cooperatives. The Soviet Union had supposedly proven the truth of this proposition. Geng Changsuo claimed to have seen the proof with his own eyes. Peasants who did not comprehend that were backward. The only proper issue was *how* to achieve collectivization. The large farming units formed in Wugong and elsewhere were halfway houses on the road to collectivization.

Lu Guang hailed the quota system. Yesterday's slackers were starting work earlier and leaving later. Extraordinary Stakhanovite efforts were encouraged as in the Soviet Union. When the leader of team eight invited women who were harvesting grain to break for lunch, Lu reported, they insisted instead on working until the job was finished. Before, members of the fifth and seventh teams were content to wait their turn to sharpen their scythes; now people brought their own sharpening stones. Moreover, members assisted each other so that a team's task was done in time. People were clamoring, Lu wrote, for tasks with quotas in order to increase their incomes.

The center took note of the achievements reported by Lu Guang. In summer 1954 the *People's Daily* described how "Communist Party Member Xu Shukuan," the wife of Boss Geng and Wugong's deputy women's leader, got women to carry food with them to the fields. It made no sense, the newspaper said, to return home to cook lunch or to take a lengthy midday break, because time lost was income lost.[12] Labor was ever more extensively mobilized.

To increase incentives, Wugong added an element to the distribution system resembling one proposed by Collectomaniac Geng Xiufeng during his 1953 visit.[13] Xiufeng always had ideas to make bigger units of labor succeed. Within each team the distribution ratio of 50 percent for land and 50 percent for labor would apply only to the first 200 catties per mu of the harvest. If yields were higher, more was distributed as a return on labor. Units that raised yields to 200–300 catties per mu distributed 70 percent of the increment above 200 for labor and only 30 percent for land. Above 300 catties, the entire increment was distributed based on labor to encourage hard work and investment in land. This innovation put into practice the principle that in socialism the entire reward must eventually go to labor.[14]

The county government praised and popularized the Wugong quota system. By January 1954 280 cooperatives in Raoyang's fourth district had adopted labor quotas.[15] Co-ops elsewhere implemented similar systems. But unlike pioneering Wugong, latecomers would not, indeed could not, win access to scarce state inputs, top administrators, and glowing publicity. Others had neither Wugong's long history of unity nor its network of personal ties to higher levels of the system. Wugong's leading role in the drama of taking the Soviet road had an inimitable aspect.

Water . . . Life

In late 1953, as China framed its first Soviet-style five-year plan, Wugong enshrined its ambitions in its own five-year plan to double grain yields to 600 catties per mu. The keys were water, state support, and toil. In 1954 Boss Geng planned to irrigate the fields with seventy-eight diesel-driven wells. With fanfare, the province offered to provide the engines.[16] Wugong was among the first to utilize the newly available technology, beginning in 1955 with two engines. But as with many heralded projects, this one was quietly shelved. Not until 1969 did Wugong acquire its next diesel engine. Provincial specialists trained nine local youths in well drilling. Wugong enjoyed financial and technical support that other villages could only dream of.

In 1954 village leaders organized a sixty-one-member well-drilling team to expand irrigation. After testing the soil with bamboo poles, villagers erected a fifteen-foot-high frame crowned with a heavy wooden structure that turned like a small ferris wheel. Two men walked the wheel to provide the force necessary to slam a wooden drill into the earth. Twelve men in three around-the-clock shifts, using kerosene lamps at night, could drill a well in forty days. Turning the wheel was exhausting work; cloth shoes wore out in a few weeks, so wives of drillers sewed new shoes. Women were barred from well-drilling teams. It was believed that a woman merely approaching such a site could bring disaster.

Previously Wugong residents had had to pay outsiders approximately 10,000 catties of millet to dig a well. Now the provincial and prefectural government sent in technicians and provided Wugong with lumber and other scarce resources for the drilling rigs. In 1953 the provincial Bureau of Agriculture and Forestry dispatched two men from Tianjin to demonstrate techniques of drilling in sandy soil and to help sink Wugong's first modern well. Villagers, slighting the contribution of the outsiders, said the well was not of much use. They focused on what was won by their own grueling toil with hand tools, exposed to wind and cold, sun and mud.

The village team drilled seventeen wells in 1953 and drafted a three-year program for eighty-eight wells and 117 irrigation channels. The deepest wells in the south village penetrated 115 meters whereas those in the east went down 170 meters. Deep wells cost thousands of labor days and some 4,000 yuan partially subsidized by provincial authorities.[17] Neighboring villagers, who were not given the state-commanded technology and resources required for deep drilling, muttered that Wugong's wells were stealing their underground water. Wugong and its friends in the orbit of power seemed threatening to those not favored. Building socialism was also building a wall between the favored of the state and all others.

When some wells came up dry, boss Geng insisted on digging deeper to solve "once and for all" the problem of water. Protesting that the labor demands and costs were excessive, some villagers called for a moratorium on wells. But the decision was no longer theirs to make. Geng insisted that the drive continue. It did.

The costly drilling was conducted in the absence of any overall soil and water survey and of any cost accounting. By 1954 Wugong had ninety-nine wells and 1,050 mu of irrigated land, only 300 mu more than before drilling began. In spite of enormous efforts, the irrigated area would increase only 450 mu during the next decade. The exhausting toil produced results far short of goals and in the mid-1950s left three-fourths of village land without irrigation.

Li Guo, Hou Kun, and Zhang Wentong, whose participation in Wugong well drilling dated from the early 1950s, believed that village prosperity depended on their ability to work through the nights and withstand cold winters. They also enjoyed visiting the nearby market village of Xiaodi and distant Gucheng county, south of Wugong on the Hebei-Shandong border, to teach Wugong's methods. It was exciting to see the world. Most of those who had once traveled in search of work and markets were restricted to organized agricultural labor in the village. The broad ties of villagers to local markets and more distant cities were being cut. Legal travel started to be limited to those authorized by the state.

Tractors and Technicians

Tractor cultivation was intended as a major step on the Soviet socialist road. Tractors had opened and cultivated the virgin lands of state farms in northeast China since the late 1940s.[18] Imported tractors were introduced as the technology that had sped Soviet development and would bring prosperity to China's countryside. In 1954 Boss Geng's nineteen-year-old daughter, Sujuan, was among a dozen Wugong youth trained to drive and maintain the machines. Xu Wendong, age twenty-three, went to school in Shijiazhuang for two years to learn to repair tractors and other machines.[19] Xu loved machines and hated politics. He tried to keep out of political movements. Wugong soon boasted three more young technicians.

In 1954 the authorities sent nineteen skilled workers to look after the Wugong tractor station's three Russian tractors, including a 75-horsepower model, and to train drivers and technicians. Station personnel included agronomists graduated from Beijing Agricultural University and Hebei Agricultural University. Such skilled individuals were a scarce resource. In the station's first year of operation 180 trainees from all over North China, including forty women and fifty Raoyang youth, were sent to Wugong before being dispatched elsewhere. The phenomenon of women tractor drivers was short-lived. Tractor drivers often had to work around the clock and to travel to distant places. In China's countryside women could do neither without incurring suspicions of immoral behavior. Most of the trained women drivers quickly found themselves back at collective field work. The station, with advisers from the Sino-Czech State Farm in Cangzhou, was organized precisely like a Soviet tractor station. In 1953 all but 58 of China's 2,788 precious tractors were on state farms, plowing two-tenths of 1 percent of China's land.[20] The Wugong station, designated the First National Hebei Provincial Mechanized Tractor Station, officially served all Raoyang. But in 1954 only Wugong with its large leveled fields could utilize tractors.

The tractor station director was Shi Xishen, a former district leader in the anti-Japanese resistance from the southern tip of Hebei. With their six children, the Shis moved into the east village, where oldest daughter Guiying befriended two of Boss Geng's daughters, tractor driver Sujuan and her younger sister Huijuan. Committed to the Soviet socialist road, Shi Xishen named his newborn son Xuesu, or "emulate the Soviet Union."

In a letter to the workers of the nation published in the *Hebei Daily* in January 1954, Boss Geng quoted, using the clichés of the day, octogenarian Li Xuchen, who had left his sickbed to see Wugong's first tractors: "I don't know how we could endure without our elder brothers the workers!" Geng reiterated that "the prosperity of Soviet collective farms was a product of Soviet industrialization which enabled the peasants to carry out the mechanization of agriculture." If China, too, directed the rural surplus to the priority development of heavy industry as outlined in the first five-year plan, *then* the countryside would benefit because all villages would get tractors.

Tractor cultivation in Wugong as pictured in the media hid the family grave mounds that still dotted the fields. The pictures were meant to spur other villages toward large-scale organization as a way to take advantage of the new technology. But China lacked tractors, trained service personnel, and other modern inputs, let alone the foreign exchange to import the machines in quantity or the fuel to run them. Wugong was the unique beneficiary of a gift, a model of what few could attain.

In 1954 the Wugong leadership planned to use tractors to plow 2,159 mu, or 51 percent of cultivated land, a target it missed by 20 percent.[21] Tractor cultivation, its proponents held, by plowing deeper and faster, would win higher yields and save labor that could then be put to productive purposes. Tractors would also obviate the need to raise draft animals. And tractors, not needing to sleep at night, could work around the clock—if spare parts, fuel, and skilled mechanics were available. Wugong leaders estimated that tractors would save 5,328 labor days.[22] But in restricting villagers to agricultural work within their villages, the socialist state was blocking productive outlets in sidelines and markets for that freed labor.

That same year two other Hebei counties, Ninghe, on the outskirts of Tianjin, and Jinxian, home of the famed Zhoujinzhuang co-op east of Shijiazhuang, acquired tractor stations. The total tractor-plowed land in the province was 5,200 mu, with Wugong accounting for more than 40 percent.[23] Provincial planners dreamed that, despite its poor soil and unreliable water, central Hebei could become China's Ukraine, the North China grain bowl. Technical resources would be concentrated here and in the grain belt in the northeast where China's largest state farms were located.

Tractor plowing was not free. Villagers paid the tractor station 1.2 yuan per mu in 1955.[24] A state subsidy made possible a low price for tractors, fuel, and personnel. Tractor stations reached fourteen counties. The goal was to reach one hundred of the more than two thousand counties in a few years with tractors imported from the Soviet Union or Eastern Europe. In 1955 the Wugong station expanded its outreach to twenty newly formed or enlarged farming units in neighboring Raoyang villages. In that year seventy-two drivers with thirty-five tractors, including one 80-horsepower Stalin tractor and others imported from East Germany, Poland, and Czechoslovakia as well as the Soviet Union, cultivated 99,997 mu in Raoyang.[25] Land consolidation and mechanization in Raoyang's fourth district grew in tandem. By summer, forty-three of its forty-five villages reported single-village units. The subsidized tractor station was an incentive to form big agricultural units.

Since costly agricultural mechanization increased indebtedness to the Soviet Union, national leaders debated the viability of relying on imported oil and imported tractors. In following the Soviet socialist road, China concentrated scarce resources and foreign currency first on building a defense-related heavy industrial base centered on the steel industry. In 1954–55 a leadership majority, wanting to avoid the slaughter of animals that had accompanied Soviet collectivization, opted for gradual change. Such large mechanized units as Wugong would show the countryside its future and provide a testing ground for resolving the problems of large-scale collective mechanized agriculture. Most leaders agreed, however, that the mechanization that purportedly made collectives profitable and attractive could not be produced overnight. Mao, however, was impatient for results.

Deng Zihui, head of the Central Committee's Rural Work Department, pressed the gradualist approach favored by Lin Tie and the North China Bureau. China, Deng declared in 1954, could not soon mechanize and collectivize; it could not quickly follow the Soviet path. "We can neither manufacture tractors in large quantities ourselves nor produce sufficient petrol." Collectivization would have to wait until China could produce sufficient steel, tractors, and diesel fuel. Deng's concern was not so much delaying mechanization as continuing voluntary participation. Why pressure or terrorize recalcitrant and fearful peasants? One student told us that a few Raoyang teachers had told favored students of the millions who died in Stalin's forced collectivization.

For Deng two basic conditions had to be fulfilled if villagers were to welcome Soviet-style collectives. First, smaller co-ops that continued to pay dividends on land must reach sufficient productivity levels to provide jobs and income for every member, including adequate welfare funds for the old and disabled. Second, people must be convinced that collectives would serve their economic interests.[26]

Whereas tractors symbolized the Soviet way, more important for development in Wugong was a seventeen-member technical team led by Zhang Zuchun of the Hebei Provincial Agriculture and Forestry Research Institute that trained technicians for three years beginning in winter 1953–54. In December this team inaugurated a Wugong Agricultural Experiment Station with a 57-mu experimental field. The station eventually employed fourteen full-time technicians to work on field management, cotton productivity, soil improvement, and pest control and to train technical personnel. These technicians, with limited modern knowledge and no college-level education, planted new seed strains and tested improved fertilizers. They also introduced such pesticides as DDT and 666, applying them without regard to ecology or safety. Bugs Zhou Yuanjiu became the leading Wugong technician at the station.

Zhou, who had returned AWOL from military service in Shanxi five years earlier, was one of sixteen Wugong youth to work and study with the technicians. The jovial buck-toothed Zhou's passion for field investigation was kindled at this time. Villagers kidded him, giving Zhou the nickname "The One Whom Bugs Fear" for his work in insect control. Bugs Zhou even hung pictures of bugs over the kang. Pests and their eradication became his major topic of conversation; some complained, his only topic of conversation.

The crush of almost two hundred outside specialists and their families created a housing shortage. Many visitors lived near the tractor station on the north side of the village, some rented rooms in households, and still others moved into a simple hostel built in a walled compound near the village center. Rentals and construction jobs increased local incomes. It was yet another channel through which a model village reaped benefits.

In 1954 Wugong planned to collect 14.7 million catties of night soil from public toilets and from individual households to distribute as fertilizer. The target was 3,000 catties of fertilizer for each mu, up from 2,000 in 1953. The effort relied on expanding pig raising, with old people from each team in charge.[27]

Officials also tried to clear away cultural barriers blocking modernization. Wugong was located close to an epicenter of locust cults. Popular belief held that when swarms of locusts descended, the only recourse was to burn incense, prepare sacrifices, and ketou to heaven. To touch the insects invited pestilence. Killing locusts ensured infestation by larger numbers of locusts.[28] In the 1950s state-provided pesticides made possible an effective attack on insects.

The government was undermining more than the economically irrational aspects of culture. The attack on tradition, which destroyed temples in the late 1940s, continued in the 1950s with the weakening of markets, which eroded popular culture. The Yanggezhuang Drama Troupe, which had long traveled all over the region, stopped touring because it lacked official backing. The state was pressing a war on tradition. The indigenous culture that survived was enormously popular. In 1954, at the annual Zoucun temple fair, a Tianjin theatrical troupe performed Hebei opera to audiences of fifty thousand. There was comic dialogue, lantern slideshows, drum playing, stilt walking, and lion dancing. These and other aspects of traditional culture helped bind and delight the community.

But a government-initiated campaign splintered society. In summer 1954, Mao had vilified literary critic Hu Feng as a counterrevolutionary traitor for requesting a free press to check state corruption and prevent popular cynicism. Thereafter, educational units were instructed to ferret out people with hidden ties to counterrevolutionary traitors. In Baoding prefecture, a leader in the campaign in Hebei, thousands of individuals were immediately seized, mainly ordinary people who had worked for previous governments. They were locked away in burgeoning political prisons.

"Learn from Geng Changsuo"

In December 1953 the provincial government had convened a conference in Baoding on co-op formation, the theme being uniting poor and middle peasants. This approach had served the small Wugong co-op well. One slogan of the drive was "Learn from Geng Changsuo." The Raoyang fourth district secretary, Zhang Yugang, reported that more than 6,100 households, 84 percent of the district population, had joined 355 co-ops. The idea was that "Old co-ops help new ones, new leaders learn from old timers." Others followed Wugong in forming larger units coinciding with the village.

Qiao Wanxiang, bookkeeper of the original co-op, and Geng Lianmin, the accountant in the big unit, visited other villages to help set up accounting systems. Accountant Geng had the same paternal grandfather as Boss Geng Changsuo. Their lineage grave mounds stood side by side. Whatever the national policy, Boss Geng was making Wugong a loyal family political machine with close political ties to patrons and such allies as Zhang Yugang in Xiaodi, the county party committee in Raoyang, and Zhang Kerang and Lin Tie in Baoding.

By April 1954 the fourth district in Raoyang county became China's first to proclaim 100 percent cooperativization.[29] In June Hebei Party Secretary Lin Tie reported that more than 60 percent of Hebei's rural population had organized mutual-aid teams, although most were just getting started. In all Hebei, only 11,400 households belonged to co-ops, with fully one-half in Raoyang's fourth district.

As in Wugong, larger units that pooled land, animals, and even cash had to devise schemes to keep tillers working hard. The problem was that state pressures for more socialism in 1954 and 1955 seriously reduced returns on land, animals, and tools invested in the semicollective. Given the usual angry divisions between labor-poor and other households, quarrels and violent fights exploded. Many Chinese villagers, whatever their class label, experienced these large units, known as da she, as more exploitative than fair. Villagers feared being taken. Yet if one worked intensely while others shirked, and if all were paid similarly from a common pool, then to work hard was to play the fool.

Farm work demanded seasonal timeliness. The fields had to be sown at a precise moment to maximize output. But in the big units, plowing was hastily done and in poor large units, people, not animals, pulled the plows. When the land was not their own and they were paid only for the completed task, villagers rushed through the work, resulting in haphazard plowing and seeding. In these bigger units, the da she beginning to take the traditional Soviet socialist road, there was no easy way to link actual economic results with pay differentials.

Once enrolled in big units, many Raoyang villagers experienced the loss of household control as personal loss. Members had to obey commands as to what to plant, when, where, and how, and with whom to work. They had to deliver the entire crop to the state's local agents to satisfy quotas, taxes, welfare, and investment requirements before receiving a share of what remained. It was difficult not to feel undervalued.

The State Takes Control

As the campaign to increase size gathered momentum in the years 1953–55, the state tightened its grip over the rural economy, positing that large units of pooled labor and shared distribution would be more productive because such units would eliminate the supposed exploitation, competition, and irrationality of small household farming and the market. Socialism, that is, large-scale production and state investment of the surplus, had to be more productive than capitalism. Hence, Mao and his allies assumed that even without tractors and other modern inputs, big socialist units were both economically and morally superior. Ever larger units and state control would substitute for smaller units and markets. A December 16, 1953, Central Committee directive called for wiping out "merchants, grain hoarders, speculators and usurers." It specified that "agricultural producers cooperatives are not permitted to engage in trade."[30] The state would act rationally with the rural surplus as the market could not. The market, increasingly equated with chaos, was suppressed.

Wugong, with its "victory" over peanut entrepreneur Li Hengxin, was presented as proof that the direct sale to the state of grain, peanuts, cotton, and other produce led to enrichment. Actually, as early as the late 1940s, Wugong villagers lost from the crushing of sidelines and the shriveling of markets. But the loss was made barely acceptable because of the exceptional leadership of Boss Geng and his special access to state resources. Elsewhere villagers would not be so fortunate. They lost from market closure. In answer to the state's propaganda against the market as chaos, they quipped, "Open, it's chaos; closed, it's death."

In December 1953 Adviser Lu Guang's team worked out the details for the state's newly promulgated regulations for the Unified Purchase and Supply of Grain, capping Wugong's per capita grain distribution at 360 catties, bare subsistence. The income due to each household was paid in grain and other agricultural commodities supplemented by a small cash payment. All grain produced above 360 catties per person was sold to the state. Villagers feared that too little would be left for them. This was deadly serious since tight state control over grain meant that hungry people could no longer count on buying in the open market in case of shortage. Co-op leaders assured nervous villagers that if there were a dearth, welfare funds would be allocated to raise the income of poorer households to subsistence. There would be enough even for people with large appetites, Geng promised.

The state called on other villages to emulate Wugong, to be patriotic and sell the state large quantities of grain and other crops. Just before the festive tenth-anniversary celebration, Wugong had sold the state 50,000 catties of grain, most of it coming from the big co-op. In return the state guaranteed the big co-op scarce insecticide and fertilizer. But by winter 1953–54 not enough grain remained to feed hungry villagers. Many households had exhausted their grain. By spring the hungry outcry led the state to sell 50,000 catties back to Wugong, an embarrassment not reported in the press, which told only of Wugong's high sales. The press was a cheerleader for state policies, not a truthful recorder of socialism's contradictions.

In some regions prodded to act as express locomotives on the socialist road, the state monopoly on grain sales, combined with attempts to prod people into large-scale socialist farming units, resulted in malnutrition and discontent. In 1954 Zhejiang provincial officials pressured peasants to form big units, suddenly increasing their number from 3,298 to 53,114.[31] The economic dislocation caused by the attempt to cut "tails of capitalism" in fifteen Zhejiang counties forced villagers to rip bark off trees and dig up roots in search of food to stave off famine. Some starved to death.[32]

Villagers could no longer readily cross administrative boundaries seeking a better price for grain and cotton. Instead all cotton had to be turned over to the state at the fixed low price for ginning. As in the centralization of peanut processing, this cost villagers the residue previously used in fertilizer. The same fertilizer loss occurred as the state took over and centralized in cities the processing of peanuts. Villagers were left more dependent on state largesse for fertilizer, bereft even of the materials needed to make cooking oil.

With prosperity ever more dependent on state favor, Boss Geng worked at cultivating his ties to the powerful. He led a return delegation of agricultural labor models to Tianjin, where he met his friend Wei Zhenhua, the model laborer in a Tianjin cotton-oil factory, who was said to know the premier. Villagers who could not tap access to state-commanded scarce resources were legally reduced to selling their grain to the government at a fixed low price. They could no longer even choose to sell fine grains for a high price and live on lower-priced coarse grains. Villagers dared not trust survival to a distant entity now in control of grain that promised to provide surplus grain to all in need. A covert grain market flourished. In Raoyang a large and stable black market could be found in almost every village. In 1954 wheat cost ten cents a catty, millet and sorghum eight cents. The state's purchasing price for wheat was eight cents a catty.[33] When the state took too much grain and created an artificial shortage, most villagers got through the bad times by purchasing grain at black markets called secret markets.

Li Peishen was one of thousands in Raoyang who frequented such markets. Born in Wugong in 1913, Li married at age fifteen, but his first wife died childless three years later. He married again in 1934. Unable to support his growing household, in 1940 Li accepted an apprenticeship in the Japanese occupied port of Tianjin. His elder sister had moved there with her husband a few years earlier, joining many other petty merchants and workers from Raoyang.

After one year of working only for his keep, Li began to buy and sell for the merchant who employed him. He scrimped and saved and eventually began peddling by himself. He traveled between Tianjin and Jinan in Shandong, soon clearing 200 yuan a year, all of which he sent back home to provide for his family. Alone in Jinan, Li Peishen joined the quisling Yiguandao secret society. Each harvest season Provider Li, as we called him, went home to Wugong to harvest his 2 mu of vegetable land and 12 of grain. Home in 1945 when Japan surrendered, he stayed in Wugong. He was classified as a middle peasant during land reform. During the grain shortages of 1954–55 Provider

Li had to find grain for his parents, wife, son, and two daughters. Like so many others he found the manna in the black markets in Yanggezhuang, Zoucun, and Xiaodi.

Yanggezhuang was particularly ill served by grain-first antimarket policies. Its people had long survived on sandy soil by growing peanuts for the market and engaging in such sideline occupations as noodle making. Over forty villagers were traveling pig castraters, a local specialty. State control of the market forced pig castraters and others with market skills to return home to farm. As markets contracted and the state insisted on food self-reliance, Yanggezhuang villagers were forced to plant grain in sandy soil more suitable for peanuts for fear they would be left with no grain at all. The result was a descending economic spiral of less cash and less nutrition hidden by misleading, albeit accurate, reports of higher total grain output. Without the income of peanuts, processing, peddling, and handicrafts, and with the decline of its weak market, Yanggezhuang was left as a ward of the state.

The state's unified purchase and sale of grain failed to meet the consumption needs of the poorest. Although grain-poor households were promised grain to make up for deficits, the supplies, when they came at all, typically came in lumps, not in the variety needed for local diets. Either one engaged in a second economy, or one's household suffered.

In the mid-1950s, concurrent with its antimarket drive, the center also transferred handicrafts based on the processing of agricultural commodities from rural households and communities to urban factories. This devastated reemerging local cotton spinning and weaving, silk reeling, oil pressing, and many other rural sideline and handicraft activities that could not compete with the state for raw materials.[34] For Wugong, the loss of its booming peanut-oil sideline was the heaviest blow. It was as if a third world commodity producer surrendered processing and marketing to the economic powers. In China, the rural hinterland was the periphery; the state was the exploitative center. The leadership view was that the countryside was temporarily sacrificing itself for industrialization. The transfer of critical resources from the countryside to urban heavy industry, and from the peasantry to the state sector and the city, deprived many rural communities of the margin of surplus required for their development and prosperity.

Not every Wugong sideline was eliminated. The county supply and marketing co-op guaranteed a stable supply of hemp for the village's rope sideline and bought the entire supply of rope. Wugong also added one approved new sideline. In 1954 an orchard was planted on the site of the Southern Li burial grounds situated in an ancient riverbed whose sandy soil could not sustain grain crops. Old Militia Xu Yizhou, who was pushed out of the leadership by Boss Geng after the 1953 imbroglio over splitting the big co-op, was put in charge. The state bought the entire fruit crop, and Wugong cut ties to the market. Neither orchard nor rope co-op earned much.

In 1954 a small county-run grain station was constructed in Wugong using ancient techniques. The brick walls were lined with mud and straw to keep out water. Indigenous methods were used to limit dust and contamination and to prevent major losses from insects and rodents. Zoucun, the traditional site of the local periodic market as well as the regional granary, was gradually being replaced by model Wugong, which was cushioned from many of the blows associated with state monopolies and socialist policies. Zoucun, like Yang-gezhuang, suffered economic setbacks.

Winners and Losers

In spite of technical, administrative, and financial support, the big unit brought Wugong no rapid breakthrough in productivity or income. Increases in grain yields, supposed proof of the wisdom of new policies, often turned out to be a chimera, obscured by a veil of manipulated units that made the numbers ethereal. Among the constantly changing variables rarely mentioned in official yield claims publicized through the media were the size of the land unit (there was a 10 percent difference in size between the larger official mu and the natural mu); the use of husked or unhusked grain and raw or ginned cotton; the inclusion of sweet potatoes in grain production figures; the calculation of both summer and autumn crops as opposed to just one or the other; and the inclusion of a grain equivalent of nongrain crops. Equally important, yields were cited with no reference to the value of excluded alternatives, to capital costs, or to labor inputs. Model communities functioned in a milieu demanding Paul Bunyanesque claims. The imperatives of statistical accuracy and economic rationality paled before political necessity.

Grain yields in 1954 increased to 352 catties per mu in the big unit, up from 282 the preceding year, before dropping back to 283 in 1955. These figures were far below the best performance of the small co-op (478 catties per mu in 1951), but far above ordinary yields in the poor central Hebei plain. Many Wugong households nevertheless experienced deprivation. The Soviet road required high investment in production to fuel the locomotive, leaving little for the passengers to consume. In both 1954 and 1955, as a result of high production costs and high rates of accumulation, the big unit distributed just 90 catties of grain per mu to members, compared with 152 in the original Geng co-op in 1951. Grain production in the big unit in 1955 actually fell 69 catties per mu from the 1954 level. Even villagers on an express train were not enamored of riding the Soviet socialist road.

In 1955, following the suggestions of its technical advisers, Wugong more than doubled cotton acreage to 624 mu. Yields zoomed from a 1954 high of 30 catties per mu to achieve a village record yield of 74 catties per mu of ginned cotton. Cotton was the main export in the region, North Korea the chief importer. The government, seeking to expand cotton growth and the textile industry, publicized Wugong's performance, but continued to pay low prices for cotton.

In spite of the bumper cotton crop, villagers were short of the cash needed to purchase household goods, to fulfill cultural expectations for proper marriages, funerals, and rituals, and to meet consumption needs; grain yields fell and the low state price made cotton unprofitable. One further reason for the low 1954 and 1955 distribution was that Wugong initiated services Boss Geng had seen in the Soviet Union, a nursery and day-care facility, a pharmacy that dispensed Chinese medicines, and a health station for women and children that brought safer childbirth to the village. It also subsidized an old-age home operated by a sixty-year-old woman, but that soon closed.[35] The big unit cared for forty-five destitute households, including seventeen that received special treatment as military dependents or the families of military martyrs. Ten destitute households were short of labor; fourteen had little land; and eleven lacked experience in agriculture, that is, they had been forced to abandon such occupations as carpenters, peddlers, and shopkeepers to earn a living in agriculture.

For urban workers and state officials, the system granted pension and welfare benefits and provided costly subsidies, but there was no systematic rural welfare. Resource-strapped villagers had to provide their own or do without. Wugong's large welfare effort was quite special. In 1954 Wugong allocated 38,000 catties of grain to its destitute households. Adviser Lu Guang, impressed by the scrupulous care local leaders paid to welfare problems, forwarded to the central authorities an upbeat report on welfare in Wugong. But welfare programs in communities short of resources cut into the earnings of co-op members and created the danger of backlash from productive workers.

Riding High

Wugong's fame inspired screenwriter Hu Su to complete his script based on the Geng co op. In June 1954 he finished "Boundless Earth," a highly politicized version of the orphans' tale. The story tells of a poor old man named Rocky Wei who is about to die. The only surviving members of his family, a grandson and a granddaughter, face an uncertain future. In an attempt to seize control of the old man's scraps of land, his nephew, an unsavory rich peasant, feigns concern. The old man suspects the worst and desperately seeks a secure future for his grandchildren. The wise co-op leader, Vast Sea Tian, is summoned. On his deathbed Wei confesses that he should have joined the co-op long ago and pleads with Vast Sea to admit the orphans. But many co-op members oppose the idea on the grounds that enlarging co-ops is a bad idea. Vast Sea argues that Rocky Wei is the flesh and blood of their own class, while his hateful nephew is the class enemy. In the end, the co-op admits the orphans. Rocky Wei dies and is given a dignified funeral at co-op expense, the plot of the class enemy is foiled, and the co-op expands.

Hu Su intended to revise "Boundless Earth" and submit it to a film studio. Wugong villagers were fascinated by the idea that their story would appear on screens throughout the nation. But Hu Su was transferred out of Raoyang in late 1954, and eventually he lost interest in the project. Villagers waited patiently for the movie, but it never came.

Nevertheless, Wugong and Geng Changsuo continued to rise. In September Geng traveled again to Beijing, this time as a delegate to the First National People's Congress, China's rubber-stamp parliament. As Wugong moved up, its leaders won opportunities to travel on the state circuit. Qiao Liguang, who had risen as Geng Changsuo's good right hand, joined a 1954 youth delegation to North Korea. He returned with stories of progress in agricultural development in a land that had recently been destroyed by American imperialism.

Other educated young people were on the rise. In 1954 Yang Tong, a future village party secretary, was tapped to supervise a village night school, the People's School, organized by the youth league. The young man from the west village, who spread enthusiasm and got along well with people, boosted student enrollment from fifty-two to ninety-three. The school was the center of cultural activities for educated youth. By 1954 Wugong boasted that 86 percent of school-age children were in elementary school. Six young people were enrolled in the middle school in Raoyang. Youngsters put out a fortnightly magazine, *Co-op Members' Life,* with poems, stories, and discussions of village life. Its finest poet was precocious Shi Guiying, the twelve-year-old daughter of the head of the tractor station whose mother, Niu Yuhua, encouraged her writing, excusing her from some household chores. The new village reading room contained the provincial newspaper and several magazines and collected four hundred books. Fifty-five young people joined Wugong's drama and opera troupe, which performed "The Women's Representative" and other contemporary plays. The vivacious Li Tuo won a reputation for her singing and performing throughout the district; she and Yang Tong married. Women were particularly active in the cultural renaissance that flourished when peaceful progress permitted villagers to restore much of the cultural life they loved. Whereas men in traditional villages used to play male and female roles, now women played the parts of women. Some accomplished troupes from neighboring Hejian county were paid when they toured.

Party member Qiao Wenzhi, the leader of the village women's organization for the preceding fifteen years, went to her first big meeting in 1954. The thirty-three-year-old Qiao, who grew up in the east village, was married to Xu Lianzheng of the west end, reinforcing the territorial links of the marriage between west villager Xu Shukuan and east villager Geng Changsuo. Like many women leaders, Qiao was childless, which was seen as giving her time to mobilize women. She joined over one thousand other Hebei women in Baoding, which she remembered for its beautiful pagodas. Whereas women's leader Qiao later visited Shijiazhuang, Beijing, and Shanxi province, most village women had no opportunity to leave the village except for occasional excursions to their native villages.

The delegates to the Hebei Women's Federation ratified delegates to the national Women's Federation. The chief of the Raoyang Agricultural Bureau was a woman, He Jinxue. At the meeting Qiao reported on women's issues in Wugong, emphasizing the expansion of women's economic roles. There was no official discussion of the erosion of the marriage reform movement or of the structural obstacles to women's equality and its low position on the state's agenda. We heard enough accounts of the violence to believe that wife beating remained common practice. It was said to occur even in public, especially when a husband felt a wife's action had embarrassed him.

The state promoted education for girls, who regularly did better than boys in Raoyang schools. In the 1950s both girls and boys received primary education and some girls even became class leaders. But as possibilities for junior high school education began to open up, some village fathers insisted that their daughters remain at home. Some of the brightest broke down as they watched classmates prepare for the junior high entrance exam. A few ran away. More were forced into early marriages. One went mad. That pathetic figure wandered in Raoyang, hair matted, half-naked, dirty, singing, laughing, and lying down in the middle of the streets. The Women's Federation did not intervene. Even in cases where husbands publicly beat wives with hands or shoes or farm tools, unless a member of her family such as its lineage head pressed charges, the party authorities would not intervene.

Spice was added to village life when foreigners visited Wugong. The first travelers in 1954 were from North Vietnam. They were followed by a group from Czechoslovakia and by tractor technicians from Poland.

The Geng Family

Lunar New Year 1955 began auspiciously for Boss Geng's extended family. All gathered at home. The children had new clothes. Xu Shukuan cooked a huge batch of pork dumplings. Visiting the Geng family, whose house walls were covered with pictures from Baoding, Beijing, and the Soviet Union, was film director Wu Tianzuo of the Central Documentary Film Studio in Beijing.[36] Boss Geng had met Wu the previous September while in Beijing attending the First National People's Congress.

Film director Wu found the fifty-four-year-old co-op leader thin and frail, with a narrow face and a slender build. Geng neither smoked nor drank. He played no games, not even Chinese chess. He neither gestured nor raised his voice. But when Geng spoke in his confident low voice in a down-to-earth way about adapting Soviet collectives to China's backward conditions, Wu claimed to be captivated. He also found a studio job as an electrician for Boss Geng's son Delu.

In 1955 Xu Shukuan broached with her husband marriage for the orphan girls she had raised. Surveying possible partners for Li Zhuan, she thought of Song Daman, the son of Song Tanyuan, who had survived the war years by fleeing to Wugong, where he grew close to the Geng family. Xu asked Li Zhuan what she thought about this marriage. When Zhuan quietly smiled and did not say no, Xu set off on a one-mile trek to see the girl's maternal grandmother to obtain consent. Final arrangements were then made with Song Tanyuan. Finally, Daman was informed that he would marry Li Zhuan.

Xu then turned her attention to the younger orphan, Li Xiuying. She had already made up her own mind, and had a close friend break the news to Xu. Xiuying and Qiao Gang, the son of Qiao Wanxiang, the most prosperous of the original four co-op members, had decided to marry after performing together in the village drama group. A few young people, with parental approval, chose partners within the village. As Wugong became more prosperous, young women were eager to marry into the village rather than into poorer neighboring communities. The ties of the model village to less-favored places were thus strained.

A double wedding was quickly arranged. It took place in the courtyard of the party committee and was billed as a new-style wedding. The accent was on simplicity. In keeping with socialist opposition to traditional religion, there were no ketous to elders and in-laws, no expensive traditional costumes, and above all no bride price. Many villagers looked askance at such departures from customary practice.

Bursting with pride, Xu Shukuan recalled the loss of her own mother when she was nine. She remembered the clothes and shoes she had sewn for the orphans, and the visits to the doctor. "No matter how hard things were," she recalled, "we had always managed to have dumplings for the orphans on festivals."[37]

The marriage of Xiuying and Gang reinforced the alliance of newly powerful east-end lineages, the Gengs and Qiaos, who had first united in the small co-op a decade earlier. Previously marginal lineages like the Gengs and Qiaos in the east and the Xus, Yangs, and Zhangs in the west entrenched their new position with strategic marriages. Indeed, intravillage marriage spread throughout the county following collectivization as extravillage networks were severed and household protection required strengthening ties with team and brigade officials. All over Raoyang, invisible but firm networks were entrenched.

Boss Geng got his new son-in-law Qiao Gang a job as a truck driver for the Water Bureau in Dezhou in Shandong province, a six-hour drive to the east. It was a coveted job on the state payroll. China's inefficient and weak transport system often left trucks without loads, while many individuals and units eagerly sought ways to move goods. Deals could be struck with drivers and favors earned as the government cracked down on private commercial and transport activity and scarcities were piled on shortages.

A state job meant relatively good pay, free medical care, a pension, and an end to insecurity and hard labor in the fields. People called it "eating the state's grain." Most who held jobs outside the county could return home just once or twice a year for a total of three weeks. Rural households nevertheless used every means to get a member on the state payroll. Each of Geng Changsuo's five sons-in-law, as well as the husbands of the two orphan girls he raised, secured state jobs. He took equally good care of his own sons and daughters. Those tied to the state did best.

The marriage of the female orphans was not a windfall for everyone. Tanzi, Li Zhuan's troublemaking younger brother, failed to get on with the new husbands. When the women married and left, he remained alone. Tanzi, who had defecated on the grinding stone, became ever more a public nuisance.

Potholes on the Socialist Road

The honeymoon years following land reform were ones of family restoration, marriages, births, and rising incomes for many. In better-off Wugong, villagers happily noticed the decline in single adults, commenting that in contrast to the bad old days, only the insane were unmarried. Nevertheless, even in the mid-1950s not all Raoyang men earned enough to marry. Those whose land was poorest, or who lived in communities where income had been linked to the market and were now forced to engage in subsistence grain production, were too poor to attract brides. As in the 1940s, "bare sticks" in such wretched places remained bachelors. Their sacred obligations to ancestors would go unfulfilled. The gap grew between the favored of the state and those victimized by economically irrational policies.

Wugong paid a price for its prominence. There was widespread discontent on moving from the successful small co-ops and mutual-aid teams to the big unit, opposition to the demanding drive to drill wells, unhappiness about state pressure to grow more low-priced cotton, murmurings against the forced abandonment of lucrative sideline enterprises and the pressures to defer consumption while expanding sales of grain to the state at low prices. These policies reduced incomes for many and generated losses.[38] The complex reality of life on the Soviet socialist road was disguised because, as with diesel pumps and high grain sales to the state, only triumphs could be publicized.

At the highest levels of the party, Mao's closest associates argued for emulating the achievements of places that had advanced farthest on the socialist road. Meanwhile, Deng Zihui and his allies warned against blind optimism and coercion that ignored the realities of production, consumption, and consciousness in a society of peasant households limited to hand tools. Whereas Mao focused on what special places achieved, Deng stressed the need for a voluntary and gradual process to win support throughout the countryside. Invoking Lenin's slogan of "fewer, but better," Deng pointed to the coercion that lay behind big alienating co-ops in Daming county in Hebei and to famine in Zhejiang.[39]

When Mao early in 1955 sent his bodyguards to visit their home villages, one went to a village in Raoyang's neighboring Anping county. He reported back to Mao that villagers had been coerced into joining bigger units by the party's insistence that their choice lay between the socialist path of big units or the old world of Jiang Jieshi. Threatened with socialism or starvation, the units grew bigger, but morale and productivity fell. Mao acknowledged to Lin Tie that the Anping village experience was probably widespread.[40]

With the state rewarding success in building socialism, many rural leaders felt pressed in 1954 and 1955 to copy big units. Rural officials, feeling a need to prove their zeal, forced twice as many villagers to enroll in co-ops in the first three months of 1955 as had in the prior twenty-four months. Local leaders found it dangerous to careers to seem backward. Panic began to spread in the Chinese countryside.

State-imposed grain shortages combined with market closure to raise anxieties among villagers. Some slaughtered animals. Some hoarded food. Prices in the remaining private and secret markets rose. Movement in the direction of Soviet-style collectives terrified many. Worried that above-average earnings would be confiscated and the somewhat better-off scapegoated as class enemies, some villagers grew passive. Among the large number of rising independent tillers, so-called middle peasants who had the most to lose, many held back from spring plowing.[41]

Public security forces across North China moved to quell opposition. In spring 1955 Hebei public security cracked down on six religious sects charged with "trading, transport, fortune telling and therapeutic practices." The Chinese state scapegoated "Daoist chiefs" and their followers, charging them with destroying farm tools and poisoning livestock in attempts to destroy fledgling cooperatives.[42] At a meeting in Beijing, Geng Changsuo asked Lin Tie whether Wugong should advance even farther and abolish dividends on land. Hebei First Party Secretary Lin equivocated. Geng took that as no.

Wugong was not immune to currents of resistance. One July night in 1955, five hundred cotton plants in the north village were uprooted. The demobilized soldier and activist in the terror land reform, Fierce Zhang Duan, was unleashed to find the culprit. He investigated every class enemy who might have a grievance, but no criminal was apprehended. Zhang's strong-arm approach ensured acquiescence to ever more collectivistic, state-imposed ways of life. The sabotage highlighted the strains inherent in undermining the burgeoning economy fostered by tax reform and land reform. Membership in big, more collective units did not feel like family. Imposing ever larger units as a step toward Soviet-type collectivization and abandoning the peasant household economy and small voluntary co-ops were both economically inefficient and politically alienating for villagers.

Voluntary Participation

The big farming units set up in Raoyang presaged the impact of collective farms in village China. In a familial society that valued landownership, even Wugong, with all its historical advantages and official assistance, had a hard time making the big unit work. Most Hebei communities in spring 1955 had but recently formed small mutual-aid teams. Fewer than 10 percent of Chinese villagers had joined cooperatives of a dozen or more households. Many people remained outside even the most rudimentary cooperative networks. Handling issues of remuneration, division of labor, and morale in fledgling co-ops that lacked the technical and material support lavished on models kept officials hopping.

In line with the views of Rural Work Department head Deng Zihui, that spring Hebei leaders warned against pressuring recalcitrant households to join co-ops.[43] The press exposed cases of coercion that led to the death of neglected draft animals. It described co-ops that collapsed under the burden of declining grain yields and low morale. In March the party announced a "three fix" policy guaranteeing peasants the gains of higher yields. 1955 tax quotas were cut.[44]

The party's Third National Agricultural Work Conference, noting the "tense situation" in the countryside, on April 21 criticized the excessive speed of co-op formation and the numerous violations of the principle of voluntary participation. The conference resolution called for consolidating existing co-ops and disbanding failed co-ops, including fifteen thousand in Zhejiang and five thousand in Hebei.[45] In May Hebei Party Secretary Lin Tie reined in officials who were "too impatient, preoccupied with quantity, size and higher forms of cooperation."[46] Acknowledging that the forced pace of the preceding year had resulted in much coerced participation followed by economic collapse, the Hebei party committee announced that no new co-ops would be organized in 1955. Consolidation and voluntary participation became watchwords. Hebei dispatched fifty thousand officials to the grassroots to shore up struggling co-ops.[47]

Lin Tie and his subordinates focused on the issue of fair remuneration. The *Hebei Daily* headlined the quota system Wugong pioneered in 1954, commending individual responsibility systems (*geren ziren zhi*) that established individual production quotas within co-ops. Responsibility systems were hailed as maximizing individual efforts by providing tangible material rewards for outstanding workers. Provincial authorities singled out Wugong's team six in the village center for its achievements in individual responsibility sys-tems for weeding.[48]

Wugong wooed villagers to the big unit by doing more than solving technical and administrative problems. Boss Geng called for provision of security for the indigent elderly who lacked family support networks. Tradi-tional familial ethics defined what was just. Geng also sought to reassure the able-bodied that their labor would be fairly rewarded. Boss Geng acknowl-edged that the first principle of welfare was self-reliant work. He told able-bodied workers that the old and the weak contributed to the commonweal and were not loafers. In summer 1955 he reported that eighteen of the forty-five welfare households requiring support from the big unit had produced sufficient surplus to sell the state 4,000 catties of grain.[49] Workfare was meant to reassure households with abundant labor power that the weak were not getting a free ride, the shirkers were not taking advantage of workers. The village guaranteed bare subsistence for those unable to survive on the com-bination of income from land invested in the big unit plus labor and family support networks. Team one, the heart of the original co-op, led the way. The seventy-year-old mother of Collectomaniac Geng Xiufeng was too old to work in the fields or even in the team's pigsty. Team leader Li Yantian had a pigsty built in her courtyard and gave grandmother Geng a piglet to care for on behalf of the co-op. That year she earned forty-six labor days. Other teams followed suit so that ten such households raised fifty-nine pigs at home for the co-op. Team six organized an old folks work group and sent its six members wherever there was light work to be done. Although much in the traditional culture was not life enhancing, such as the parochialism, nativism, and pa-triarchy that made life miserable for those with physical disabilities and facilitated nasty chauvinism and wife beating, socialism in the countryside still worked best when it harmonized not with imported Soviet organizations and policies but with China's peasant household economy and traditional values.

Hunting rabbits with an old-fashioned rifle. Photo: autumn 1980, Paul G. Pick-owicz.

Winter wheat harvested by hand in Wugong in early summer. Photo: summer 1978, Paul G. Pickowicz.

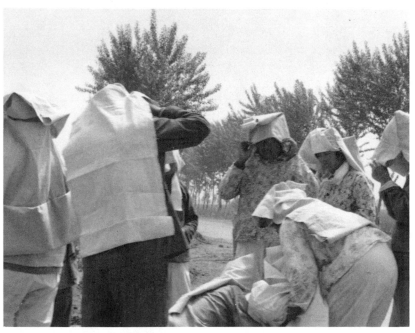

Bereaved women dressed in traditional-style white mourning garments assist a member of the funeral party who has been overcome by grief. Photo: spring 1983, Paul G. Pickowicz.

A typical residential area in Wugong, with homes facing south and courtyards surrounded by mud-brick walls. Photo: west end of Wugong, summer 1978, Paul G. Pickowicz.

Boys are taught to love the army and to participate in displays of male vigor, such as this tug-of-war. Photo: summer 1978, Paul G. Pickowicz.

The traditional method of plowing used in the 1940s and earlier by those who had access to draft animals. Photo: autumn 1980, Paul G. Pickowicz.

A traditional outdoor barber shop specializing in head shaving. Photo: Zoucun market, summer 1978, Paul G. Pickowicz.

Traditional cone-shaped earthen graves and white memorial wreaths located in a cemetery that was once owned by Wugong's Southern Li lineage. Photo: summer 1978, Paul G. Pickowicz.

Spinning rope on hand-operated equipment is a traditional Wugong cottage industry. Photo: spring 1983, Paul G. Pickowicz.

For centuries hand-powered grinding stones have been used in Wugong to process food. Photo: autumn 1980, Paul G. Pickowicz.

Elderly boundfoot women use wooden canes to hobble around Wugong. Photo: autumn 1985, Paul G. Pickowicz.

Traditional foot-powered wooden water-drilling rig. Photo: summer 1978, Paul G. Pickowicz.

8 ❖ AGAINST COOPERATION

In the summer of 1955 Mao propelled Chinese villagers down the Soviet socialist road. Voluntary cooperation and preparation to assure mutual benefit were thrust aside. Emphasis was placed on class struggle. Ignoring the large and growing middle group fostered by tax reform, rent reduction, and land reform, Mao claimed that only collectivization could prevent future polarization between a few rich and many poor.[1] Whereas Stalin, in coercing villagers into collectives, had declared war on peasants who produced a surplus, Mao acted to preempt the supposed inevitability of the emergence of a small minority of rich and a deprived and declining mass. Charging the head of the party Rural Work Department, Deng Zihui, with rightism, Mao appointed Chen Boda deputy head of the department. Chen cited data on land sales from Baoding prefecture and elsewhere as proof of the threat of polarization. Collectivization, Chen promised, would prevent class polarization and promote growth. But Chen's own data reveal that land sales actually had declined in 1953 and had almost halted by 1954.[2]

Instant Collectivization

In an October speech, Chen Boda cited Wugong to show that big units held the key to rapid growth. Wugong's grain yield, Chen claimed, had leaped from 419 catties per mu in 1954 to 463 in 1955. He predicted that yields in Wugong would soon exceed 500 catties,[3] proving that even in such poor counties as Raoyang, big units could quickly achieve high yields. Although 1955 yields in Wugong actually fell, success had to mean higher yields. Chen's numbers were concocted. Even now it is hard to know what Wugong's grain yield was from 1953 through 1955. Different figures appeared in the press at different times. The high numbers cited by Chen, if they had a basis, treated peanut production in terms of grain-equivalent estimates, with no public mention that grain yields for 1954 and 1955 were artificially inflated by this method of calculation.[4]

In October 1955 the center called for immediate universal collectivization. Ownership and management of land, draft animals, wells, and machinery would be transferred from households to the party-run collective, eliminating dividends on property.[5] The Central Committee's Sixth Plenum, declaring that the small producers of a peasant household economy were inherently capitalistic, promoted collectivization to block polarization. But many peasants experienced collectivization as theft. The issue was not confined to the loss of land title or work autonomy. People were abused. Zhang Xinfa, working in the Rural Work Bureau of Shijiazhuang prefecture, found that villagers resented being forced into collectives. Rural writer Ge Wen, who thought the small co-ops fine, saw big collective units as unworkable, as accentuating the bad. Corrupt personal connections became more central. Yuan Zhenwu of the Rural Work Department in Wuyi county discovered that collectives, in emulating the Soviet model, imposed a "forced accumulation" that left little possibility for income gains for villagers. An agricultural researcher in Beijing told us that almost half the new collectives, lacking experienced leaders and accountants were unable to set up reliable accounting systems. They simply doled out equal harvest shares.

But no one dared state such truths at the time. With critics and resisters labeled bad elements, with the party-state insisting that collectivization was the only path out of misery, villagers fell silent.[6] They enrolled. With state pressures for collectivization mounting, Geng Changsuo, confronted by village dissension and economic decline caused by the big unit, searched for ways to assure that Wugong would remain in the vanguard. He sought out Hebei Party Secretary Lin Tie.

"How are things with Wugong?" Lin Tie asked.

"Backward," Geng glumly responded.

But Lin Tie would not press Wugong, his favorite model. "After the distribution following the autumn harvest," he told Boss Geng, "let the co-op members fully discuss it again. We want genuine comprehension as well as enthusiasm. If conditions ripen then you can move to a higher stage co-op [collective]."

Lin Tie, however, could not long delay or continue the freeze on new co-ops. In October he criticized himself for the 1953 cutback in which 2,150 of Hebei's 5,800 cooperatives were disbanded or downgraded to mutual-aid teams.[7] That was when the Wugong big unit was slashed. Lin then called for 25,000 to 30,000 new co-ops by spring 1956. Still, Hebei provincial leaders tried to proceed cautiously. On December 3, 1955, when the *Hebei Daily* formally introduced collectives that eliminated land dividends and transferred land ownership and management from households to a villagewide entity, the authorities proposed organizing only 113 of the enormous units in 1956, all based on such successful older co-ops as that in Wugong.

There were sound reasons for caution. Collectives severed the bonds between household ownership and income. Although the share of land dividends in co-ops had dwindled over the past two years, no Hebei farming group had ever based income exclusively on return to labor. Hebei sought to experiment rather than impose an untried system. But the center demanded collectivization everywhere, regardless of local conditions. According to Chen Boda, 78 percent of China's rural households had abandoned household farming by January 1956. Of these, 24 million, or 26 percent of China's 90 million rural households, were in collectives.[8] Provincial party caution surrendered to the center's insistence on zeal. The media reported that by January 1, 1956, seven thousand collectives had *already* been formed in Hebei.

Officials impeding instant collectivization could be branded rightists. 50,000 collectives were mandated in Hebei before spring planting![9] Zealous officials soon exceeded the center's size targets. In September 1956 Party Secretary Lin Tie reported that 33 percent of Hebei's 24,249 collectives were multivillage or even multitownship units.[10] Two-thirds took the village as the organizational unit. The average Hebei collective had 340 households. Even where land reform was but recently completed and where there were few experienced cooperatives, villages were collectivized in a matter of months (see table 7).

Model Misgivings

Wugong leaders, who faced smaller and less threatening changes than most, did not immediately organize a collective. Because Wugong was nationally prominent and politically useful, its patrons wanted to ensure against injury by rash action. While other villages were forced headlong into collectivization, Wugong sent out investigators to analyze the problems encountered. The major problem discovered was persuading people that the new payment scheme and the transfer of landownership would not hurt them. Many of those with adequate or better landholdings would not believe it. Still less would the elderly, the infirm, and others with little or no labor power who relied heavily on income from their land.

Geng Changsuo focused on convincing those jeopardized by a loss of income from their land. Assuming high daily pay, he claimed that 363 out of 426 households would earn more in the collective than they had in the big unit, where income was based on a return on land as well as labor. Less optimistic investigators suggested that with the elimination of land dividends, 246 households might earn higher incomes, but 173 stood to lose. Even at Boss Geng's optimistic calculation, at least 56 labor-short households, with ninety-six people, would lose.

Taking seriously the real peasant economy based on a household division of labor, Geng's concern was labor-short households, not the hypothetical poor peasants or land-poor households.[11] Collectivization, pivoting on re-

Table 7   Agricultural Cooperation and Collectivization in Hebei, 1950–1956

| | % Peasant Households | | | | | | |
	1950	1951	1952	1953	1954	1955	1956
Cooperatives	0.0	9.9	9.1	0.7	7.3	34.9	0.0
Collectives	0.0	0.0	0.0	0.0	0.0	0.0	99.4

Source: Shi Jingtang, *Zhongguo nongye hezuohua yundong shiliao* (Beijing: Sanlian shudian, 1957), pp. 1000–1019.

ward for labor rather than for land or capital, would shortchange labor-poor households, including the old and the ill, unless collectives not only achieved substantial productive gains, but also increased member incomes and implemented redistributive welfare measures. Wugong would stress welfare for the weak. In most rural communities, however, higher yields, income gains, and effective welfare benefits would not soon materialize.

The abolition of land dividends would leave five Wugong households with nine people who were too old, weak, or incapacitated to do any work and who had no household support, with no source of income. The leaders allocated 2,500 catties of grain for their support—however, at 277 catties per person, that was well below subsistence. An additional twenty households, comprising the old and the weak who could do a little light work, would require 16,802 yuan in assistance.[12] Although leaders framed social welfare plans, even in Wugong, with more than two years of large-scale organization and mechanized tractor-driven agriculture, villagers were anxious. If instant collectivization was indigestible to many in well-prepared Wugong, where the imposed change from big unit to collective was less drastic than in 99 percent of China's villages, then the trauma elsewhere must have been far greater.

It required courage to voice doubts. Collectivization made awesome the already great power of party secretaries and militia chiefs. If one thought the party secretary unjust and complained to Raoyang, the county party asked the local party to look into it. The accused would be judge and jury.

One horrifying result of the monopoly of power in the hands of local rural officials was a plague of rape. A few village officials in Raoyang county became wantonly lawless. The negative aspects of a local culture fraught with violence and patriarchy conspired with the state's institutionalization of secret unaccountable power to make prosecution of the rapists nearly impossible. With gossip spreading about the sexual violence, villagers in the worst areas feared that if the story got out, then the virginity and marriage prospects of all village girls would be in question. Powerful and powerless alike had a stake in a coverup.

Obviously China's rulers did not mean to foster criminal rapists. But the new system reinforced nasty elements in the old culture. Two of Mao's former bodyguards who took high office in the Hebei port city of Tianjin forced themselves on powerless, vulnerable women. Many new powerholders from Beijing and elsewhere dropped their wives of many years and took up with attractive young females. By 1953–54 the party center tried to crack down on these delegitimating practices. The former bodyguards were executed, as well as one Tianjin-area official. Rules about divorce and marriage for officials were promulgated. Top leaders tried to undo the unhappy consequences of the power system they had institutionalized.

Villagers were ever more dependent on the goodwill of the party secretary for everything from recommendations for getting sons into the military or family members into the party to securing jobs outside the village. With collectivization, the party secretary controlled all job assignments. Party leaders tended to reserve better jobs for relatives and allies. Real plums, such as working with Soviet oil-drilling teams in the nearby North China oil field, went to the children of high officials.

With unaccountable party power a base for favoritism, nepotism, and corruption, many villagers experienced the call for collective members to work for all as hypocrisy. A corrupt leveling collective created massive disincentives to hard work. Although Boss Geng and his followers used their positions to take care of family members and political allies, compared to most local leaders, they were honest, self-abnegating, and disciplined.

The widest gaps in wealth and privilege between leaders and led grew in impoverished villages where the poorest women tended to resist collective field work. Raising chickens at home earned far more than the pittance from miserable collective labor. Unmarried girls seeking peer and male companionship still went to the fields. Whereas local rulers enjoyed privileged access to state resources, ordinary villagers had ever less access to cash as markets closed and barter replaced money. By 1957 earnings in Hebei from sidelines were 25 percent lower than in 1949. Earnings from animal husbandry had decreased to almost half that. Cash was ever more scarce. Powerholders responded by greatly expanding secret shops where scarce top-brand commodities were available at a fraction of market prices to those within the privileged orbit of the state.

Peasants found themselves the lowest priority in a system that siphoned off their output to provide cheap food for urban dwellers and to subsidize industrialization. The state's command of resources created scarcities, a pyramid of state-society stratification, and corrupt social relations. Members of collectives lacking ties to those who controlled resources had no way to get what they needed from the command economy. A popular jingle vented anger toward those who commanded resources and exchanged things among themselves.

First rank folk
Have things sent to the gate.
Second rank folk
Rely on others.
Third rank folk
Only fret.

The first-rank folk in Wugong found their call for collectivization in late fall 1955 opposed by 126 brave households, including those with more or better land as well as some who had many mouths to feed but few able-bodied laborers. The opponents included martyr households, army dependents, and families without sons to count on for support in old age. They included households that owned trees and draft animals. As in the 1953 debate over the big co-op, opponents of collectivist socialism included many old revolutionaries and people of the humblest origins, not just the traditional elite and the new rich, as claimed in official categories of capitalistic class polarization.

Wugong's leaders reassured the scared, angry, and wavering that their interests would be protected after abolition of land dividends. Li Huiting, who in 1951 had incurred Geng's wrath when he bought 4.3 mu of land, would not be placated. He lamented, "If I get nothing from my land, what will I eat?"[13] In 1954 Li's household earned 592 yuan, including 200 yuan in land dividends. If dividends were eliminated and the household's two able-bodied adults worked three hundred days per year, the leader explained, at 1.1 yuan per labor day, household income would total 660 yuan.[14]

The collective's promise of great prosperity was empty. Li Huiting was one of many whose incomes declined as a result of collectivization. Whereas the 1955 value of a labor day in relatively well-off Wugong co-op was .74 yuan, it would be more than twenty years before a Wugong collective labor day consistently surpassed 1955 pay. In most Raoyang villages, which were much poorer, the value of a labor day in the early years of collectivization was barely ten cents, paid in kind. There was no cash income. Some Wugong households with abundant labor would gain as a result of the shift in income based exclusively on pay for work. But the promise of immediate wealth for all could not be met.

When word spread about the plan to abolish land dividends, former independent tiller Xu Pingwen was so upset that he refused to leave his house for several days. All his life he had scraped and worked to improve his land. Now it would be taken from him without proper payment. His daughter was prodded to explain to him that compared to the previous year, when the household had received 235 yuan for land and 243 yuan for labor, next year, with no land dividends, the collective would more than double the daily wage for labor. Xu would earn 304 yuan more than he had the preceding year. The numbers were absurd. Boss Geng tried another tack, stressing the instability and vulnerability of the former petty producer economy. The big unit had ended that insecurity. The collective would do even better. But Xu, whose household's 20 mu had shrunk to just 7 mu in the early 1940s famine, remained unmoved.[15]

Old Li Zhuanruo in the east village had barely survived the 1943 famine, which took the life of his wife. In the early 1950s his three sons promised the old man security in his old age based on income from their land, a promise maintained in the first years of the big unit when dividends were paid on land. Li Zhuanruo's land was his pension. In the collective, he would have to depend on income provided by his children or on collective welfare. The new system eliminated some of the props of the old, including props sustained in the big unit. Boss Geng, and such central leaders as Deng Zihui, sensitive to the moral and economic crisis posed by collectivization, sought ways to reassure and restore security for people like Zhuanruo.

With rumors flying, heated arguments erupted. Li Shunian owned land with many trees. He urged that trees remain private property. Village authorities, insisting on collectivizing trees, agreed to pay a fixed sum for each tree. But four fearful households cut down their trees and sold the valuable wood. A formula was then devised by which the collective would receive seven parts and the owner three parts when the wood was sold. Many owners felt cheated.[16]

Village leaders explained that people would be compensated for draft animals, orchards, wells, and other items taken over by the collective. But villagers could see there was no money for such payments. Lu Zhenxing insisted on keeping his ox rather than see it pass to the collective. He vowed to turn to private transport as a source of income. But private transport and commerce had been undercut. The matter of the Lu Zhenxing ox was settled within a few days when the beast mysteriously died. Throughout Hebei the numbers of draft animals dropped from 4.2 million in 1955 to 3.3 million one year later.[17] Villagers ate their animals rather than have them appropriated.

Wugong's leaders tried to persuade resisters that collectivization was in everyone's long-term interest. More than a dozen tractor station workers and county officials went into homes to win over skeptics. Tractor technician Zhang Gengtuo, who later rose to head Hengshui prefecture's Agricultural Bureau, and Wang Yukun, from the administrative office of the county party committee, each moved into homes in the recalcitrant village center. Opposition was strong in teams four, five, six, and seven in the village center, with its better land and superior irrigation, the highest concentration of former vegetable-farming independent tillers, and the stronghold of the Li lineage. Officials, such as the trained propagandist Li Wanyi, failed to convert the village center. Li lineage members feared the consequences of concentrating more power in the officials who had brought down the Lis. Misgivings and fears remained, but all had to fall in line, surrender land, animals, trees, and tools, and collectivize.

Deeper Entrenchment

On New Year's Day 1956, one thousand visitors attended the inauguration of the Wugong collective. Changsuo's good right hand, Qiao Liguang, who had been in charge of production in the big unit, announced that Boss Geng had been selected as its head. The appearance of visitors was nothing new. Wugong's monopoly of tractors had made it a tourist attraction. Fathers loved to take their sons to gawk at the mechanical wonders.

Gao Jian, Raoyang's rising party secretary, congratulated Wugong for upholding the principles of "voluntary participation and mutual interest." He praised Wugong for resolving such complex issues as membership investment shares, ownership of trees, and care of the orphaned, the old, and the weak. The words were ritual incantations; many villagers were not reconciled to collectivization. Opposition raged in the now relatively prosperous east end, which was the core of the original Geng co-op, and the village center, home of the long-dominant Li lineages. As in the formation of the big unit, members of the Geng co-op stood to lose most as a result of pooling and redistribution. Assurances that they would be paid full value for their draft animals and equipment persuaded few.[18]

Beginning in 1955, a system of population registration and control under the aegis of the Public Security Bureau bound rural people to the village of their birth, now reorganized as their collective, or in the case of married women, to their husbands' collective villages. By 1956 all villagers were tied to land they no longer owned and could not leave and to jobs assigned by party-appointed village leaders.[19] With a virtual end to easy rural labor mobility, to travel for seasonal employment, and to household sidelines, the gap between the state-endowed metropolitan regions and their suburbs and those locked into the rural hinterland grew ever wider.[20] In return for collective labor, members received a share, mainly in kind, not cash, of value produced. Some fled the poorest communities to resettle in the northeast. Most who experienced collectivization as expropriation had no recourse.

A few households tried to secure urban jobs and urban household registrations. State investment, pricing, wage, and welfare policies favored the metropolitan regions. Chinese factory workers were guaranteed inexpensive housing, pensions, sick leave, and shorter hours; they received food, health, and myriad other subsidized services. These gains exceeded benefits in neighboring developing states.[21] But the broad rural hinterland enjoyed none of these benefits.

Wugong regulations stated that the collective would pay fair value, meaning prevailing market prices, for draft animals, carts, water pumps, plows, and trees. Even in relatively prosperous Wugong it was two years before any payment was made, and even then the recipients felt the sums were paltry. It was worse elsewhere. Most collectives set purchase prices very low and never delivered promised reimbursement for confiscated property. Most collectives had no reserve funds. They were subject to heavy pressures to invest the little they had to expand grain sales to the state. For a household to demand promised payment was to expose its members to charges of being rightist and anticollective. Such beginnings would not persuade people to work loyally and hard for the collective.

As in the Soviet Union, collectivization was coupled with small private plots, a concession to the peasant household economy and recognition of the limits of collective agriculture to efficiently produce and market meat, fruit, vegetables, and other nongrain crops. The Wugong collective charter formally guaranteed each household a private plot limited to 3 percent of collective lands. But politically ambitious Wugong did not permit any private plots. In virtually eliminating the private household economy, model Wugong tried to live by the fundamentals of communism. The state rewarded zeal.

With the land collectivized, Wugong began unified land use for housing. Decisions passed out of the hands of households. Village leaders allocated housing plots, in theory based on the number of members and priority need. In practice, the enhanced power of party leaders intensified the dependency and fawning of villagers. At a whim officials could decide whether households could comfortably expand or divide when a married son moved out.

With the collective controlling house building, Wugong launched an ambitious village reconstruction that began to eliminate winding lanes. Straight lines and squares seemed efficient, modern, socialist. The plan featured straight rows of solid brick houses, each with its own wall-enclosed courtyard.

A Wugong nursery school was set up in 1956. It was merely custodial and not a happy option for mothers with young children. Grandparents remained the preferred alternative in child care for households in which mothers engaged in collective work. With family labor underemployed and seemingly costless, villagers viewed such costly collective projects as subsidized child care as stealing from laborers to support those with soft hands.

Geng Changsuo was again a delegate to the National People's Congress, which met in June 1956. To demonstrate the humanity of Wugong's collective welfare system, Geng told the congress about the infirm Li Xingcai. Not only did the co-op supply Li with grain and fuel in old age, but when he was sick it also delivered wheat noodles, called a doctor, and provided nursing care. When Li died, the co-op dressed him in a new suit and new shoes, bought a wooden coffin, and laid him to rest. "If this had been the old days," Boss Geng said, "there would have been no one to look after Li Xingcai. After he died they would have just wrapped him in some old cloth and laid him in the ground."[22] The message projected to villagers nationwide was that the collective was moral, a bigger, stronger, and more secure family. Those who died penniless and without kin would still receive a decent burial from officials who were surrogate parents, "mother and father officials."

The Wugong collective charter offered security against work-related accidents. Those injured on the job were guaranteed half-pay for up to three years, as were the dependents of an income earner who died on the job.[23] In practice, however, the village would not be able to make good on costly welfare provisions.

Written into the Wugong charter were guarantees of the sanctity of cemeteries and burial practice. Members were guaranteed rights to dig graves in cemeteries and to maintain them for the deceased. The document recognized that families are eternal. But most of rural China, struggling to solve the numerous technical, morale, and administrative problems of collectivization, lacked the money, experience, unity, leadership vision, and state support to build similar welfare systems and to pay heed to cultural values.

Deng Zihui saw welfare as a key to peasant attachment to private land, for if a villager was "to lose his ability to work, and if no remuneration could be obtained for his land, the livelihood of his family would be affected."[24] Nothing in Mao's call to speed up collectivization addressed these issues. The state offered rural people no retirement pensions or welfare. Priority tasks were to organize the economy, accumulate, sell crops to the state at fixed low prices, invest more, and assure equitable remuneration. Under the circumstances, collective welfare was no more than a pittance.

In 1956, east-ender, Geng Shupu, who had introduced Boss Geng into the party, became village branch party secretary, but collectivization made west-ender Zhang Duan the most important figure on Boss Geng's team. In 1955 and again in July 1956, when villagers who were angry at the low state price for cotton uprooted fifteen hundred cotton plants, Fierce Zhang and his militia vigorously investigated. Zhang alerted villagers against "special agents." Suspicion fell on one person who died soon thereafter. Although Li Maoxiu was then away in prison, the "landlord" was later forced to confess to the deed. Combining a class-struggle approach to crime with a medieval insistence on confessions institutionalized vigilante scapegoating and torture of purported class enemies. Zhang Duan's zeal in the cotton case commended him to officials at a time of great tension. In spring 1956 he was appointed militia commander and head of public security. He acted as an unstinting Geng loyalist.

Zhang Duan was born in a poor family in the west village in 1926. When he was three, flood struck. His father, Zhang Wangchen, fled south to Guangdong province, leaving his wife to bring up Zhang Duan. After a decade Wangchen returned and in 1938 became an early member of the village Communist party. The family had been too poor to pay school tuition, but education was free in the local school run by the party-led resistance, so teenager Zhang Duan entered primary school. He never learned much, but in his first year, towering over his younger classmates, Zhang became head of the village Children's Corps and a political instructor. At age eighteen he served in the militia and joined the Communist party. In the land reform of 1946 Zhang's household was classified as middle peasant. After playing a militant role in the subsequent leveling terror phase of land redivision, he joined local forces fighting alongside Eighth Route Army troops in southern Hebei. On returning to Wugong, Fierce Zhang rose through the militia.

Zhang felt the pressure of his new police responsibilities. He hated reading documents. Splitting headaches never seemed to go away. He pushed his two fists hard against his head to relieve the pressure, shaking his head vigorously to free it from pain. He took silent walks in the orchard. But nothing helped, and the pain got worse. At times Fierce Zhang released the pain by exploding at villagers. He was a take-charge public security official with a penchant for swift action. Other illiterate or semiliterate village males identified with Fierce Zhang.

Moving up in the militia in the village's east end was burly Li Shouzheng. His father, Li Gen, had joined with Geng Shupu in party work in the thirties. Li Gen enlisted in the Eighth Route Army in 1945 when his small co-op collapsed. Like Zhang Duan, Shouzheng was hard on those who broke rules. People said he carried himself with "male airs." We therefore referred to Shouzheng as Macho Li.

Li married Zhang Fang from Xiyanwan village in 1956. She rode to Wugong in a horse-drawn cart with pillows, blankets, and chairs. On the eve of the traditional wedding, bride and groom dined separately with her or his own party. As the sun rose, the wedding began. Zhang and Li bowed to each other, to Li's parents, and to other relatives and honored guests. Customary teasing of the bride accompanied the rituals. Presiding was Gao Xuezi, a *quanren,* a complete person. That is, Gao had procreated both male and female. That augured well for the new couple. Zhang Fang gave birth to four sons, the first born within a year.

Tough young boys who did not take to school, such as Boss Geng's oldest village grandson, Zhang Mandun, made macho men like Zhang Duan and Li Shouzheng into heroes. Adolescent males competed in tests of virile strength. The inherited traditional culture and the new political culture mutually reinforced their emulation of tough male leaders.

Li Shouzheng was an intimate in the Geng Changsuo political family. With Geng's older son Delu working in Beijing, and the younger boy still a child, Macho Li became the mature son in Geng's home. Because Geng's wife, Xu Shukuan, was busy with political work, Macho Li, who had long been close to the Geng lineage, assisted Shukuan's eldest daughter, Geng Xueren, in raising the other children, including the orphans. The Li family home was on the same dirt lane as the Geng family home. The center's policy of collectivization did not stop the further entrenchment of loyal political networks.

New Burdens

Collectivization came to the countryside simultaneously with Mao Zedong's January 1956 National Program for Agrarian Development, which projected ambitious twelve-year construction targets for 1956–67.[25] Regions responded with plans to harness labor to realize these targets. When Hebei Party Secretary Lin Tie proclaimed that in 1956 Hebei would increase grain yields by 36 percent, a major stride toward grain self-sufficiency, the key was mass labor for waterworks projects. Between winter 1955–56 and May 1956 Hebei people drilled 720,000 wells, twice the total of the previous six years. This enormous expenditure of labor and funds added 16 million mu to irrigated land. Lin Tie, however, soon acknowledged that wells had been drilled too quickly and that some were useless.[26] National targeting slighted local realities.

In January 1956 Wugong village announced its development program. It began a ten-year project to level the land, fill in ditches, and turn its thirty mu of dry riverbed into flat and fertile fields, to "gardenize" the land. No longer would the village be pockmarked with the sandy knolls that had shocked the visiting writers in 1953. Xu Shukuan led a winter drive to collect natural fertilizer by digging silt from ditches and ponds. Throughout the winter, villagers filled in and leveled dry riverbeds. More land was exchanged with other villages; fields were reconstructed and reapportioned. Xu Shukuan prodded and embarrassed people to get them to work for the collective. Despite the frost biting into her bound feet, she led women into icy pits, her tiny steps making her look as if she were constantly running.

Xu embraced the party's view that the collective was a bigger family. Having lost her own family early in life, Xu dedicated her considerable energies to this new larger family, throwing herself into the most demanding tasks, always striving to work harder than others. She was a source of awe, even inspiration, for some. But for others who sought to preserve family lives as centers of ultimate commitment, for those leery of the burdens of large-scale collectives, for those who bridled at officious bosses, for those who sought assistance in times of disaster, Xu was a busybody, an irritant, and worse. Hers was a form of leadership that shamed supposed slackers. The pressure could not be resisted by the old, the infirm, or the pregnant any more than it could by strapping youths. That first collective winter, villagers exhausted themselves digging four thousand cartloads of silt to level and improve land.

This imposed activity generated its opposite, passivity and irresponsibility. Villagers who had used their resourcefulness and strength in the household economy now waited until collective leaders issued orders.[27] They felt that control of their fortunes and farms had been taken from their hands. All over China people resigned themselves to that fate.

In spring 1956, after three years in the village, the Lu Guang work team and the nineteen agricultural specialists who had introduced Wugong to rudiments of scientific farming were withdrawn. Lu went to work in the Organization Department of the party's North China Bureau, which was responsible for personnel appointments throughout the region. Zhang Yugang, deputy head of the Raoyang party in charge of propaganda, replaced Adviser Lu as Wugong's direct link to the county and to Shijiazhuang prefecture. On August 1, Raoyang assigned twenty-two-year-old Zhou Tiechuan from nearby Gengkou to live in Wugong, to stay at Geng Changsuo's side, and to write regular news reports for the prefectural and provincial press, the army paper, and the *People's Daily*. A higher elementary school graduate, Zhou came to Wugong after serving as youth secretary in the township government. He remained at Geng's side for the next eighteen years as a public relations representative and a link to higher authority.

That year Boss Geng arranged the transfer of one of Wugong's educated youth from his position as a scribe in the fourth district government. More socialism required more administrators. West-ender Zhang Chaoke, nicknamed Ball-Bearing Brain by villagers for his sharp mind, was twenty-six years old. He had recently begun to read systematically such classic Chinese novels as *The Three Kingdoms* and *Water Margin*. Brains Zhang supplied agricultural expertise and the ability to handle documents. He was the only child of once dirt-poor west-village parents who spoiled him by feeding him sweets. To try to make ends meet in the harsh 1930s, the father gleaned and peddled candy outside the village. The Zhangs moved up. Chaoke followed his father into the fields, where he learned from a frugal, hard-working, and shrewd farmer. By the time he was eleven, in 1941, following the party's tax reform, the family's situation had improved, helped by the silent revolution. The three Zhangs eventually owned 15 mu of land and rented three more.

In 1942, when the Japanese swept through the village in search of Eighth Route Army soldiers, Chaoke wandered out of the family courtyard. The soldiers grabbed and beat him. His hero became Geng Tiezheng, who fought back against the Japanese at a market fair.

At fifteen, with his aunt as go-between, Chaoke married a distant relative four years his senior from Beiguan village, a few miles northeast of Wugong. There was no bride price. The bride brought two wooden chests. The wedding cost the Zhangs 700 yuan, the going price. As a rural intellectual with a secular and universalistic outlook, Zhang was impatient with the irrational costs of tradition. But rural intellectuals had to respect customary mores, he felt, because otherwise their households would confront public shaming, ridicule, and loss of face. Married, Chaoke left to continue his education. Chaoke became a party member in higher primary school at age seventeen in 1947.

He was called home from junior high school in Raoyang in 1949. The family wanted his labor. The next year Brains Zhang became a teacher in Yanggezhuang. But in 1951 he happily returned to work on the land, having found teaching little children more pain than pleasure. In 1952 he brought his family, which was classified as middle peasant during land reform, into a small co-op in the west village led by his kinsman, the militia activist Fierce Zhang Duan. In 1956, the Wugong leadership took in the thin, crewcut, sunken-cheeked Zhang Chaoke. Along with a number of other well-connected house-holds, in 1952 the Zhangs had their class label reduced to lower middle peasant, thereby magically turning Chaoke into a proper leader of the poor. Brains Zhang, who showed an enormous capacity for alcohol during celebra-tions, was a zealous supporter of the collective. He was also skilled in translat-ing the nuances of a party document and the subtleties of a policy debate at the state center into concrete options so that village leaders understood the signals from on high.

The state promoted cotton production in Hebei in 1956. Before his transfer, Adviser Lu Guang urged Wugong to expand cotton acreage and to cut back sharply on grain. Wugong, which had only grudgingly conceded to previous pressures to plant more of the low-paying crop, tripled its cotton acreage from 624 to 1,988 mu. The area planted in grain in 1956 dropped from 3,101 to 2,261 mu, whereas double cropping expanded. In a hoped-for little leap forward, in line with the Lysenkoan view that there was no inherent competition within a species, Wugong zealously planted six thousand cotton seeds per mu. To reach high grain targets, as testimony to success in collectiv-ization, Wugong increased the use of chemical fertilizer on millet. The village enjoyed unique access to scarce chemical fertilizer.

Disaster

In late July and August in year one of collectivization, the exhausted, dis-pirited, and alienated villagers met another disaster. Following a good wheat harvest and the usual long spring and early summer dry spell, the skies opened. Water flooded parched fields. The flood affected 15 million people in North China. In Hebei alone 45 million mu of land were damaged. Histo-rians recalled the floods of the Daoguang era of the late Qing dynasty and of 1939, if only to make favorable propaganda for the socialist government's response.[28]

Employing traditional techniques, working around the clock, villagers led by Fierce Zhang Duan and the militia built a mud wall two meters high and two meters wide around the perimeter of the residential center. The wall did not burst. Homes were spared. But peanuts, cotton, and other autumn crops were inundated by several feet of water. The cotton yields dropped from the 1955 high of 74 catties per mu to just 24. Wugong sold the state only 33,000 catties of cotton. Not for a quarter-century would Wugong plant as large a cotton crop or obtain as low a yield.[29]

Ten-year-old Li Zhongxin excitedly scooped up fish more than a foot long as water subsided from the fields. Villagers caught nearly 100 catties of fish. Young Li had returned in the honeymoon years from the northeast with his mother, who had fled with her husband, a veterinarian, in the economic decline of the 1930s.

Not all the water in the fields rained down from above. To save Tianjin from flooding, officials in Shenze county, thirty miles west of Wugong, under orders from the provincial government, opened the river dikes. The regional water control official in Tianjin had authority over and above Hebei provincial officials. The city was spared, but water poured across the countryside. It appeared as if both Anping and Raoyang counties were covered by a lake of Hutuo River flood waters.

The dikes banking the Hutuo were higher and stronger on the north side that protected Tianjin and Baoding. Raoyang war hero Zhang Nian headed the county Water Conservation Bureau. Local people called the bureau by its Qing dynasty name, the Flood Prevention Headquarters. The power of the headquarters was fearsome. To prevent inundations where the government did not want them, Zhang and his people created local floods elsewhere. As waters rose, Zhang, after consulting top officials, opened the dikes on the south bank. Young fighting males, on hearing that Zhang's people were coming to their village, resisted with force. In theory, Zhang had the power to shoot those who blocked his efforts. Surrounded by bodyguards, displaying a large pistol at his belt, and carrying himself like a warlord, Zhang actually had resisting villagers strung up on trees and flogged. Zhang Nian was hated.

With no government cars in poor Raoyang, Zhang rode out on horseback accompanied by militia members and the dozen soldiers in the army platoon stationed at the county seat. The soldiers' regular job included guarding the county jail, which, as in the era of Japanese occupation, remained a building in the old Tian lineage compound now serving as county government headquarters. The soldiers also accompanied convicted local residents to the big prison in Shenxian county just to the south.

To breach the dikes and to avoid popular resistance, Zhang's armed band sought surprise. They arrived unannounced and acted swiftly, thus avoiding violent confrontations with young men who would fight to keep their village's fields from being flooded and their crops and their homes from being destroyed. On occasion unsuspecting villagers drowned.

Even in the face of the ruinous 1956 flood, rural folk said, "Don't say the Hutuo River brings only disaster. One flood, one wheat crop, and people are happy." An August flood brought fertile silt that permitted tillers, after the water subsided, to sow winter wheat with expectations of a bumper harvest.

Flooding, however, also eroded house foundations and destroyed mud-brick walls as well as crops.

Zhang Duan collapsed after leading Wugong's flood control effort. Boss Geng accompanied him to a hospital in Tianjin for treatment available to party people with connections. The collective offered to pay his bill, but, people were told, Fierce Zhang adamantly insisted on paying it himself. With cash scarce because households were unable to sell goods on the market, Zhang borrowed the money from the credit co-op.[30] His stay in the hospital was just one day. He could not afford more. A villager in an urban hospital could be broken financially by bills. Collective welfare did not cover hospital care, and rural people had no state health insurance.

Although this flood was less destructive than the 1952 drought, it still devastated much of Raoyang, especially the low-lying northern and eastern areas. In places water ran six feet high. In Luotun and Fucun along the southern bank of the Hutuo, land was covered by sand. Even such minimally lower-lying villages as Gengkou were hard hit. Wugong responded philanthropically by sending animal fodder to worse off places. It did not please suffering charity takers to see fortunate Wugong praised for generosity while they were slighted. People in Gengkou were irked that the press treated less-affected Wugong, which was on higher ground, as a heroic conqueror of flood, but ignored the labors of beleaguered Gengkou. Palpable favoritism made people cynical about claims for the feats of models. Young males in Duankou village found their marriage hopes dashed when a once prosperous economy collapsed beneath the weight of fundamentalist zeal. Angry bachelors, led by a former war hero, formed a gang that warned the families of prospective brides against marriage.

Even Wugong villagers faced a hungry winter. The 1956 grain harvest was 629,000 catties, barely half the 1954 level and just 70 percent of the 1955 output. While the press applauded Wugong's heroism in fighting the flood and its generosity to other villages, Li Dalin, a scapegoat in land reform, grumbled that there was no food for the hungry, including his family.[31]

As disasters mounted in late 1956, Liu Zhenqing, a "prosperous middle peasant" with a history of commercial activity, attempted to leave the collective. Complaining to county and even to provincial officials that the collective was poorly run, Liu appealed for the return of his land. Poor peasants Li Sanxun and Zhang Zhuan joined Liu in voicing grievances and demanding their land and the right to farm it. Boss Geng responded, "Sure you can leave, but your land must stay!" The commercial route had closed. It was not only land that now belonged to the collective; so did the laborers.[32]

Wugong's northern neighbor, Wangqiao, before collectivization had three hundred men working in Beijing, Tianjin, and Shijiazhuang. Most were compelled to return to their natal villages because of collectivization and population registration restrictions. Yet between 1955 and 1957 Wugong's population plummeted from 1,912 to 1,711. One reason for the decline was that the tractor station dispatched workers and their families elsewhere. In addition, some villagers who were already working outside dropped from Wugong's registers. Another one or two dozen people quickly won urban registrations, fearing that flight from the collective would become legally impossible.[33]

But population decline in Wugong was also caused by the deadly impact of socialist policy. The collective lashed people together in exhausting labor, irrigating and reconstructing fields. It forced many new workers, including women and the elderly, into field labor. With administrative costs, sales to the state, capital construction, and other investment up, with grain acreage cut way back, and with the flood destroying autumn crops, little was left for villagers. Local leaders deny it, but our household survey shows that part of the 1956 population drop in Wugong was a result of the toll on the elderly and infants, of decreased pregnancies and increased miscarriages of women weakened by the combination of exhausting toil, malnutrition, and natural disaster. More pregnancies were prematurely aborted, and infants were left without mother's milk or medicine. In famine, marriages are delayed because money is lacking for a proper wedding. In famine, women do not menstruate regularly and sexual appetites fall, resulting in reduced births at the same time that infant mortality soars.[34]

Wugong tried to help its needy. After the flood, 20,000 catties of grain were distributed to thirty-eight households that were added to the relief roll. In addition, twenty-five army, martyr, and five-guarantee households were helped. Overall, 10 percent of village households survived on welfare. With market activity curbed and most crafts collectivized or nationalized, hungry, proud, rural people were forced onto the collective dole.

The dearth was far worse in places that lacked the Wugong collective's relative legitimacy, unity, stored grain, financial resources, and advantageous high land. Poor villages like Yanggezhuang, with wretched soil and unreliable water, were hardest hit by anticommercial food-first policies and enforcement of collective discipline. The poor, with no surplus, most needed items to sell for cash that could be turned into grain on the black market. Income from handicrafts, processing, and services had long provided the difference between survival and disaster for many rural households and entire communities. Fundamentalist policies wiping out the household commodity economy forced households into semilegal and illegal economic activities.

Such poor villages as Yanggezhuang implemented the five guarantees to assure the welfare of the indigent. But when natural disaster struck, the welfare fund was quickly wiped out. And even when relief was forthcoming, peasants frequently muttered that it was humiliating and a pittance. The "five guarantees" (wu bao) were widely ridiculed: "Wu bao, wu bao, better to die now." A tale circulated of officials in one north Raoyang village who were in such a rush to be finished with caring for an old man who had no living relatives that they put him in a coffin when he was still breathing. Villagers did their best to avoid the onus of becoming five-guarantee families. Lineage ties were the real welfare system.

In 1956 all Raoyang was a disaster area. For the first time the central government flew in emergency grain relief. Provincial aid followed.[35] In spite of the loss of much of the autumn crop, the press reported that Wugong had rejected 8,000 yuan in state aid to draw on its own slender reserves. The model was made to look self-reliant. Actually Wugong received rice and wheat flour from the state and was exempted from its grain-sale quota.[36] Power-holders played up Wugong's rejection of relief to discourage requests for state relief.

Hebei's 6.8 million-ton 1956 grain harvest was well below precollectivization 1955 levels. Per capita production of 384 catties was lower than in any of the four preceding years.[37] The provincial government, which had projected a leap in grain output, had to allocate 336 million yuan in direct relief and loans. This was more than 50 percent above the total value of agricultural taxes that Hebei peasants paid in an ordinary year. To feed Hebei's destitute, 3.6 billion catties of wheat were distributed.[38]

Promoters of the collective blamed the 1956 disaster on poor weather and insisted that only state and collective aid prevented famine. Actually people sought grain in markets. Because the floods were localized, areas of Hebei such as Baoding had surplus grain that quickly reached private markets in Raoyang, the very markets the state was attempting to crush. Corn was available at 15 cents a catty in the private market, roughly double the state purchasing price. With the governmental apparatus geared to shipping grain out of Raoyang to the big cities, Raoyang villagers perforce turned to private and semilegal grain markets when disaster struck.

But efficient alternatives to the inefficient antimarket policies of the state were being wiped out. The temple fairs and rural markets collapsed. As the local market dried up, even rock plates used for school slates disappeared. Carpenters and craftspeople who used to travel far and wide for winter jobs were instead chained to the land. The large number of small entrepreneurs doing well in Yincun were turned into poor farmers. The Raoyang economy shriveled, and with it, local culture. The wonderful local amateur opera troupes that had been traveling through the county since the honeymoon years disappeared. So did the traveling animal show that had delighted children.

In many parts of Raoyang, particularly in northern villages near the Hutuo, men customarily went downstream by boat to Tianjin in search of work each fall at the start of the agricultural slack season. The three to five day trip made stops at Xianxian and the industrial town of Bozhen, which boasted China's first match factory and was located at the intersection of the Hutuo River with the old Grand Canal and the Tianjin-Pukou railroad. Collectivization and travel controls eliminated the cycle of winter work in Tianjin, and the building of reservoirs upstream on the Hutuo in 1956–57 and 1957–58 subsequently eliminated the river as a commercial link between Raoyang and Tianjin. Throughout China many inland waterways were eliminated as transport links as the state's efforts to expand water conservancy ignored the communication and transportation functions of rivers. Trying to make each small area economically self-sufficient in order to wipe out the linkages of capitalism devastated the connections among areas that brought vitality and diversity to the economy.

Still, no railroad or paved road reached Raoyang. A few trucks were used as buses. From Raoyang's major market center of Yincun to Beijing, in harmony with the traditional marketing cycle, one truck left every fifth day. It took one day to reach Beijing or Tianjin. A dirt strip airport began to be constructed in eastern Raoyang, which was to be used for aerial spraying of crop pests.

In 1956 angry and fearful Wugong voices asked a defensive Boss Geng why "eating bread and milk" had not come to pass with the collective as he had promised on returning from the Soviet Union. "They did have bread, milk and meat at every meal and tile buildings to live in," he insisted. "But mind you, that kind of happiness did not drop from the sky. It was the result of Soviet peasants working hard for over thirty years."[39]

Some villagers recalled 1956, the first year of collectivization, as the low point of their economic fortunes. Although the data remain fragmentary, it seems that Wugong, as with many Hebei communities, suffered a catastrophe exceeded in living memory in its toll on human life only by the great famine of 1943, which spurred the formation of the first small co-op.

Whereas collectivization of agriculture and nationalization of the market badly hurt the rural poor, the state's goal was to help the poor and to protect the poor from exploitation by unscrupulous merchants. Raoyang, as a poor county in Shijiazhuang prefecture, had a relatively low tax burden. In 1957 it received a subsidy partially to compensate for the losses of 1956.

The disaster was not willed. It was the combination of an institutionalized process that carried counterproductive aspects of the traditional Soviet model to fundamentalist extremes. In 1956, China's rulers generated impossible targets and political zealotry, squeezed out sidelines and commerce, eroded labor incentives, ended grain markets, exhausted people in labor corvées, bound people to the land in imposed collectives, and was slow to deliver relief. It previewed a tragedy.[40]

Return to Reform

In September 1956 Geng Changsuo returned to Beijing yet again, this time as a delegate to the Eighth Party Congress, the first newly selected since 1945. The congress celebrated China's rapid transition to collective and state ownership and set new priorities,[41] at the same time proclaiming the end of the tumultuous period of class struggle and sweeping institutional change of land reform and collectivization.[42] The emphasis, speaker after speaker asserted, would shift to economic and technological development and to improving living standards.

Patriotic intellectuals again were invited to play a significant role to spur growth and undercut bureaucracy. The party also approved more cultural openness, including popular culture. Symbolically, the Hebei literary journal that had resumed publication in 1954 adopted a vivid name, *The Bee,* to replace the gray bureaucratic name *Hebei Literature and Art.* In like manner, the Shanxi journal became *The Spark* and the Henan journal, *Torrent.* This liveliness of the antibureaucratic reform was a manifestation of the Hundred Flowers movement. Journals promoted Chinese national forms and derided Soviet approaches and influences. Teachers became more active. Writing on "The Good and Bad of Satire" in *The Bee,* Wang Fenghui made a name for himself ridiculing the long, vacuous meetings run by the party. He suggested carrying suitcases to meetings. People might still be put to sleep, but at least they would be prepared to rest comfortably.

Economic reformers, in this more open atmosphere, criticized the state-imposed collectives for abandoning the commitment to "voluntariness and mutual benefit." The collectives were accused of creating chaos in farm management and plowing and promoting a downward leveling of hardworking, able, somewhat better-off farmers who lost their enthusiasm for labor. Mao's opponent on swift collectivization, Deng Zihui, called for building again on systems of contracting labor, equipment, and funds to small groups or households in order to restore that sense of responsibility and efficient management essential to a thriving agriculture. In the name of opposing adventurism, the economic reform agenda included making more consumer goods available and freeing up markets and credit.[43]

By spring 1956 China's pig population had dropped from 100 million to 87 million as people slaughtered pigs rather than risk losing them to the collective. With reform, pig procurement prices were raised substantially. Household pigsties were encouraged under the slogan "private ownership, private raising, public support."[44] Nationwide the number of privately owned pigs rose rapidly, aided by a hefty price increase suggested by Minister of Commerce Chen Yun. But Wugong had initiated collective hog raising and collective night-soil collection from thirty big pits the previous autumn. It rejected the reform urged by the Eighth Congress of promoting private pig raising to boost household incomes, meat consumption, and fertilizer supplies. The Wugong collective continued to restrict income opportunities in the household sector.[45] Having nearly been burned in the 1951 peanut scandal, Boss Geng eschewed the private sector, even when the state sanctioned it to compensate for some of the negative impact of collectivization and nationalization.

With mobilization pressure down, Wugong did cut by 40 percent cotton acreage and seeds planted per mu. In late 1956 the village increased investment in sidelines, that is, collective ones, launching ten small enterprises, including a woodworking shop, an oil press, a transport team, and a forestry team.[46] Wugong's unique financial reserves provided the capital for the sidelines. Still, at year's end, per capita income had dropped by 30 percent from the preceding year to just 44 yuan. Even this meager income was possible only because the collective distributed 97 percent of its net income in 1956, holding back almost nothing for investment. It was the first time that the value of per capita income had fallen below 60 yuan since the founding of the big unit and the lowest distribution of any year from 1953 to this writing. Moreover, just two yuan was paid in cash. As sons were needed for households to live ethically and to continue a lineage, so money was required to purchase necessities ranging from home repairs to funerals to furniture for wedding dowries. Raoyang villagers said, "As sons do not die, so money does not disappear." But in fact the collective, by squeezing out cash, was making it difficult for families to live in morally proper ways that required many cash expenditures. Villagers did not live by grain alone.

The happiest cultural news of 1956–57 was the success of Hejian county's sixteen-year-old Pei Yanling. Her fame as a stellar performer in Hebei opera, even playing old male officials, won command invitations to display her talents in Beijing to top national leaders, including Mao Zedong and Zhou Enlai. People in Raoyang and neighboring counties praised Pei as a worthy successor to a fine regional tradition.

As recovery from the 1956 disasters proceeded, young and old relished traditional cultural activities. Wugong's drum corps performed with four villagers playing each of the big drums and lion dancers cavorting to their rhythms. Wugong sent teams of young performers to Zoucun's temple fair, when twenty thousand people poured into the market for the grandest gathering of the year. Shi Guiying, daughter of the tractor station head, sang a paean to the collective and a number about cleaning up after the flood.

In early spring 1957 Geng Changsuo left Wugong for Eastern Europe. Once again he traveled with a government agricultural group. They flew from East Germany to Czechoslovakia and were taken the first evening to a cultural program that included formal ballroom dancing. Geng found the customs of Westerners riveting. But, he later told Wugong villagers, the Chinese tour leader chided their Czech host, saying that he had not come from China to see such performances; he was here for serious international socialist purposes. Soon the two were going at each other with the Czech insisting that the dances were respected local traditions. Geng Changsuo laughed silently. The parochialism of some urban officials never ceased to amuse Wugong's peasant leader. Villagers relished the story about the bungling official.

In East Germany Geng visited collectives and offered to engage in friendly competition. After his return, letters arrived, but they were written in German, so the Chinese villagers could not respond. Other than seeing what more modern Czechoslovakia and East Germany looked like, nothing human transpired. The same barriers that have kept foreigners from seeing Chinese reality kept Geng from seeing the reality of Soviet-dominated Central Europe in the wake of the crushing of Hungary's 1956 revolution.

On his return, Geng spoke to students in Raoyang. A feeling of international solidarity pervaded the gathering, beginning with an emotional singing of "The Internationale." Youngsters were moved by high ideals. The throng thrilled to a simple story Geng told about a conversation with an Italian Communist, indicating that the world's people were with the Chinese. If China had problems, then these young people listening to Geng wanted to contribute to solving them and to furthering the cause of peace and social justice. Neither the hope won by the revolution nor identification with the socialist state had dissipated.

The reforms injected more life into the 1957 Zoucun temple fair. Those happy spring days, however, ended in a melee. In settling accounts Zoucun representatives asked a visiting opera troupe to acknowledge that it had used but not paid for village coal. Troupe members got into a shouting match and then a fight with local people. The head of the opera troupe, a demobilized soldier who had lost a leg in combat, tried to calm both sides. Instead he was attacked. The case became a matter of prefectural and provincial concern when assertive local army people insisted that insults to the patriotic military not go unpunished.

Although the power structure, including the army, grew more entrenched, reforms in 1956–57 sought to reverse the losses caused by the economic irrationalities of the collectivization campaign. Hebei Party Secretary Lin Tie acknowledged that excesses in the mobilization drive launched early in 1956 had resulted in setbacks. As acting director of water conservancy in Hebei, he sought more central funds for construction to contain the Hai River and its tributaries. In line with economic reforms, collectives were to introduce the piecework systems that Wugong had earlier pioneered to increase incentives, and multi-village collectives were to cut back to village scale.[47] Within one year Hebei eliminated all multi-village units. But whatever the ameliorating effects of the reforms, the collective and the political system remained firmly in place.

Socialist Networks

Wugong's model status was sustained through a network of ties to officials at various levels of authority who controlled scarce resources. Models were linked by sinews of career and loyalty to higher officials and by marriage and social bonds to local and regional networks of villagers in their own and neighboring communities.

In late 1955 Mao included an article on Wugong in *Socialist Upsurge in China's Countryside*, a three-volume compendium on more than one hundred exemplary co-ops that he edited and annotated to promote collectivization. But Wugong was not in the condensed one-volume edition that circulated throughout the countryside. Perhaps Wugong's climb seemed insufficiently dramatic, lacking the flair of bitter class conflict. Perhaps because its co-op originated with commercial sidelines and then advanced with mechanized agriculture courtesy of the tractor station, it did not capture Mao's preferred tone of self-reliance, manual labor, and food first. Perhaps Wugong's stress on quotas, rewards, and incentives did not seem sufficiently selfless and communistic to Mao.

Yet Wugong's leaders felt slighted to find Mao, whom they revered, stressing the achievements of Nanwangzhuang (South Kingsboro), just an hour's jeep ride west of Wugong in Anping county. What leadership had its new boss, Wang Yukun, shown? His small co-op had fallen apart! Several dozen families quit, leaving only three households of Wangs to help each other.[48] Nevertheless, on February 7, 1956, the South Kingsboro leader was rewarded with a meeting with Mao, who hailed the failed co-op of three neighbors. The two Hebei villages that Mao singled out, Wang Yukun's South Kingsboro and Wang Guofan's Xipu, were rewarded, as Wugong was not, with huge infusions of new resources.

Mao had written comments in his own hand in the margins of the article about Wugong prepared for the compendium. He knew Wugong had built a co-op of more than four hundred households, but he chose not to single out Wugong for highest praise. Still, once included inside the circle of the favored of the state, one was not lightly pushed out. Archivists from Beijing's Museum of Revolutionary History went to Wugong in 1957 to collect memorabilia of the early co-op, land reform, and the first big unit.[49] Known to Chen Boda, Lin Tie, and other promoters and patrons, Wugong continued to receive state attention and support.

Model status brought Wugong myriad benefits. In 1956 the Zoucun clinic, the largest in Raoyang outside the county seat, began to move to the outskirts of Wugong. Eventually based in Wugong, it would serve twenty villages in southern Raoyang and be subsidized by the prefecture. The move testified to the supremacy of the state's new model over the old market center.

Bringing modern medical care into the village did not please everyone. The nationalization of medicine forced the closing of Li Kuanyu's traditional pharmacy. With commerce commandeered by the state, the open market in Chinese medicine was eliminated. It continued as a remnant black market, with many households growing their own medicinal herbs. But many valued medicines were not available in Wugong with its tight ties to the state and its allergy to the market. Worse yet, although the clinic offered traditional as well as modern treatment, Wugong's traditional practitioner could not get supplies and was forced to abandon his practice. Elderly people complained that it was difficult to walk to the new clinic on the western outskirts of the village. They did not like the strange doctors, did not like waiting in line, filling out forms, and paying registration fees. When ill, they wanted to be visited at home by their familiar practitioner. They wanted herbal medicines they trusted. Nationalizing commerce and centralizing medical care ended that. If one pointed out the real gain of a local clinic with a modern doctor, many villagers, ever mistrustful of outsiders, complained about the loss.[50]

In like manner, if tractors now plowed the fields, harvesting remained hand labor, with short scythes used to cut the grain. Peasants believed that by using the hand tool they would harvest every grain coming to them. Beginning in June 1957, and continuing every summer and fall for the next two decades, Wugong was the beneficiary of unpaid student labor from Raoyang to help bring in the harvest. The high school organized truckloads of students to the famous model village to help with the harvest. No other Raoyang village received such assistance. The system further enriched the already privileged.

Boss Geng worried about his relation to higher-ups. He believed Wugong was made to look bad by promises and predictions in the press about expected high harvests that were not achieved. Geng concluded that outsiders were the sources of this embarrassment, especially newspaper reporters who would ask one person after another to estimate the forthcoming Wugong harvest, eventually publishing the highest number offered. Geng told fellow leaders and villagers that he no longer wanted them to bow down to ignorant outsiders and say "yes, yes, yes" to the claims and suggestions proffered by the outsiders. Stubborn Geng, who liked his reputation as a "hard head," wanted outsiders to experience Wugong as populated by people who could not be bullied or ordered around.

The state could push powerless people around. When the authorities built a small airport in east Raoyang, they seized the land of peripheral villages with no proper compensation. As with those in Hebei who lost land for dams to prevent further flooding, such households suffered economic decline. People commented darkly, "Two people have to eat out of one bowl."

Education

Wugong's primary school added grades five and six in 1956. Then a new two-year junior high school attracted students from neighboring villages able to pay an annual three yuan tuition. In the Raoyang countryside, education through eighth grade became available only in Wugong. The junior high had

240 students and thirteen teachers and staff. The single high school in the county remained in Raoyang town.

Education expanded, but opportunities for girls were constrained. When it came time to hike to Raoyang town to sit for the three-day high school examination, some girls were told by illiterate parents that their education had ended. One girl, facing a parental ultimatum to proceed with an arranged marriage to an unknown mate, joined her boyfriend in a double suicide.

The waste and loss of the little leap forward of 1956–57 led to budget cuts that hit education. In 1957 only one-fourth of the three hundred Raoyang junior high graduates could move up to high school. Goals of universal education were limited by government priorities, strained resources, and traditional morality. At one Raoyang junior high, after the authorities announced how few would be permitted to go on, students vented their rage on dormitory walls and blackboards:

> Raoyang junior high student
> Nine years strived in vain.
> Did not pass into high school;
> Normal School takes no students.
> The future has only one path:
> Go home and work the land.
> No way to fulfill one's ambition,
> Anger is too hard to calm.

Such frustrations fueled a response during the liberalization of the Hundred Flowers campaign. Critics condemned corrupt officials for living high off the hog while education was starved of funds.

The Anti-rightist Movement

In the summer of 1957 the party launched an anti-rightist campaign to silence and punish those who spoke out during the preceding Hundred Flowers movement when the party invited openness, criticism of bureaucracy, and reformist suggestions. In July Mao called for attack on "the counter-revolutionary activities of landlords and rich peasants," a category quickly extended to all who questioned collectivization or other policies.

In the anti-rightist movement powerholders cracked down on those who had pointed out ineffective and corrupt leaders or flaws in policies, or who had complained that dictatorship was destroying popular enthusiasm. People targeted in the past would be scapegoated yet again. Rural targets centered on those who bore such class labels as landlord, rich peasant, and even middle peasant, as well as intellectuals. Peasants who showed children which plots of land had once been theirs could be beaten, labeled, or jailed. Throughout the nation hundreds of thousands of people were sent to labor camps where many would die, while the survivors were cruelly mistreated for two decades or more. Hundreds from Shijiazhuang were shipped to dangerous coal mines in neighboring Shanxi province as virtual slave labor. Millions more were labeled rightists. Such people became a stigmatized caste, disenfranchised with their households and progeny. Two members of the Hebei party committee were branded rightists. One had exposed corruption, and the other had defended a colleague who had been framed as a "counter-revolutionary."[51] People learned that to criticize authorities exposed oneself and one's relatives to an endless hell. Only silence and sycophancy were safe.

In late summer word spread that rightists would be the target of a rectification campaign at the Wugong tractor station. The four graduates of agricultural colleges who worked at the station grew silent. They asked friends, "What is a rightist?" Some guessed that a rightist must be someone opposed to collectivization, the road the tractor station had pioneered. It turned out that all educated people were vulnerable to class degradation.

Thirty reporters throughout China who had written stories exposing the expanding network of popularly resented secret shops for officials were branded rightists and sent to labor-reform camps in poor places. All the writers for the Hebei literary journal *The Bee* were denounced as rightists and members of an antiparty group. One-third of the members of the Hebei Literary Association were condemned. The *Beijing Literary News* targeted Sun Li, the famed writer of novellas about the Hutuo River region, as an opponent of collectivization. Pleading illness, Sun announced that he would write no more.

Popular culture was again attacked as feudal superstition. A Hebei writer of works on traditional martial arts was criticized, helping to spark a national struggle against such practices. Temple festivals were condemned. 1957 was the last time for decades that Wugong people could enjoy the region's most famous traditional storytellers. Zoucun villagers came to believe that patriots and veterans standing up for the soldier who had been beaten at the spring festival melee got the government to punish local people by closing down the market festival. Zoucun, once a walled market village and vital center for government, commerce, medicine, education, and philanthropy, was reduced to stagnation.

The state treated as revolutionary those who pushed the class struggle line of the 1947 land reform and those who subsequently infringed on villagers' interests by collectivizing agriculture and handicrafts, suppressing market activity, and crushing rural culture branded as feudal. In spite of the harm unto death that such people caused, they were treated at worst as overzealous or ahead of their time. On the other hand, critics of the terror and alienation of popular support caused by these policies risked being branded as rightists, enemies of socialism, and counterrevolutionaries. To expose malfeasance, seek democracy, or favor more economic initiative for households was to risk arrest or attack as a political criminal, an enemy of the people. Behavior that could be labeled rightist was dangerous to self and to career. Leftist mistakes could be forgiven; rightist mistakes could not.

The hunt for rightists in Hebei was aimed at schoolteachers. In Raoyang town the anti-rightist campaign went on at the high school. As in the anti–Hu Feng campaign, officials were pressed to see educated individuals as enemies of the people. Three of the forty teachers were labeled rightists. Sparking zealotry in witch-hunting, higher levels rewarded local officials who found more than 5 percent rightists in their units. Those who had earlier responded to the Hundred Flowers campaign to expose corruption or to propose reforms were vulnerable. The corrupt now turned on their critics. The system penalized idealistic and democratic people and rewarded vengeful ones. Victims were jailed. Some were beaten. Many were given black labels. Primary and middle-school teachers were brought to Raoyang town from throughout the county to denounce rightists in their midst. More than fifty teachers were singled out for vicious personal degradation rituals. Local officials became wary of educated outsiders teaching peasant youngsters.

The state insisted that peasant life was the good life, but it punished teachers dubbed rightists by sentencing them to life as peasants, sending some to distant villages, a form of permanent internal exile. Even high-school students were seized by the police and publicly degraded until it was determined that state policy precluded labeling high-school students as "black elements." One student nevertheless was expelled from the high school.

Local peasant leaders, long mistrustful of the educated and of outsiders, tightened their bonds to each other. They would not seek to replace the rural schoolteachers lost in the anti-rightist movement. The party center circulated documents insisting that class struggle was still needed against imperialism and the bourgeoisie. Intellectuals were targeted as bourgeois class enemies guilty of rightism, of standing for democracy and individual liberty instead of socialism and common prosperity. If class loyalty was what the state prized, then illiterate or semiliterate rural leaders increasingly would trust and reward only those with honest, thick, local accents like themselves, and mistrust and exclude those educated folk who talked like the mandarins of old. Local networks of poorly educated veterans tightened.

Although people learned how to play safe, these political vicissitudes did not create disillusionment in areas that had been bases for the Eighth Route Army. The revolution had transformed loyalties. People tried to make sense of events within a framework of allegiance to Mao, socialism, and the party's army, the protectors of the people. Against such ultimates, the injustices and tragedies of the moment faded. Loyal people said that those victimized by the party should see themselves as children wrongly punished by caring parents. The few who complained about their punishment were silenced.

In 1957 Fan Shufang, the wife of Wugong's "landlord" Li Maoxiu, had difficulty acting as a caring parent and wife. She and her eleven-year-old son Li Wei returned to Wugong from the security of her natal village. The boy's legal residence was Wugong, his father's village, so Li Wei could attend school only in Wugong. Fan's husband was about to finish serving five years at hard labor for the crime of flight. Patriarchal tradition dictated that Fan be in Wugong when he returned. On moving back in with her ill mother-in-law, the wife of former village chief Li Jianting, Fan found little food, certainly little to spare for a counterrevolutionary, criminal, landlord household. Fan stood up to the Wugong leaders, calling attention to her dead brother and insisting she had a right to good treatment as a member of a martyr's household. She was told she was a landlord element, a very black one. Besides, ever since she had moved to Wugong twelve years earlier and begun to lash out at her mother-in-law, villagers were put off by Fan's arrogance. They pitied her mother-in-law. During land reform the largest portion of the Li family courtyard had been divided up to house the destitute. The Lis crowded into a few small rooms. In 1956 the authorities confiscated another room for a village store. Fan petitioned the authorities, who spurned her request. She marched off to the county town to report that Wugong's leaders were letting members of martyr families go hungry. Raoyang officials asked Wugong leaders to check. The village party branded Fan a landlord element, a slanderer, and a troublemaker out to ruin socialism.

When the anti-rightist campaign began, Fan Shufang was dragged to the courtyard behind the rooms where Adviser Lu Guang's work team had lived. Public security chief Li Zhiting and militia chief Zhang Duan took charge. Young Li Zhongxin and his boyfriends crowded in to view the spectacle. Li Maoxiu, just back from prison, watched glumly from the rear of the crowd. Fan was brought on stage in bonds and forced to bow before the whole village. She was ordered to confess that she had connived to undermine socialism. The atmosphere was tense. People started pushing, hurting, and bullying her. After much physical abuse Fan confessed, but her tormentors rejected her confession as lacking sincerity. She would have to learn to be sincere. The brutal spectacle continued. Fan Shufang never again complained publicly.

Fierce Zhang Duan spearheaded Wugong's anti-rightist crackdown. To the usual group of black elements, he added Provider Li Peishen, who had lived in Japanese-held Tianjin, joined the quisling Yiguandao secret society, and like so many others, illegally bought grain on the black market at times of shortage. Although state rules did not make criminals of mere members of the Yiguandao who had participated in no treasonous acts, in August 1957 Li Peishen was seized and marched to Raoyang with the Daoist Li Jinzhua and other black elements. Hundreds of people from all over the county were forced to camp out in the courtyard of the Public Security Office.

Divided into groups of fourteen, each supervised by a police official, they met daily to engage in criticism and self-criticism. Weeks later, Li Peishen was marched back to Wugong. Fierce Zhang told Li he was now black element Li. In September Li was sentenced to three years of supervised labor beginning with two months of forced labor in Zoucun. He would discover that his black label and his forced-labor term would not end after three years or even seven times three years. Li Zhiting took charge of Wugong's forced laborers.

Li Yutian was dissatisfied, alone, hungry, and angry after collectivization. He had pulled out of the original co-op and never recovered from the famine of 1943. His wife left him. We were unable to learn his fate during the 1957 campaign that branded him a rightist.[52] Some leaders claimed there was no such person. Nor could we discover the fate of Li Dalin, who was persecuted during land reform and was again singled out in 1957 for complaining about hunger, thereby undermining the collective. We were told that he was still alive, but too ill to receive visitors. Since we did succeed in learning the fates of others who had been degraded, bullied, branded, beaten, and sentenced to forced labor, worse fates probably befell Li Yutian and Li Dalin. Li Heiyan, Li Yuqing, and all the other black elements were linked to the once powerful Li lineages.

As the state increased its demands on villagers, Fierce Zhang Duan again came to the fore to keep people in line. The élan, unity, and committed cooperation of the era of the resistance war, the silent revolution, and the honeymoon were undermined. With Boss Geng presiding, with Fierce Zhang and the militia alert, and with the state demanding suppression of class enemies, villagers learned to fear being cruelly penalized for even complaining about starvation. Calling attention to state-imposed disaster was taken as an attack on socialism, so cries of hunger and despair were choked off and swallowed. Class enemy labels could be pinned on anyone who opposed what the state defined as the only road to communism. Wugong and China were in deadly trouble.

9 ✤ A LIFE
AND
DEATH
STRUGGLE

In spite of all the institutional change, beginning with tax reform in the late 1930s, daily life for Raoyang villagers entering 1958 was still mired in premodern poverty. If it rained, lanes flooded, imprisoning people in their homes. There was no pipe drainage. Food was simple and unvaried. Breakfast was millet gruel. Coarse grain cooked for lunch was eaten again at dinner. There was little meat, fowl, fish, or fresh vegetables. Homes lacked chairs, sofas, beds, radios, and clocks. Women did washing using a rock and icy water drawn from a distant well. Cooks continuously fed straw to a brazier in the middle of the house. The fumes and dust dirtied the dwelling and filled the lungs. Coal powder used for heating had a similar polluting impact. A latrine behind a courtyard wall served even the elderly and the ill in rain, snow, and freezing cold. Simple comforts such as sanitary napkins and toilet paper did not exist. There was no running water and no electricity.

Modernization and Miracles

Citizens and officials welcomed modernization. Baoding officials transferred to Shijiazhuang enjoyed it as a more modern city, where new government buildings installed steam radiators instead of Baoding's coal fires. Raoyang leaders predicted productive wonders as a result of the 1958 aerial spraying of 666 insecticide. In Raoyang insecticides were credited with eliminating the perennial plagues of lice and bedbugs. Villagers hoped for a chemical that would wipe out fleas.

Targeting corn pests, demobilized Air Force pilots stationed in Tianjin flew in to the new Raoyang county air strip. Tents were prepared for the pilots, but the fliers spurned the hospitality, returning instead after work to the comfort of Baoding or Tianjin. Raoyang inaugurated aerial spraying, targeting corn fields where youngsters wearing masks and excitedly waving red flags directed the pilots. The spraying continued for a couple of weeks and drastically reduced corn pests; it unintentionally also diminished fireflies, foxes, and snakes. With their natural predators gone, mosquitoes and rats grew as plagues, the rats competing with villagers for scarce grain.

In spite of modernization, traditional attitudes remained deeply embedded. Although the government propagandized against feudal superstition, legitimate marriages remained patrilineal and patrilocal; marriages within five generations on the patrilineal side remained taboo, regarded as incest. Yet modern sports readily took hold. Tianjin sports leaders saw themselves as pioneers, having introduced basketball in 1896, right after its invention in the United States. Provincewide sports competition began in 1952. The October 1958 Hebei games were divided among the cities of Tianjin, Baoding, and Tangshan. Based on Tianjin's power, Hebei rose in the 1959 national games to finish third in swimming. A peasant from south of Raoyang won regional fame for records in the pistol competition. As traditional martial arts declined, denounced as feudal superstition in the anti-rightist campaign, the youth league popularized modern sports, especially basketball and ping-pong. When rural schools were built, construction workers first put up the basketball court so they could enjoy the modern sport.

China's supreme rulers sought socialist modernization. Mao now saw the traditional Soviet road as leading to an elitism of educated Soviet-style officials. In contrast to reformist officials who in 1956 tried to reverse the losses caused by the forced shrinkage of markets and the disincentives and rigidities brought by collectivization, leaders aligned with Mao. Believing that "only socialism can save China," they sought a path to socialism built not on moneymaking but on the fundamental values of communism.

Such leaders made Xushui county in Hebei, just north of Baoding, their model. From all over China, rural leaders were sent to Xushui to emulate it. Xushui leaders won renown in winter 1957–58 for water conservation work that mobilized rural labor, combined with a drive to enliven militia work. More new acreage was irrigated in China in 1957–58 than in the prior eight years. Young militia members acted as a Stakhanovite labor corps, digging dikes and dams. Claiming they could save the nation as the revolutionary army had a decade earlier, idealistic youngsters sang patriotic songs while working. Writer Kang Zho was sent in to chronicle Xushui's selfless militarized march toward communism.

Mao argued that correct attitudes liberated miraculous productive energies. In January 1958 he declared that all who criticized rapid collectivization as "adventurist" were anti-Marxist rightists. Once rightist thought was overcome, he held, productive wonders would flow. Mao was buoyed by reports of the success of the big units and big mobilizations of labor for dam construction and irrigation not only in Xushui, but also as orchestrated in Henan province by its provincial party secretary, Wu Zhipu, and by Chen Boda.[1] These reports proved to Mao that Rural Work chief Deng Zihui was wrong in arguing that hand tools and limited managerial know-how made small units, mutual-aid teams, and even household farming suitable and efficient for China. Chinese villagers, Mao insisted, would rally to communist ways of doing things: leveling rich and poor, doing away with money, militarizing labor, wiping out the market, and ending commodity production, in sum, abolishing all forms of private property and exploitation.[2] When Deng Zihui would not be convinced, he lost his right to speak. Virtually all senior leaders supported the communistic initiatives of Henan Secretary Wu.

Communist Mobilization

Although policy changed, networks of loyalty were entrenched. In February 1958 the Hebei co-op leaders Mao had earlier singled out for highest praise, the Pauper co-op's Wang Guofan and South Kingsboro's Wang Yukun, were featured in a Hebei magazine. On the cover in color, bedecked with party medals, was the favorite co-op leader of Hebei First Secretary Lin Tie, Geng Changsuo.[3] Boss Geng acted on Mao's line of struggling against elements of capitalism to advance toward communism. In April 1958 "prosperous middle peasant" Li Qingyong was arrested for plotting to sabotage production. Li was accused of fabricating charges against team leader Li Shuxing, of poisoning team leader Li Zhuang's family pigs, and that ubiquitous act of protest, of uprooting cotton plants. Li Qingyong was prosecuted and jailed. The following month "prosperous middle peasant" Li Can allegedly circulated clandestine leaflets. The Wugong militia seized Li Can. He, too, was jailed.[4]

When Lin Tie did not press Hebei to the forefront in mobilizing labor and imposing communist institutions, Lin was compelled to resign his concurrent post as governor. The new governor, Liu Zihou, presented a budget at the Hebei People's Congress in May projecting monumental growth. Liu, a Hebei native, was expelled from school in 1931 for protesting Japan's seizure of northeast China. He became a Communist in 1936 and served in guerrilla units in southern Hebei and central China. After 1949 he rose as an administrator in central China under the tutelage of Li Xiannian. When Li moved to Beijing in 1954 to become finance minister and to join the Politburo, Liu succeeded him as governor of Hubei province. In January 1956 Liu was made first secretary of the mammoth Sanmen Gorge irrigation, power, and flood control project.[5] As with Boss Geng's network, so the Liu Zihou–Li Xiannian connection remained intact through numerous large changes in policy.

In May, at the Second Plenum of the Eighth Party Congress held in Beijing, Geng Changsuo heard Mao's heir apparent, President Liu Shaoqi, proclaim "Hard work for a few years, happiness for a thousand."[6] Mao pledged that big collective units would let China accomplish in a day tasks that took others twenty years. China would swiftly surpass Britain, and then, in eight more years, the United States.[7] Mao turned to gargantuan collectives to send China's economy leaping forward. Meeting at Baoding in June, the State Statistical Bureau was ordered to release only numbers likely to launch high production sputniks, human creations touted by Mao as more important than the mechanical sputniks recently launched by the Soviet Union. Statistical Bureau members became cheerleaders.

On June 14 Mao made clear that the issue was not mere growth but true communism, negating all private property. Treating the family as a remnant of private property, Mao targeted the peasant household for destruction as an economic unit. Household plots of land should be wiped out, as should household sideline production. To replace the social functions of the family, nurseries should be established to raise children and collective dining halls created to end eating as a family unit. Such measures, Mao said, would inaugurate a pure and perfect society. Perhaps, he speculated, men and women for purposes of procreation, need stay together only for a year.[8] Party propaganda shifted from focusing on high growth to emphasizing building communism.

In July, in the inaugural issue of *Red Flag,* editor Chen Boda styled the mammoth units of Xushui county and Henan province "communes." He claimed that the leap to communes would open a road to communism. Communism meant the end of money. Food was to be free. For villagers, this meant that what was stored or otherwise available could be freely consumed.

To those fired with enthusiasm by official exhortation, by stories about Xushui and Henan, and by an expected bumper crop, communism, with its promise of abundance, seemed imminent. Local black-market prices for grain, which had been running at twice the state price, fell precipitously. Other second economy prices followed this trend.

In August Mao toured experimental units in Xushui and Dingxian counties in Baoding prefecture on the Beijing-Wuhan railway, and nearby Anguo county, all readily accessible to leaders in Beijing.[9] Xushui became one of two key points for national emulation. With the Hebei provincial capital and Party Secretary Lin Tie transferred in 1958 from Baoding to Tianjin, leaders in Baoding, who had been promoting big units and communist forms such as eating in common rather than as private families, could more readily press the fundamentalist line in the region. In spring 1958 Xushui built separate dormitories for men and women. The destruction of the peasant household economy was carried into organizing life as the big collective organized labor. Although the press did not report on the separate dorms, visitors spread the story. Only a few most zealous places would emulate it.

The other key point, Henan province, was said to be sending up high production sputniks. Mao singled out Henan's big units as organizational forms for a transition to communism. Henan made its Statistical Bureau a subunit of its Bureau of Propaganda.[10]

During his tour of Baoding prefecture, Mao was accompanied by Yan Dakai, agricultural chief of the party's North China Bureau, and Xie Xuegong, a rising fundamentalist member of the Hebei party committee in charge of commerce and finance. Mao, his pants hitched high on his portly belly, heard that Xushui expected a fantastic autumn harvest of 550,000 tons of grain. Mao asked, "How can you consume all this food? What are you going to do with the surplus?" He advised taking land out of grain to grow oil-bearing crops and a variety of vegetables to upgrade the diet. "Plant a little less and do half a day's work. Use the other half day for culture; study science, promote culture and recreation, run a college and middle school."[11]

Mao's instructions sped via telephone conference and newspaper. *Within two days* Dingxian county in Baoding prefecture reported setting up 2,300 fertilizer plants.[12] After leaving Baoding, Mao promoted large organs of labor in Henan. His terse comment, "People's communes are good," echoed across the nation. Mao then went to a Central Committee meeting at the Hebei seaside resort of Beidaihe and declared that the large units he had witnessed proved that China could soon realize fundamentals of communism. Chen Boda proposed doing away with money and commodities, promising that, with the state replacing the market, large rural units would permit the realization of communist distribution, a free supply system giving to each according to need.[13] The leadership endorsed these policies. The Central Committee predicted a great leap in grain yields to 1,000 catties per person and approved the formation of communes, enormous militarized collective organizations that combined labor in industry, agriculture, commerce, education, and military affairs. Slighting the productive promise of scientific agriculture in market economies, Mao promoted reorganization and vast labor mobilization to win common prosperity. Divisions between town and country and between industry and agriculture would vanish. Communes would provide "the golden bridge to communism." In Raoyang that fall people were taught to sing:

Communism is heaven.
The commune is the ladder.
If we build that ladder,
We can climb the heights.

Ignoring the lesson learned by Wugong adviser Lu Guang that propaganda alone could not get villagers to work hard and well, the party nationally exhorted villagers to harsh semimilitarized labor. In Wugong village, reward and retribution, carrot and stick, were used to induce hard work. Those who worked long hours gathering the most manure were publicly praised. Those who did not meet high targets were publicly humiliated. Where exhortation failed, party leaders, whose careers depended on delivering the goods, tended to resort to more coercive means.

From August 23 to September 1 the *People's Daily* featured a "Eulogy to the People's Communes in Xushui." When Agriculture Minister Tan Zhenlin signed an article in the *People's Daily* promoting Xushui, Hebei officials concluded he was Xushui's patron. Its seven communes averaged forty to fifty thousand people. A reporter in Nanliyuan village in Xushui described four hundred women workers, "many wearing jackets of red cloth with pink flowers or white cloth with blue flowers," together with six hundred men, organized as a militia "labor shock brigade." Armed with rifles, they marched to the fields. Drill preceded and followed work. Leaders shouted drill commands, "one, two, three, four," to push militarized labor. Since 1957 Xushui had been presented to the nation as a model of militia-building, as Mao put it, of "militarization, combatization and disciplinization." Militias were then promoted throughout the countryside to prepare for a defensive war and to accelerate labor mobilization.[14]

Cultural institutions throughout Hebei were reorganized to serve the war communism of the Leap. People were called to defend the nation and destroy its enemies. Defenses were built on both sides of the main north-south railway through Hebei. Hebei's literary journal, *The Bee*, was shut down in June and replaced in January 1959 by the national defense oriented *Literary Guard*. Not only its name was militaristic. The cultural policy attendant to the march into communism was to propagate the theme of war preparedness. Written works that did not strengthen the nation's fighting spirit became political targets. Liu Zhen's *Yingxiong yuezhan* (A parade of heroes) was criticized for portraying war as hell, which could lead people to shrink from fighting. Hebei people were told that the highest value was steeling themselves to fight enemies. With militarization a central goal of the Leap, writer Ouyang Shan was attacked for writing as if there were a common human nature, instead of distinguishing enemies from friends by building on notions of class war so that people would learn to hate the enemy. In 1959 Hebei writers were summoned to Beijing to learn to write militantly to serve a communism fit to survive war.

Dasigou village in Xushui embodied communism in its four dining halls with "twenty cooks in white caps and aprons" to serve its 124 village households. In Xiefang village the reporter from the *People's Daily* found a kindergarten, "a tall white building" serving 173 children between ages three and seven, most of whom stayed overnight. "The boys are all dressed in blue shorts and white vests with red flowers. The girls are all dressed in white blouses with blue skirts, with colored flowers on their blouses." Twelve old folks were cared for in an immaculate "Happiness Home."[15] China's notion of communism harmonized with its traditional culture of rigid gender divisions and great respect for the elderly.

Since China suffered scarcities of textiles, lumber, and other building materials, news of Xushui's uniforms and buildings caused panic. Villagers guessed that Xushui had traded its grain for the pretty cloth used to make its colorful outfits. The swap, according to the rumor mill, caused grain shortage in Xushui. Worried that the state was confiscating all the private property it needed for construction, villagers rushed to sell property before the state seized it. The market was glutted; prices plummeted. Wood beams used to construct buildings lost 90 percent of their value, bringing a price of only five yuan.

Henan's Party Secretary Wu Zhipu was cited in the national press for promoting deep plowing to achieve wheat yields of 7,000 catties per mu. The top yield in Wugong was but 400 catties. Xushui county proclaimed that by plowing seven feet deep, sowing 1,000 catties of seeds per mu, and applying 300,000 catties of manure followed by scarce chemical fertilizer dressing, it would produce 120,000 catties per mu. Foreigners were sent to Xushui to see communism.

The state organized units of ten thousand or more households throughout the countryside. Private plots were eliminated along with most private markets. The logic of collectivization, transferring control of the economy from the household to party-designated managers, was carried yet further. At Beidaihe the Central Committee had called for immediate expansion of collective activities, including mess halls, kindergartens, nurseries, sewing groups, barber shops, public baths, homes for the aged, agricultural middle schools, and "red and expert" schools.[16] Chaotic and costly construction followed. The wish was translated into policy that China could quickly stop being a poor place whose development was blocked by scarcity piled upon bottleneck, a place that lacked everything from capital and transportation to skilled technicians, modern agricultural science, and farm machinery.

Veterans were urged to recall that earlier mobilizations had made possible victories against Japan's war machine and the forces of the Nationalist party, Chinese troops had even fought America to a standstill in Korea. Most villagers had happy memories of the gains following land reform. History bred a faith that gave birth to a season of enthusiasm, especially for the young.

Workers were dispatched far from home. Raoyang sent workers to the iron and steel city of Baotou in Inner Mongolia. Villagers who obtained state-sector steelmaking jobs did their best never to return to collectivized farms. A 120-member Hebei opera troupe was dispatched to entertain thousands of Hebei workers patriotically serving in Inner Mongolia. The troupe encamped in the Baotou suburbs in the vicinity of a plant working on China's hydrogen bomb project. The influx of Han workers into Inner Mongolia seemed to Mongolians to threaten their land, culture, and opportunity. Mongols, according to an informant from Inner Mongolia, became nostalgic about the Japanese invaders. National leaders presented the Han influx as closing the economic gap between coast and hinterland. Industry moved inland would reduce China's vulnerability to attacks on coastal cities with heavy and military industry.

Labor corvées of unprecedented scale tried to reduce Hebei's water problems. In subsequent decades central Hebei relied on the reservoirs and canals built in 1958–59 with the labor of millions using picks, shovels, and handcarts. Following Mao's denunciation of experts at a March meeting at Chengdu, water conservancy stressed mass creativity.[17] The hectic efforts at times backfired, misusing the water table, increasing salinization and alkalinity of the soil, and bringing waste and great loss.[18] As a horrendous flood in 1963 soon showed, the claims of great success for the labor corvée work were much exaggerated.

Reliance on mass energy and folk wisdom was presented as truly communistic in contrast to the traditional Soviet way, which was now said wrongly to rely on an elite of officials and highly educated technicians. In Shijiazhuang, officials sought other work for teachers of Russian. Throughout Hebei the schools used to educate illiterate local officials were closed. In August educators from Raoyang and other Hebei counties were called to Tianjin to rewrite textbooks in order to remove unhealthy Soviet influences and to highlight China's communistic reliance on masses, not elites.

Although water control was welcome in flood-prone areas of Raoyang, rounding up and dispatching laborers far away to work for strangers was alienating and destructive. "Shock brigades" toiled around the clock, pushing animals and humans to, and beyond, their physical limits. Loss could exceed gain. To build a dam to irrigate the plain around Shijiazhuang, in 1958 engineers from the Ministry of Water Conservation trekked into the mountains west of that city to Xibaipo, where the 1947 land reform conference had been held. The houses of the top party leaders and the meeting room for the Central Committee still stood. They would be washed away by the planned Gannan reservoir, as would the village of Xibaipo. Residents were peremptorily informed of how the Great Leap would affect them.

Furniture and other historical artifacts of the party leadership, which had been headquartered in Xibaipo between May 1947 and March 1949, were packed and taken to Beijing for safekeeping. Xibaipo households were told to rebuild higher in the hills. The Gannan reservoir flooded the fertile Xibaipo plateau. The state provided little compensation. The county's best land was lost. Even ten years later, villagers stagnated in poverty worse than before the land reform.[19]

In a political atmosphere of zealotry that precluded caution or realism, on September 10, 1958, President Liu Shaoqi arrived in Hebei's model county, Xushui, which claimed to have achieved communism. President Liu applied for commune membership along with Wang Guangmei, his wife, and other family members. Announcing grain yields of 2,000 catties per mu, Xushui implemented a free supply system. All food, clothing, and services were to be provided at no charge.[20]

Zealotry

Following six years in which provincial per capita grain output declined 1.8 percent per year, Hebei proclaimed a big leap forward, announcing three-year goals of 2,000 to 3,000 catties per mu.[21] Beginning in the small leap of 1956, this chronic grain-deficit province whose 1957 grain yields were the second lowest in China, reduced acreage planted in grain. In 1958, officials projected tenfold productivity increases and discussed reducing grain acreage by 50 percent. Anticipated wealth would fund forestry, orchards, animal husbandry, and economic crops, as well as schools, hospitals, and services.

Pondering imminent grain yields of 2,000 to 10,000 catties per mu, Mao Zedong urged a "three-thirds system." "Planting one-third is enough; another third may be turned into grass or forests; let the remaining third lie fallow. The whole country will thus become a big garden."[22] Some Raoyang officials recognized the three-thirds idea as that of Soviet agronomist Vasilii Robertovich Villiams, who was born to American parents named Williams.[23] In spite of the attacks on Lysenko in the Soviet Union and an open forum in China in 1956 to assess his worth, Stalin's Lysenkoan dogmas still dominated in North China's agricultural circles in the wake of the anti-rightist onslaught against critics of Stalinism. Close planting was fervently promoted as proof that, within a species, members cooperated and therefore prospered. In 1958 and 1959 poor North China peasants, hoping that such tricks as close planting would produce a great leap in yield, heeded Mao's call and dangerously cut back grain acreage.

Leaders competed in zealotry. Hebei promoted units of ten thousand households in plains areas and even sanctioned some units of fifteen thousand and twenty thousand households. Echoing Mao in Xushui, the Hebei government directed communes to run nurseries, kindergartens, primary schools, and junior high schools, and even colleges. "Within ten or fifteen years, all people now below twenty-five years of age may reach the cultural standards of a college student."

The euphoria was not universal. Mao privately noted that in Hebei "thirty-five percent basically accept the communes but with objections or doubts on particular questions. Fifteen percent oppose or have serious reservations about them." He blamed the opposition on local leadership in the hands of "prosperous middle peasants or even undesirable elements."[24] Following the fearsome anti-rightist movement of 1957–58, it required courage to voice common sense doubts about the gargantuan collectives. The following year Wugong tractor station chief Shi Xisheng argued that deep plowing broke expensive blades and brought up less fertile soil to the surface. He insisted that the pressure to do jobs quickly and to keep the plows going without servicing produced shoddy work and ruined costly, irreplaceable machinery. Provincial authorities were called in to squelch Shi's disbelief in the Leap. He was dismissed and sent to a factory in a neighboring county. During the subsequent twenty-seven years Shi was seldom permitted to return home to be with his family other than during the New Year.

Hebei's administration was reorganized to further the transition to communism. The provincial capital was moved from Baoding to Tianjin. To facilitate large-scale water conservancy, 147 counties were amalgamated to 80. The North China Bureau temporarily stopped functioning. As illustrated by Raoyang, the organizational upheaval brought administrative chaos.[25]

> In March 1958 Raoyang was transferred from Shijiazhuang to Cangzhou prefecture.
>
> On April 28, 1958, Cangzhou prefecture was abolished. Raoyang became part of Tianjin prefecture.
>
> On December 20, 1958, Raoyang and Wuqiang counties were incorporated in an enlarged Xianxian county administered by Tianjin municipality.
>
> In January 1960 three former Raoyang communes in the east remained with Xianxian county. The rest were transferred to Shenxian county.
>
> On July 9, 1961, the enlarged Shenxian county was broken up. Anping county, which had been incorporated into Shenxian in 1958, was reestablished. The former Raoyang county was taken from Shenxian and given to Anping to the west—except for the three communes that remained in Xianxian.

In 1959 Zhang Kerang, chief of the Hebei Department of Agriculture, was transferred to Beijing to serve as head of the Rural Work Department in a revived North China Bureau. Zhang, Wugong's patron since the 1940s, did not visit Wugong again for fifteen years. Despite organizational chaos, Wugong still had friends in high places. Networks of power held firm.

Red Flag over Wugong

The Red Flag People's Commune, headquartered in Wugong, was proclaimed on September 9, 1958. Soon renamed the Wugong People's Commune, it joined fifty thousand people in the four townships comprising the old Raoyang fourth district. Geng Changsuo was named chairman. But Geng could not effectively lead a unit comprising one-fourth of the county. Transportation was primitive. No motor vehicles were available. Geng could not even ride a bicycle. So wearing his coarse gray shirt and black pants, a customary white towel wrapped around his head, he walked from commune headquarters in Wugong to Zoucun, almost two miles east, or Xiaodi, five miles southwest. When his comrades presented the fifty-eight-year-old Geng with a donkey, he rejected it. Walking made Geng look unprivileged. Ubiquitous petty corruption was a minor irritant in Wugong, but the consequences of unaccountable power secretly commanding resources were disastrous elsewhere. Neighboring Yanggezhuang's decline into misery was made more painful by a rise in the brutality and thievery of its leaders. To older people, incorruptible Geng remained "the rope-seller from the market." He won a reputation for incorruptibility, walking when others rode, repairing his sandals when others bought new ones, rejecting favors (such as sweet melons), even when they were offered to all officials.

In theory the commune was a way to pool resources, to enlarge the scale of labor, and to defend against catastrophe. By combining the wealth of thirty-six villages, an enlarged accumulation fund could purchase electric power, trucks, factories, and well-drilling machines that no single village could afford. The countryside would catch up with the city, field laborers with mental workers, the destitute with the rich. Massive labor mobilizations would make it possible to level and square the land, improve the soil, dig irrigation canals, construct dams, drill wells, and build roads. Mechanization would then prove profitable. Factories would dot the countryside. Peasant scientists, no longer misled by bourgeois scientists, would sow with improved seeds and develop superior planting and plowing methods.

In practice the enlarged administrative unit threatened Wugong villagers who had recently grown far richer than their neighbors. They stood to lose more by amalgamation than had members of the original co-op in 1953 when they were merged into the big unit. The August 29 Hebei directive inaugurating communes stipulated that collective property would be transferred to the commune for unified management and equal distribution.

The thirty-six villages of Wugong Commune were renamed brigades. Wugong village's ten teams were reorganized into three. The former teams one, two, and three in Boss Geng's ropemaking east end comprised a new team one. Teams seven, eight, nine, and ten, comprising two incest-bounded regions divided by a lane, formed the largest of the new teams, the third, in the west village where Old Militia Xu, Brains Zhang, and Fierce Zhang resided. Teams four, five, and six in the discontented vegetable growing center, which was the old bastion of power of the Li lineages where independent tiller households and old water wells were concentrated, constituted team two. The center west, including some of the richest and strongest of prereform Li households, was split off from the center to become part of team three, the largest team. The village center was composed of 90 percent Li households, while the east end and west end held a bare majority of Li households.

In Wugong's split, weakened, and disgruntled village center, now called team two, the 1958 yield was 50 percent lower than in the west end, team three. Despite propaganda about the commune as the unit for organizing labor and distributing income, the three enlarged teams served as the main units not only for labor but also for income distribution. The west end and east end resented and resisted villagewide distribution that meant sharing with the once powerful, but now economically lagging, politically ostracized Li lineages of the village center.

Wugong's intravillage reorganization into larger work units was feasible, if far from popular or efficient, because of a history of enlarged cooperation and mechanization based on neighborhood and lineage. For most of rural China, the gargantuan scale of the new organization was irrational in light of the lack of bonds of trust required for income pooling and labor organization. Big units artificially mixing dozens of villages lacked legitimacy, provided few economies of scale, ignored the imperatives of hand labor appropriate to small fields, and ultimately were alienating.

Wugong village benefited, however, as commune headquarters. Resources were monopolized by nodes in the state hierarchy. An insect control station was established. The thirty-bed county branch clinic with its staff of twenty, previously located in the Zoucun village market, sped up its move, begun in 1956, to Wugong. This would become a bonanza for Wugong when the prefecture richly subsidized Boss Geng's clinic. The Raoyang county clinic, like most rural clinics, became a resource-starved disaster, lacking any claim to an enhanced state budget share, lacking even antiseptics to wash the floors on which patients had urinated because of the absence of toilet facilities. Villagers had no place else to turn for medicine because socialist policy prohibited private doctors from practicing. Politics, however permitted the reporting and predicting only of advance and success.

Between October 25 and 28, 1958, Geng Changsuo attended Hebei's Second People's Congress in Tianjin and heard Governor Liu Zihou praise "high production 'Sputnik' fields," the more than one thousand units whose reported yields exceeded 10,000 catties per mu! Wugong's 382 catties in 1958 did not win sputnik status. Yan Dakai, who had taken Mao to Xushui, then came to Wugong. "You're a model unit. Wugong must become a 'red satellite,'" he told Boss Geng. That is, Wugong should report higher figures than others. But Geng, who in earlier years went along with some exaggerated figures, refused this huge inflation of Wugong's figures. Given his recent tirades against colleagues for declaring embarrassingly high targets, local credibility made it difficult for Geng to trumpet high figures. Yan fumed. "You keep on like this and we won't print a line on Wugong in the press for three years."[26]

The threat was real. Political standing was the source of access to state-monopolized scarce resources. For two years, between early 1958 and spring 1960, Wugong disappeared from the provincial and national press.[27] Still, Geng Changsuo retained his status as a national peasant leader. In November

1958, Geng, as well as Hebei Party Secretary Lin Tie, were again among the Hebei representatives to the National People's Congress.[28]

For Lin Tie, Wugong's top province-level patron, the Leap was meant to further "four changes" essential to the modernization of agriculture: mechanization, irrigation, electrification, and fertilization. State resources should contribute to these goals. While state propaganda highlighted self-reliance, state structures rewarded the well connected. Lin Tie, without publicity, arranged an extraordinary two million yuan allocation to Wugong to build a power station, expand the tractor station, construct a brick and tile factory with a daily capacity of four hundred thousand bricks, and establish an agricultural tool repair shop and vehicle team. When Mao called on Chinese scholars to record histories of working people in the village, family, commune, and factory, Nankai University in Tianjin sent ninety students to Wugong commune. Living with villagers, laboring in the fields, and conducting interviews at night, they remained from August through December.

One student, Zuo Zhiyuan, later a professor at Nankai, reached Wugong as the commune was established. Zuo concluded that the secret of Wugong's success lay in its origins. From the outset its officials were relatively honest and hardworking, implying a negative assessment of most rural leaders. While in Wugong, Zuo participated in tree planting, part of a national afforestation campaign. The trees planted on both sides of roads provided timber, income, windbreaks, and shaded beauty. Zuo saw ditches dug for irrigation and fields leveled and squared. With so many men away with labor shock brigades, the village was quiet.

Zuo noted that surrounding villages had difficulty accepting Wugong as their leader. No matter how they labored, these villagers could not catch up. If there was a drought, Wugong could count on water from dozens of deep wells drilled with state support; other villages had only a couple of shallow ones. Other villages coveted and lacked Wugong's leadership, unity, and, above all, Wugong's public accumulation fund and ties to the state. Wugong had these, others said, because it got started earlier. There was no way to emulate what counted most in the model experience: being rewarded by the state for being first. Hence, the call for model emulation sounded hollow.

In 1959 the Hebei authorities sent another team of historians to Wugong headed by writer Wang Lin and Wu Senlin. Qin Zheng went along to do sketches. A manuscript of two hundred thousand words was prepared.[29] Fundamentalist domination of the media kept the Nankai historians and the Hebei writers from immediately publishing on Lin Tie's model village.

Exploiting Labor

During the Leap, night and day, people were thrown into back-breaking labor. In 1958 Wugong Commune conscripted thousands to build major north-south and east-west dirt roads to link its villages. In keeping with military discipline, each team had to obey the "commander-in-chief," who sent people far and wide according to a "strategic plan." The project ignored equitable remuneration, popular support, physical limits of endurance, and conflicts among units. Where a project promised direct benefits to one's own village, then low wages and physically punishing work might not pose insuperable problems. Returns would come later in higher productivity and income. But in numerous cases there were few local benefits. Whereas the Great Leap promised to expand cooperation, after an initial burst of enthusiasm, overworked and abused people instead turned inward to protect themselves; mistrust and parochialism intensified.

Workers on Wugong commune-organized projects in 1958 received .20 yuan per day. In 1958 the value of the labor day in Wugong village dropped to .49 yuan, down from the three preceding years when it ranged from .71–.85 yuan. Between 1955 and 1959, the number of labor days doubled, yet per capita income fell. The state exploited labor as a limitless free good. In September 1958 workers from Wugong and other villages trekked several miles west to Sangyuan to dig an irrigation channel. That winter Wugong people opened 1,980 meters of irrigation channels and dug fifteen wells. Cement replaced bamboo tubing to line increasingly deeper wells. Water seemed to be fleeing.

Precious resources were frittered away. Contemporary reports claimed that in 1958 China constructed 6 million commune factories, about 125 new factories per commune in one year.[30] Whatever the exaggeration in the figures, labor and materials were strained to the breaking point. Scarce resources were dissipated; little of value was produced; money was lost. The damage was most acute in poorest places where a surplus was hard to generate.

In August and September 1958, Mao focused China's industrialization drive on iron and steel. Villagers built more than one million crude blast furnaces, known in the west as "backyard steel furnaces." By early September more than twenty million had joined the campaign; eventually ninety million people took part.[31] Every Raoyang commune was ordered to send two hundred to three hundred men to make steel. In September Wugong village sent forty-five men to the industrial town of Bozhen, ninety miles east, to make steel. People brought their own tools. There was no accounting. Sometimes horses and carts were left at the work site when people returned home. The Wugong middle school constructed a primitive blast furnace. Activists collected "waste" iron and steel to smelt. The state sent teams from cities to pressure villagers all over China to surrender that waste. Wugong villagers were forced to turn in supposedly useless stoves, broken cooking pans, and broken farm tools, anything that could be melted down to feed the furnace. Wugong students at school elsewhere were pressured to convince their parents to donate raw materials. In many communities all pots and pans were melted down, usually including the unique cooking equipment a village could draw on to prepare special banquets for important ceremonies. Youngsters were dispatched from schools in Raoyang to find bricks to build steel furnaces. Surviving temples were destroyed for their bricks, and the ancient town wall of Raoyang was completely dismantled. Even school-building walls were pillaged beyond repair for bricks. Hebei villagers were traumatized and alienated when the quest for fuel led to a seizure of scarce timber, valued wooden gates, and even precious coffins. Since class struggle was touted as the way to communism, in many villages the graves of once prosperous families were pillaged. The bricks were used to build kilns fueled by the coffin wood. Still, the low-quality iron and steel produced was valueless.

The height of the campaign coincided with the autumn harvest. It drew away tens of millions of experienced hands when their labor was needed in China's fields. Skilled farmers made bad steel. The harvest and the planting of winter wheat were left to inexperienced field hands, many of them women. Given the magnificent 1958 weather, record harvests were in the offing. Zhang Kerang told us that 1958 yields of 152 catties per mu were the highest Hebei attained in the 1952 to 1961 decade. In Raoyang, as in many localities, however, with so much labor sent elsewhere, grain was left to rot in the fields.

In poor villages that did not even have sickles, the wheat had to be wrenched out of the soil, root and all, by hand, resulting in callused, bleeding, and cut skin. The roots were used for fuel. The stalks were used to make mats, cushions, and mattresses. Inexperienced, weaker workers were not up to the task. More important, if the roots were not pulled up slowly by hand, thereby loosening the soil, seeds for the next crop could not be planted simply by hand. Many poor places lacked draft animals for plowing. Consequently the poor 1958 harvest augured not only an immediate decline in cash, comfort, and fuel but also a poor next crop from bad seeding. This prolonged catastrophe struck water-rich rice regions as well as the northern hinterland because both suffered similar irrational organizations of labor.

By October, as food grew scarce, it became obvious that mass steelmaking was a costly disaster. Within two months furnaces were dismantled. Mao made a token innerparty self-criticism for having launched the campaign without investigation. While this one irrationality halted, the campaign frenzy continued. Villagers were prodded into a campaign of deep plowing. Customarily, peasants used shovels on a section of land to dig up clay to mix with sandy soil that could be made into more fertile soil in three to five years. It was grueling toil, averaging a square foot of work per labor day. The race into communism had no patience for slow, partial efforts. Success was needed now. Hebei Governor Liu launched a movement to "sow wheat by shock attack," assuring villagers accustomed to yields of 100–300 catties per mu of 1959 yields of at least 1,000 catties per mu. Liu's slogan was "Learn from

Henan, catch up with Henan, press ahead consistently and win first position."[32] Liu directed villagers to plow some fields to a depth of even six feet. But the raw clay soil brought to the surface was not fertile.

In autumn 1958 and spring 1959 Wugong and neighboring Yuanzi pooled labor in a "shock attack." Thousands of men and women dragged plows through the fields. Working day and night, they turned up 2,000 mu of Wugong's rock-hard soil to a depth of 1.5 feet, in a few places 3–5 feet. For two weeks, young militia members from neighboring villages were drafted to deep plow in Wugong, to help the advanced. Such draft labor was deeply resented, so Geng Changsuo halted what he called empty efforts and sent the youngsters home. To the visiting youth, Boss Geng seemed an honest traditional peasant. He greeted them, thanked them, and even sat on the ground with them and shared a typical lunch of mantou, preserved vegetables and soup.

Wugong's technician, Bugs Zhou, without defending the Leap, later claimed that previous plowing to depths of .7 or .8 feet was inadequate for corn and wheat, whose roots penetrate to a depth of 1.5 feet. Deep plowing allowed roots to sink and leaves to grow better; it facilitated irrigation and raised yields. Subsequently, every five years, using tractors, Wugong would deep plow to a depth of 1.5 feet.

The state's demand for "rational close planting" multiplied the disastrous errors of 1956. Wugong, whose highest cotton yield was 74 catties per mu, sowed 5,000 seeds per mu in search of yields of 1,000 catties. In sweet potatoes, the number of plants reached 20,000 per mu, and in corn 12,000 plants. The result was that plants suffered as each stole nutrients from the other. Wugong leaders later found that yields improved from moderately closer planting.

While the Great Leap unleashed an explosion of activity, one sphere was cut to the bone: trade and the household sidelines associated with it. A 1958 Tianjin rectification campaign attacked "capitalist spontaneity" among small traders and shopkeepers. Enterprises and services that had already been squeezed were snuffed out. Services declined or disappeared.[33] Throughout Raoyang home spinning wheels to make cloth for clothes and for bags to hold grain were idled. New clothes grew more expensive, old clothes more patched. Women were de-skilled.

Each commune was directed self-reliantly to fulfill basic needs so that commercial units had only to allocate the commune's output among members, dispensing with buying and selling among localities. Each place wastefully sought to produce what could be purchased at higher quality and less cost elsewhere. A new contract system, consistent with Chen Boda's 1958 call to eliminate commodity production, curtailed monetary exchange.[34] Eliminating commodities and money was to bring closer a transition to communism. In theory, the multipurpose commune would produce all it needed—

even ball bearings. In practice, crucial gaps widened, production suffered, and cultural imperatives went unmet.

The Zoucun market was forced to stop its big temple fair, which had attracted twenty-thousand people a day in spring. The fair was banned as a manifestation of "feudal culture." Periodic markets shriveled when private plots were eliminated, peddlers and craftspeople were yoked to collective units, and money no longer flowed into the countryside. The destruction of markets was most devastating in the poor mountain areas of north and central China. Leaders proved their faith in Mao and the commune by destroying sidelines and markets root and branch. Tiny surpluses that these poor regions produced were squandered. Food disappeared. People were exhausted. With local markets wiped out, it could take five days to walk to a factory, an intermediate market, or an administrative center to acquire everything from salt and clothing to economic inputs.

Investigators sent to Henan in late 1958 found bare subsistence yields where 7,000 catties of grain per mu had been announced. Worse yet, they found officials so zealously competing in selling grain to the state that almost no grain was left in villages. By January 1959 many places had nothing to eat and no crop to harvest until late spring. And that poorly planted crop could not help but be minimal. Beggars began to flood Henan's cities. Visitors to the communes of Hebei's Xushui county likewise discovered grain shortages and hunger even as the press trumpeted bumper harvests. Villagers fleeing to cities revealed a massive death toll in the making.

Although even Mao was skeptical now of inflated claims, no one dared expose the state's disastrous fundamentalist policies. The political atmosphere smothered criticism of anything presented as leftist, advanced, and socialist. To be critical was to be a rightist, an enemy of progress, a reactionary. It was to be on the side of all the old evils that socialism supposedly was transcending. Anyone who did point to economic irrationality, decline, disaster, and hunger would be accused of throwing cold water on the enthusiasm of the masses and forced to criticize oneself, or suffer far worse humiliation and abuse for stifling the energies China needed to build a better future. Stories circulated about the recent anti-rightist campaign. Few villages lacked victims like Wugong tractor station chief Shi Xishen or hungry Li Dalin and Fan Shufang, or pure scapegoats like Provider Li Peishen. Calling attention to the famine-inducing facts would only make oneself and one's family victims who would share a degraded fate. The sound of politics had the ring of death. The countryside fell silent.

Over the Brink

Instead of slamming on the brakes to save lives, those driving the socialist super express slowed just a bit, still careening dangerously. On December 25,

Boss Geng was a member of the presidium at a congress in Beijing of six thousand village representatives of advanced units. Along with Wang Guofan of the Pauper's co-op and Li Shunda, who had accompanied him to the Soviet Union, Geng heard of new decisions to adjust commune affairs. Mao, in December, agreed to pull back from the brink by allowing some commodity production, restoring some household plots, raising more pigs, limiting what the state could take for investment, and utilizing some responsibility systems that would more directly link a worker's effort with pay. But these suggestions were given neither political priority nor institutional form. No campaigns promoted these suggestions. Gargantuan organizations remained intact. Few North China villagers had private plots to fall back on, most having been abolished in 1958. Mao would not allow China to enter the world grain market to purchase food for the starving. Officials continued to publicize places such as Xushui and Henan as advancing rapidly toward communism. The Great Leap hurtled over the brink.

Winter 1958–59 brought no rest. People were dragooned into land leveling and well drilling. Men were dispatched to join large construction brigades and water projects. Night workers in Wugong received an extra meal. Wugong planted 400 mu in sweet potatoes just in time to avert starvation. But at lunar New Year, when villagers traditionally took stock, they found themselves in difficult straits. There were few meat-filled dumplings, although even the poorest households made sure they had some dumplings, often substituting sorghum for wheat flour.

Nonetheless, the favored displayed loyalty. Model villages increased grain sales to the state. In 1959, under the leadership of Zhang Duan, the thirty-four-year-old militia leader who took over as party secretary in April, Wugong sold to the state 180,000 catties, more than twice the preceding peak. Village grain reserves were exhausted in the hungry winter of 1959–60 when more work brought less income. When the commune was organized, the leaders had seized all private stores of grain. Households now had nothing left and nowhere to turn.

The disaster was far worse in Yanggezhuang and other neighboring villages, where grain yields fell to just over 100 catties per mu, below the average harvest prior to the founding of the People's Republic. Yanggezhuang would stagnate at the miserable 1959 level for more than a decade. Generally, the poorest places with bad soil took longest to recover. The worst hit were zealous villagers in such northern and central provinces as Henan and Anhui whose sons had bled to win the revolution and who hoped that Mao's policies of close planting, market abolition, and labor mobilization could save them from poverty.

Governor Liu Zihou declared that Hebei's 1958 autumn harvest broke records. The food-grain harvest was claimed to be 45 billion catties, more than double the fine 1957 harvest. Cotton statistics were more fantastic.[35] By comparison, Wugong's 1958 production gains looked pitiful. Xushui and other model counties near Baoding claimed to have quintupled grain yields and promised to double that the following year.[36] Whatever the yield, the inability to harvest the crop, hold on to it, or distribute it made Hebei a disaster area. Per capita grain output actually declined from 470 to 404 catties, and that figure masks the fact that famine was averted only by a late sweet potato crop. Grain output (excluding potatoes) fell from 402 to just 264 catties per person, starvation levels. The bumper harvest claims masked a disaster.[37] A quarter of a century later, Hebei would not yet come close to yields of 1,000 catties per person as claimed in that first frenzied year of the Leap. In fact, usable output declined, capital and labor were exhausted, and people were left hungry, tired cynics. The original enthusiasm disappeared.

In 1959 the state reduced its exaggerated national production claims for 1958. Hebei officials still insisted that 1958 grain and cotton yields had increased by 23 and 12 percent, respectively, over 1957. No mention was ever again made of Governor Liu's claims of increases five and fifteen times as large. Hebei's harvest actually declined.[38]

The central government took half-measures that did not deal with the worsening famine. The government told villagers to economize on food and suggested that local leaders approve some use of private plots and household sidelines. The state insisted, however, that villagers pay taxes in grain, sell grain to the state on the basis of inflated reports, and hew to targets and obligations based on impossibly high grain numbers.[39]

Focusing on grain yields—almost the only measure of productivity publicized by the state—could disguise a disaster, even if the reporting was accurate. Wugong reported a 1959 record grain yield of 430 catties per mu. Yet per capita income was 46 yuan, compared to 57 in 1957. Income fell, as did exhausted villagers. Fixed assets dropped from 73,000 yuan in 1957 to 47,000 in 1959. Draft animals dropped dead and machines burned out. The state demanded higher investment and higher grain sales. Leaders were pressured to trumpet the high-unit grain yield and to squelch news of empty grain bins and empty stomachs.

Facing a lean winter and impossible targets, local leaders ordered exhausted people to grow crops that would permit them to survive and could be reported in terms of expected production of grain equivalent. Raoyang sent people to see models of sweet potato success in Baoding prefecture, home of the Xushui model. Villagers were also told that in Henan other crops had been cut down and sweet potatoes planted. In Raoyang villages where corn or other crops were doing well in summer 1959, officials commanded commune members to do as people had in these model areas. Coerced, women cried as they cut down good crops in order to grow potatoes. Planted too late, the sweet potatoes often were as small as a finger. The food tragedy intensified. Some Raoyang tillers lay down in the field and refused to work. Some repeated the saying, "If people cheat the land, the land will cheat people's stomachs."

In August, at a Central Committee meeting in Lushan, Defense Minister Peng Dehuai finally tried to make China's top leaders confront the deepening disaster. In a visit to rural areas of his home province of Hunan the preceding winter, Peng recorded his concerns in a poem:

Grain scattered on the ground, potato leaves withered,
Strong young people have left to smelt iron,
Only children and old women reaped the crops;
How can they pass the coming year?

At Lushan Peng pointed to the economic collapse of Mao's favorite Hebei model, the communes of Xushui.[40] Although many leaders had come to share Peng's misgivings about the Leap, most either kept silent or joined in when Mao lashed out at Peng. Mao declared that the issue of halting or continuing Great Leap policies was "a continuation of the life and death struggle between the two opposing classes, bourgeoisie and proletariat."[41] To take issue with Mao was to risk being branded as a class enemy. At Lushan few besides Peng Dehuai would risk that. To speak the truth was to court danger. Raoyang people invoked the popular saying, "Disaster exits through the mouth, illness enters through the mouth."

Mao stripped Peng Dehuai of executive positions in army, party, and government and labeled him a right opportunist. Mao then installed Lin Biao in Peng's stead as minister of national defense. Former members of the North China Bureau were, like Peng, criticized for rightist conservatism. Members of the Hebei Bureau of Agriculture who had tried to check the Leap's economic irrationalities were similarly criticized. Rather than pull back from the brink, Mao made the life and death decision to plunge ahead with fundamentalist policies.

In September 1959 Mao promoted Hebei Governor Liu Zihou's idea of sputnik fields, a reference to extraordinary yields claimed for intensive cultivation of 10 percent of commune land.[*] Despite the dearth, in 1959 Mao ordered another cut in grain acreage. The area planted in grain was reduced by 12.5 million hectares, 9.5 percent of the total area. Great Leap pacesetter Henan reduced its sown grain acreage by 14 percent.[43] A 7 percent reduction in 1959 brought Hebei's total reduction since 1956 to 1.3 million hectares, 14.5 percent of its grain acreage.[44]

The 1959 grain dearth was intensified because the state extracted record sales of 66.5 million metric tons from villagers. Although China's grain output fell 15 percent below 1958 levels in 1959–60, the state would procure 32 percent more than it had in 1958–59.[45]

Mao, having approved some cutbacks from fundamentalism and having arrived at Lushan open to more concessions to necessity, after clashing with

Peng, suddenly ordered officials to continue to institutionalize communist fundamentals. This meant abolishing private plots, eliminating the household raising of pigs, chickens, and ducks, recruiting more labor for big water projects, and creating more collectivized mess halls, in sum, pressing forward with "sharp class struggle in the villages."[46] All China was urged to leap ahead on the model of the original Sputnik Commune in Henan's Suiping county, which continued to report fantastic successes.

In Hebei that winter, Huailai county villagers were reduced to eating leaves. In mountain areas near Zhangjiakou, people stopped working and even slaughtered draft animals to stave off starvation. But the state, instead of combating the famine, pushed Chinese villagers over the brink.

A Miniature Cultural Revolution

As in the 1930s, economic decline deprived households of the wherewithal to act morally as tradition dictated. Lineages and communities came unglued. Fighting within the family grew nastier. People invoked the expression "qiong jia," the poor fight. Family bonds disintegrated; more families divided. Adding to the sorrows of villagers this time was a state-directed war on popular culture. During the Leap Chen Boda and other fundamentalists launched a cultural revolution linked to Lenin's call to combat "the survivals of the middle ages" in the minds of Asia's peasants. Minds full of feudal superstition were to be refilled with socialist ethics and science. Chen called for a campaign to expose and eliminate religion in order to liberate productive forces.[47]

In 1958 the Catholic church in Xianxian, which earlier had been converted into a hospital, was turned into a factory. The Japanese had only desecrated the church. Chinese patriots defensively claimed to us that in Zhending, just north of Shijiazhuang, the Japanese had done worse by cutting off forty-two arms of the giant bronze goddess of mercy, smelting the arms into bullets in a Tianjin factory.

The fifty-one-year-old Roman Catholic bishop of Baoding, Monsignor Peter Joseph Fan Xueyan, was arrested in 1958 and sentenced to fifteen years in prison. Bishop Fan, one of the last Chinese ordained by the Vatican in 1951, became a prisoner of conscience for his continued loyalty to the pope.[48] Raoyang's surviving Daoist and Buddhist temples were demolished. In one north Raoyang village the three remaining temples, one Buddhist, one dedicated to the land god, and a third to Guan Di, the god of war, were destroyed in the 1958 steel campaign. The temples' wooden ramparts and rafters fueled the furnaces.

Most believers continued ritual activities at home, thus binding and defining the family as a sacred preserve secure from state intervention. Some older people stubbornly went to sites where temples once stood in order to burn incense and to worship. Security forces often beat such people away. In a few villages, older women whose sons had died fighting with the Eighth Route Army felt they had the right to resist anyone daring to challenge their public worship. Powerholders were frequently among the most superstitious and least vulnerable to adverse consequences of public display of ritual. When the father of a Raoyang commune party secretary died, the son summoned a Daoist priest. Brandishing a ceremonial sword, the priest directed the soul of the deceased heavenward. The party introduced a "revolutionized" spring festival at the 1959 New Year. After eating dumplings in the morning, villagers had to work as usual. Ritual obeisance to elders and other traditional practices for celebrating the two-week New Year holiday were banned.

Wugong's leaders still acted on traditional ethical imperatives. When Li Laohan, a father of six daughters, died at the start of the Leap, he murmured, "If there had been but one son, things would be much better."[49] The household's income now rested on the earnings of a widowed mother of six. She could never save enough to provide proper dowries for her daughters. With state policies making cash scarce, a penniless widow rearing children faced humiliation unless local leaders helped with school books, new clothes at the New Year, and a penny for a sweet when school friends went to a store.

The village provided welfare to Li Laohan's daughters. Having worshiped at Buddhist temples with his mother and having suffered the ignominy of a marriage without ceremony, Boss Geng felt the weight of traditional culture. But since 1948 he had responded loyally to the party's pressure to secularize and sanitize village culture. Nonetheless, Geng helped the fatherless girls find work. Two became army officers, one was given a job at the co-op pharmacy, and a fourth was made a minor village official. Using power to prevent families from disintegrating was how a good patriarch should act. But in less united, less well-off villages, leaders could not halt the decline toward family disintegration.

With the county virtually bankrupt and traditional culture under attack, Raoyang authorities recalled their opera troupe from Inner Mongolia. No longer able to afford to feed the entire troupe, Raoyang disbanded three-quarters of the members. The popular Hebei operas, a glory that had been restored in the honeymoon period, almost disappeared. As in Hejian county, local people were proud that they at least kept the opera going.

No Wugong leader tried to tell fellow villagers that they were backward feudal reactionaries. Although the local credit co-op stopped loans for weddings, funerals, and holiday celebrations, the cultural issue was presented as leaping forward economically. In summer 1959 Wugong Party Secretary Zhang Duan assembled villagers to discuss removing burial mounds from the fields. He proposed moving graves to a common site, originally the ninety-mound Southern Li lineage cemetery on the village's southern outskirts. By removing the graves, Fierce Zhang contended, they would be both keeping faith with the party that had done so much for them and helping themselves. Revolutionary consciousness could produce wealth. More land could be leveled; irrigation and mechanization would improve. Zhang suggested using burial material for productive purposes, but no one wanted to use the lumber. The smell of the grave permeated coffin wood. Of course no woman was invited to dig up a grave. Death was associated with yin, the female element. For auspicious outcomes in mourning, the female dirt had to be balanced by male (yang) activity.

Zhang invited villagers to move ancestral remains. He then opened the meeting for discussion. No one said a word. Villagers were asked to raise their hands if they agreed to move the burial mounds. Everyone raised a hand. But the democratic process was a sham. Even village powerholders sat silent. Almost everyone, especially the elderly, had misgivings, but the party had spoken.

Larger Wugong lineages had their own burial area. The lineage heads met and opposed moving the mounds. Three days later, undeterred, Zhang Duan dug up his grandparents' bones, placed them in a small wooden chest, and carted the load to the Southern Li cemetery for reburial. Under party pressure the lineages subsequently agreed not to oppose the removal of burial mounds. The eighteen mu of Northern Li burial ground were leveled for cultivation. Sections of the Southern Li burial ground were allotted to other lineages. Each would continue to bury its dead with its own lineage members.

The redivision of cemeteries paralleled changes in power. The Northern Li, in decline for nearly a hundred years, lost its burial ground. The Southern Li, whose power was broken in the twentieth century, lost its monopoly on the village's largest burial ground. Its geomantically favored spot was shared with the Gengs, Qiaos, Yangs, Xus, and Zhangs who came to power in the revolution, as well as with the Northern Li.

Almost everyone knew where fathers and grandfathers were buried, but many were unable to locate earlier generations. After removing recent remains, the land was leveled. Each family decided how many generations to move. A few brash people leveled the land without bothering to move the bones.

To show how class warfare produced wealth, Geng insisted that even the dead rich kept living villagers poor. He claimed that the tombs of the more prosperous took as many bricks to build as an average house, some twenty thousand. When villagers balked at using dismantled tombs for home building, village leaders ordered the bricks used in water control. That too was resented. Boss Geng commandeered bricks from a large tomb for irrigation construction. The widow's son-in-law was an army officer, who threatened to report Geng to higher authorities for commandist abuses. But Geng pointed out that the widow, too, had raised her hand in favor of using graves for economically productive purposes. Checkmated by the empty democratic form, the soldier dropped the case.

The transfer of graves by the end of 1959 increased cultivable land by 60 mu.[50] Still, numerous mounds dotted the fields. Old people opposed moving burial mounds. The leaders hoped that pressure and the promise of wealth would eventually win all burial mounds to the village cemetery. In other Raoyang villages, digging up graves was far nastier. Coercion undermined community. Since villagers were supposed to be working for communism and not acting on material incentives, no recompense was offered to families that removed ancestral grave mounds from the fields. Some village leaders simply ordered the mounds to be leveled. Other leaders consolidated cemeteries around their own lineage grave site. To salvage something, some households dug up graves, disposed of the bones, and used coffin wood for fuel. Many attempted to find the wherewithal to reinter parents in wooden coffins. Some outraged households insisted on preserving their grave mounds. A few let it be known that anyone who dared move their lineage graves would be killed. To resist state-imposed cultural outrages, villagers relied on the more parochial and violent aspects of tradition.

Tradition included physical abuse. Male patriarchs saw a bloody thrashing as a cure for disobedience. Raoyang men said, "kneading makes good dough; beating makes good wives." Village social relations were still violent. Just prior to the 1959 lunar New Year, Dog Li and some junior-high friends played hooky. That took courage. A report of an unexcused absence could result in a beating by a father that could bloody a child.[51]

Dog Li skipped over to the Zoucun market to buy yellow powder for homemade firecrackers. Halfway back to Wugong, he climbed a tree to set off the packed powder, but it fell from his hands. When he climbed down for the explosive, it went off in his hands. Li's friends ran to find their teacher, who raced to the accident site and carried the bloodied boy to Zhang Ping, recently returned from the army where he had studied first aid. Zhang put antiseptic on the arm stumps, bandaged them, and took the boy to the miserable Raoyang County Clinic, where what was left of his hands were amputated.

Villagers helped Dog Li make a normal life. Teachers rigged up hooks on his arms so he could turn book pages. He practiced using his hooks and mouth to manipulate small tools. Over the decades Li became an adequate repairman. For a wife Dog Li was presented a mentally retarded woman who could do household chores. The Lis raised two healthy children. Life went on with a modicum of decency and self-respect in harmony with Chinese cultural norms.

Revived traditional norms took religious forms. Sects with Islamic and martial arts rituals spread in neighboring counties. In Raoyang a secret eclectic religious sect, combining the teachings of Daoism, Buddhism, and

Confucianism, spread. Young people joined in large numbers. The leader, named Qi and known as the king, was a venerated calligrapher. His family members became lower-ranking royalty. Married women were welcome, but girls who would later marry out of a village were not allowed to join. Local people spoke of "Marrying out a daughter, like pouring out water." All sect members had to go through initiation rituals. Special prayers and ceremonies celebrated marriage and honored the dead. A few times, at midnight, hundreds met secretly, burned incense, spoke in tongues, and prepared for the arrival of a savior. Then the members shared a communal dinner. To prepare for their savior, members had to act honestly and honorably. As bonds fell apart, villagers sought the glue of traditional culture. While crime spread and temptation heightened, sect members supported each other in acting ethically.

The removal of the graves and other such jarring fundamentalist policies as elimination of the temple fair, the destruction of temples, the cutback in traditional opera, the loss of traditional medicine and traditional cooking utensils, and the coerced shrinkage of the market that had brought the goods needed for ritual celebrations all alienated villagers. Raoyang villagers spread the story of one particularly nasty local official who used force, going house to house, to stop the ketou to elders. But when he went to his parents' home for New Year's dinner, his frail mother told him that there would not be even one meat-filled dumpling for the son until he would ketou to every family member. The humbled son did as the elderly mother insisted. Villagers took satisfaction in this small triumph. In many villages, officials outraged people by forcing them to do corvée labor even during the New Year holiday. And the cultural revolution that made war on Chinese culture had barely begun.

Eating out of One Big Pot

After Mao praised an Anhui commune in which it was "not necessary to have money to eat," the state called for mess halls to substitute for families eating together.[52] After the 1958 autumn harvest, Wugong village established collective kitchens at ten locations, subsequently consolidated in one place, the former Southern Li lineage temple, but quickly redivided into three mess halls, one for each team. The militarized mess halls had no tables, no roof, and no warmth. Bricks were piled up outdoors and covered with bare planks. People carried their stools, bowls, and chopsticks. In autumn 1958, with so many men away working on construction projects and women forced to bring in the harvest, many welcomed the mess hall with its big stove and cauldron since there was little time to cook. Some young people relished a chance to join friends at meals as a break from subordination to elders in hierarchical households.

Nevertheless, families disliked having to eat with strangers. Defiant households brought containers to the kitchen and carried food home. Some angry households ate the little grain they had hidden away rather than eat "free" in the mass mess. To many frugal older people, eating free and eating as much as you wanted seemed immoral. Folk wisdom had it that one ate today thinking of the potential natural disasters tomorrow. "If you pass bumper years like lean ones, in lean years you won't starve." It was painful for the elderly or the infirm to walk to the mess for each meal. It was also hard for mothers with breast-feeding or napping children who had to mesh multiple needs with a common eating time. Food for the ill and elderly gone cold by the time it arrived home was hardly appealing. Rain and the long winter made every- thing worse.

Many poor Raoyang villagers nonetheless ate their fill at the free mess halls after the fall harvest, happily commenting, "This is communism." Some mess halls even offered meat, but meat and grain swiftly disappeared. By the dearth of winter 1958–59, villagers considered themselves fortunate if they had held back a pot from the iron and steel campaign. Most villages in Raoyang kept their mess halls open through winter 1959–60. Wugong kept its three mess halls going a bit longer.

Brains Zhang Chaoke, who embraced the communist vision of the Leap, believed Wugong's public kitchens were a good thing. "When times were hard in 1959 and 1960, they may have saved some from suffering or even from having to go begging," he recalled. But, he said, they never became places with which people identified. In fact, they became soup kitchens, a communism of state-imposed poverty.

The mess halls were linked to a free-food policy that made food available with few restrictions and little bookkeeping. Wugong Commune, like others, printed blue food coupons that allowed the holder to eat free anywhere in the commune. Economist Xue Muqiao later observed that with free supply, some peasants ate until "the skin on their bellies was tight," consuming a year's supply of grain in three months. As a result, "people were hungry in com- munes throughout the whole country, and in some villages quite a few people starved to death."[53] Sun Yefang of the National Institute of Economics investigated Hebei's Changli county in early 1959. He found that mess halls were "not in keeping with the habits, customs and level of consciousness of rural people, that waste resulted and that it went against national feeling."[54] Mao, however, insisted that continuing these wasteful and resented institu- tions was a matter of class struggle.

Wugong cautiously tried to restrict free supply, deducting meal costs from the income owed each household. Still, people ate too many vegetables in the mess hall. Moreover, as economic conditions deteriorated, strangers came to eat in Wugong's mess halls. More prosperous communities such as Wugong village and neighboring Wangqiao experienced free supply as robbery since the fruits of their labor became handouts to strangers. The dearth caused by the Great Leap set village against village, household against household. Increasingly villagers relied on customary ties. Lineage members in less badly off villages helped worse-off relatives.

Explaining Famine

Local officials were instructed by the party center on how to explain the famine. They were to blame the catastrophe on bad weather. A grizzled Wugong old-timer told us, "it did rain, but not even enough for water logging." The state scapegoated the Soviet Union for its summer 1960 withdrawal of aid. But people starved to death long before that, trapped and killed by a system promoting rapid progress toward communism. The Great Leap death toll was not a sudden, one-time error resulting from unique policy blunders in 1958, 1959, and 1960. Rather, it was the culmination of institutionalized processes, values, and interests that had previously generated frightening consequences, as in the terror phase of the 1947 land reform and the anti-rightist movement of 1957. State-contrived local combat was celebrated as "class struggle," with the party rewarding zealots. A generalized disaster was made more likely when the state foreclosed ways that villagers could earn money and expand the economy, ending grain markets, eliminating rural handicrafts, sidelines, and processing, and imposing large, alienating, abstract collectives. The cruel treatment of individuals and their families who were branded as class enemies for pointing to hunger and disaster forced people and officials to swallow their cries.

President Liu Shaoqi, an early supporter of the Leap, privately acknowledged that "people starved and families were torn apart" because the state took so much grain away from the peasantry.[55] Peasants were informed, however, that the party was blameless and that Mao shared their suffering. He had ordered his chef to give up meat. Mao would dine on sparrow and not waste a kernel of grain. Village army men tended to believe the best of Mao.

By late 1959 Wugong villagers were reduced to eating cornstalks. There was little fuel and no cooking oil. It would be two decades before cooking oil became readily available. That winter, vegetables grown in fields fertilized by excrement often had to be eaten uncooked. Sickness and hunger plagued even proud Wugong. Some villagers whispered that "the commune is not as good as the co-op and the co-op was not as good as going it alone."[56] Privately a few Raoyang people muttered that Mao was doing everything fine, yet they had nothing to eat. Some recalled that during the revolutionary war party officials said their purpose was to see that people could eat their fill. Now bellies were half-empty. If an official approached complaining villagers, they swiftly shut up. One careless Raoyang villager was publicly criticized and dismissed from the party after muttering, "I want to tell Mao face to face that we are hungry." And Raoyang, whose officials had restrained Great Leap zeal, fared better than the most desperate regions.

In worse-off regions, weakened, dispirited villagers left some of the meager crop to rot in the fields. By winter and into the next spring, there was no nutrition and no medicine. Sick people died; so did infants and the elderly. By contrast, hungry Raoyang was much better off. With the condiments of cooking gone, rolls and buns in Wugong had no consistency and fell apart in one's hands. With grain stores exhausted, people began to scavenge, grabbing unguarded food. Writer-songstress Shi Guiying, daughter of the former tractor station chief, stole turnips. Villagers rationalized thieving with a ditty, "Lower rations; squash and greens instead of grain; who doesn't steal gets what he deserves." Starving Henan peasants fled to Hebei.[57] Officials tried to record what the hungry took from Wugong fields, hoping someday to be reimbursed. No repayment ever came.

Many Henan wanderers were women forced out of their husband's village so food would be left for blood relatives. Beggars became ubiquitous. In Hebei's Cangzhou prefecture hungry villagers crowded into train stations hoping to exchange possessions for food coupons. In Raoyang, a few husbands sold wives for food and cash. The poorer the region, the greater the amount of wife selling. To hide the shame, the wives were called cousins. As in the famine fifteen years earlier, in some of the worst-hit areas children with placards around their necks were left at busy places, in hopes that some better-off family would take in the starving young. If the top family earner died, a teenage daughter might be sold to the highest bidder in a distant place to obtain grain to keep the rest of the household alive. Prostitution, which had declined in the early 1950s, revived. One instance of wife selling in Raoyang became notorious when years later the husband returned to reclaim the woman. She refused to budge, so he went to court to collect on his property rights. The court decided for the wife.

Muslim robber bands attacked the grain station in Hejian, just north of Raoyang. Troops were ordered in to the starving region with barbed wire and machine guns to guard grain stations. Along the rail line running from Hebei to Shandong, bands attacked trains in search for food. The state responded by placing twelve guards on each train.

Hungry villagers could see that many were afflicted with dropsy. Facial skin became swollen and shiny. If any pressure forced the skin in, it no longer had the resilience to bounce back. Weakened by hunger, Wugong leaders fell ill. Collectomaniac Geng Xiufeng retired to Wugong with tuberculosis and prematurely prepared to "go and see Marx." Wugong reserved its scarce oil for pregnant women. Healthy young people got by, but the elderly and the ill were in deep trouble. According to Accountant Geng Lianmin, a dozen elderly villagers died prematurely.

Even some in the normally prosperous rural suburbs of Shijiazhuang starved. It was far worse in poorer areas across the border in Shandong and further south in Henan and Anhui. The worst famine counties in Hebei were Yongnian, southwest of Raoyang, and Baxian to the north. Villagers forced themselves to eat things they ordinarily would not feed even to dogs or pigs. Starving, diseased pigs went wild or dropped dead if famished villagers did not risk eating them.

Matters hit bottom in Hebei in 1960. Wugong's yields plummeted to 310 catties per mu. Total village grain production of 720,000 catties barely reached two-thirds of the 1959 total. Grain sales to the state were cut way back. Still, Boss Geng in 1960 loyally sold the state 20,000 catties of wheat. Wugong's 1960 individual grain allocation dropped to the lowest figure since the founding of the big co-op, just 270 catties per person. Facing starvation, villagers turned in desperation to the black market just as prices were driven up by the combination of grain shortage, heavy demand, and the state's crackdown on the market.

Wugong's poor neighbor Yanggezhuang had embraced the Great Leap policy of grain first. Its sidelines had long been squeezed out, its market eliminated. Peanut acreage had fallen 60 percent. In North China from 1956 to 1978, the acreage sown in peanuts fell by 30 percent.[58] For Yanggezhuang the displacement of peanuts and other commercial crops meant less value produced, less cash available, and less oil in local diets. It meant an uneconomic growing of grain in soil better suited for peanuts.

Following collectivization, with no cash and nothing to exchange, Yanggezhuang experienced a chronic grain crisis. In 1958 the poor villagers threw themselves into the Great Leap, hoping to solve their grain problem. By 1960 Yanggezhuang was a disaster, its grain yield barely reaching 100 catties per mu. The prices on its black market skyrocketed as a huge hungry regional demand chased a diminished supply. Corn rose to eighty cents per catty, sorghum from eight to sixty cents, millet from eight to fifty cents, and wheat went from ten cents to well over a yuan—if wheat could be found. The price for a goat soared from 15 to 150 yuan. In one year, real food prices in the hidden economy rose by 600 to 1,000 percent or higher; few had cash.

Some brigades with no food in spring 1959 issued certificates to villagers granting them permission to go begging. The certificates, stamped with the brigade seal, attested to the bearer's good class credentials and explained that begging was caused by the failure of the harvest in the village. This practice continued in periodic hard times in the decades to come.

Throughout Wugong Commune 1960 grain yields averaged well under 200 catties per mu. With less land under cultivation and far more people than during the bad 1930s, when yields averaged just under 200 catties, the crisis was acute. By 1960 and 1961, China produced less grain, cotton, oil-bearing crops, and hogs than in 1951, far less per capita given the rapid population growth of the 1950s.[59]

Thousands of Hebei peasants fled to the northeast along famine routes pioneered earlier in the twentieth century. Migrants opened frontier land. Some formed new collectives to facilitate the legal transfer of registrations to the northeast, an act that permitted migrants to be joined by family members at first left behind in Hebei. Villagers maneuvered within and around the system.

The semilegal movement of traders and refugees carried stories into Rao-yang about peasants in neighboring provinces rising in arms to obtain food. Travelers said that many were killed in Shandong in a historically rebellious region and that the state executed former Nationalist party officials who were in prison, falsely charging them with inciting the rebellions.

The first party secretary of Henan province, Wu Zhipu, who continued to report fantastic production numbers for famine-stricken Henan into 1960, was removed and permanently barred from higher office but never prosecuted or arrested. A few party secretaries in the most devastated counties who reportedly refused to issue travel passes to villagers so they could flee to cities for food and work, and who insisted that all was well and no relief was needed, were publicly tried. Although Mao was exonerated, local officials in Suiping, Xinyang, and other devastated Henan counties were publicly executed. The official word was that local bad elements and counterrevolutionaries who deliberately sabotaged the correct line of the party were to blame for the famine deaths. Soldiers received mail from home describing starvation, family deaths, and the rape of wives; the party explained to them that local toughs were to blame and would be executed. From the famine areas, travelers passed on news of public executions. Informed village gossip seemed more reliable than empty party claims.

A story circulated about a woman in Shanxi province leading starving peasants in the seizure and distribution of grain in the region where Li Zicheng had begun his second uprising against the Ming dynasty three centuries earlier. President Liu Shaoqi subsequently commented, "If we do not take emergency measures, we will be back in the situation of the Soviet civil war," when Bolshevik policies of war communism provoked peasant uprising.[60]

The most hair-raising tales reached Raoyang from Henan and Anhui. From Anhui, the province with the highest percentage of famine deaths, came descriptions of starving people digging up corpses for food. From Henan, once the pacesetter in the Great Leap, now the province with the largest number of famine deaths, the tales of horror were almost too numerous to absorb. Each returnee claimed that the county he had been in had been hardest hit. Some said Xuchang, some Xinyang, some yet others.[61] Reports circulated of villagers where everyone had died. Others told of villages where all the elderly had died. Soldiers doing relief work found people lying on the ground. Some were dead, some dying. Many were too weak to carry in the relief supplies the soldiers had brought. The soldiers rushed those who might be saved to hospitals. Throughout China twenty to thirty million people died, the largest death toll from famine in human history.[62]

The Hebei rural poor were especially interested in news of Henan villages in which everyone had died. Some were looking for open land to which they could escape. The death toll from starvation was so devastating that the government reportedly sought settlers from overpopulated regions to re-populate devastated villages. Some hundred Raoyang volunteers resettled. Travelers said that a depopulated region of Henan was being turned into a mammoth labor camp. A campaign to induce villagers in the crowded North China plain "to go to the pass to the west" led to a large exodus from Hebei's poorer western neighbor, Shanxi province, to the thinly populated, poor northwest. Minorities in Inner Mongolia and Xinjiang made way for Han settlers.

Balloons from Taiwan, where Nationalist forces had fled after losing the civil war, were carried by strange winds over the Hebei plains. Villagers hungrily opened the packages inside the balloons desperately seeking food. Instead they found propaganda leaflets, toys, and medicines. Once villagers stared skyward to watch military aircraft crisscrossing the heavens trying to shoot down the balloons.

Yet even as the famine deepened, the state constructed monuments cele-brating the first decade of the People's Republic. Hungry villagers gossiped about well-fed urbanites building the headquarters of the central government, the Great Hall of the People. It was rushed to completion in Beijing for National Day, October 1, 1959. On that day the military parade in Beijing featured massed militia and modern weapons made in China, symbolizing how communism kept China independent and strong. China also proved its vigor in international sport competition in 1959 by winning a world cham-pionship. The victors in men's table tennis were given a heroes' welcome in the new Great Hall. Proudly heralded victories in international sport competi-tion, military achievements, and continuing growth of urban heavy industry were presented as proof that China could no longer be ridiculed as the sick man of Asia.

In spite of the worsening rural disaster, the Hebei government, at a re-ported cost of 17 million yuan, began erecting a virtual palace to house high-powered official guests in Tianjin. Similar construction went on throughout the nation. The Tianjin complex was equipped with a large ballroom, luxury carpets, and a film projection room.[63] Young women were brought in to dance with officials. The movies shown included what Chinese considered erotic material. The socialist state graded by levels of secrecy what it considered obscene. The higher the leader, people quipped, the more pornography was available. As with other scarce and expensive consumer items commanded by the state, those at the higher echelons of party, army, and government had priority access. Ordinary villagers were excluded. In Tianjin, as in Raoyang and all of China, the networks of power that channeled resources to those within the orbit of the state were so deeply structured that not even the catastrophe of massive famine could budge them.

10⟡THE STATE
OF THE
REVOLUTION

The first Eighth Route Army soldier sneaked into Wugong in 1938 to be hidden by his east-end brother-in-law Prosperous Qiao Wanxiang, who then formed a party branch by linking up with others in his lineage and his neighbors. When these lineages then linked up with other outside lineages from the village's west end, the Xu, Zhang, and Yang, the Wugong party branch became a star in the orbit of the state on high. The revolutionary war had quickly entrenched a system that guaranteed privilege not merely by traditional personal networks, but also by location in regional and institutional structures. Villagers in the suburbs of a metropolis who shared in the power of such urban centers as Beijing and Tianjin to command resources would not starve during the famine. In like manner, the Hebei mountain district of Zhangjiakou, however badly wounded by the economically irrational and culturally alienating politics of the Great Leap, still fared better than other hinterland areas because it was a major military base and the military commanded priority access to scarce resources.

The Privileged and the Marginalized

The army preferred to enlist loyal, tough patriots from poor early liberated regions, dispatching them to sensitive posts. Soldiers from Raoyang served from the distant border with India to the national capital, Beijing. Parents of soldiers were awarded work points as if the son were home working, and soldiers received a few yuan in cash as pocket money. That, too, might be sent home to help parents through hard times. When the party center in 1960 finally began to deal with the famine by returning to more economically rational policies such as contracting private plots of land to households, the state's hierarchy of privilege gave pride of place to service families.

If one's standing in that statist hierarchy of privilege fell, however, as did Baoding's in 1958 when the Hebei capital moved to Tianjin, then local residents lost status and wealth. Baoding lost the ability to command the resources for its own growth. It began a decline from the province's number-one city—excluding Beijing and Tianjin—to its number-four city, after Tang-shan, Shijiazhuang, and Handan. With top places monopolizing scarce resources, smaller, less-favored cities got last and least, often providing residents a life little better than that in such poor counties as Raoyang. Socialist propaganda focused on classes, but individuals, families, and villages calculated opportunities in terms of a structured hierarchy of places and networks of officials.

Given its high standing with the Lin Tie network in Hebei, Wugong village would not suffer as badly as its neighbors in the Great Leap famine. In 1959, as hunger worsened, Wugong celebrated the tenth anniversary of the People's Republic by inaugurating an electric power station underwritten by Lin Tie's subsidy. Some families connected their homes to electricity; a few obtained scarce radios. Lights were strung to permit night work by shock brigades.

Four teenagers formed a film projection team. They were to do political education using homemade slides. An amphitheater was built at the north end of the village for showing outdoor movies. The medicinal herbs that had been destroyed during the Great Leap were quickly replaced as new seeds for the plants were made available to the Wugong Commune. Wugong's two small generators of 80 and 300 kilowatts, the electric power station made possible by Lin Tie's huge Great Leap subsidy, made it the first village in the region to enjoy the benefits of electricity. Three specially trained local technicians kept the generators in good repair. Electric power permitted machine processing of grain and fodder and, more important, electric powered pump-wells that irrigated the fields and drove machines in village workshops. For the favored, even in hard times, life opportunities expanded.

Li Mengjie, the youngest orphan raised by Xu Shukuan, escaped the local dearth by enlisting in the army. Shi Guiying, whose vilified father had been transferred out of the Wugong tractor station, still benefited from her local ties to state-favored Wugong. She was assigned to the surviving opera troupe in Raoyang and then sent to study in a short course at the Hebei Academy of Arts in better-off Tianjin.

Boss Geng's eldest son, Delu, sent home from Beijing in February 1958 as the government tried to cut costs, was one of those put in charge of the power station in October 1959. He had already been put back on a state payroll a year earlier as a member of a team showing movies. In 1958 Delu's wife won a state-payroll job in the Anguo County Agricultural Bank. The following year Lin Qingying transferred to Wugong and a state-payroll job as a bookkeeper for the Raoyang branch of the Agricultural Bank. Transferring up the ladder of places required connections. People sought to hold on to the highest and most favored rung on the state's ladder, even at the cost of dividing families.

Even village truck drivers and village factory workers tried to transfer on to state-farm payrolls. State farms kept losing money, but the state subsidized the losses and provided state-farm workers with free housing, free medical care, a little cash, and pensions.

One reason Wugong was politically strong was that neighborhood and lineage linkages had been built into a stable villagewide coalition embedded in personal networks of power. In contrast, communities splintered by the state's various vigilante campaigns were left powerless. Those feeling themselves unfairly at the bottom looked at those higher in the hierarchy of privilege with envy and disdain.

At lunar New Year 1960, when Raoyang villagers took stock, most lacked cash for firecrackers. The dead market no longer provided the delicacies and entertainments that made the holiday a delight. Meat-filled dumplings hardly existed. Life had been impoverished.

When ruling groups in 1960–61 relaxed the state's stranglehold on the market in order to reenergize the economy, people still experienced trade in terms of state-structured relations that benefited some and locked out others. In the pyramidal command economy, the national capital, Beijing, could commandeer food from throughout the nation. The Hebei capital, now Tianjin, could commandeer food from throughout the province. All goods, from fine grain to books to bicycles, were distributed in precise hierarchical relationship to closeness to the center.

Hungry peasants reduced to sweet potatoes bridled when urban dwellers complained that they did not have enough fine grain. In that catastrophic winter of 1960 even people in Beijing adopted such traditional strategies for coping with famine as stripping the bark from trees. The government instructed city dwellers to lie in bed and use as little energy as possible so as to reduce food requirements.

Country people talked about the immoral and undeserving character of city people. In Raoyang, people recalled the Qing dynasty ditty about "the slick operators of Beijing, the fast talkers of Tianjin and the hired thugs of Baoding." Villagers retold unsavory tales about the treachery of Baoding people who had served the Japanese invaders.

Hungry Raoyang villagers silently raged at the sight of commune credit officials biking in at harvest time, then calling in a truck to cart away grain to fulfill quotas or repay debts. Officials, they grumbled, took everything, leaving villagers only the dregs.

> First round: return loans.
> Second round: deliver state grain.
> Commune members share the leftovers.

Banks called in all debts for repayment. If not enough grain remained to get residents through the winter, villages applied to purchase food from the state. Villagers lost good wheat and got back sorghum, or even dried sweet potato that was mixed with water and made into tasteless buns called *wowotou*, which turned the throat terribly sour and painfully burned the stomach. Villagers ate the sweet potato wowotou only when there was no alternative.[1] Now even city dwellers in Hebei had to eat wowotou.

Villagers with food relished the tough terms they could impose on urban dwellers who came to the countryside for food. Urbanites exchanged cloth coupons for grain coupons at five feet of cloth for one catty of grain. From Baoding, which had been devastated by devotion to the Leap, some resident military families born in Sichuan and Hunan came looking for red peppers. They returned to the city cursing the black market price of pepper, which they said had soared from five cents to five yuan per catty. Villagers bargained their grain coupons for watches and other prize brand consumer items that they believed were monopolized by the privileged. Brand consciousness was intense, brand being proof of position in the state's status hierarchy. Almost anyone could rattle off the ascending quality of brand-name cigarettes, bicycles, and radios. A few villagers refused to exchange with or sell to anyone on the state payroll, claiming they would take less and do business only with ordinary folk like themselves.

In spite of a prolonged struggle in the name of socialism against superstition and proclaiming a "dictatorship of the urban proletariat," peasant culture shaped consciousness and action in most traditional ways. Outsiders to the village continued to be experienced as strangers and sources of injustice. Commune officials lived in a separate compound and were almost never invited into a village family's home or life. Raoyang natives still felt the shame imposed when they were forced to sit silent so country accents would not provoke public ridicule. Young male toughs, especially those from military families, presented themselves as the community's conscience as they resisted water control officials who would flood and devastate the community. Tales of high prices charged to city folk searching for food were popular.

The life chances of villagers surviving by their wits were structured quite differently from Boss Geng's, whose goal was to strengthen vital ties to the state. Boss Geng served the state by downplaying need. Wugong proclaimed a 65 percent increase in 1959 grain yield over 1958, although the accountant's book presented to us in 1978 shows only a 13 percent increase. In the continuing rural dearth, even villagers in favored Wugong cried out for state relief. Not only were eggs, pork, and cooking oil nearly unobtainable for the second consecutive year, but staples, grain and vegetables, were also in short supply. The Geng leadership group served the hard-pressed state by keeping demands on it to a minimum.

Xu Shukuan tried to squelch cries of suffering and disillusion, saying, "We're in heaven compared to 1943," when she and others had gone begging, been forced to sell children, and watched loved ones starve to death. Other leaders contrasted the old days, when no government cared and families were split asunder, to the present, when taxes were remitted to spare villagers their food.[2] Village leaders compared the community's situation to praying in a Buddhist temple. The prayers would be answered. No one would starve. Boss Geng brushed aside villager requests that 40 mu of unirrigated cotton land that had not properly sprouted because of frost be replanted in food. He insisted on loyalty to the state, saying, "The national plan is to grow cotton. Even if the yield is not high, we should do our best."

In helping to mute anger against the state, Wugong's leaders, looking forward to reward from the state, told villagers that if they would work hard, drill new wells, and upgrade irrigation pumps using the new electric power source, all losses would be recouped. Growth would resume. Wugong villagers took great pride in their ties to the state, feeling superior to people who lacked such ties. Regions and villages better integrated with the state or capable of two or three solid harvests and, thereby, of generating a surplus that could be sold, were not so badly off once fundamentalist policies were halted.

Villages in Raoyang stationed guards to watch the crops day and night. But starving people took risks. All strangers were suspect. Often people suspected the guards. Trust declined. Anyone suspected of stealing was searched. Since no one dared search party officials or their children, they were popularly blamed for the ubiquitous theft that plagued the countryside as morale and morality declined and a gulf deepened between villagers and officialdom.

The Wugong fruit orchard had to be protected against thieves and angry households who wanted to divide it up. Wugong built a wooden fence around the orchard, with a single gate secured with a heavy lock, the key carefully controlled. Iron Man Li Duolin, a security worker and long-time confidant of Fierce Zhang Duan, was put in charge. The tie between Boss Geng and Fierce Zhang, who never criticized Geng, not only helped join the east- and west-end lineages, but also kept the village united since Zhang had good ties to the Li lineages of the village center, especially through his wartime comrade and long-time drinking companion, Li Wanyi.

Carrying a knife and followed by his mongrel, Li Duolin, who had married the beggar woman in the famine twenty years earlier, commanded a rotating group of militia members guarding the Wugong orchard. They carried mats to the orchard to rest on during the night shift. Wugong tried to keep its precious food from being snatched by starving strangers. Although Boss Geng threatened dire consequences for any leader found pilfering even a penny, villagers gossiped that nothing could safeguard the fruit from leaders.

In nearby Gengkou village, the Wugong orchard fence seemed another proof of privileged access to state resources. Ordinary villages like Gengkou could not obtain scarce and expensive lumber to fence in orchards. Gengkou villagers said they could not stop Wugong youngsters from stealing their fruit.

The fence in Wugong and its absence in Gengkou revealed two worlds, a favored one protected and absorbed into the orbit of the state, and another world abandoned to its fate. Gengkou villagers picked their apples before ripening to keep them from expected thieves.

Villages throughout Raoyang hired militia to watch crops at harvest time. In some villages guarding became year-round, including patrolling the lanes at night and safeguarding trees and all other collective property viewed as fair game by the hungry or angry. Usually two militia members were stationed at party headquarters to respond to emergencies. With two people, each could keep an eye on the other. Young male toughs in these security forces often became lawless bands unto themselves. When they broke in on gamblers, after physically abusing men and women alike, they would take the money for themselves. Gamblers seldom reported thefts. To be lawfully locked up in the windowless room used as a village jail usually guaranteed beatings.

Peasant culture, at times empowering and enriching, at other times was cruelly constricting. Children were brought up to fear gossip that could shame the family if traditions were violated. Consequently Brains Zhang Chaoke had spent just the right amount on his wedding and Macho Li Shouzheng included a complete person in his. At times the nastiest elements of the culture reinforced the cruelest consequences of the socialist system that made powerholders unaccountable. When rape increased, villagers believed that some members of the hired militia abused women. Victims and their families dared not report the crimes. Life as a single woman in the countryside was bitter, and the prospects of marriage for rape victims dim. Anonymous letters were passed to higher party officials begging for redress. One Raoyang village militia leader known as the king was a notorious rapist. Eventually, after many anonymous letters finally brought a high-level investigation, the rape king was sentenced to fifteen years in Number Three Provincial Prison in Shenxian county. Run by the Provincial Labor Bureau on wasteland in Weiqiao Commune, the prison was surrounded by a huge wall and electrified wire, housing thousands of prisoners, eventually including King Qi, the venerated calligrapher who headed the Raoyang secret religious sect.

A nonparty person could be executed for rape, but party and military officials were often invulnerable to criminal prosecution. When officials were punished, it was usually through special party tribunals, not the courts, and punishment frequently involved merely job transfer or demotion. Justice was not blind. The fifteen-year sentence for rape reflected the state's view of the prerogatives of a local official in the light of popular anger at a spate of heinous crimes.

In every walk of life the system discriminated against those least attached to the state. When the state gave top priority to developing atomic bombs and rocket technology, the military and the relevant bureau in the Ministry of Heavy Machinery had first rights to the graduates of Qinghua and China's other top science and engineering universities. Here and everywhere, the command economy created scarcities for the less favored. With state-favored units monopolizing scarce personnel and resources, massive redundant waste was how the privileged assured themselves of what was needed when it was needed. The draft animals given Boss Geng in the late 1940s, the tractors sent to Wugong in 1953, the electric power installed in 1959, and special access to fertilizer and medicinal herbs all reflected a political logic of privilege that was not conducive to economic efficiency.

Limited Reform

In 1960 and 1961 China's government moved away from communist fundamentals in the economy, allowing a resurgence of private activities and market transactions. At the same time, the center continued to propagandize through the military for the ethical superiority of communist fundamentals. Through all the contradictory change and hesitant movement, the entrenched socialist system continued to mold life's prospects. The forces shaping daily life were far too complex to be understood simply as the victory of a single unified government policy.

In 1960 Raoyang party branches were ordered to hold meetings for villagers to recall how much worse the old days had been. Many people remembered how good things had been in the honeymoon era after tax and land reform and before collectivization. In May, faced with a mere ten-day supply of grain in Beijing and a seven-day supply in Tianjin, the socialist state at last permitted villagers to drop the most destructive Great Leap policies that had devastated the countryside and the national economy.

Wugong's Zhang Chaoke reported back from a county meeting that each village could decide to modify the distribution system. Wugong transferred administrative power from the villagewide brigade to work teams one, two, and three. Following the earlier demise of wasteful backyard steel furnaces and unpopular mess halls, the hastily erected and poorly staffed schools, clinics, and day-care centers were dismantled. Time, equipment, funds, resources, trust, and life had been squandered. In Raoyang all the new factories closed except the East Wind Machine Factory. Built during the steel drive, its skilled workers continued to repair tools.

The state-funded home for the elderly and retired in Raoyang did not close down. It provided food that met urban standards, and there was great demand for access to its more than forty beds. Entry was restricted, however, to those with impeccable political connections. Favoritism ruled, whatever the party's policy line. The state took care of its own. Wugong received the lion's share of the county's scarce fertilizer. Poor Gengkou searched everywhere for fertilizer, but found none. Raoyang villagers mocked the system that forced them to bow to power to survive:

Flatter shamelessly: eat delicacies and drink hot stuff.
Don't flatter: starve to death for sure.

Villagers not in state-favored units had life shaped in ways distinct from
Wugong people. Whereas the privileged village's three management teams
administered units of 150 to 200 households, proof that the Wugong party
still supported big collective units, ordinary neighboring villages set up
smaller teams, only one-sixth the size of Wugong's. These village leaders tried
to woo people who had been alienated and scarred by gargantuan unproduc-
tive units. In most communities, villagers paid in kind for collective field work
had little way to earn needed cash. Any enterprise or sideline that paid cash
was seen as a better job. More and more youngsters did not want to learn how
to farm. Villagers began to say, "Only the stupid work the land."

In the anxious spring of 1960 even reforms heightened tensions in poor
Raoyang villages. County officials disbanded collectivized handicrafts and
reduced collective investments in an attempt to motivate laborers by leaving
more of the fruit of their work in their hands. However, many village party
leaders did not give any cash or resources to craft workers who were suddenly
left to their own devices. Seen as weaker farmers, many were not allowed to
work on collective land or given a share of collective distribution. They then
took up not quite legitimate commercial pursuits neglected by the state and its
collectives. In Zoucun and elsewhere, small market fairs came to life. Even
people without cash walked to markets to savor the excitement and to enjoy
free opera and martial arts.

The 1960–61 reforms improved life, famine receded, and China's rural
economy moved ahead. The agenda of the Rural Work chief whom Mao had
silenced, Deng Zihui, was acted on again. As in the early 1950s and in 1956–
57, villagers were urged to use responsibility systems, including the kind of
piecework and quotas that Wugong had pioneered under Adviser Lu Guang.
Beginning in devastated Anhui and Sichuan provinces and in poorer areas
across the countryside, villagers welcomed yet more far-reaching reforms,
including household contracting of land. The reforms encouraged the resurgence of the household economy and the market.

Zhang Kerang, the Hebei agricultural leader who had been Wugong's
patron, worked in the Rural Work Department of the North China Bureau in
Beijing. This made him a subordinate of the vindicated Deng Zihui, who still
championed incentives and organizational forms that harmonized with peasant rationality. In Hebei, permission was won to lease as much as eight mu to
households in some experimental villages. The major Hebei promoter of
contracting responsibility fields to households was Hu Kaiming in Zhangjiakou prefecture, deputy governor to Lin Tie prior to the Great Leap.

By early 1961, as emergency measures in response to the high death toll,
the party center agreed to permit household sidelines and local markets and to

no longer treat the utilization of experts or quota systems as the crimes of class enemies.[3] Deng Zihui's right to speak was restored.[4]

In May, Zhang Kerang responded to Deng Zihui's policy initiatives by convening prefectural heads to discuss responsibility systems. Zhang found Deng, who was a southerner, to be short, talkative, hard working, and a fanatic on grass-roots investigation. Reports heralded Hebei reform successes, especially those of Hu Kaiming in Zhangjiakou. The reforms introduced responsibility systems for field management, leased land to poor households for three years, and even leased land for raising sheep and horses. An Agricultural Work Conference concluded with recommendations for more use of responsibility systems except in plowing, sowing, and harvesting. These reforms were said to have been especially successful in bringing the famine regions of Anhui province back to life. Hebei authorities ratified the new policies, and the poorest regions in Pingshan county and Xingtai prefecture immediately put them into practice. In four neighboring counties, Hengshui, Wuyi, Zaocheng, and Shenxian, land was allocated to households for cultivation in 1961.

Another sign of a return to normalcy in the world of village China was the end of the cultural revolution attacking so-called feudal traditions. Once again throughout the county customary rituals revived to mourn the dead. This cultural normalization was reflected in the elite sphere in Tianjin, where in June the literary journal *Hebei wenyi* resumed publication. Intellectuals were no longer targeted.

Most Raoyang villages had eliminated private plots in 1958. In 1960 they were restored and, in some cases, expanded to 5 to 10 percent of village land. Villagers pressed to expand household plots. Wugong villagers heard stories of initiatives in nearby Shenxian county, where households were allotted cultivation rights not only to private plots but also to untilled wasteland. The policy was an invitation to a broad definition of wasteland. Neighboring Wangqiao village responded to the invitation.

Although the reforms restored some sense of community, the institutionalized catastrophe continued to unleash emotional rage. Tensions erupted into angry disputes over ownership of homes and courtyards. Lineages, having lost control over farmland, animals, tools, and handicrafts, focused inheritance calculations on the surviving legal property, the household residence. Parents dared not bequeath property to a daughter for fear that other family members would seize it. Whatever the constitutional guarantee of gender equality, a daughter was viewed as a member of another lineage by her eventual marriage. She therefore had no village standing and no lineage support network. Inheritance disputes simmered. People feared buying and selling houses. A returning urban worker who bought an empty house could soon find it the target of rock throwers and arsonists. With lineage heads now lacking the legitimacy to settle disputes among surviving brothers, the brothers innovated. Some, with the wisdom of Solomon, literally split the house in two. With law irrelevant and lineage authority weakened, property disputes regularly exploded in violence.

Raoyang remained so poor and peripheral that no cars were available to officials. Even the party secretary biked to work. Coping on their own with the economic disaster, people saw all those favored by the state as unfairly better off. People gossiped about corrupt officials who reserved the best jobs for family members.

Wugong people were fortunate that at the villagewide level of governance, Geng Lianmin, a close relative of Boss Geng, kept the post as accountant that he had first taken twenty years earlier. Accountant Geng's integrity facilitated some trust and unity between leaders and led. The continued employment of a substantial independent tiller from the days prior to the establishment of the People's Republic (Accountant Geng would serve until his death in 1984) even while the state insisted that only the once poor should be trusted and promoted, reflected the special concern with unity and honesty that marked Boss Geng's leadership. Indicatively, when Wugong west enders muttered about corruption by their treasurer, he was removed and Li Zhimin, a recent junior-high graduate, was appointed team three treasurer. Accounts were publicly posted on a bulletin board, ending secrecy. This was called democracy.

To regain popular confidence and to consolidate his power, in 1961 Boss Geng appointed burly Li Shouzheng, Geng's east-end neighbor, to head the village militia. After Shouzheng's hungry elderly mother scavenged for food in violation of a ban on gleaning in collective fields, to cleanse his disgrace Li dropped down in front of the family's residence and wailed aloud his humiliation to all passersby. If anyone other than his own recently widowed mother was causing him trouble, Li Shouzheng would have smashed and cursed the culprit. Li virtually worshiped his mother and was a most filial son. Li also favored swift physical action. Poor families in the east end, who seldom spoke in public, whose homes had no books, and whose children left school as quickly as possible, looked up to Macho Li Shouzheng. He tried to help their sons get into the army, which was a way onto state payrolls for the rural poor. Further helping tie Macho Li to Boss Geng's political family was a plan to marry Shouzheng's younger sister, Li Kuanzhe, to Geng's eldest village grandson, Zhang Mandun. Family ties still made for political bonds.

Against Reform

Whereas those outside the privileged orbit of clientelist state favoritism survived by maneuver, market, and mobility, such zealously loyal leaders as those in Wugong welcomed more fundamentalism that delivered resources through the state channels they monopolized. Although fundamentalists justified the war on remnants of capitalism as facilitating common prosperity, in reality the war on the survival mechanisms of the excluded further privileged the already favored. The ironic consequence of a continuing struggle against the market and the private was to further wound the weak and to more strongly empower the privileged. More socialism in practice brought more polarization, locking the poorest into their poverty while strengthening the grasp of the zealous on the state's supply of resources.

An immediate result of Macho Li Shouzheng's militia post in favored Wugong was a paid trip to a militia conference in Tianjin. It was the first time Shouzheng had set foot in a city. Without money or a way to obtain food and residence, all of which required an official pass and ration coupons, villagers were excluded from travel. Although leaders and led alike blamed the corrupt and praised the incorruptible, it was an institutional structure that defined the gap between the favored of the state and ordinary villagers.

In November 1960 the state reestablished six regional party bureaus. Hebei was again under the North China Bureau, now headed by Li Xuefeng, a fundamentalist ally of Chen Boda. Outside the Li-Chen group, bureau leaders who favored meaningful material incentives and gradual transition in tune with popular consciousness, including Lin Tie and his allies, had less clout. Political winds still blew in the fundamentalist direction of Great Leap policies. The Lysenkoan geneticists still ran their institutions. From 1960 Lin Biao, who succeeded Peng Dehuai as minister of defense, headed a campaign to turn the army into a model of communist fundamentals, which the Rao-yang military command vigorously implemented. Since 1938 Raoyang young men had intertwined with this military. Wugong would heed the call of the military to serve as a model of communist virtue. Its militia went furthest in adapting military terminology and the ways of tough army patriots. Young men like Boss Geng's grandson, Zhang Mandun, and recently returned from Manchuria Li Zhongxin rallied to Mao's patriotic cause in the village militia.

Geng Changsuo's most politicized daughter, Huijuan, a student at Rao-yang High School and a militia activist, met regularly with Li Guochang, an ally of her father who headed the Raoyang Military Commission. Li Guo-chang spearheaded Lin Biao's campaign to promote Mao's thought in Rao-yang. Huijuan was also seeing, and moving toward marriage with, fellow student Zhang Ping, whose father, Zhang He, the Raoyang deputy party secretary, was another ally in the Geng political family. Zhang He, like Boss Geng, a straight talker who was admired for not using campaigns to attack others, was part of the power group that had kept Raoyang out of the most deadly Great Leap campaigns.

Boss Geng kept Wugong out of the most economically enlivening reforms. He stuck to the big collective and kept a distance from the market. Geng and Party Secretary Zhang Duan urged villagers to improve the collective fields in the difficult winter of 1960–61, but many were too exhausted. The target was leveling and reclaiming 200 mu of new crop land.

Complaints were harshest in the west end, where many resented team leader Xu Lianzheng as a vituperative bully. West enders were furious when Xu, the husband of women's leader Qiao Wenzhi, forced them into such energy-wasting physical toil as leveling frozen ground. Geng's good right hand, Qiao Liguang, suggested that the work be restricted to the easiest 100 mu. Steady Xu Mantang argued that in such cash-poor times, nothing should be allowed to get in the way of sideline work, money-earning work. Finally Boss Geng compromised and conceded that just 100 mu should be leveled that winter.

With the leadership pointing in both reformist and fundamentalist directions, Boss Geng, as in 1953 when he took his big gamble, did not go where the reformers pointed. Apprehensive about the future, he became a heavy cigarette smoker. He stifled village discontent and household aspirations and loyally hewed to Mao's call to consolidate communes. Geng declared not only that all Wugong homes could afford fuel for heat in winter and to boil water for tea, but also that the mess hall and nursery had liberated female labor for work outside the home. Geng's account of the superiority of the collective economy made the press. While fundamentalist leaders in the military and North China Bureau found increasing reason to back him, some villagers suspected that Boss Geng was advancing his career at their expense.

Not long after Geng championed the success of the Leap, the famine recipes that failed to sustain him in 1943 took their toll once again. He collapsed. His left arm grew numb. The paralysis remained for several days. He had dropsy, his vision was going, and his intestines were a mess. His legs began to swell painfully, and his hearing further deteriorated. In short, unlike many other leaders, Boss Geng shared the suffering. But unlike ordinary villagers, he was rushed to what remained of the clinic in Zoucun.

The commune party committee decided to help the sixty-year-old hero through his bad times. They sent him duck eggs, which many Chinese believe to be especially salutary in restoring vigor. In line with press reports about good leaders, Geng gave the eggs to patients who were worse off. In the clinic he mulled over the lessons of recent years for the political future of his village. A journalist friend who helped promote Wugong visited Geng during his half-month in bed and presented him with a large-print edition of the recently published fourth volume of Mao's *Selected Works*. Geng found much of the book beyond his capacity, but he tried to figure out what loyalty to Mao meant.

Soon after Geng Changsuo left his sickbed, Lin Tie invited him to a January 1961 meeting at the Beijing Hotel, the capital's finest, to discuss income and grain distribution. That, is, Lin wanted to discuss how to motivate work and end the resistance and passivity triggered by Leap policies and the dearth. There Geng met Chen Yonggui of Dazhai village, whose achievements had been trumpeted in the *People's Daily* the preceding August. A close political friendship began.

Rural leaders, a group blessed by state favors and biased against market solutions, were invited to discuss ways to increase food output. The discussion touched on the overexpansion of costly welfare and educational programs and the lack of work enthusiasm. Reports circulated of places where leaders had resorted to violence to get tillers back to work in collective fields. Some conferees commented that villagers welcomed reducing collective impositions and responded positively to contracting land to individual households. Household contracting and the resurgence of markets restored incentives for hard work. Others argued that proper reward for labor within the traditional Soviet-style collective structure would do the job faster and more equitably. Geng Changsuo strongly favored appropriate reward for collective labor, but when some discussants seemed to take reward for labor as an absolute, Geng grew agitated. He reasoned that if socialism meant helping the poor who could not help themselves, then in bad times, when ill and exhausted people could hardly labor, the proper policy was to distribute by need rather than by value produced, the opposite of what was being proposed. Geng Changsuo believed that collectives must care for all regardless of natural disaster, personal adversity, or lack of labor power. Actually no one dissented from the consensus that households in difficulty, especially labor-poor households, must receive collective relief. But the priority task of 1961 was reform to invigorate China's failing economy.

The tone of the discussion confused Boss Geng. He understood Wugong, with its long history of cooperation and state support, not the poorest, hungriest regions where unpopular and poorly managed collectives presided over declining incomes and the issue was household survival. The Great Leap had squandered Wugong's collectively accumulated resources, worn out its machines, killed its animals, exhausted human labor, and left villagers hungry and demoralized. To restore Wugong, Geng believed, villagers had to reinvest in their collective future, providing guarantees for all. But Geng heard people in Beijing suggest diametrically opposite policies. Distribute more, they said; allow greater initiative to households and the market; worry less about collective investment.

Disoriented, Geng got up and strolled around. His head buzzed. Perhaps he had misunderstood some of the discussion; his hearing had deteriorated and he had only recently left the clinic. Though normally silent at meetings, Geng felt he had to speak. He stressed the need to provide guarantees for all, then broke off, saying, "Let's eat," and walked out. No one followed. Geng withdrew to his hotel room and was not called back. Three days later he was told to go home, but to say nothing about what he had heard. Suddenly, on issues of distribution, Geng was at odds not only with his patron, Lin Tie, but also with Hebei Governor Liu Zihou, who agreed that, to pull through the famine, China had to expand individual economic incentives and markets.[5]

In spite of the continuing dearth, the press presented the 1961 lunar New Year in Wugong as a happy time. Geng contrasted his family's present good fortune with 1943, when his elder daughter Xueren was sold for 45 catties of sorghum. Geng told of returning home on New Year 1961 to find his younger daughter Xiujuan listening to a phonograph record, laughing, playing under the electric light, and awaiting pork-filled dumplings.

A Central Work Conference at Guangzhou in March dropped the stress on economic leveling. But the same conference also called on local leaders to study Mao's thought. The party simultaneously promoted both ideological education, to encourage people to act as revolutionaries and win the promise of communism, and economic and administrative reforms, to help people work their way out of the famine disaster. Within the party people took the combination of revolution and reform to mean "left in politics, right in economics."

The call to revolutionize attitudes left in place the institutions that fostered fear and fawning and dampened initiative and innovation. The reforms helped end the Great Leap disaster, but no policy grappled with historically inherited problems, from the bad soil and worsening land-population ratio, to growing corruption and the need to identify, train, and empower talented people. Reform in Hebei was slow. According to Zhang Kerang, in 1961 when other provinces began to recover, Hebei's grain production fell to 113 catties per mu, its lowest level in a decade (see table 8).[6]

Following the Guangzhou meeting, central leaders went to the countryside to study the impact of the Leap. Zhou Enlai, accompanied by representatives of the Hebei party committee, conducted a three-week investigation in Wuan and other Hebei counties, On May 7, 1961, he reported to Mao in Shanghai that individuals and animals were still too weak to labor fully and that villagers wanted to be allowed to return home to eat. The mess halls, free supply system, and distribution of earnings from large units that people did not identify as their own made no sense. By June the remnants of these programs, touted throughout the Leap as the means to achieve communism, were disbanded.[7]

Team three in Wugong closed its mess hall. Yang Tong had run it well enough to win grudging respect. Even Brains Zhang Chaoke, who still supported communist fundamentals, acknowledged that the communist institution was unwelcome. "As soon as we learned that maintaining it was optional, we abolished it." In spite of popular suffering, fear and zealotry were so institutionalized in the state's career structure that some officials maintained discredited institutions rather than risk a move that could label them antisocialist.

Table 8   Hebei Grain Yield

Year	Official Shi Mu
1952	138 (drought)
1953	120
1954	116 (state purchase at low prices)
1955	136
1956	119 (collectivization, flood)
1957	137
1958	152
1959	140 (famine)
1960	122 (famine)
1961	113 (famine)

Source: Data provided by the office of Zhang Kerang.

Only under pressure of crippling famine did rulers abandon a policy of maximizing local, regional, and national self-reliance, finally expanding domestic trade and, for the first time, importing grain. Mao had earlier argued that grain imports from capitalist countries by Yugoslavia and the Soviet Union proved them dependent on imperialism. Actually, grain imports permitted the state to reduce the burden it had placed on the backs of villagers to feed state officials, the army, and urban dwellers. Less food was requisitioned, so more grain was available for peasants in the hard times. Grain prices, which had soared by 1,000 to 15,000 percent between 1958 and 1961, fell by 35 percent as a result of reforms in 1961. The dearth ended.

Nonetheless, reformers could not openly and fully pursue the logic of their project. Mao warned that such reforms as household responsibility systems in farming and energizing the rural market, if pushed too far, would lead to capitalism. Reforms would reverse revolutionary gains that socialism should guarantee. That reversal, he concluded, was what Tito had produced in Yugoslavia. Mao opposed allowing people to "go it alone"; he believed instead in fostering "common prosperity" the collective way.

A new struggle was brewing. Hebei Party Secretary Lin Tie was associated with Peng Zhen, Liu Shaoqi, and other officials at the state center who were sobered by recent catastrophes. They sought to move China away from fundamentalist policies. But other national leaders such as Chen Boda, who had allies in the Baoding region and the party's North China Bureau, as well as Minister of National Defense Lin Biao and his subordinates in the Raoyang military, promoted class struggle to propel the revolution closer to communism. The January meeting at the Beijing Hotel that Geng attended provided a forum to explore both traditional Soviet-style and reformist alternatives to fundamentalism.

In the early 1960s Geng Changsuo seemed to be gravitating ideologically and politically toward the fundamentalists. Although his personal style and concern for people's livelihood had not changed, by mid-1961 his patrons began to put out publicity releases announcing that "Geng Changsuo never forgets to read Chairman Mao's books" and claiming that his attitudes had been revolutionized, since "whatever Chairman Mao says, Geng does." For Geng, Mao was the one who founded the new state, destroyed the old evils, ended chaos, and held China together.

These crosscurrents of revolution and reform at the national level had their counterparts in Wugong village. Agricultural machine repair specialist Xu Wendong, who kept away from political movements, was delighted that his machines would no longer be abused and ruined. But some villagers experienced the end of Great Leap policies as a loss. Young Li Zhongxin's career hopes rode on the success of Great Leap creations. In 1961, when no cash was available and households were putting all their energies into getting through the dearth, Zhongxin, who was about to enter junior middle school, along with twenty fellow students was pulled out of school and sent home. The Li family valued education. Zhongxin's elder brother taught junior middle school in neighboring Gengkou, their mother's natal village. Schools all over rural China, which had so recently expanded, were cut back. Zhongxin and his fellow returnees were told that their families needed them at home temporarily to help during the hard times. Zhongxin's veterinarian father, who returned at this time from a quarter-century in the northeast, wanted his son to prepare for the exam that would win him entrance to a better school in the northeast. His mother wanted Zhongxin to prepare to enter an agricultural college. But the dearth left the bright young man with little strength to study.

Zhongxin considered himself fortunate to have attended one of the rural agricultural schools hastily set up during the Leap. The school, in neighboring Zoucun, had good teachers sent down from urban schools. Li identified his career hopes with a creation of the Great Leap Forward. Oblivious that fundamentalists had gutted education, Li saw that he would never have the chance to resume schooling cut short by reformers ending a revolutionary policy that had offered him better career prospects.

Still, even in Wugong, villagers grabbed the new economic opportunities opening up as reforms released some of the state's stifling grip on the economy. Although Boss Geng succeeded in banning the household responsibility system, Qiao Yong, the almost adopted son of war hero Qiao Hengtai, and numerous other villagers so chafed at being kept from sideline production and market earnings that they threw themselves into such efforts despite the jeremiads of Boss Geng, Fierce Zhang, and Xu Shukuan. Tensions grew. All over the countryside, energetic youth used every possible device to escape the collective to avoid being tied to the land and kept subservient to autocratic officials who regimented them as farmhands working for bare subsistence.

The village party branch organized meetings to explain why Wugong would never permit families to take priority over the collective as was occurring all over the region. Wugong, too, believed in the importance of family. But, Party Secretary Zhang Duan declared, Wugong relied on a bigger, stronger family—the collective. If people would eat less in the winter slack season, if they would grow more sweet potatoes to tide them over the short crisis, then, Fierce Zhang predicted, with the commune no longer forcing villages into costly and unwise large-scale activities, Wugong would again progress rapidly. As before, benefits would flow to all. The new economic policies promoted by Zhang Kerang in North China for Rural Work chief Deng Zihui had no impact in Wugong. In fact, except for the revival of small household plots, Raoyang county retained collective cultivation.

Still, for the poorest Raoyang villages, the lifting of heavy state controls in the aftermath of the famine expanded opportunities. Some fled low-paid field labor on overcrowded collectives, even settling in distant frontiers. The frigid northeast and distant northwest frontiers seemed to some lands of opportunity. Migrants included people with craft skills who were treated as capitalist remnants in orthodox Raoyang.

During the dead season traditional peasant households yoked to farm work sought off-farm jobs whose earnings could be turned into fine white flour for feasts on special occasions, or solid wooden chests so that daughters would have proper dowries and suitable marriages. For Boss Geng, working within the state system, a very different logic was at work.

The State Ladder

The dense networks of personal loyalty that constituted the strata and sinews of the state could keep outsiders from penetrating the truth, even about the disaster borne of the Great Leap. Defense Minister Peng Dehuai had learned of the catastrophe in his home province because Hunan Party Secretary Zhou Xiaozhou wanted him to know. Zhou fell when Mao purged Peng. In Hubei, Politburo member Dong Biwu discovered little because Party Secretary Wang Renzhong concealed much. Wang remained secure in his post. His province eventually constructed what was purported to be the largest labor camp in all China, located in the Shayang region.

Even agricultural chief Zhang Kerang, who prided himself on his intimate knowledge of Geng Changsuo, was kept from seeing the real Geng. In the presence of Zhang, who in 1961 worked under Deng Zihui in Beijing, Geng stifled his biting wit about bumbling urban officials. Zhang wrongly concluded that Geng was so somber he never even smiled.

In early 1961, when leaders set out to discover what was going on in the countryside, they found villagers too petrified to tell the truth, showing only obeisance to unaccountable state power. Mocking the need to jump when leaders barked, Raoyang villagers said:

Higher-ups let out a fart, underlings try to look smart;
Leaders move their lips, commune members run off their hips.

Deng Zihui found that despite massive popular discontent with Great Leap policies, "officials, fearful of being labeled rightists, did not dare respond factually in informing higher levels" of conditions in their area.[8] President Liu Shaoqi made the same discovery when he visited his native village in Hunan, where only his own relatives would level with him. One high official who had participated in the 1947 land reform, on returning to a village in an old base area in which he had served, was greeted by a peasant falling to the ground and banging his head and bones on the floor in a ketou.

The powerless tried to keep out of harm's way. Raoyang teachers were afraid to discipline students from Wugong. Neighboring parents warned their children against fighting with Wugong youngsters. Wugong villagers seemed like bullies and cheats because powerless people found fairness an impossibility in dealing with those within the privileged orbit of the state.

The statist structuring of hierarchies was accentuated by the precise way the organs of the command economy differentially distributed the commodities it controlled. As goods disappeared in the great dearth, the state elaborated a five-tier supply system for officials. Special supplies went to the military by rank. Officers in Raoyang got the most precious medicines, meat, nutritious food, and such scarce higher-quality brand-name consumer durables as bicycles and sewing machines. This distribution was handled by the special military supply bureau of the Ministry of Commerce, which kept large stores of prized wine, sugar, meat, and oil. At Chinese New Year, deliveries were made directly to the doors of high-ranking military and civilian officials, precisely graded by rank.

The finest goods distributed to civilian officials went to those above rank thirteen in the twenty-six-grade scale of officialdom. That usually meant prefectural level or above. No civilian official in Raoyang received the top benefits. A few top civil officials in Raoyang qualified for a third level of deliveries, those reserved for ranks fourteen to eighteen. No one in culturally poor Raoyang qualified for the next level of deliveries, which went to outstanding artists and other cultural luminaries.[9] But a good number in the county received the fifth and final level, reserved for those signaled out for achievement in many fields, from labor models to mechanics. The few civil and military officials in Raoyang who received high levels of distribution had enough to trade and sell to secure obligations and favors that further cemented personal networks. Some valuable medicinal and nutritional products were reserved for individuals in desperate medical need. The attempt to secure minimum guarantees for the needy was offered as proof of the superiority of socialism in serving the poor. Just as the system of special stores was consolidated, a comprehensive rationing system went into effect for the general public. Even in the countryside coupons were required to purchase cloth and grain. Implemented supposedly as a response to crisis, rationing expanded over the coming decades.

Wugong could expect to prosper again through its ties to the state, but ordinary villages had to make the most of the reforms that lifted restrictions on the market and the household. Whereas Boss Geng at first resisted the state's instruction to expand the household economy and distribute more income, most villages immediately cut collective investment and expanded the private sector to ensure that all would be fed and that farmers, receiving more of the fruits of their labor, would again see a link between effort and reward. To get food and other commodities flowing, the state relaxed market controls, even those on private grain markets.

The state's network of party, army, and government officials into which Boss Geng was tied evinced loyalty to an ascetic vision of patriotic belt tightening so that state and the collective could stay strong. Raoyang leaders proclaimed that villagers would sell the state all grain after retaining 360 catties per person, bare subsistence. Villagers were not persuaded that 360 was enough. "Gou bu gou, sanbailiu" (Enough or not, it's 360). Throughout Raoyang older people told each other that in the old days, when they were young and strong, in a single five-day market cycle they could earn as much as 150 catties of grain, nearly half of what many could expect in an entire year. In autumn 1961 Boss Geng learned that Dazhai, the fast-rising Shanxi model village led by Chen Yonggui, had also sold all grain to the state above this 360-catty subsistence minimum. He immediately made Wugong's subsistence 359, one catty less than Dazhai, and sold the rest to the state. In spite of the Great Leap disaster, the logic of the entrenched system still led people such as Geng to seek ways to display revolutionary zeal to please state leaders.

Boss Geng and his colleagues acted in accord with the rules of political competition structured by the state to win what the state monopolized and distributed. That was how Wugong had gotten tractors, technical assistance, and the power station. It was no secret that President Liu Shaoqi had presented leaders in model Xushui with a brand-new Moscow television set. Only higher levels of the state system could deliver such scarce commodities.

Consequently, political wisdom led Boss Geng and his local patrons to link up with the Wang Yukun leadership group in nearby South Kingsboro that Chairman Mao had singled out during the collectivization drive. Blessings of association with the national leader flowed into South Kingsboro. A paved road connected the village to the prefectural capital. A bus line carried passengers to and from the prefectural capital and beyond. Specialists, seeds, and subsidies produced a magnificent fruit orchard in South Kingsboro. Wang himself, however, became something of a village tyrant. Other leaders and villagers quaked in his presence. He soon sported a large watch with a gold-tinted band. Foreign visitors were bused to South Kingsboro to see the fruits of the supposed self-reliance that Mao had singled out. In comparison with the benefits rained on Wang Yukun's village or Wang Guofan's, Boss Geng's Wugong was starved of state inputs. The central government poured far more into Xushui and other key-point Hebei counties intended for national emulation. Already in 1958 a few Hebei places such as Jinxian county, home of the famed cotton-growing village of Zhoujiazhuang, had state electric power lines run in from nearby Shijiazhuang.

Geng Changsuo concluded that among peasant leaders, Wang Guofan, head of the Pauper's co-op, best understood Mao's message. That message centered on the inviolability of large collectives and curbing the household sector and the market. It was of little moment to Geng how neighboring villages, lacking silken ties to the socialist state, used reforms to liberate household, market, and sideline energies. What he noted was that some model villages were outperforming Wugong in winning state resources. Geng's peers were not the powerless peasant poor but the favored of the socialist state.

Geng did not dwell on how the state showered resources on Wugong in contrast to neighboring villages such as Yanggezhuang, Zoucun, and Geng-kou. Lin Tie's Great Leap subsidy to the Wugong Commune seemed to Boss Geng a pittance compared to what flowed into Wang's Guofan's Jianming Commune. Geng's goal was to win for Wugong what Wang got for his locale. In 1958 Jianming Commune, without fanfare, received enough help to build its own fertilizer factory, the only one of its kind in Hebei. Wang Guofan, whom Mao had singled out for special praise in 1955, rode the currents of the Leap to ever greater fame and fortune. His commune, eighty-five miles northeast of Beijing in Zunhua county, was a uniquely blessed once-poor area. Two of its villages, Xipu (The Pauper's co-op) and Shashiyu (Sand Stone Hollow), which had been among the first to organize co-ops, were becoming popular touring places for Chinese leaders. The Hebei commune most lavishly endowed by the state was presented as a model of what all China, particularly poor rural communities, could accomplish by self-reliance. While ordinary villagers might become privatized and cynical when challenged by such empty claims, other model village leaders strained to figure out how their villages could be as fortunate as Xipu and Shashiyu.

As peers looked to peers, so models looked to models. Boss Geng looked to Wang Yukun, to Wang Guofan, and to Chen Yonggui. Wugong production specialist Brains Zhang Chaoke was dispatched to the most successful model collectives. To strengthen ties and to increase output by studying everything from soil enrichment to labor management, Zhang went south to a leading cotton producer, Liuzhuang village in Qiliying Commune in Henan, east to Yangyuxue in Shandong, and north to Shashiyu in Wang Guofan's commune. Boss Geng himself visited Wang, and the two began exchanging letters.

The dilemmas confronting ordinary Chinese villagers seeking to ensure survival and improve life for their families through the opportunities of physical mobility, the second economy, the peasant household economy, and the enlivened market were a world apart from the challenges confronting those leaders maneuvering inside state networks to tap special resources. Fundamentalists tended to see the survival acts of the excluded as selfish and capitalistic; these sprouts of capitalism were taken as threats to be extirpated by revolution: changing attitudes, mobilizing the masses, and launching more-purifying class struggles. Opponents of fundamentalist initiatives at the state center found it difficult to legitimate the traditional socialist model in the 1960s when the traditional Soviet Union became China's enemy. Reformers had an even harder time legitimating policy preferences that could be called capitalistic, hence supposedly leading to exploitation, immiseration, and polarization, thus discarding the common prosperity the revolution promised. Whereas reforms facilitated economic recovery from a fundamentalist disaster, Mao increasingly saw reform as subversive of revolutionary goals. Boss Geng saw it the same way. The socialist state structured ideas, interests, and institutions that weighed against reforms that might empower or enrich the overwhelming majority of Chinese villagers.

⊰⊱ CONCLUSION

In 1978, during the first of our nineteen visits to the Chinese countryside, Hebei officials introduced us to Boss Geng's Wugong village and two more-prominent model villages in neighboring counties, Wang Yukun's South Kingsboro and Yao Fuheng's Houtun. Our hosts also took us to the village of Yanggezhuang. Its stagnation was attributed to a lack of good leaders and a self-defeating commitment to the market. Officials also permitted a trip to the nearby Zoucun market. Although it used to accommodate some twenty thousand people in the spring, the market was dead. In the legend spun out on that first visit to Raoyang, major credit for Wugong's achievements went to its leader, its mini-Mao, Geng Changsuo. There was no mention of Collectomaniac Geng Xiufeng and his innovative ideas. No one as much as whispered about Lin Tie's Great Leap subsidy.

It took a decade of research to acquire the data on years of state inputs and to make contact with Lin Tie, Zhang Kerang, Hu Su, Zuo Zhiyuan, Zhou Tiezhuan, the Zhang Duan family, the Wei Lianyu family, the Li Maoxiu family, Li Peishen, Li Jinzhua, Shi Guiying, Shi Xisheng, Geng Huijuan, Geng Xiufeng, Ge Wen, and numerous others unknown or unavailable to us on that first visit. These people helped us understand the structural dynamics of China's socialist development. Over that decade, numerous visits to Yanggezhuang, Zoucun, Gengkou, and other villages whose stagnation was a product of the socialist system revealed the life and treasure wasted by policies and movements that systematically hindered development in many poor communities. None of these data were made available in that first month-long stay of interviewing in Hebei.

Without Lin Tie later volunteering the data, there was no way to deduce the existence of his two-million-yuan Great Leap subsidy to Wugong. If Geng Changsuo had not subsequently called attention to it, an investigator could not have divined the yet larger state subsidies to Wang Guofan's village of Xipu. It took a household survey to reveal a postcollectivization population decline of young children that outsiders could not see and insiders would not disclose. It has been sobering to learn the limits of what can be elicited through on-the-spot interviewing.

Four Continuities

People who conceive of the People's Republic of China as totalitarian may conclude that their view is confirmed by this book's discussion of state penetration of village life and of domination by top-down bureaucracies and a mobilizing one-party dictatorship, all producing a growing gap between the powerful few and the powerless many.[1] As no previous study of rural China has, this book depicts the cruel weight of pervasive security, police, and militia apparatuses. But to see China as totalitarian fails to capture the significance of the political strife among leaders committed to reform socialism, traditional socialism, and communist fundamentalism.[2] It obscures how local power spread, entrenched itself, and defended parochial interests. It also keeps one from seeing how factional networks took on a life of their own.[3] Most important, the theory of totalitarianism presupposes a self-replicating totality, whereas this study discovers a contradictory system whose tortured logic tended to delegitimize the state and alienate society. The socialist body politic, already in embryo during the pre-1949 resistance struggle, whatever its inhumanities, was not a timeless self-replicating totality. It was far from being a monolith of total control. Even in embryo it generated the elements that would give rise to a state-society gap that eventually had to anger the alienated majority.

There were deeply structured elements that resisted change, that held firm whether buffeted by the policy winds of fundamentalists or those of reformers. Neither effort transformed the inherited political culture, challenged police state controls, or undermined locally entrenched networks. Political culture, state controls, and local networks were too deeply structured to be readily destroyed by particular policies.

The research for this book discovered a powerful and pervasive culture in which consanguinity and community, family and residence shaped power relations as much in 1984, when Boss Geng's eldest Wugong grandson became village party secretary, as in 1938, when Eighth Route Army contact Jin Qinglian hid in his sister's house and built a party based on ties of lineage and neighborhood. The unpopular campaigns against tradition of both the Nationalist and the Communist party were unsuccessful. Official socialist culture was so alienating that primordial loyalties actually grew stronger and more sacred even as they perforce became invisible. Such passions and commitments could explode and reshape politics if state controls weakened. Surprisingly little had changed in human relations and understanding in spite of the war against landlords, private property, and market, in spite of mass campaigns and catastrophes.[4] When villagers maneuvered within and around the new structures of socialism, they did so using traditional values and ties.

Villagers thought and acted on the basis of inherited institutions and values of lineage, religion, and village, of traditional norms embedded in cherished customs. The irrationality and experienced immorality of certain state actions led villagers to turn ever more to traditional norms and forms. Life was shaped by complex interactions between a diverse, defensive peasantry and a conflictive state apparatus trying to penetrate society in order to attack tradition.

Tradition is too large and complex to be reduced to good or bad. Tragically, as with patriarchy, sexism, and violence, life-negating elements in the inherited culture could reinforce the worst aspects of the new system of arbitrary power, making the bad yet worse. But traditional cultural and economic practices were not merely irrational. Such practices embodied much that was economically useful and even lifesaving, from dividing labor within the family to coping with natural disaster by preparing famine recipes. The peasant household economy even facilitated certain forms of cooperation. Party policy through the honeymoon years of the early 1950s built on some healthy forces in peasant tradition. But foreign economic dogmas that treated household farming, sidelines, and commerce as evil and exploitative, while treating increasingly statist and collectivist control as liberating, hurt the economy, alienated villagers, and undermined peasant household rationality. Frugality and industriousness declined; authoritarian dependence and patriarchy were strengthened.

In villages splintered by political vigilantism called class struggle, communities and families were left lost and powerless. Such losers reacted to units better linked to the orbit of the state, which monopolized resources, with silent anxiety and nasty gossip, warning their children not to fight with those favored by officials and blaming theft on privileged villagers. Those struggling alone deemed it hypocritical to be asked to emulate those whose path was greased. Survival for those outside the state's orbit required dissimulation, fawning, personal connections, and powerful patrons. Perhaps Boss Geng Changsuo voiced an important truth when he explained the socialist system to his adopted daughter Li Xiuying as the old family order writ large.

Yet the state attacked culture and ritual that signified meaningful moments in life's cycle, including birth, marriage, and death as well as those communal experiences associated with temples, lineages, and festivals, thus desecrating much that gave meaning to Chinese lives. These private bonds were social glue.[5] To mourn and to celebrate is to be human. To share joy, grief, and pain is humanizing.

An unintended consequence of the state's war on village culture and the peasant household economy was that villagers, expropriated of so much they treasured, clung more tightly to surviving, virtually sacred, household resources, from the home to the lineage to the marriage bond. These embattled traditions burrowed deeper, at times surfacing in secret societies and sects. Families turned inward to preserve what they cherished. The party weakly preached equality across gender and generation, declaring that marriage was an individual free choice. Yet antimarket collectivist socialism locked peasants within the village and kept out of the village forces of individual mobility and of the market that elsewhere have weakened conservative elements in peasant household culture. To survive, maintain dignity, and avoid impoverishment, many rural families acted in ever more patriarchal and autocratic ways. So did powerholders. Socialism was increasingly infused with much that was worst in the tradition.

Nothing in the system generated action to deal with a deepening ecological crisis. Well drilling ignored environmental factors; the water table kept falling. Chemical fertilizers were used to the maximum possible; the impact on human health and the survival of other species was ignored. A rat plague spread. As rats devoured ever more of the grain crop, demand for rat poison spread. No acknowledgment of a need to deal with the worsening ecological crisis came from China's socialist leaders.

The change in local leadership styles and personnel that ended the revolutionary honeymoon can be conceptualized in terms of the historiographical debate over whether the revolutionary mass is more crowd or mob.[6] The issue should not be conceived as seeking the essence of backward folks.[7] Our findings show that hinterland villagers are not inherently irrational. In the early years, when socialist-oriented leaders harmonized with the needs of the crowd that formed the Association in Wugong village, they called forth respected new leaders in tune with positive and unifying aspects of village culture. In the silent revolution and the honeymoon years of the late 1940s and early 1950s, a dignified life in harmony with cultural expectations again became possible. But when outside leaders turned toward violence and terror that split the community, they brought to the fore mean and vengeful toughs who could mobilize mobs but could not unify the community. Life-enhancing and life-negating tendencies coexisted in traditional village life. The worst consequences were fostered by state policies that strengthened authoritarian repression. One sees this transformation in Wugong village in the 1950s rise of Fierce Zhang Duan and his aide, Iron Man Li Duolin, and the scapegoating of Li Maoxiu, Li Peishen, Li Jinzhua, and Shi Xishen. Most other villages we have studied, lacking Wugong's unified leadership and economic cushion from state support, suffered far more violence, scapegoating, misery, cruelty, and repression.[8]

In seeking a general understanding of how villagers reacted to such traumas, the book does not choose sides in the debate over whether peasant society is to be comprehended as moral economy or rational economy.[9] Moral economists do not deny the weight of economic realities, and rational economists accept the relative autonomy of local culture. If rational economy is taken to mean, however, that villagers act as atomized individuals, then this book's central data on the immediacy and primacy of residential and lineage groupings contradict a basic premise of rational economy. And if moral economy is taken to mean that peasants are rooted tillers concerned only with subsistence, then this book's data on the centrality of markets, sidelines, temporary labor, and remittances must weigh against an essential element of moral economy. But as with the old debate on peasant mobilization between those stressing nationalism and those emphasizing economic reform, this moral versus rational economy debate now seems somewhat forced.

Traumatic state policies thundered down on communities whose economic relations remained embedded in multigenerational, culturally defined household relations. But after 1952, extravillage relations once mediated by the market and by travel were attenuated by statist restrictions. Entrepreneurial individuals and mobile nuclear households did not multiply. Travel to markets and festivals shriveled. So did economic effort, as grain production in Hebei plummeted in 1954 because of the state's takeover of the grain market and its imposition of compulsory low prices. The result was grain yields lower than in any subsequent year except the 1961 famine. Ironically, the fundamentalist war on peasant culture unintentionally strengthened parochial elements by restricting life to the village and to familial culture.

Weighed against the values of that culture, the collective seemed a waste that did not deliver the goods. With the collective and the state blocking outlets for mobile labor, underemployed household labor grew. Peasant households, experiencing extra household labor time as cost free, were willing to work hard and exploit themselves. Hence the relentless expansion of collective activities was felt as theft from households that believed they could do the job cheaper and better. With cash-poor collectives seeming inefficient and unjust, peasant households sought needed cash by striving to get a household member a salaried job on the state payroll, anything that earned cash. To get by, the peasantry adapted.

This traditional materialist pragmatism was condemned in the post-Mao era by intellectuals who harked back to China's great writer Lu Xun and contended that such adaptability produces spineless complacency rather than active resistance to injustice. In considering why villagers did not actively resist the disasters imposed on them, these analysts found that familial socialization to patriarchal authority facilitated the worship of tyrannical political leaders and the production of local tyrants capable of drawing from the culture support for anti-intellectual, anti-urban anger. It is true that from the 1947 terrorist leveling to the Great Leap, plenty of envious country people responded vengefully to calls to reduce others to their level. Fundamentalist policies strengthened these crude and cruel elements in peasant culture.

Over time and over areas, honeymoon unity gave way to nasty divisions. In fact, projecting from interviews with land-reform activists who served in regions that redistributed land in one swift act after national power was conquered in 1949, quite often these young urbanites, instructed to liberate the poorest and target their enemies, helped install the most vengeful individuals as new village powerholders. This outcome was far less common in such early-liberated areas as Raoyang where a locally rooted party could help shape land-reform targets in a more gradual process. In the later-liberated regions, vengeful young toughs full of rage and hate shattered villages so cruelly through personal vendettas that, by contrast, such splintered villages in Raoyang as Gengkou almost seem tranquil.

Still, if democracy is compatible with cultures as varied and as authoritarian as Greek Orthodoxy, Roman Catholicism, Judaism, and Shintoism, not to mention the Buddhism of Mongolia and the Islam and Hinduism of South Asia, then there is no reason why Confucian culture should be uniquely incompatible with democracy. In fact, democracy has grown, however fitfully, in Confucian areas to the east of the China mainland. China's inherited peasant culture, which was compatible with the self-governing co-ops of the precollectivist era, need not foreclose major progressive political options.

Legitimating the new system in village China was not democracy but the superpatriotism of rural males. In spite of painful socialist economic policies, from state capture of the grain trade at depressed prices to the outlawing of markets and the expropriation of household land in the name of collectivization to the Great Leap famine, the new state remained legitimate with the rural poor. The patriotic experience of peasant fighters linked into traditional attitudes toward leadership. The young men may have hated local tyrants and economically irrational policies, but the new nation was their nation, Mao Zedong their champion. Victims of a system can be loyal, however discontented.

The young people who sang while they labored in Xushui Commune, the Raoyang teenagers who thrilled to hear the strains of the Internationale resonate with Boss Geng's report of international solidarity in Eastern and Central Europe, the North China village youths who threw themselves into Lin Biao's campaign to build a pure and selfless militia, all sought to prove themselves worthy heirs to the heroic sacrifice and achievement of the revolutionary generation. Idealism on behalf of country and communism ran high among China's young.

This legitimating nexus of leader, values, and institutions, of Mao, military "macho-ness," and the army-militia, harmonized with structured tendencies in the socialization of young men. Young militia males competed in feats of strength. In Wugong such rising militia leaders as Boss Geng's grandson Zhang Mandun and recently returned Li Zhongxin competed in lifting a cauldron filled with water using only fingers pressed tight against the outside of the huge pot. Handsome, tall, and wiry Li Zhongxin displayed admirable virile power. There was continuity in the legitimating political culture.

Yet the Great Leap undercut legitimacy. Collectivist socialism held no appeal for young men using every wile and way to find an employment alternative to the stagnant collective. Villagers began to mock leaders and mutter about how things were getting worse. In Raoyang, when peasants knowingly referred to *zhu-mao,* it was no longer the revolutionary leadership of Zhu De and Mao Zedong. They were recalling a fortune-teller's prophecy from the turn of the century that a pig (*zhu*) and a cat (*mao*) would bring hard times.

Villagers noted that urban workers protected from the famine did not dare tell the truth because to do so risked loss of their food guarantees, the so-called iron rice bowl. But peasants who had nothing had nothing to lose. Some villagers muttered that although everything about Mao might be great, the great leader did not let people eat; Jiang Jieshi, the head of the defeated Nationalist party, might by rotten, but he did not interfere with your stomach. Villagers who were denied the right to beg or to earn money pointed out that in the old days no one needed such permission.

For many others, including the families of victims, it was hardly conceivable that Mao could do wrong. Most villagers only wished Mao knew of their plight. He was their last hope and ultimate savior. It was he who, in the war against Japan and again in the silent revolution ending in land reform, had won them their start in life. For much of the poor peasantry, Mao, army, and nation still symbolized a way to a life of dignity.

Yet contrary forces were at work. We found an early strain in socialist dynamics and structures that eventually, as it grew stronger, produced brutal outcomes. These seeds were planted well before 1949 in such systemic factors as a security force set to arbitrarily and mercilessly crush those dubbed counterrevolutionary and a notion of socialism that treated all accumulated wealth as resulting from exploitation. Mao did not suddenly go wrong with the injustices of the 1957–58 anti-rightist campaign or the economic irrationality of the Great Leap. In Wugong, arbitrary and unaccountable power was already manifest in the outside work team's imposition of economically irrational distribution schemes in 1944, in vengeful scapegoating, in the co-op's ability to seize a donkey from a powerless veteran in 1948 and expel him from the party, and in the continuing growth of heavy-handed police power in the 1950s that left innocent victims devastated and without recourse. Some of these poisons originated in Chinese traditions, many more in imports from the Soviet Union. But during the famine, victims primarily blamed particular corrupt and careerist local officials. Rulers at the center, however, strove to focus outrage on foreigners and traitors.

The nationalism of poor peasant males, premised on the notion that their army and its state had saved the poor, precluded attacking the system. This nationalism evoked a positive response when Mao blamed famine on the Soviet Union's 1960 withdrawal of aid. Geng Changsuo believed that patriotic villagers had saved China in the 1950s when they tightened their belts to defeat the American economic embargo. He readily concurred that peasants had also saved the country in the 1960s when they tightened their belts further to resist the attempt of the Soviet Union to exploit China's famine to force concessions. Viewing the soldiers who defended China as their boys, the rural poor were deeply patriotic. Rulers of the socialist state, symbolized by Mao and the army, successfully stirred nationalist embers into chauvinistic fires. The data generated in our research reveal the error in conceiving Mao as singularly fixated on equitable economic development. In fact, he was preoccupied with military matters, chauvinist appeals, and such utopian goals as annihilating all private property, including the family.

Identities forged in China's nation-building process would long retain their salience. Students of the French Revolution agree that in significant areas of France the political divisions established in the 1789 revolution—and sometimes going back to seventeenth-century religious divisions or peasant rebellions—continue to shape French politics in the late twentieth century. In China, too, new identities continued, whatever the policies imposed from Beijing. This patriotic identification with the project of their state was so deep that North China rural youth eagerly responded to the 1960 call of Lin Biao's militia to help Mao achieve an independent nation serving its poor. This passionate idealism was tapped in 1961 both to scapegoat the Soviet Union and to condemn county-level officials, who were held accountable for the recent famine and executed.

Beyond peasant culture and the new nationalism, a third continuity that transcended shifting policies and factional ups and downs was embedded in the personal bonds of loyalty that gave substance to the structures of the system. These grew ever more entrenched. Wherever one was situated in socialism's hierarchies of people, places, and institutions, one sought further to entrench oneself.

An ironic life story captures the determining power of a tie to the state as the secret of success. During the anti-Japanese war, party authorities asked the Raoyang resistance to send a villager to Yan'an to report back on life at the heartbeat of the resistance. But villagers had no interest in trekking off to a poor, strange, distant land. A miserable beggar from Caozhuang village nicknamed Little Dog was paid to go. His location at the center of power made his fortune. With the establishment of the new government, he moved to the capital that commanded resources, becoming an official in Beijing.

The political prisoners, permanent outcasts, and black elements, whose sons had difficulty finding a mate and whose family line therefore faced extinction, lay in a hellish pit into which people sought not to fall. Officials clung fiercely to their rung of the state's ladder and painstakingly tried to climb. Their combined weight created a system of extreme stability, virtual immobility. In this socialist system, merit, innovation, skill, energy, and dedication tended to count less than locale, personal connections, and political status. This volume has shown how personal networks originated, operated, and became institutionalized in villages and through connections to higher levels of party, government, and military.

Because the system was one of structures, the asceticism of particular individuals did not alter it. Boss Geng Changsuo may well have lived an austere life, but he lived it within the privileged circle of the state. Rulers praised self-reliance and common prosperity but bestowed rewards on a favored few. For those outside the circle, those not blessed with the scarce resources, life would not improve because Boss Geng declined a phonograph or because his village practiced a leveling form of sharing the wealth.

Those within the circle obtained the newest, best, and scarcest resources. They had the ties. For those outside the circle to be told that sharing and leveling brought wealth was to be asked to believe a lie. Villagers did not appreciate city people who made fools of them. The more the state preached ascetic equality, the more it exposed itself as hypocritical to the many excluded, who were forced to live austerely, while the privileged manifestly profited from the entrenched system. Whereas the excluded sought to survive outside the walled-off socialist system, any favored unit was compelled by the structure of the system to try to grab everything, no matter how redundant. The favored, logically, favored more socialism.

Although Gengkou villagers looking at the Wugong orchard fence could see that the favored of the state, through institutionalization personal networks, took care of their own, the gap between favored and forgotten in Raoyang county was actually far smaller than in most places. Boss Geng correctly noted that such model villages in Hebei as Xipu, South Kingsboro, and Zhoujinzhuang all received far more state largesse than did Wugong. And numerous outsiders observed that the Geng leadership, which had rebuffed such state offers as a central market and free labor, was much less greedy, more honest, and more concerned not to further alienate neighbors than most privileged leaders elsewhere, who took all they could get. The structured system built and consolidated major inequalities, hierarchies, and yawning economic, social, and political gaps. A study of Raoyang county only hints at how much worse things were elsewhere.

A fourth and final deeply rooted continuity reflected persistent historical problems and the limited resources available for resolving them. China's state leaders, from the Qing dynasty through the decline of the Republic, sought talented local people to contribute to the general welfare so the nation would grow wealthy and strong enough to withstand foreign threats. Even hinterland Raoyang was affected by these modernizing reform efforts. Yet throughout the late Qing and the Republic, even as taxes rose, the land-population ratio worsened, corruption and violence intensified, and foreign countries imposed their will on China. To patriotic Chinese, the establishment of the People's Republic seemed a total break with that humiliating past.

But the rupture turned out to be less than complete. Although the new government mobilized nationalist sentiments, built a strong state, and accelerated heavy and military industrialization, deeply structured problems remained unresolved and some were even intensified. The land-population ratio grew far worse as China's leaders rejected family planning as a Malthusian deception. No all-out effort was made to employ educated and talented people in suitable jobs. New forms of corruption became entrenched. Fundamentalists spurned world market opportunities and derided modern values and education.

Popular educational reforms that began in the late 1930s, at the outset of the decade of silent revolution, continued in the 1950s as Raoyang primary and middle school education expanded for both boys and girls, although only a small percentage of graduates could move on to high school. But so many educated people, including rural schoolteachers, were condemned in the anti-rightist repression of 1957–58 that intellectual and cultural endeavors were chilled. Local leaders treated outside educated people as potential traitors. The Great Leap, which began with an expansion of schools, brought bankruptcy that forced local governments to close numerous schools. After the Leap, fundamentalists offered patriotic rural youth militia work, labor corvées, and political campaigns. The system proudly based itself on loyal uneducated political activists.

Some Chinese scholars in the post-Mao era saw Mao's failure as similar to that of the mid-eighteenth-century Qing dynasty. In that perspective, while chauvinism and orthodoxy flourished, the nation rejected the world's advanced science, thereby drastically limiting China's ability to solve its problems. The economic stagnation of the rural poor in the post-honeymoon era was but another failure in two centuries of failures. Generations of rulers could entrench themselves by appeals to proud nativists. But in the 1960s, while China remained mired in historical dilemmas, much of East Asia raced ahead.

Controversies

The data in this book, focusing mainly on the hinterland of the North China plain, cast light on some important controversies about the nature of China's diverse countryside. Villagers in more literate wealthy suburbs view such places as Raoyang as culturally and economically backward. The 15 percent living in suburban villages or along transportation arteries had happier economic experiences. Villagers from southern water-rich rice regions with easy multiple cropping, whose sons did not fight in the Red Army and who had minimal acquaintance with Japanese troops, experienced a very different reality from that of poor patriotic northerners. Some villagers in the northeast, while carrying out the 1947 land reform, found the Nationalist army marching down upon them. They killed all who might reveal what cruelties had just transpired. They, too, had a different history. The 9 percent residing on state farms enjoyed security and benefits that produced yet another experience. And things were far worse for the 25 to 30 percent in the poorest mountain areas, the northwest, and the southwest, far from modern transportation and communication. In any nation, political conflicts and alliances reflect regional differentiation. In a socialist system that locks people into their village and region, these realities take on added weight.[10]

Scholars debate whether the revolution was inevitable, whether the happenstance of foreign invasion prevented the Nationalist government from ending chaos, decline, and a compromised sovereignty. Without gainsaying the transformation facilitated by the army of Japan, such as the opportunities it permitted the hitherto crushed Communist party in Raoyang and across the North China Plain, it is nonetheless true that the Nationalist party had failed to mobilize already powerful elite patriotism, let alone reach the peasant majority; after 1937 the Communist party succeeded on both scores. The Nationalist party failed to contain disintegrative forces within villages; the united front tax reforms of the Communist party succeeded.

Some scholars have attributed peasant nationalism to popular reaction to Japanese atrocities. This book shows rural as well as urban Chinese seeking nationalistic solutions *before* the Japanese arrived. Indeed, Japan's inhumanities had major mobilizing consequences because existing presuppositions led patriots to treat such incidents as paradigmatic. Otherwise the atrocities could have been seen as isolated excesses of bad individuals or as inescapable tragedies that occur in all wars.

A broad stratum of rural educated people was nationalistically oriented by the 1920s when the Northern Expedition reached North China. Even illiterate villagers in the hinterland were susceptible to antiforeign mobilization. As early as the Boxer Rebellion many villagers viewed as illegitimate both foreign religions and Chinese politicians who quavered before foreign threats.

As the debate on the relationship between nationalism and socialist revolution continues, some scholars have argued that collectivization was the only way to end the polarizing decline decimating peasant households. But in the rural hinterland that included Raoyang, the long-term decline was not polarizing. The biggest losers were marginalized, pushed off the land and out of villages, and left too poor to marry and continue the family line. Some ran away or died. But the record in North China belies the notion of land concentration in the hands of an ever richer landlord minority. The more prosperous also declined. In the hinterlands almost everyone seemed to be hurtling downward. Subsequent Communist party policies of protecting the families of soldiers from poor villages permitted marginalized males to keep their families alive. Vengeful village toughs, many from poor households with weak kinship bonds, were most responsive to the destructive initiatives of fundamentalist leaders whose policies required political scapegoats and bred a climate of fear. This book charts how this tough rural stratum intertwined with the army and militia to further a perverse and pervasive political culture.

The party's wartime reforms gave new hope to the rural poor through social revolution. The reversal of position in the Raoyang social order can be encapsulated in the contrast between 1938 and 1946. By 1946, better-off lineage members, weakened by tax reforms, sought tax shelters by surrendering land. In less than a decade, ownership had been dispersed, creating a world of relatively equal, small-holding, independent tillers. This dispersion of landownership contrasts with prior epochs of crisis in which the poor sought "tax shelters in powerful households by donating their lands to the latter," thereby facilitating "the concentration of land ownership."[11]

Party fundamentalists treated the success of the silent revolution between 1938 and the early 1950s in building a dynamic and more equitable society almost as if it had never occurred. Seeing themselves leading a class war to socialism and equality by replacing the peasant household economy with a collectivized and nationalized economy, many party leaders treated peasant values, practices, and social relations as exploitatively capitalist, with capitalism portrayed as inevitably creating a few rich and an immiserated mass. Party leaders were so committed to the Soviet path that they never assessed the significance of their own innovations. The silent revolution of the 1940s could have but did not provide an alternative to Soviet dogma. The ideas in the heads of leaders had large consequences. Driven by a vision of socialism based on state industry, party leaders did not draw generalizations from the particulars of their rural experience of liberating the productive energies of an egalitarian peasant economy.[12] Party historians scarcely mention the humane basic reforms carried out over fourteen difficult years from 1938 to 1952 that reunified families and villages, transformed rural life in ways compatible with peasant ideals, made the party legitimate, permitted a symbiosis of household and mutual aid, brought broadly shared consumption gains, and released economic energies, thereby increasing productivity. China had not merely mobilized for war. In fact, reknit families, restored culture, and continuing economic gains stretched into the honeymoon era. The establishment of the People's Republic in 1949 was not a great rupture for villagers who had experienced a decade of silent revolution. Unfortunately for villagers, however, socialist notions of a need to wipe out peasant property and culture also bridged the establishment of the new state.

Starting in 1952–53, socialist policies curbed markets and captured the rural surplus for urban industrialization for the military, and for the support of a rapidly growing bureaucracy. Beginning with curbs on long-distance trade, the state secured a monopoly on grain and cotton at imposed low prices. Their presuppositions precluded party rulers from understanding how their policies caused shortages and bred corruption. Instead, China's leaders experimented with more state control and ever bigger agricultural units.[13] Finally, in 1955–56 the party abandoned many of the finest achievements of the silent revolution and honeymoon years to go down the Soviet socialist road of imposed collectivization. This tragic reversal was made disastrous for villagers by Great Leap fundamentalism.

Collectivization was not then a natural outgrowth of the empowering force of enlarging and enlivening the peasant household economy, but an economically costly and politically alienating rupture. It broke with policies that had harmonized with rational aspects of the peasant economy. Farming has many diverse tasks—plowing, seeding, weeding, irrigating, fertilizing, harvesting, storing, marketing, and so on. Each requires timely action. Yet value is earned only in exchange with a purchaser. There is no way to determine the percentage contributed to the result by the weeder versus the waterer or to measure and properly reward superior contributions. The precise value of each partial contribution to the whole effort defies calculation. Unless affective bonds or passionately held commitments bind farm workers, any collectivist pay system will seem unjust and therefore act as a disincentive.

In 1953 Adviser Lu Guang began to seek alternatives to the leveling distribution schemes on Wugong's big unit (da she). Between 1953 and 1955, he devised intricate piecework and bonus systems to compensate for the disincentive of a leveling large unit. Some pay schemes were less alienating than others. None removed the persistent sources of tension, the passivity, and the experienced injustice of the big unit, a halfway house on the road to collectivization. The focus of this volume on the failed experiments with big units helps clarify why yet more socialism, that is, collectivization, made matters worse.

This book builds on the pioneering contribution of the French scholar Jean-Luc Domenach, who investigated how big units were the experimental forms that became collectives and communes. Starting in 1953 Mao and his associates paid close, yet ahistorical, attention to these big units. Focusing on unique instances with great state backing, they insisted that achievements of such special places were universally generalizable. Mao's mobilizational agenda and pressures for rapid accumulation and development joined to push rural people as rapidly as possible—indeed, more rapidly than possible—into ever larger and more communistic organs of labor. But large state-imposed work units could not bring prosperity to an impoverished Yanggezhuang, a stagnant Zoucun, a decommercialized Yincun, or a divided Gengkou. They and most other villages traveled alone down a rough road that had been smoothed for such favored units as Wugong. The politics of promoting models promoted illusions about the future of most Chinese villages.

The alienating impact of collectivization need not have caused ultimate economic catastrophe. That required economically irrational fundamentalist policies and fearsome police practices, some of which had already been introduced in the 1947 terror land reform. This cruel politics reached new horrors in the 1957–58 anti-rightist movement, turning 1958 into a year of no truth, as people called it. The subsequent famine was the product of elite zealousness and coerced popular silence, added to the economic irrationalities of alienating Soviet-type collectives and compounded by a fundamentalist war on popular culture, money, commodities, household sidelines, and the market.[14] This fundamentalism intensified China's departure from the reform policy path that had earlier created the hopes of the honeymoon years.

Self-inflicted Wounds

Some historians take this record of socialist failure as evidence that a non-Communist government would have better served the Chinese people by founding a strong state, utilizing world market opportunities, and building on the strengths of the peasant household economy. But there was no alternative group capable of winning national power and building such a state.

Because prior ruling groups and movements failed to establish a state strong enough to defend China, Soviet expansion in Mongolia and Japanese military intervention in Manchuria disrupted trade and livelihood even in peripheral Raoyang in the first half of the twentieth century. Decline in the rural hinterland continued in part because the Nationalist party could not defend China. Still, early-twentieth-century world market involvement and the attendant development of the northeastern provinces, as well as of Tianjin, Shanghai, Fuzhou, and other spots, did expand economic opportunities, even to marginal tillers in peripheral areas about to go under, thereby cushioning the speed and agony of their decline. Earnings in areas tied to the world market, however unstable, allowed Old Militia Xu Yizhou to return home to Wugong from Fuzhou and start a family. Some marginal families, such as that of Provider Li Peishen, could remain intact on earnings remitted from Tianjin. Such earnings also permitted the parents of Li Zhongxin to survive in the northeast and then return to their home village. Although the politics of world market penetration strengthened competing warlords and legitimated conquest, thereby wreaking plunder and devastation on rural China, that world market, to the extent it can be treated as a pure economic phenomenon, also helped some villagers to survive. Indeed, survival in the densely populated North China plain required supplementing the meager fruit of the harvest with sideline, commercial, or industrial incomes associated with the market or the city.

The Communist party built a strong state, but a Korean War embargo temporarily barred that state from deep involvement with the capitalist world market. Starting in 1952, however, the Chinese government treated not only foreign investment, but even long-distance domestic trade, as exploitation to be extirpated. Consequently the new state imposed injuries that invite comparison to those inflicted by conquerors and plunderers who had disrupted the market and devastated the economy.

To be sure, the return of long-distance trade in the early 1950s, after a century of turmoil, permitted some traders huge profits. There are, however, numerous ways to limit excess profits, including taxation, regulation, and competition. These keep the goose laying golden eggs. China's rulers instead killed the goose by waging a war on the market. Villagers bore the brunt of the economic losses caused by crushing markets and concentrating resources in the centralized state.

Tragedy was foreshadowed in the 1947 class struggle land reform, when all villagers whose standard of living had improved, even the beneficiaries of party-promoted cooperative efforts, were looked on with a jaundiced eye. Treating the propertyless poor as the singular source of energy needed to create communism made even the less-poor Geng co-op an exploitative rich-peasant organization. In the name of siding with the poor, this kind of socialism would destroy the prospering and level wealth. Such purportedly pro-poor policies worked against development that alone could create wealth for all. Although the poor benefited from a onetime distribution of wealth, the repetition of such leveling policies retarded growth for all, locking poor regions and disadvantaged households into poverty.

Analysts who saw China's pre-1955 policy of voluntarism, gradualism, and small self-governing co-ops as a commitment to an alternative path missed the party's unswerving commitment to taking the Soviet road, in which modern state-run industry was premised on collectivized agriculture. In the North China hinterland, socialist leaders stuck to the Soviet road, where the state commanded the rural economic surplus. Mao and Deng Zihui agreed on that. Whereas Mao was impatient to take the Soviet socialist road, Deng hoped that rising peasant incomes would gradually fund the modern inputs that would supposedly make collectivization voluntary because materially benefi-cial to all villagers. In contrast, Mao, like Stalin, pressed for collectivization as state intervention in a purported class conflict, taking the side of an expand-ing, exploited poor majority against a minority of exploiters.[15] Research for this book, however, discovered no data to lend credence to this imported dogma that legitimated collectivization as the socialist alternative to polariza-tion. Given the large middle sector fostered by the revolution, whatever else caused poverty or blocked development in the 1950s, it was not increasing exploitation by rich peasants.

The problem of building socialism is not only an economic issue. Given the great and relatively autonomous power commanded by the state, particularly following the nationalization of the economy, the war on religion, and the repression of physical mobility, politics were decisive. In 1945, imposition by a party team of a new distribution formula on the co-op in Wugong alienated peasant households and split the co-op. Geng Xiufeng knew that many would experience as unjust a more socialistic distribution scheme that slighted the need to reward land and capital, but he could not buck party superiors. The result was the loss of half the member households, bringing the co-op to the brink of collapse.

Once Mao called a halt to experimentation with routes to the Soviet road in 1955, all villagers were compelled to follow one path imposed from the state center. Only a few places could make co-ops work. But diversity violated the Leninist presupposition of a party whose leaders, through Marx's science, led all on a correct path toward communism. Critics in China called this orthodoxy of party-imposed single truths "the cut of a single knife." With one path imposed on all, there could be no autonomous quests for progress, prosperity, or justice. Life itself was collectivized and nationalized. Local initiative was drained. Villagers found themselves dependent. The traditional socialism of the Soviet model could not empower the powerless majority who had few ways to control their destiny.

The centrality of state power and leadership preferences in socialist China made the nature of state goals and organizations decisive. There were no institutional checks on arbitrariness, coercion, and abuse of power. By joining a Marxist logic of progress through class struggle, a Leninist belief that the democratic centralism of the party-state embodied higher forms of democracy, and Stalinist institutions and policies, the party-in-power-taking-the-socialist-road rendered patriotic supporters in the countryside victims of an unmitigated disaster. This book calls attention to alternatives inherent in the revolution's history and the costs associated with both the traditional Soviet and the fundamentalist path eventually chosen. Fundamentalist mobilization policies of ever more communism, although legitimated as helping the poor, repeatedly blocked avenues by which the poor might escape poverty, even before the founding of the new state in 1949.

The Old History and the New

This book does not choose sides in the debate, going back to the Enlightenment critique of frivolous court nobles, between the old history and the new, between a stress on decisive political events at the state center versus a focus on more deeply structured forces. Each approach captures important, albeit partial, realities.

In harmony with the new history's focus on anonymous masses shaped by impersonal processes, this study found social disintegration, a prolonged economic decline, and a weak national government as major long-term tendencies facilitating the success of revolutionary nationalism. But, as suggested by the old history, politics could also be decisive and autonomous. Mao's imposition of rapid collectivization and the forced march to communism overwhelmed the gradualist approaches associated with Deng Zihui and restructured the life chances of Chinese villagers. Mao's 1959 removal of Defense Minister Peng Dehuai and promotion of Lin Biao were not merely court politics. They permitted a continuation of catastrophic Great Leap policies that devastated millions of poor, vulnerable Chinese villagers. Struggles and decisions at the apex of power have large consequences.

But this study also highlights the rich narratives of rural households struggling to survive the disastrous consequences of state decrees. The choices and strategies of villagers were shaped by deep continuities, ranging from mistrustful, patriarchal strains in peasant culture and a virile, xenophobic nationalism, to rich traditions of family and culture, all conditioned by climate, soil, and the land-population ratio. Villagers made history in terms of their values and sense of dignity.

In contrast to new historians who argue for research on the demos rather than the elite, or for interpretation, meaning, and continuity in discourse, rather than cause, effect, and ruptures with outmoded pasts, this volume seeks to bridge the world of popular culture and the social development of family, lineage, and village, on the one hand, and the world of the state, dominant ideologies, economic command, and political history, on the other. Local officials lived within the village mores in which they had been socialized. Survival strategies utilized lineage linkages as well as state structures. The structure of power was also a network of familial relations. Less-than-modern aspects of China's socialism, such as the violent, parochial, and patriarchal energies of tough, young, semiliterate village males, did not emanate from the works of Marx or Lenin, the institutions of Stalin, or even the commands of Mao. The research reveals complex relations between the modernizing socialist state and traditional rural society, an interactive and dynamic web of human action, belief and structure, a strained and straining whole.

The entrenched system was replete with delegitimating forces. A system that during the Great Leap dearth secretly delivered New Year delicacies to the gates of a few high officials, while most villagers lacked dumplings and firecrackers, would erode its legitimacy when the secret deliveries became known. The system contained the seeds of its own delegitimation in the form of institutionalized hypocrisy that would cause massive cynicism and self-seeking, a universalization of corruption that began to spread in the wake of the Great Leap famine.

This system of hierarchy and privilege embodied feudal and traditional elements that collided with the imperatives of a modernizing world.[16] Powerholders in Wugong village, Raoyang county, and Hengshui prefecture, however, explicitly rejected our analyses depicting collectivization as entrenching a feudal-like system. They rejected the comparison of villagers tied to soil they did not own and could not leave with serfs living under feudal lords, tillers who had no rights. Local officials insisted that socialism guaranteed rights for laboring people. Tillers could no longer be dispossessed by landlords. The collective, they argued, paid fairly for labor and served the interests of all members, above all the once-poor. A socialist state could not and would not exploit. All villagers enjoyed equal rights in property and economic progress. Socialism was proclaimed to be a fair and inclusive system of distributive justice.

Yet the ruling party in the collective era openly legitimated itself in language laden with feudal overtones. Leaders proudly proclaimed that they were parents (usually fathers) and the people—or even lower officials—were children. In a republic, by contrast, it is assumed that citizens are adults, not children who need to be chided, corrected, and punished into obedience. The victims of the anti-rightist campaign were portrayed as children punished by caring parents. In fact, as serfs and outcasts, their status was a matter of blood, something passed on by marriage and birth, not by individual behavior.

In arguing against conceiving of the socialist state as feudal-like, officials slighted the experience of villagers in less-favored places such as Gengkou, Yanggezhuang, and Zoucun, and the ever-expanding number of "nonpersons" throughout the nation who bore black class labels. The excluded and neglected were separated by an impenetrable wall from the favored of the state. The Raoyang airport, constructed in an area without good political connections, brought a ludicrously low level of compensation to those deprived of land. Among the compensations usually requested—but rarely received—by people whose land was seized were jobs for sons within the privileged orbit of the state. Villages bereft of a powerful patron received scant compensation when the state pushed them off land required for prisons, offices, roads, dams, factories, and other projects.

A people's republic was meant to realize for the powerless poor the material blessings that, Marxists held, a mere bourgeois republic could not deliver. During the honeymoon era, the state began to make good on its program of improving life and bringing services to the poor, offering land, health, and education. But quickly, as with compulsory crop sales at low prices and collectivized land, the state reappropriated benefits. Military hospitals open to high officials maintained international health care standards, but resource-starved rural clinics, like the one in Raoyang, stagnated or actually declined. There was no consultation on budget with the citizenry. There was no way for the excluded to make known, still less to impose, their budget priorities on elites secretly deciding funding. The information needed for reasoned choice was kept from the populace. Political participation was reduced to ritual. Rest houses and sanatoriums built for working people were soon reserved for model workers and then only for officials. The best jobs and coveted positions in the state sector were inherited by the children of officials. In fact, the freezing of class status and the inheritance of class labels, in addition to a mistrust of the market and individual energies, froze most children into the status of their parents.

The government regularly acted on feudal-like criteria. In spite of inherited wealth, old-boy networks, and private clubs, liberal republics do create space for meritocratic careers open to talent. Competence should—and often does—prevail. But as the socialist state consolidated its networks of power, it made nepotism, personal ties, and unquestioned loyalty decisive in determining who moved ahead. Such a socialism, which ignored the criteria of competence, was bound to conflict with the imperatives of modernization and discredit its rulers.

In a republic, all are supposedly equal before the law. A socialist state would transcend the bourgeois reality in which the rich buy legal protection denied to the poor. But the party, which eliminated property-based structures of inequality, institutionalized its own stratified inequalities. Rights were distributed according to hierarchical positions in state networks. Penal sentences, the data of this book reveal, were decided by political position and not by the nature of the crime. Privilege, even law itself, was determined by a stratified status hierarchy. The principal axis that privileged some and excluded others was access to hierarchically ordered power and resources. A most unequal and frozen statist reality structured life's opportunities.

A republican practice of public governance, including a meritocratic civil service, is meant to negate personal, private, and secretive government. It is supposed to negate bonds of feudal-like loyalty and further an open, transparent, and public political order. However far actual liberal democracies are from that ideal, the socialist state grew ever more personal, secretive, and opaque.

Rural people nevertheless took pride and found legitimation in inclusion in new political rituals that excluded others. Even meetings where villagers raised their hands to ratify decisions already taken in secret by higher-ups did not seem empty. Poor villagers invited to attend meetings that excluded black elements, among them the previously prosperous and powerful, at first experienced the new system as lending them dignity and removing them from a world where they had been invisible and powerless. Even if the meetings were boring and rigged, the ritual signified a promise that the once poor were part of the deserving and good.

Reform-minded scholars in post-Mao China have argued that feudal-like elements of the socialist state made sense to peasants by harmonizing with their traditions and expectations. There obviously is significant truth in this contention. Yet this book finds something more. It comprehends villagers also as ethical agents, not merely as backward remnants. Early party policies harmonized with, built on, and fostered peasant strengths. Later party policies not only attacked the peasant household, its values, and its culture but also, when carried to fundamentalist extremes, built cruelly on the envies and tensions also inherent in a complex village culture. Mao and the commanders of the peasant-based army well understood the historical angers of this peasant culture. Persistent patterns of hierarchical authority, of patriarchal gender relations, and of quick resort to violence were reinforced both among China's conservative villagers and in state power. That conservative popular culture has had major political consequences. The cultural thrust of traditional, virile rural males shaped both army and village. Those cultural factors retard progress toward gender equality and democratic practice.

In the villagers' categories of experience, both before and after the consolidation of socialist power, urban people were often indistinguishable from fools, traitors, and exploiters. Officials were seen as living soft lives in comfortable offices with chairs, sofas, lights, steam heating, windows, and toilets. None of these material blessings existed in the village. Such suspect people not only luxuriated in what was stolen from hard-working country people, but they also hypocritically bragged about their role in uplifting others. Symptomatically, some Wugong villagers and virtually all the Raoyang leaders in Boss Geng's political network resented the only somewhat more urbane and educated Geng Xiufeng for claiming responsibility for the rise of the village. He seemed too glib, and almost alien in his knowledge of documents and outside connections. Although Boss Geng also successfully cultivated outside contacts, Collectomaniac Geng was more readily discredited as a threatening outsider than as a proponent of mobilizational collectivism.

Mistrusting talkers, rural tillers believed that their silent suffering and bravery in the resistance war and their dirty, hard outdoor work had made everything possible. Villagers and unschooled local leaders enthusiastically welcomed fundamentalist attacks on supposedly ignorant experts and pompous intellectuals. Boss Geng Changsuo knew how to identify with such popular passions, as did Fierce Zhang Duan and Macho Li Shouzheng, who held charismatic appeal for the uneducated poor. We watched Shouzheng stroll down a lane filled with his people and heard those east-enders murmur, "Shouzheng's come! Shouzheng's come!" as they delightedly reached out to touch him.

When Mao preached a communistic self-reliance that excluded non-toilers, markets, and money, villagers understood Mao to say he was with them, with their boys who put their lives on the line in the patriotic army. The myth of the resistance war did not focus on the tax reform that created a world of independent peasant tillers in the silent revolution of 1938–46, but on the camaraderie and heroism of poor, illiterate village soldiers. Peasants translated Mao's appeal to mean that their sacrifice would be rewarded, that urban exploitation would end so that at long last villagers would enjoy the full richness of their labor and the fruits of communist abundance. The economic disasters brought on by this communist fundamentalism forced many peasants to choose such semilegal survival strategies as peddling, migrating, and seeking urban work, thereby rendering them more vulnerable to attack as antisocialists. It was Catch-22. Politically, however, fundamentalist passions continued to unite the supreme leader with the poor rural masses. For many of the hinterland poor, the socialist project remained largely legitimate even as it became more repressive and destructive, promoting mob violence, hate mongering, scapegoating, demand for loyalty to and worship of the leader, and mistrust of the city, markets, intellectuals, the prospering, and the sophisticated.

Neither the Great Leap famine nor the post-Leap economic reforms basically redefined the socialist project. China's socialist rulers still assumed that anything related to markets and private households had to be exploitative and bad for the poor, even while using those means to restore a ravaged economy. Traditional socialists who looked to the Soviet experience, as did the overwhelming majority of China's leaders, shared these presuppositions with fundamentalists. Leaders who wanted to reform the system to build on the gains of the silent revolution had a hard time legitimating their project. Deng Zihui, with his vision of the virtues of the peasant household economy, never had a chance, not least of all because he shared with Mao and other leaders a belief in the ultimate goal of collective agriculture. What was economically rational in the predispositions of the peasant household economy could not be conceived as such by most ruling socialists.

The logic of the system trapped leaders and led alike. By the early 1960s some leaders, shocked by the famine, began to discern structural flaws both in the traditional Soviet socialist way and in the communist fundamentalism of the Great Leap. But it was not easy to legitimate the reform alternative. As with Lenin's New Economic Policy following the disasters of war communism in the Soviet Union, conceding to peasant households and markets might be necessary to avert famine, but it seemed a turn away from socialism. The peasant household economy seemed inherently capitalistic, that is, precisely what communists should negate. The reforms of the post-Leap early 1960s could be only a temporary tactic to overcome a supposedly passing problem.

"Right in economics, left in politics" was an internal party slogan legitimating economic reforms to breathe life into a devastated economy in the early 1960s. It was neither a stable compromise nor a long-term policy. Politics remained in command, the politics of antimarket, antihousehold economy, the politics of fundamentalist, mobilizational collectivism. Raoyang party and military officials with ties to fundamentalist leaders at prefectural and provincial levels were hardly alone in seeing that the safe course was zeal on behalf of ever more communist fundamentals. Reformers could not readily cultivate local models of economic rationality and cultural integrity when local party people knew that political zeal offered the sure way to win career rewards.

In addition, powerholders identified the hierarchy of personal networks created by the new state as the institutions of socialism, that is, as the only agencies that could win a world of abundance without exploitation. One could target for criticism individual bad apples but not the walled-off socialist orchard that produced them. A search for exploitative class enemies who supposedly kept people poor could not lead to an attack on the budget system that siphoned off funds to build a cultural palace in Tianjin for elites while Raoyang villagers dwelled in hovels. That search for exploiters led instead to attacks in Wugong on landlord son Li Dalin, landlord son Li Maoxiu, Geng's election competitor in 1952, Wei Lianyu, Daoist Li Jinzhua, Provider Li Peishen, educated technicians at the tractor station and tractor station chief Shi Xishen. These were not powerful exploiters but the vulnerable, the scapegoats, and the targets of personal grudges. And Boss Geng's leadership group was less vindictive and more concerned about popular welfare and unity than many local leaders.

In 1947, the class-struggle land reform threatened to rip life into shreds. Revenge against the heirs of the old elite became institutionalized. Religious people, indeed almost any unlucky soul, even a disliked army veteran with a donkey, could be scapegoated. The powerful could use mobilization campaigns to pursue personal vendettas against those who angered them. The struggle after 1949 to catch the unscrupulous and corrupt officials who had abandoned the people mainly ensnared the unlucky or unprotected. Beyond attack, beyond question, was the systemic and structured dynamic of the socialist state that intimidated and impoverished millions of patriotic and loyal villagers.

This book traces the painful consequences of an incapacity to solve historically rooted problems. It analyzes achievements, failures, costs, and roads not taken, the interaction and impact of deep continuities amid changing currents. The promise of early liberating reforms went unfulfilled; a system became entrenched. The structures of that system were shaped by peasant tradition, a new nationalism, and socialist networks connecting village and state in ways that privileged some, peripheralized many, and stratified all as it defined rules of conduct for both socialist state powerholders and many millions of powerless villagers. Although militarism, retrogression, and fundamentalism are inherent dangers in all statist modernization, the feudal-like elements of Soviet-style socialism and the political culture of tough, authoritarian Chinese males fostered the least progressive outcomes.

Seeking ways to change China and yet remain Chinese, to deal with the challenges of modern and powerful foreign forces while improving the lives of poor, conservative villagers, patriotic Chinese would continue the tortuous struggle going back to the Qing dynasty. For the heirs of the great civilization that was China, as for Lu Xun's wanderer in his poem "Wild Flowers," the voice ahead still beckoned, "push on."[17]

APPENDIX

Table A1. Crop Area, Yields, and Output in the Geng Changsuo Cooperative, 1944–1952 (Area in Mu, Yield in Catties per Mu)

Year	Corn		Millet		Sorghum		Wheat		Late Corn		Sweet Potatoes		Per Mu Grain Yield	Gross per Capita Grain Output	Peanuts		Cotton	
	Area	Yield	Area	Yield	Area	Yield	Area	Yield	Area	Yield	Area	Yield			Area	Yield	Area	Yield
1944	7	220	6	210	8	180	15	130	15	155	1	1,000	223	375	3	250	0	0
1945	33	200	35	210	30	180	80	130	80	150	5	1,800	215	368	35	250	0	0
1946	12	210	12	220	11	200	40	135	40	165	4	1,900	285	549	25	280	0	0
1947	10	140	12	200	10	190	53	135	53	155	5	1,800	234	382	30	280	3	25
1948	20	210	20	200	18	200	80	135	80	160	5	1,900	291	621	35	280	5	30
1949	22	230	20	200	20	200	80	140	80	185	5	1,500	329	681	35	280	5	30
1950	20	230	20	200	19	200	80	150	80	190	5	2,000	336	662	30	280	5	35
1951	25	245	20	220	23	250	100	170	100	200	5	2,200	478	1,008	40	280	6	40
1952	15	174	20	185	15	179	180	194	180	45	5	1,140	237	497	40	134	10	62

Table A2.   Population and Labor Utilization in
the Geng Changsuo Cooperative, 1944–1952

Year	Total Population[a]	Male Population	Female Population	Total Labor[b]	Full Male Labor	Full Female Labor	% of Labor Force Male
1944	22	9	13	7	4	3	57
1945	107	52	55	22	17	5	77
1946	41	20	21	16	11	5	69
1947	55	27	28	20	13	7	65
1948	67	33	34	22	14	8	64
1949	71	35	36	24	15	9	63
1950	73	36	37	26	16	10	62
1951	82	41	41	31	20	11	65
1952	112	55	57	49	28	21	57

[a]Population refers to all members of participating households, including children, as well as adults working outside the village.
[b]This includes individuals rated as partial labor power, so two individuals each rated as half a labor power are counted as a full labor power.

Table A3.   Cooperative Income in Geng Changsuo
Cooperative, 1944–1952 (in Thousand Catties of Grain)

Year	Gross Crop Income[a]	Gross Sideline Income	Percent of Income from Sidelines	Gross Income Total[b]	Gross Per Capita Income (catties)[b]
1944	9	0.4	4	9.4	427
1945	49	47.0	49	97.0	906
1946	31	30.0	50	61.0	1,488
1947	29	25.0	47	54.0	981
1948	58	21.0	26	79.0	1,179
1949	61	50.0	45	111.0	1,563
1950	73	60.0	45	133.0	1,821
1951	107	47.0	30	154.0	1,878
1952	79	7.0	8	86.0	767

[a]Gross crop income includes grain, cash crops (such as peanuts and cotton), and some miscellaneous crops not included in table 1.
[b]Gross income total and gross per capita income figures do not take into account production expenses, accumulation for investment, and taxes paid to the state.

Table A4. Crop Area, Yields, and Output of Major Grain, Cotton, and Oil-Bearing Crops in Wugong Village, 1953–1961 (Area in Mu; Yield in Catties per Mu; Output in Catties)

Year	Corn Area	Corn Yield	Millet Area	Millet Yield	Sorghum Area	Sorghum Yield	Wheat Area	Wheat Yield	Sweet Potatoes Area	Sweet Potatoes Yield	Cultivated Area	Irrigated Area	Grain-Sown Area	Grain-Yield per Mu	Total Grain Output	Gross per Capita Grain Output	Crop-Sown Area	Peanuts Area	Peanuts Yield	Cotton[a] Area	Cotton[a] Yield
1953	400	297	300	207	200	229	1,100	125	60	3,420	3,400	450	4,600	282	958,800	572	5,590	500	283	230	21
1954	700	347	700	205	340	219	1,300	202	240	2,300	3,390	n.a.	4,600	352	1,193,300	712	5,540	600	239	250	30
1955	490	332	859	225	352	314	1,315	206	150	1,500	3,101	1,100	4,915	283	877,600	481	5,863	822	377	624	74
1956	183	271	404	190	0	0	1,414	233	168	2,300	2,261	1,200	5,089	278	628,600	329	7,186	110	284	1,988	24
1957	207	438	616	256	81	269	1,497	152	139	2,060	2,772	1,200	4,262	300	831,600	486	5,980	528	335	1,190	55
1958	340	502	615	308	125	473	1,178	195	185	958	2,988	1,500	4,416	382	1,145,200	656	5,747	579	246	752	46
1959	322	502	590	306	984	212	871	252	400	580	2,492	1,500	3,313	430	1,071,600	614	4,643	600	235	700	69
1960	713	293	455	134	230	152	800	430	650	1,084	2,258	1,500	3,058	310	700,000	378	4,298	450	66	780	59
1961	1,300	360	456	273	210	248	850	215	250	602	2,296	1,500	3,144	437	1,003,400	527	4,254	260	191	850	62

[a]Cotton figures are for ginned cotton.

Table A5. Population and Labor Utilization in Wugong Village, 1944–1961

Year	Total Population	Male Population	Female Population	Total Labor	Full Male Labor	Full Female Labor	% of Labor Force Male	Labor in Industry and Sidelines		
								In Teams and Brigades	Outside the Team	In Brigade
1944	1,400	690	710							
1945	1,430	705	725							
1946	1,480	720	760							
1947	1,520	737	783							
1948	1,600	767	833							
1949	1,650	792	858							
1950	1,620	827	793							
1951	1,640	856	784							
1952	1,650	870	780							
1953	1,675	905	770	428	265	163	62			
1954	1,675	933	742	558	379	179	68			
1955	1,823	954	869	586	405	181	69			
1956	1,912	961	951	627	380	247	61			
1957	1,711	833	878	717	398	319	56		40	40
1958	1,745	844	901	744	398	346	53	21	40	40
1959	1,744	845	899	685	330	355	48		40	40
1960	1,853	887	966	695	330	365	47	25	60	60
1961	1,904	890	1,014	702	346	356	49		60	60

Table A6. Income and Income Distribution in Wugong Village, 1955–61 (in Thousand Yuan)

Year	Gross Crop Income	Gross Sideline Income	% of Income from Sidelines	Gross Income Total	Net Income Total	Total Income Distributed	Cooperative Membership	Average per Capita Distributed Income (yuan)	Average per Capita Income Paid in Cash (yuan)	Value of Labor Day (yuan)
1955	151	10	6	162	126	113	1,823	62	8	.74
1956	101	14	12	115	88	85	1,912	44	2	.71
1957	149	19	10	168	109	99	1,711	57	5	.85
1958	137	14	9	151	124	81	1,745	46	2	.48
1959	162	19	10	181	134	91	1,744	52	3	.78
1960	128	19	13	147	114	100	1,853	54	5	.52
1961	174	27	13	201	146	129	1,904	68	15	.59

Note: Per capita distributed income is the estimated cash value of distributed collective income including income paid both in kind and in cash.

Table A7.   Crop Sales to the State in the Wugong Cooperative
and Wugong Brigade, 1952–1961 (in Thousand Catties)

Year	Wheat	Coarse Grains	Total Grain	% of Gross Grain Output Sold	Per Capita Grain Sales (catties)	Cotton	Peanuts
1952	0	0	0	0	0	0	0
1953	0	60	60	11	49	10	150
1954	0	70	70	6	42	17	140
1955	20	50	70	8	38	33	180
1956	0	0	0	0	0	33	0
1957	20	25	45	5	26	57	100
1958	30	50	80	7	46	20	60
1959	50	130	180	17	103	33	80
1960	20	0	20	3	11	40	0
1961	30	40	70	7	37	47	10

⚜ ABBREVIATIONS
USED IN NOTES

DSSCT *Di sishi chuntian* (Shijiazhuang: Huashan wenyi chuban she, 1983)

FBIS U.S. Foreign Broadcast Information Service

GMRB *Guangming ribao*

HBRB *Hebei ribao (Hebei Daily)*

HKDYZ *Huakai di yi zhi* (Tianjin: Tianjin renmin chuban she, 1963, 1973)

JDSJ *Zhonghua renmin gongheguo jingji da shi ji (1949–80)* (Beijing: Zhongguo shehui kexue chuban she, 1984)

JPRS Joint Publications Research Service

NCNA New China News Agency

RMRB *Renmin ribao (People's Daily)*

SCMP *Survey of the China Mainland Press* (Hong Kong)

WGRM Nankai daxue lishi xi, Wugong dadui cun shi bianxie zu, eds., *Wugong renmin de zhandou licheng* (Beijing: Zhonghua shuzhu, 1978)

ZZYS Zhonggong zhongyang yanjiu shi, *Guanyu jianguo yilai dang de ruogan lishi wenti di jueyi* (Beijing: Renmin chuban she, 1985)

❖ NOTES

Introduction

1 Prasenjit Duara, *Culture, Power, and the State: Rural North China, 1900–1942* (Stanford: Stanford University Press, 1988), details this disarticulation of the traditional culture in the pre-Communist era.

2 Sidney D. Gamble, *Ting Hsien: A North China Rural Community* (1954; Stanford: Stanford University Press, 1968; Gamble, *North China Villages: Social, Political, and Economic Activities before 1933* (Berkeley: University of California Press, 1963).

3 For a discussion of the early history of Raoyang, see Zhang Yongfu, "Raoyang shi kao," *Hengshui ribao,* September 27, 1980.

4 Luo Ziwen et al., *The Great Wall* (New York: McGraw-Hill, 1981), p. 22.

5 The reader is invited to compare this work with other studies that analyze data on Wugong. See Marsh Marshall, *Organization and Growth in Rural China* (New York: St. Martin's Press, 1985), and Keith Griffin and Ashwani Saith, *Growth and Equity in Rural China* (Singapore: Maruzen Asia, 1981).

6 Anita Chan, Richard Madsen, and Jonathan Unger, *Chen Village: The Recent History of a Peasant Community in Mao's China* (Berkeley: University of California Press, 1984); Richard Madsen, *Morality and Power in a Chinese Village* (Berkeley: University of California Press, 1984); Ezra Vogel, *Canton under Communism: Programs and Politics in a Provincial Capital, 1949–1968* (Cambridge: Harvard University Press, 1969); William Parish and Martin Whyte, *Village and Family in Contemporary China* (Chicago: University of Chicago Press, 1978); and Bernard Frolic, *Mao's People* (Cambridge: Harvard University Press, 1980); Jean Oi, *State and Peasant in Contemporary China* (Berkeley: University of California Press, 1989).

7 After the initial joint five-week field trip in May–June 1978, each author took responsibility for drafting material on particular topics and periods. The chance to return in November 1978 led to a quest for additional information. Eventually we visited Raoyang eighteen times. Except for 1981 and 1982, when the authorities prevented research in Raoyang, between 1979 and 1987 we made at least two visits every year, ranging from a few days to three weeks. On two visits two researchers went together. On one visit three traveled as a group. All four visited Raoyang at least four times. Although she generously shared notes and insights, bad health prevented Kay Johnson from writing chapters. As each author time and again used new material to rework all chapters, the book became genuinely collaborative both in its conceptualization and in its continuous redrafting.

8 The structured logic of how more communism created an ever-widening gap between those favored by the state and all others is explicated in Michael Schoen-

hals, "Saltationist Socialism: Mao Zedong and the Great Leap Forward, 1958" (Ph.D. diss., University of Stockholm, 1987), pp. 110, 167.

9   Paul A. Cohen, "The Post-Mao Reforms in Historical Perspective," *Journal of Asian Studies* 47:3 (August 1988), p. 519.

10   Fei could see what was missing when he reinvestigated the village of Kaixian'gong after collectivization because his 1930s investigation had revealed the importance of sidelines, trade, and transport to the peasant economy. Only by returning could Fei see what was gone.

11   C. K. Yang, *A Chinese Village in Early Communist Transition* (Cambridge: MIT Press, 1959); William Hinton, *Fanshen: A Documentary of Revolution in a Chinese Village* (New York: Monthly Review Press, 1966); Isabel and David Crook, *Ten Mile Inn: Mass Movement in a Chinese Village* (New York: Pantheon, 1979); Yuan-tsung Chen, *The Dragon's Village: An Autobiographical Novel of Revolutionary China* (New York: Pantheon, 1980).

12   Notes are provided for publicly available documents and archival sources. The wide array of interviews, surveys, and other data that exist only in our private files are not annotated. Since much of the printed material is politically informed, when we cite a published source it is because investigation persuaded us of the plausibility or reliability of that particular fact. If the facts cannot be established, individuals are presented offering their personal views.

13   More than half of the villagers of Wugong are surnamed Li. Since there are few lineage names in the village, to keep names straight, and in accord with the widespread use of nicknames among villagers, we frequently use local nicknames. Where we introduce nicknames of our own invention, these are explained. Li Guanghui was the Raoyang official in charge of our first visit and the only county-level Li we dealt with. He became, for us, County Li.

14   Access was facilitated initially by helpful professionals at the Friendship Association in Shijiazhuang and Beijing, and later by officials of the Hebei provincial government. Especially important were Xu Fu, Zhang Fengtong, and their colleagues in Raoyang and Hengshui.

15   Duara, *Culture, Power, and the State,* concludes that "alleviating the tax burden was the most pressing demand of the masses" (p. 252). Jerome Ch'en's forthcoming *The Highlanders of China: A History, 1895–1937* (Armonk, N.Y.: M. E. Sharpe), describes the centrality of tax reform to Communist success in the highlands of south central China.

16   Frederick Teiwes, "The Origins of Rectification," *China Quarterly,* no. 65 (January 1976), pp. 32–49.

17   There is much archival data in such recent work on the career of Deng Zihui as Jiang Boying et al., *Deng Zihui zhuan* (Shanghai: Shanghai renmin chuban she, 1986).

18   Jean-Luc Domenach, *Aux origines du Grand Bond en Avant* (Paris: Presses de la Fondation Nationale des Sciences Politiques, 1982).

19   Fei Xiaotong (Fei Hsiao Tung), *Chinese Village Close-Up* (Beijing: New World Press, 1983), pp. 158–96.

20   Roderick MacFarquhar, *The Origins of the Cultural Revolution,* vol. II, *The Great Leap Forward, 1958–1960* (New York: Columbia University Press, 1983); Thomas Bernstein, "Stalinism, Famine and the Chinese Peasants," *Theory and Society* 13:3 (1984), pp. 339–77.

21   Chalmers Johnson, *Peasant Nationalism and Communist Power* (Stanford: Stanford University Press, 1962).

22   Robert Marks, *Rural Revolution in South China* (Madison: University of Wisconsin Press, 1984); Mark Selden, *The Yenan Way in Revolutionary China* (Cambridge: Harvard University Press, 1971).

23   Loren Brandt, *Commercialization and Agricultural Development: Central and Eastern China, 1870–1937* (Cambridge: Cambridge University Press, 1989), contests the notion of decline.

24   Philip C. C. Huang, *The Peasant Economy and Social Change in North China* (Stanford: Stanford University Press, 1985); Kang Chao, *Man and Land in Chinese History: An Economic Analysis* (Stanford: Stanford University Press, 1986).

25   Ramon Myers, *The Chinese Peasant Economy: Agricultural Development in Hopei and Shantung, 1890–1949* (Cambridge: Harvard University Press, 1970). See also Prasenjit Duara, "Power in Rural Society: North China Villages, 1900–1940" (Ph.D. diss., Harvard University, 1983).

26   The explanations of the economic crisis have come in many forms. Chao, *Man and Land in Chinese History,* has argued for a centuries-long ecological decline. Mark Elvin, *The Pattern of the Chinese Past* (Stanford: Stanford University Press, 1983), argues for a technology trap. Prasenjit Duara, "State Involution: A Study of Local Finances in North China, 1911–1935," *Comparative Studies in Society and History* 29:1 (January 1987), pp. 132–61, has discovered a financial crisis. E. L. Jones, *The European Miracle: Environments, Economies and Geopolitics in the History of Europe and Asia* (Cambridge: Cambridge University Press, 1981), contends that the seeming political security of extensive growth and internal colonization kept the rulers of the Ming dynasty from risky but necessary innovations. Chinese scholars have argued that the long-term economic crisis was caused by misguided political leaders. In accord with the post-Mao reform policy, Xiao Jiefu argues that by the midseventeenth century the Qing closed its doors, threw out missionaries, repudiated the theories of Copernicus and Kepler as heresies, and imposed a feudal cultural dictatorship. It rejected as a path to national awakening earlier policies of cultivating talents and welcoming such foreign knowledge as mathematics, calendars, and mapmaking. "The Open Policy in Historical Retrospect," *Social Sciences in China,* no. 4 (Winter 1986), pp. 31–42. Although all these and other explanations of the long-term crisis remain contested, the data presented in this book are at one with the notion of a long-term secular decline.

27   Building on the work of Alexander [Vasil'evich] Chayanov, such scholars as Basile Kerblay and Teodor Shanin have investigated why peasant household culture and economy persist in feudal systems, capitalist societies, and socialist states. This line of research permits one to see peasantries as persistent partial societies with intrinsic strengths that are not defined by, equal to, or obliterated by feudalism, capitalism, or socialism. Cf. A. V. Chayanov, *The Theory of Peasant Economy* (Madison: University of Wisconsin Press, 1986), and Basile Kerblay, "Chayanov and the Theory of Peasantry as a Specific Type of Economy," in *Peasants and Peasant Society,* ed. Teodor Shanin (Baltimore: Penguin, 1971), pp. 150–60.

28   Peter Perdue, *Exhausting the Earth: State and Peasant in Hunan, 1500–1850* (Cambridge: Harvard University Press, 1987).

29   For data on the subsequent shredding of those bonds, see Chan, Madsen, and Unger,

Chen Village; Gao Yuan, *Born Red* (Stanford: Stanford University Press, 1987); and Anne Thurston, *Enemies of the People* (New York: Alfred A. Knopf, 1987).

1   The County Declines, Villages Disintegrate

1   This account of Raoyang in the eighteenth century is based mainly on a local gazetteer, *Raoyang xianzhi,* edited by magistrate Shan Zuozhe and published in 1749.

2   On the early history of Raoyang, see Zhang Yongfu, "Raoyang shi kao," *Hengshui ribao,* September 27, 1980.

3   Pierre-Etienne Will, *Bureaucratie et famine en 18e siècle Chine* (Paris: Mouton, 1980), p. 176.

4   See Jen Yu-ti, *A Concise Geography of China* (Beijing: Foreign Languages Press, 1964), pp. 72–75, and Ramon Myers, *The Chinese Peasant Economy: Agricultural Development in Hopei and Shantung, 1890–1949* (Cambridge: Harvard University Press, 1970), pp. 8–12, for summaries of geographic conditions.

5   World Bank, *Waterlogging, Salinity and Drought: North China Plain* (Washington, D.C., 1983), p. 12.

6   A catty is equal to 1.1 pounds, a mu to one-sixth of an acre. In the *Raoyang xianzhi* (1749) the figures are given in units called *dan,* or piculs. There were 30,000 dan in the central granary and 14,000 dan in the suburban granaries. We calculate that in Raoyang a picul contained 100 catties and a *dou,* or peck, 10 catties.

7   See the discussion of cannibalism during the 1887 famine in Dingxian in Sidney D. Gamble, *Ting Hsien: A North China Rural Community* (1954; Stanford: Stanford University Press, 1968), p. 446.

8   Compare Susan Mann, "Widows in the Kinship, Class, and Community Structures of Qing Dynasty China," *Journal of Asian Studies* 46:1 (February 1987), pp. 37–56.

9   Cf. Vivien W. Ng, "Ideology and Sexuality: Rape Laws in Qing China," *Journal of Asian Studies* 46:1 (February 1987), pp. 57–70.

10   Gamble, *Ting Hsien,* p. 437.

11   Stephen MacKinnon, *Power and Politics in Late Imperial China: Yuan Shikai in Beijing and Tianjin, 1901–1908* (Berkeley: University of California Press, 1981), p. 172. We are grateful to Professor MacKinnon for sharing his research notes on Zhili.

12   *Zhili tuchan biao* (1904), in *Beijing xuebao* (1905), *Kexue conglu,* 4, *Diaocha,* no. 1, p. 91.

13   MacKinnon, *Power and Politics in Late Imperial China,* pp. 93, 103, 147; Sally Borthwick, *Education and Social Change in China: Beginnings of the Modern Era* (Stanford: Stanford University Press, 1983), p. 78.

14   United International Famine Relief Committee, *The North China Famine of 1920–21* (Beijing, 1922), pp. 6, 9–11, 13, 26.

15   According to G. William Skinner, the areas most vulnerable to depopulating forces were famine-prone densely populated places on the North China plain. See "Social Ecology and the Forces of Repression in North China: A Regional Systems Framework for Analysis" (Paper presented at ACLS workshop, Rebellion and Revolution in North China, July 27–August 2, 1979, Harvard University).

16   Edwin Moise, "Downward Social Mobility in Pre-revolutionary China," *Modern China* 3:1 (January 1977); Carl Riskin, *China's Political Economy: The Quest for Development since 1949* (Oxford: Oxford University Press, 1987), pp. 24–25.

17   This account of Raoyang politics in the years 1925–33 is based in part on Raoyang xian geming lieshi shiliao bianxie zu, ed., *Qian gu ying lie* (Raoyang, 1984).

18   "Raoyang xiuzhi Hutuo he yijian shu," *Hebei sheng jianshe ting* (December 1932), 65–66. We are indebted to the Academia Sinica, Taibei, Taiwan, for a copy of this article.

19   This account of Raoyang economy and society in the mid-1930s is based on a field survey entitled "Hebei sheng Raoyang xian difang shiqi qingkuang diaocha baogao," *Jincha diaocha tongji congkan* 1:4 (October 1936), pp. 112–22. According to economist Kang Chao, the technological infrastructure had deteriorated (*Man and Land in Chinese History: An Economic Analysis* [Stanford: Stanford University Press, 1986], pp. 89, 203, 207, 214, 215). The proliferation of taxes is discussed in Prasenjit Duara, "Power in Rural Society: North China Villages, 1900–1940" (Ph.D. diss., Harvard University, 1983), pp. 214–17, 329.

20   *Hebei sheng mianchan diaocha baogao* (1936), 157–58.

21   "Raoyang diaocha," p. 115.

22   The low rates of tenancy in North China are well documented in Linda Arrigo, "Landownership Concentration in China: The Buck Survey Revisited," *Modern China* 12:3 (July 1986), pp. 259–360, esp. pp. 270, 287, 298, 321; Joseph Esherick, "Number Games: A Note on Land Distribution in Prerevolutionary China," *Modern China* 7:4 (October 1981), pp. 323–36; Philip C. C. Huang, *The Peasant Economy and Social Change in North China* (Stanford: Stanford University Press, 1985); and Chao, *Man and Land in Chinese History.*

23   *Les Missiones de Chine onzième année* (1933–34), pp. 85–87. Jean-Paul West, Coordinator for Maryknoll Fathers and Brothers, and Donald MacInnis, Maryknoll Coordinator for China Research, generously provided information on the church in southern Hebei.

24   Sidney Gamble, ed., *Chinese Village Plays from the Ting Hsien Region* (Amsterdam: Philo Press, 1970). For a fascinating explanation of why the Dingxian operas contain so much material that defies traditional norms of behavior, see David Arkush, "Love and Marriage in North China Peasant Operas," in *Unofficial China: Popular Culture and Thought in the People's Republic,* ed. Perry Link, Richard Madsen, and Paul G. Pickowicz (Boulder, Colo.: Westview Press, 1989), 72–87.

25   Thomas Gottschang, "Railways, Foreign Trade and Pre-modern Transportation at North China Ports in the Early Twentieth Century" (Paper presented at the annual meeting of the Association for Asian Studies, March 23, 1985, Philadelphia).

26   Gamble, *Ting Hsien,* pp. 230–34.

27   *DSSCT,* p. 175.

28   *WGRM,* p. 4.

29   "Raoyang diaocha," p. 118.

30   The total of 80 mu of privately owned land that was rented was divided among 25 households. We estimate that approximately 50 households rented the 150 mu of lineage and temple land.

31   See the discussion of hired labor in nearby Dingxian in Gamble, *Ting Hsien,* pp. 79–80.

32   Grain rations in China in the 1970s were equivalent to 300 catties. See Philip C. C. Huang, "Analyzing the Twentieth-Century Chinese Countryside," *Modern China* 1:2 (April 1975), p. 134.

33   Thomas Gottschang, "Economic Change, Disasters and Migration: The Historical Case of Manchuria" (Ph.D. diss., University of Michigan, 1985).

34   Gamble, *Ting Hsien,* pp. 398–425, contains a discussion of popular religious practice in Hebei in the 1930s. Also see Arthur H. Smith, *Village Life in China* (Boston: Little, Brown, 1970), pp. 98–105.

35   Gamble, *Ting Hsien,* p. 409.

36   *HKDYZ* (1963), p. 329.

37   Gamble found wedding costs in Dingxian also to be about the equivalent of one year's household income, with costs ranging from approximately 135 silver dollars for poor households, to 300 dollars for middle income to 600 dollars for prosperous households. In poorer Wugong, weddings tended to be less elaborate. *Ting Hsien,* p. 383.

38   *HKDYZ* (1963), pp. 177–78.

39   Ibid., p. 329; *WGRM,* p. 7.

40   See Prasenjit Duara, "State Involution: A Study of Local Finances in North China, 1911–1935," *Comparative Studies in Society and History* 29:1 (January 1987), pp. 156–57.

41   For a discussion of crop-watching organizations in North China, see Smith, *Village Life in China,* pp. 119–24.

42   *WGRM,* p. 8.

43   Ibid.

44   Ibid., p. 13.

45   Ibid.

46   Ibid., p. 16.

2   Bonds of War

1   See Linda Grove, "Economic Change and Social Transformation: The Case of Central Hebei" (conference paper, Tianjin, 1984), pp. 22–46.

2   This and subsequent paragraphs draw on biographies of Lu Zhengcao, Peng Zhen, Huang Jing, Nie Rongzhen, and Song Shaowen in Donald Klein and Anne Clarke, eds., *Biographic Dictionary of Chinese Communism, 1921–1965* (Cambridge: Harvard University Press, 1971), and Lu Zhengcao, *Jizhong huiyi lu* (Beijing: Jiefang jun chuban she, 1984).

3   *Nie Rongzhen huiyi lu* (Beijing: Jiefang jun chuban she, 1984), II, pp. 380–81.

4   Harrison Forman, *Report from Red China* (New York: Holt, Rinehart, and Winston, 1945), p. 142.

5   Ross Terrill, *The White-Boned Demon: A Biography of Jiang Qing* (New York: William Morrow, 1984).

6   Zhongguo renmin jiefang jun Hebei junqu zhengzhi bu, ed., *Jizhong kangri zhanzheng jian shi* (Hebei: Renmin chuban she, 1958), pp. 1, 24–28. We are grateful to Linda Grove for making available a copy of this book.

7   This account of early county resistance activities is based on Raoyang xian geming lieshi shiliao bian xie zu, ed., *Qian gu ying lie* (Raoyang: 1984), pp. 2–9, 28–42, 47–51, and on local interviews.

8   Ibid., p. 29.

9   Hebei sheng di ming bangongshi, ed., *Hebei zhengqu yange zhi* (Shijiazhuang: Hebei kexue jishu chuban she, 1985), p. 326.

10   See Wei Hongyun, ed., *Hua bei kangri genjudi jishi* (Tianjin: Tianjin renmin chuban she, 1986), for material on the newspaper effort (p. 71) and for statistics on the education effort (pp. 254, 260).

11   *Qian gu ying lie,* p. 29.

12   For the rape of a thirteen-year-old Hebei girl by eight Japanese soldiers in 1937, see Lloyd Eastman, "Facets of an Ambivalent Relationship," in *The Chinese and the Japanese,* ed. Akira Iriye (Princeton: Princeton University Press, 1980), p. 296.

13   The following people played leading roles in other mass organizations: Zhang Duan (children's corps), Qiao Wenzhi (Women's Anti-Japanese Patriotic League), Li Wanyi (Cultural Corps), and Qiao Hengtai (Worker Anti-Japanese Patriotic League). *WGRM,* p. 16.

14   *Zhong gong dang shi ziliao* 27 (1988), p. 195.

15   *HKDYZ* (1963), p. 40.

16   *WGRM,* p. 21.

17   Grove, "Economic Change and Social Transformation," pp. 22–46. For a detailed discussion of wartime economic reforms in central Hebei, see Nankai daxue lishi xi, ed., *Nankai shixue: Hua bei kangri genjudi shi zhuanji* (Tianjin: Nankai daxue chuban she, 1984), pp. 189–241.

18   *WGRM,* p. 19.

19   Ibid.

20   *Selected Works of Mao Tsetung* (Beijing: Foreign Languages Press, 1967), II, pp. 441–49.

21   In poor mountain village areas, which were far worse off than Raoyang county, and in parts of southern Hebei, as much as 70 percent of the households were tax-exempt. Isabel and David Crook, *Revolution in a Chinese Village: Ten Mile Inn* (London: Routledge and Kegan Paul, 1959), pp. 46–47.

22   *WGRM,* p. 19.

23   Carl Dorris, "Peasant Mobilization in North China and the Origins of Yenan Communism," *China Quarterly,* no. 68 (December 1976), pp. 704–9.

24   *Nie Rongzhen huiyi li,* II, pp. 38–82; Dorris, "Peasant Mobilization in North China," p. 697.

25   *Nie Rongzhen huiyi lu,* III, p. 541.

26   Lu, *Jizhong,* p. 203; *HKDYZ* (1973), p. 82.

27   Wei, ed., *Hua bei,* p. 317.

28   *HKDYZ* (1963), p. 12.

29   *WGRM,* p. 21.

30   *Jizhong kangri zhanzheng jian shi,* p. 89.

31   Ibid., p. 84; *Nie Rongzhen huiyi lu,* II, pp. 530, 534.

32   Committee members included Communists Li Zhenhai, Qiao Molin, and Li Fuxiang, as well as Li Dianfeng, Geng Ruchang, Li Takai, Li Sanzhu, Xu Xiufeng, and Yang Laiyi. All were from the middle-income ranks of the independent farming group with the exception of Li Fuxiang, Li Sanzhu, and Xu Xiufeng, who were from relatively poor households.

33   *WGRM,* p. 19.

34   In contrast, the polarized village of Zhangzhuang in Shanxi was the site of a Japanese fortification in a community that had no prewar Communist organization. This fragmented village would experience a violent land reform.

35 Linda Grove, "Economic Change and Social Transformation," p. 23.
36 *WGRM*, p. 23.
37 Yu Qiuli, "A New Creation," in FBIS, *Daily Report*, March 23, 1983, K 13.

3   Strains of Socialism

1   Theodore H. White and Annalee Jacoby, *Thunder Out of China* (New York: William Sloane, 1961), pp. 166–78; Jack Belden, *China Shakes the World* (New York: Monthly Review Press, 1970), pp. 61–70.
2   *WGRM*, pp. 30–31; *RMRB*, March 19, 1952.
3   *HKDYZ* (1963), p. 147.
4   Ibid., p. 35.
5   Ibid., pp. 42–50. *Qingzhu Wugong renmin gongshe jitihua ershi zhounian huibian, 1943–1963* (Hebei: Renmin chuban she, 1964), pp. 26–28.
6   *HKDYZ* (1963), pp. 163–71.
7   Ibid., pp. 36, 50–55.
8   Ibid., pp. 55–57.
9   Ibid., p. 1.
10 *RMRB*, January 7, 1954, March 19, 1952; *HKDYZ* (1963), p. 45.
11 *HKDYZ* (1963), pp. 13, 37.
12 Ibid., p. 37.
13 *RMRB*, March 19, 1952; *WGRM*, pp. 31–32.
14 *Shehuizhuyi zhi hua* (Hebei: Renmin chuban she, 1956), pp. 1–2; *HKDYZ* (1963), p. 38.
15 The original text is in *HKDYZ* (1963), pp. 339–40. See *RMRB*, March 19, 1952.
16 *HKDYZ* (1963), p. 166.
17 Geng Changsuo, "Guoqu he xianzai," in *Yongyuan bu yao wangji* (Tianjin, 1961), pp. 56–59; *WGRM*, pp. 9–10; *HKDYZ* (1963), pp. 10–11, 15–16.
18 *HKDYZ* (1963), p. 152.
19 Ibid., p. 11–12.
20 Ibid., pp. 68–69, 297.
21 See Philip C. C. Huang, *The Peasant Economy and Social Change in North China* (Stanford: Stanford University Press, 1985), p. 257.
22 *HKDYZ* (1963), p. 65
23 *WGRM*, p. 18.
24 *HKDYZ* (1963), p. 69.
25 Ibid., p. 13.
26 *WGRM*, pp. 30–31; *HKDYZ* (1963), p. 13.
27 *HKDYZ* (1963), p. 39.
28 Tongjibo, 1944–59, Raoyang Archive.
29 *HKDYZ* (1963), p. 48.
30 Ibid., p. 1.
31 *WGRM*, p. 33.
32 Ibid., p. 35; *HKDYZ* (1963), p. 39.
33 *HKDYZ* (1963), p. 39.
34 Ibid.

35 Mao Zedong, "Zuzhiqilai," in *Mao Zedong ji* (Tokyo: Hokubosha, 1970–73), IX, pp. 85–94.

36 Wei Hongyun, ed., *Hua bei kangri genjudi jishi* (Tianjin: Tianjin renmin chuban she, 1986), p. 497.

37 *HKDYZ* (1960), p. 10.

38 *Shehuizhuyi zhi hua*, p. 1; Tongjibo.

39 *RMRB*, January 7, 1954.

40 Tongjibo.

41 *HKDYZ* (1973), p. 302.

42 *RMRB*, January 7, 1954; *WGRM*, 37; *HKDYZ* (1963), pp. 166–69.

43 Tongjibo.

44 *HKDYZ* (1963), pp. 152–57.

45 Ibid., pp. 115–19.

46 Ibid., pp. 315–18.

47 Ibid., p. 40.

48 *RMRB*, March 19, 1952; *WGRM*, pp. 37–38.

49 *WGRM*, p. 38.

50 *RMRB*, January 7, 1954.

51 *HKDYZ* (1963), p. 40.

52 *WGRM*, p. 38.

53 Ibid., pp. 38–39.

54 Tongjibo.

55 *WGRM*, p. 40.

56 *Geng Changsuo zouguo de lu* (Tianjin: Hebei renmin chuban she, 1966), p. 33.

57 *WGRM*, p. 40.

58 Ibid., p. 39.

59 *HKDYZ* (1963), p. 117.

60 Ibid., p. 51.

61 Ibid., p. 50; *WGRM*, p. 41.

62 *WGRM*, p. 43.

63 Lin Tie, "Wo yu Geng Changsuo tongzhi he ta chuangban de Wugong dadui, Wugong gongshe de guanxi he jidian kanfa" (Memoir prepared for the authors, December 1979); Donald Klein and Anne Clarke, eds., *Biographic Dictionary of Chinese Communism, 1921–1965* (Cambridge: Harvard University Press, 1971), I, pp. 574–75.

64 Wei, ed., *Hua bei*, pp. 520, 521.

65 *Hebei sheng Raoyang xian geming lieshi yingming lu* (Raoyang, 1981), p. 53, lists seventeen Wugong wartime martyrs, and identifies nine as party members.

66 *WGRM*, p. 41.

67 Tongjibo.

68 *Geng Changsuo zouguo de lu*, p. 36.

69 *Shehuizhuyi zhi hua*, p. 4; *RMRB*, March 19, 1952.

70 *WGRM*, p. 42.

71 *HKDYZ* (1963), pp. 126–31; Hsiao Ping, "A New Kind of Peasant," *China Reconstructs* 43:1 (January 1964), p. 33.

72 Geng Changsuo began to act as the head of a political machine. Although villagers

called him a host of names—Ropemaker, Uncle, Co-op Leader—we call him Boss Geng to capture the political role that Changsuo learned to play very effectively.

73   *HKDYZ* (1963), pp. 51–52.

74   *WGRM,* pp. 42–43.

75   Ibid., p. 43.

76   Tongjibo.

77   *WGRM,* p. 44.

78   Ibid.

79   Tongjibo.

80   *WGRM,* p. 44.

4   Silent Revolution, Sound of Terror

1   *Selected Works of Liu Shaoqi* (Beijing: Foreign Languages Press, 1984), I, pp. 372–78; Suzanne Pepper, *Civil War in China: The Political Struggle, 1945–1949* (Berkeley: University of California Press, 1978), pp. 246–48.

2   Mark Selden, *The People's Republic of China* (New York: Monthly Review Press, 1978), pp. 208–14.

3   Isabel and David Crook, *Revolution in a Chinese Village: Ten Mile Inn* (London: Routledge and Kegan Paul, 1959), pp. 179–80.

4   *WGRM,* p. 46.

5   For a summary of the terminology contained in the May Fourth Directive, see Pepper, *Civil War in China,* pp. 246–48.

6   Information in this and the next three paragraphs is drawn from Jizhong qu dang wei, "Jizhong qu dang wei zhixing zhongyang wusi zhishi de jiben zongjie," April 1, 1947, Bureau of Investigation Archive, Xindian, Taiwan.

7   *HKDYZ* (1963), p. 342.

8   Ibid., pp. 132–33.

9   *WGRM,* p. 52. The Wugong tax obligation was set at the high figure of 100,000 catties through 1948.

10   *WGRM,* pp. 52–53.

11   *HKDYZ* (1963), p. 342.

12   Tongjibo, 1949–59, Raoyang Archive.

13   Pepper, *Civil War in China,* p. 286.

14   "Mao Zedong 'da gong she' sixiang chusuo," *Zhong gong dangshi xueshu taolunhui lunwen,* (September 1988), pp. 1–16.

15   Frederick Teiwes, "The Origins of Rectification," *China Quarterly,* no. 65 (January 1976), p. 32.

16   For a restricted circulation discussion stressing Kang Sheng's role in promoting a more militant land policy at the Pingshan conference, see Zhong Kan, *Kang Sheng ping zhuan* (Beijing: Hongqi chuban she, 1982), pp. 96–105.

17   The text of the Agrarian Reform Law is presented and discussed in Selden, *People's Republic of China,* pp. 214–17.

18   Joseph Esherick, "Number Games: A Note on Land Distribution in Prerevolutionary China," *Modern China* 7:4 (October 1981), p. 395. Cf. Philip C. C. Huang, *The Peasant Economy and Social Change in North China* (Stanford: Stanford University Press, 1985), pp. 185–216.

19 See the text in Selden, *People's Republic of China,* and the discussion in Pepper, *Civil War in China,* p. 289.

20 *Nie Rongzhen tongzhi kaimu ci* (Jizhong: Xinhua shudian, 1947), Bureau of Investigation Archive, Xindian, Taiwan. Nie's speech is dated October 3, 1947. Wei Hongyun, *Zhongguo xiandaishi gao, 1919–1949* (Heilongjiang: Renmin chuban she, 1984), II, pp. 356–60.

21 Pepper, *Civil War in China,* pp. 312–14.

22 Tetsuya Kataoka, *Resistance and Revolution in China* (Berkeley: University of California Press, 1974), pp. 358–60.

23 Lin Tie, "Bixu jianding zheng dang fangzhen," *Gongzuo wang lai,* no. 17, December 25, 1947, 1, Bureau of Investigation Archive.

24 For an introduction to how party rectification could precipitate terror and torture, see Peter Seybolt, "Terror and Conformity," *Modern China* 12:1 (January 1986), pp. 39–74.

25 *Gongzuo wang lai,* no. 17, December 25, 1947, 4, Bureau of Investigation Archive.

26 "Jizhong qu dang wei zhixing zhongyang wusi zhishi de jiben zongjie."

27 *WGRM,* p. 48.

28 Pepper, *Civil War in China,* pp. 314–15.

29 *WGRM,* p. 48.

30 Ibid., pp. 48–49.

31 *HKDYZ* (1963), pp. 205–6.

32 *WGRM,* pp. 56–57.

33 *HKDYZ* (1963), pp. 206–7.

34 Pepper, *Civil War in China,* pp. 317–19.

35 Teiwes, "Origins of Rectification," pp. 43–46.

36 "Zhong gong zhongyang guanyu zai lao qu ban lao qu jinxing tudi gaige gongzuo yu zheng dang gongzuo de zhishi," February 2, 1948, Bureau of Investigation Archive.

37 For an account of the moderate spring 1948 land reform in a village in Wuan county, southwest of Raoyang, see Isabel and David Crook, *Ten Mile Inn: Mass Movement in a Chinese Village* (New York: Pantheon, 1979). Exploiters were redefined as those whose income from the work of tenants and laborers was more than 25 percent of their total income. The use of 25 percent of income earned from "exploitation" as a cutoff was meant to be generous to the more prosperous. When the party classified peasants in South China in the early 1930s, all those who earned more than 15 percent of their income from "exploitation" were classified as rich peasants.

38 Some such land deeds still survive. "Tudi fang chan suoyou zheng" was issued in Wugong to poor peasant Zhang Jingpu in 1948 by the fourth district government of Raoyang county.

39 *HKDYZ* (1963), p. 342; *WGRM,* p. 51.

40 *HKDYZ* (1963), pp. 1–5; *WGRM,* p. 53.

41 Dou Zhikai, *Jiefang zhanzheng shiqi de tudi gaige* (Beijing: Beijing daxue chuban she, 1987), p. 262.

42 *WGRM,* pp. 49–50.

43 *HKDYZ* (1963), pp. 326–35.

44 *WGRM,* pp. 49–50.

45 *Hengshui ribao,* October 5, 1980.

46 Pepper, *Civil War in China,* pp. 323–25.

47   *WGRM,* p. 51; Pepper, *Civil War in China,* p. 296.
48   Cf. G. William Skinner, "Marketing and Social Structure in Rural China," *Journal of Asian Studies* 24:3 (May 1965), p. 363.
49   *RMRB,* June 15, 1948.

5   Honeymoon

1   *HKDYZ* (1963), pp. 89–90; *WGRM,* p. 53.
2   "The Evolution of the North China Region (1948–1952)," *Current Background,* no. 161, February 20, 1952, pp. 1–3.
3   Donald Klein and Anne Clarke, eds., *Biographic Dictionary of Chinese Communism, 1921–1965* (Cambridge: Harvard University Press, 1971), II, pp. 977–80; Wolfgang Bartke, *Who's Who in the People's Republic of China* (Armonk, N.Y.: M. E. Sharpe, 1981), pp. 466–67.
4   See Charles W. Hayford, *To the People: James Yen and Village China* (New York: Columbia University Press, 1990).
5   *HKDYZ* (1963), p. 342.
6   Tongjibo, 1944–59, Raoyang Archive.
7   Shi Jingtang et al., eds., *Zhongguo nongye hezuohua yundong shiliao* (Beijing: Sanlian, 1957), p. 435.
8   Tongjibo.
9   *WGRM,* pp. 55–56.
10   Quoted in Mark Selden, *The People's Republic of China* (New York: Monthly Review Press, 1978), p. 235.
11   *Selected Works of Mao Tsetung* (Beijing: Foreign Languages Press, 1977), V, p. 39.
12   Shi et al., eds., *Hezuohua,* pp. 1006–11.
13   *RMRB,* March 19, 1952.
14   "Wugong cun Geng Changsuo nongye shengchan hezuoshe," in Shi et al., eds., *Hezuohua,* pp. 436–37.
15   Hsiao Ping, "A New Kind of Peasant," *China Reconstructs* 43:1 (January 1964), p. 33.
16   *HKDYZ* (1963), p. 343.
17   *HBRB,* November 28, 1950.
18   *HKDYZ* (1973), p. 315.
19   Shi et al., eds., *Hezuohua,* pp. 433–34; *RMRB,* March 19, 1952.
20   *RMRB,* March 19, 1952; Shi et al., eds., *Hezuohua,* pp. 433–37.
21   *HBRB,* March 15, 1952.
22   *RMRB,* March 19, 1952.
23   Tongjibo.
24   Shi et al., eds., *Hezuohua,* pp. 433, 437.
25   See Kay Johnson, *Women, the Family, and Peasant Revolution in China* (Chicago: University of Chicago Press, 1983).
26   *RMRB,* June 29, 1951; "Evolution of the North China Region," pp. 17–23.
27   See the discussion of agrarian socialism by the editors in *Selected Works of Mao Tsetung,* V, p. 71.
28   Shi et al., eds., *Hezuohua,* pp. 1000–1005.
29   Hu Hua, ed., *Zhongguo shehuizhuyi geming he jianshe shi jiangyi* (Beijing: Zhongguo renmin daxue chuban she, 1985), pp. 98–99. Changzhi prefecture in Shanxi province

was a source of numerous models. One of its villages is depicted in the writings of William Hinton. See *Fanshen: A Documentary of Revolution in a Chinese Village* (New York: Monthly Review Press, 1966).

30 *Selected Works of Mao Tsetung,* V, 71.

31 Shi et al., eds., *Hezuohua,* pp. 1006–11.

32 *HKDYZ* (1963), p. 343.

33 *RMRB,* December 25, 1951; *WGRM,* pp. 57–58.

34 Shi et al., eds., *Hezuohua,* pp. 1006–11.

35 *HKDYZ* (1963), p. 343.

36 Ibid., pp. 158–59.

37 *HBRB,* November 28, 1950.

38 *HKDYZ* (1963), pp. 159–61.

39 NCNA, Baoding, December 20, 1951, in *SCMP,* 241, December 21, 1951; Tong-jibo.

40 *HKDYZ* (1963), pp. 6–9, 19–21; *WGRM,* pp. 62–63.

41 *HBRB,* July 6, 1978.

42 Franz Schurmann, *Ideology and Organization in Communist China* (Berkeley: University of California Press, 1968), p. 318.

43 In her exhaustive study *Chinese Business under Socialism* (Berkeley: University of California Press), Dorothy Solinger dates the control and destruction of private rural trade from 1954. See pp. 168–92.

44 Tongjibo.

45 *RMRB,* March 19, 1952.

46 *HBRB,* January 17, 1952.

47 *RMRB,* March 19, 1952.

48 *HBRB,* March 30, 1952.

49 Ibid., April 2, 1952.

50 The Soviet trip was written up in a series of articles in *HBRB,* September 23–24, 1952. See also the lengthy account in *Jinbu ribao* (Tianjin), November 10, 1952.

51 Liu Binyan, *A Higher Kind of Loyalty* (New York: Pantheon, 1990), p. 38.

6 The Gamble

1 *Zhongguo wenxuejia cidian* (Beijing: Beijing yuyan xueyuan, 1978), pp. 348–49.

2 *HBRB,* June 7, 1952.

3 Ibid.

4 Ibid., July 15–18, 1952.

5 Ibid., March 15, 1952.

6 Ibid., April 30, 1952.

7 Ibid., May 16, 1952.

8 ZZYS, p. 296.

9 *HBRB,* May 22, 1952.

10 *RMRB,* June 7, 1952.

11 *HKDYZ* (1963), pp. 7–8, 133–34, 312–15; *WGRM,* pp. 64–67.

12 Geng Xiufeng, "Guanyu kuoda Geng Changsuo nongye shengchan hezuoshe de yijian: xiang sheng wei nongcun gongzuo bu sheng nong lin ting de baogao," Hebei

sheng Raoyang xian, renmin weiyuanhui danganshi, Wugong dadui, Raoyang Archive, Book 10, document 2, pp. 12–17.

13   *HKDYZ* (1963), pp. 24–25.

14   *HBRB,* September 18, 1952; *Jinbu ribao,* November 1, 1952.

15   Ibid., September 23–25, 1952.

16   Ibid., September 18, 1952.

17   Ibid., September 20, 1952.

18   Ibid., October 9, 1952.

19   The views expressed by Geng and other Hebei delegates were collected in a forty-four-page volume entitled *Women suo kandao de Sulian jiti* (Baoding: Hebei renmin chuban she, 1952).

20   Ibid., pp. 1–2

21   *Jinbu ribao,* November 10, 1952.

22   Tongjibo, 1944–59, Raoyang Archive.

23   *RMRB,* January 7, 1954.

24   *WGRM,* pp. 67–68.

25   Ibid., p. 68; *HKDYZ* (1963), p. 134.

26   *WGRM,* pp. 68–69.

27   *HBRB,* November 12, 1952.

28   *Zhongguo nong bao,* no. 4, February 25, 1953.

29   Shi Jingtang et al., eds., *Zhongguo nongye hezuohua yundong shiliao* (Beijing: Sanlian, 1957), pp. 1006–11.

30   *Selected Works of Mao Tsetung* (Beijing: Foreign Languages Press, 1977), V, p. 135.

31   *WGRM,* p. 72.

32   Ibid., pp. 69–76.

33   *HBRB,* November 23, 1963.

34   Tongjibo.

35   *Zhongguo nong bao,* no. 4, February 25, 1953.

36   *WGRM,* 64–67; *HKDYZ* (1963), pp. 312–25.

37   See Yue Daiyun and Carolyn Grant, *To the Storm: The Odyssey of a Revolutionary Chinese Woman* (Berkeley: University of California Press, 1985), pp. 64–68. Gu Hua, *A Small Town Called Hibiscus* (Beijing: Panda Books, 1983), contains a description of a similar forced labor group of black elements.

38   *Huakai* (1963), pp. 148–49.

39   *Selected Works of Mao Tsetung,* V, pp. 103–11.

40   A series of speeches in summer and fall of 1953 revealed the hardening of Mao's position. Ibid., pp. 103–11, 115–20, 121–29, 131–35, 136–40.

41   "The Price China Has Paid: An Interview with Liu Binyan," *New York Review of Books,* January 19, 1989, p. 31.

42   Mark Selden, *The People's Republic of China* (New York: Monthly Review Press, 1978), p. 281.

43   In September 1953 the state collected 80 percent of planned procurements. In October this fell to just 38 percent. *Zhonghua Renmin Gongheguo jingji da shi ji (1949–1989)* (Beijing: Beijing chubanshe, 1985), pp. 66–68.

44   Deng Liqun, Ma Hong, and Wu Heng, eds., *Dangdai Zhongguo de liangshi,* translated in JPRS-CAR-89-093, August 31, 1989, pp. 24–59.

45 ZZYS, pp. 300–1.
46 *Selected Works of Mao Tsetung,* V, pp. 131–40.
47 Tongjibo.
48 GMRB, December 4, 1953.
49 *Zhongguo qingnian bao,* January 8, 1954.
50 *RMRB,* January 4, 1954.
51 *WGRM,* p. 75.
52 *HKDYZ* (1963), pp. 133–35.
53 *RMRB,* January 4, 1954.
54 *GMRB,* January 3, 1954; *RMRB,* January 7, 1954.
55 *WGRM,* p. 75.
56 *RMRB,* January 4, 1954.

7   On the Soviet Socialist Road

1   *Dagongbao,* July 3, 1954. *Da she,* big units, were fostered in many areas to promote rapid agrarian socialism. Cf. Jean-Luc Domenach, *Aux origines du Grand Bond en Avant* (Paris: Presses de la Fondation Nationale des Sciences Politiques, 1982), p. 164.
2   Lu Guang, "Geng Changsuo nongye shengchan hezuoshe zuzhi she hui ping ku hu canjia shengchan zhong de jige wenti," Hebei sheng Raoyang xian, renmin weiyuanhui danganshi, Wugong dadui, Book 13, document 1, pp. 1–4.
3   "Geng Changsuo she wusi nian shengchan jihua," Hebei sheng Raoyang xian, renmin weiyuanhui danganshi, Wugong dadui, Raoyang Archive, Book 9, document 18, pp. 61–70; *HBRB,* January 11, 1954.
4   Lu Guang, "Geng Changsuo nongye shengchan hezuoshe zai san qu zhong ruhe tuixing 'baogongzhi,'" Hebei sheng Raoyang xian, renmin weiyuanhui danganshi, Wugong dadui, Book 10, document 4, pp. 19–28.
5   Ibid.
6   *RMRB,* January 7, 1954; *HBRB,* February 8, 1954.
7   Wugong dadui, Book 10, document 4.
8   Geng Xiufeng, "Guanyu kuangda Geng Changsuo nongye shengchan hezuoshe de yijian," Hebei sheng Raoyang xian, renmin weiyuanhui danganshi, Wugong dadui, Book 10, document 2, pp. 12–17.
9   *Zhongguo nongye da shi ji, 1949–80* (Beijing: Nongye chuban she, 1982), p. 24; *RMRB,* January 29, 1954.
10 *HBRB,* June 3, 1955.
11 Wugong dadui, Book 9, document 18; *HBRB,* January 7, 1954.
12 Ibid., Book 10, document 4; *RMRB,* August 7, 1954.
13 Ibid., Book 10, document 2.
14 Book 9, document 18, Raoyang Archive.
15 *HBRB,* November 4, 1954.
16 *RMRB,* January 7, 1954.
17 Book 13, document 2, Raoyang Archive.
18 William Hinton, *Iron Oxen: A Documentary of Revolution in Chinese Farming* (New York: Monthly Review, 1970).
19 *Zhongguo xinwen bao,* October 31, 1955.

20   Benedict Stavis, *The Politics of Agricultural Mechanization in China* (Ithaca, N.Y.: Cornell University Press, 1978), pp. 33–36, 58–67.

21   *HBRB,* November 4, 1954, April 25, 1955; *RMRB,* July 31, 1955.

22   Book 9, document 18, Raoyang Archive.

23   *GMRB,* April 2, 1954; *HBRB,* August 11, 1954; *GMRB,* September 30, 1954.

24   *Wenhuibao* (Xianggang), December 8, 1955.

25   *Zhongguo xinwen bao,* October 31, 1955; *HBRB,* October 18, December 8, 1955; *RMRB,* July 12, 1954; *HBRB,* November 4, 1954.

26   *Zhongguo qingnian bao,* September 1, 1954.

27   Book 9, document 18, Raoyang Archive.

28   Hsin-yi Shu, "The Cultural Ecology of the Locust Cult in Traditional China," *Annals of the Association of American Geographers* 59:4 (December 1969), pp. 731–52.

29   *RMRB,* July 5, 1954; *HBRB,* July 12, 1954; *RMRB,* November 4, 1954; *HBRB,* April 14, 1955.

30   *Cooperative Farming in China* (Beijing: Foreign Languages Press, 1954), pp. 13, 25.

31   *JDSJ,* entry of April 21, 1955.

32   Zhongguo geming buowuguan danganshi yanjiu shi, ed., *Dang shi yanjiu ziliao* (Chengdu: Sichuan renmin chuban she, 1982), III, pp. 695–99; Jiang Boying et al., *Deng Zihui zhuan* (Shanghai: Shanghai renmin chuban she, 1986), pp. 317–18.

33   The state purchasing prices given here are those in effect in 1952. Nicholas Lardy, "Agricultural Prices in China," *World Bank Staff Working Papers,* no. 606 (1983), p. 14.

34   Mark Selden, "Cooperation and Conflict: Cooperative and Collective Formation in China's Countryside," in *The Transition to Socialism in China,* ed. Mark Selden and Victor Lippit (Armonk, N.Y.: M. E. Sharpe, 1982), p. 53; *1954 quan guo geti shougongye diaocha ziliao* (Beijing: Sanlian shudian, 1957), p. 52.

35   *RMRB,* July 31, 1955.

36   *Wenhuibao,* March 22, 1955.

37   *HKDYZ* (1963), pp. 213–14.

38   *HBRB,* November 25, 1963.

39   Jiang, *Deng Zihui zhuan,* pp. 306–24.

40   Michael Kau and John Leung, eds., *The Writings of Mao Zedong, 1949–1976* (Armonk, N.Y.: M. E. Sharpe, 1986), I, p. 524.

41   Jiang, *Deng Zihui zhuan,* pp. 306–24.

42   *SCMP,* 1078, June 17, 1955, pp. 27–28; Elizabeth Perry, "Rural Violence in Socialist China," *China Quarterly* 108 (September 1985), pp. 419–26.

43   NCNA, May 14, 1955, in *SCMP,* May 19, 1955.

44   *JDSJ,* March 3, 1955.

45   Ibid., January 30, April 21, 1955; Deng Zihui, "Zai quan guo di san ci nongcun gongzuo huiyi shang de kaimu ci," *Dang shi yanjiu,* no. 1 (February 1980), pp. 2–9; Qiang Yuanjin and Lin Bangguang, "Shilun 1955 nian dang nei guanyu nongye hezuohua wenti de zhenglun," *Dang shi yanjiu,* no. 1 (February 1980), pp. 10–17.

46   *HBRB,* May 19, 1955; Qiang and Lin, "shilun 1955," pp. 12, 13.

47   Jiang, *Deng Zihui zhuan,* p. 8.

48   *HBRB,* July 25, 1955.

49   *RMRB,* July 31, 1955.

8   Against Cooperation

1   *Selected Works of Mao Tsetung* (Beijing: Foreign Languages Press, 1977), V, pp. 201–2; Mark Selden, *The People's Republic of China* (New York: Monthly Review Press, 1978), p. 342; Mark Selden, "Cooperation and the Socialist Transition in China's Countryside," and Edward Friedman, "Maoism, Titoism, Stalinism: Some Origins and Consequences of the Maoist Theory of the Socialist Transition to Communism," in *The Transition to Socialism in China,* ed. Mark Selden and Victor Lippit (Armonk, N.Y.: M. E. Sharpe, 1982), pp. 32–97, 159–214. For a valuable introduction to how precollectivization reforms reduced polarization, see Vivienne Shue, *Peasant China in Transition: The Dynamics of Development toward Socialism, 1949–1956* (Berkeley: University of California Press, 1980).

2   *GMRB,* February 3, 1956.

3   *Chen Boda wenji* (n.p., n.d.), pp. 77–78.

4   Chen Boda was not alone in using those deceptive figures to conceal the 1955 decline in yields. Raoyang Deputy Party Secretary Zhang Yugang quoted identical figures in January 1956, and Geng Changsuo in January 1957 repeated the 1955 claim of 463 catties per mu (*HBRB,* Janury 9, 1956, January 18, 1957). The figures provided by Wugong accountants in 1978 and thereafter show grain yields dropping from 352 catties per mu in 1954 to 283 in 1955.

5   Qiang Yuanjin and Lin Bangguang, "Shilun 1955 nian dang nei guanyu nongye hezuohua wenti de zhenglun," *Dang shi yanjiu,* no. 1 (February 1980), pp. 13–15.

6   *JDSJ,* pp. 153–54; Hu Hua, ed., *Zhongguo shehuizhuyi geming he jianshe shi jiangyi* (Beijing: Zhongguo renmin daxue chuban she, 1985), pp. 134, 143–45, 158.

7   *RMRB,* October 30, 1955, discusses the 1953 decision. See also "Third Conference of Hebei Provincial People's Congress Adopts Five Year Plan," Baoding, October 6, 1955, *SCMP* 1150, October 14, 1955.

8   *GMRB,* February 3, 1956.

9   *HBRB,* January 7, 1956.

10   *RMRB,* September 20, 1956.

11   *RMRB,* June 30, 1956; *Zou zai qianmian di gaojishe* (Baoding: Hebei renmin chuban she, 1956), pp. 49–54.

12   *HBRB,* January 9, 1956.

13   Ibid.

14   *WGRM,* p. 79. There are the inevitable vagaries of the data. A story in *Zhongguo xinwen,* October 30, 1955, gave Li's income as 200 yuan before joining the co-op and 532 yuan in 1954.

15   *WGRM,* pp. 77, 82–83.

16   *HBRB,* June 27, 1956; *RMRB,* June 30, 1956.

17   Kenneth Walker, *Food Grain Procurement and Consumption in China* (Cambridge: Cambridge University Press, 1984), p. 293.

18   *WGRM,* p. 78.

19   Cf. William Hinton's *Shenfan* (New York: Random House, 1983), pp. 105–7, on the issue of bondage to the land. In its initial years the system was not tightly administered. Some urban and intrarural migration continued. From 1960 forward, access to the cities would be vigorously controlled.

20   See Mark Selden, "State, Market, and Sectoral Inequality in Contemporary China," in *States versus Markets in the World System,* ed. Peter Evans et al. (Beverly Hills: Sage, 1985), pp. 275–91; Martin Whyte, "Town and Country in Contemporary China," *Comparative Urban Research* 10:1 (1983), pp. 9–20; and Ajit Kumar Ghose, "The New Development Strategy and Rural Reform in Post Mao China," in *Institutional Reform and Economic Development in the Chinese Countryside,* ed. Keith Griffin (Armonk, N.Y.: M. E. Sharpe, 1984), pp. 255, 272.

21   Nicholas Lardy, "Subsidies," *China Business Review* 10:6 (November–December 1983), pp. 21–23.

22   *HBRB,* June 27, 1956; *RMRB,* June 30, 1956.

23   For the full text of Wugong's collective charter, see *HBRB,* Janury 9, 1956.

24   "Report to the Rural Work Conference of the Central Committee, New Democratic Youth League," July 15, 1954, in Chao Kuo-chun, *Agrarian Policies of Mainland China: A Documentary Study (1949–1956)* (Cambridge: Harvard East Asian Research Center, 1957), p. 74.

25   Selden, *People's Republic of China,* pp. 357–64.

26   *GMRB,* June 25, 1956; Roderick MacFarquhar, *The Origins of the Cultural Revolution,* vol. I, *Contradictions among the People, 1956–1957* (New York: Columbia University Press, 1974), p. 127.

27   *DSSCT,* p. 21.

28   *HBRB,* February 1, 1957.

29   Ibid., August 22, 1957; JPRS DC-401, August 28, 1957.

30   *Geng Changsuo zouguo de lu* (Tianjin: Hebei renmin chuban she, 1966), p. 89; *HKDYZ* (1963), p. 89; *HKDYZ* (1973), p. 71; Hsiao Ping, "A New Kind of Peasant," *China Reconstructs* 43:1 (January 1964), p. 32.

31   *WGRM,* p. 89.

32   Ibid.

33   *RMRB,* January 29, 1957.

34   E. Le Roy Ladurie, "Amenorrhea in Time of Famine," in *The Territory of the Historian* (Chicago: University of Chicago Press, 1979), chap. 15.

35   *RMRB,* January 29, 1957.

36   Ibid., June 30, 1956; *Hengshui ribao,* October 1, 1962.

37   Kenneth Walker, "Grain Self-sufficiency in North China, 1953–1975," *China Quarterly,* no. 71 (September 1977), pp. 558, 568; Walker, "China's Grain Production, 1975–80 and 1952–57: Some Basic Statistics," *China Quarterly,* no. 86 (June 1981), pp. 231, 233.

38   *HBRB,* August 23 and 28, 1957.

39   *RMRB,* February 3, 1957.

40   The consequences of antimarket policies are assessed in Nicholas Lardy, *Agriculture in China's Modern Economic Development* (Cambridge: Cambridge University Press, 1983).

41   MacFarquhar, *Origins of the Cultural Revolution,* I, p. 91.

42   "The contradiction between the proletariat and the bourgeoisie in our country has been basically resolved." "Resolution of the Eighth National Congress of the Communist Party of China," in *Eighth National Congress of the Communist Party of China* (Beijing: Foreign Languages Press, 1956), I, p. 116.

43   *ZZYS,* pp. 260, 276, 286, 298.

44 Nicholas Lardy, *Agricultural Prices in China*, World Bank Staff Working Papers, no. 606 (Washington, D.C., 1983), lists pork prices for 1952 and 1957 as .53 and .73 yuan per kilogram (p. 14); *JDSJ*, p. 187.

45 *RMRB*, March 1, 1957.

46 *WGRM*, p. 87.

47 *RMRB*, September 20, 1956.

48 Cf. "The Direction for Five Hundred Million Peasants," *Socialist Upsurge in China's Countryside* (Beijing: Foreign Languages Press, 1977), pp. 121–34.

49 Shi Jingtang, *Zhongguo nongye hezuohua yundong shiliao* (Beijing: Sanlian shudian, 1957), p. 433.

50 *DSSCT*, p. 78.

51 Frederick Teiwes, *Politics and Purges in China* (White Plains, N.Y.: M. E. Sharpe, 1979), p. 321; *HBRB*, December 3, 1982.

52 *WGRM*, p. 90.

9   A Life and Death Struggle

1 Jean-Luc Domenach, *Aux origines du Grand Bond en Avant* (Paris: Presses de la Fondation Nationale des Sciences Politiques, 1982), pp. 148–63.

2 Hu Hua, ed., *Zhongguo shehuizhuyi geming he jianshe shi jiangyi* (Beijing: Zhongguo renmin daxue chuban she, 1985), pp. 166–71, 174–75, 177; ZZYS, pp. 318, 324.

3 *Hebei huabao,* February 1958.

4 *HKDYZ* (1973), p. 347.

5 Wolfgang Bartke, *Who's Who in the People's Republic of China* (Armonk, N.Y.: M. E. Sharpe, 1981), p. 246; Donald Klein and Anne Clarke, eds., *Biographic Dictionary of Chinese Communism, 1921–1965* (Cambridge: Harvard University Press, 1971), I, pp. 631–32.

6 Duncan Wilson, ed., *Communist China, 1955–1959: Policy Documents, and Analysis* (Cambridge: Harvard University Press, 1965), p. 422.

7 *JDSJ*, p. 212. Cf. Wilson, ed., *Communist China*, p. 424.

8 "Mao Zedong 'da gongshe' sixiang chusuo," *Zhong gong dangshi xueshu taolun* (September 1988), pp. 2–6.

9 *RMRB*, August 11, 1958.

10 Domenach, *Aux origines du Grand Bond en Avant*, p. 298.

11 *JDSJ*, p. 219.

12 NCNA, August 11, 1958, in *SCMP*, August 15, 1958.

13 ZZYS, pp. 324, 325, 328.

14 *Current Background*, no. 520, August 1958; *JDSJ*, pp. 221–22; Roderick MacFarquhar, Timothy Cheek, and Eugene Wu, eds., *The Secret Speeches of Chairman Mao: From the Hundred Flowers to the Great Leap Forward* (Cambridge: Harvard University Press, 1989), p. 427.

15 *Zhongguo nongbao* 19 (1958), p. 1.

16 Wilson, ed., *Communist China*, p. 454.

17 An October 14, 1986, *China Daily* story records the devastating consequences of the building of two water reservoirs in Hebei's Huailai and Miyun counties twenty-five years earlier. In Miyun nearly eighty thousand people were moved to other villages— they were barred from moving to cities—to make way for the reservoirs serving

Beijing. Per capita farmland was cut in half, from 1.6 mu per person to less than 0.9 mu. Both became stagnant grain-deficit counties dependent on the state dole.

18   Roderick MacFarquhar, *The Origins of the Cultural Revolution*, vol. II, *The Great Leap Forward, 1958–1960* (New York: Columbia University Press, 1983), pp. 34, 40.

19   *RMRB*, March 28, 1988, p. 4.

20   *Liu Shaoqi tongzhi zai Hebei* (Baoding: Hebei renmin chuban she, 1958); *JDSJ*, p. 222.

21   Kenneth Walker, "Grain Self-sufficiency in North China, 1953–1975," *China Quarterly*, no. 71 (September 1977), p. 55; Walker, *Food Grain Procurement and Consumption in China* (Cambridge: Cambridge University Press, 1984), pp. 28, 32.

22   *JDSJ*, p. 229. In November 1958 Mao observed that in 1959 Hebei would double grain output on one-fourth the acreage. MacFarquhar, Cheek, and Wu, eds., *Secret Speeches of Chairman Mao*, p. 447.

23   S. V. Utechin, *A Concise Encyclopedia of Russia* (New York: E. P. Dutton, 1964), p. 590. We are indebted to Lu Aiguo for information concerning Villiams.

24   *Miscellany of Mao Tse-tung Thought, 1949–1968* (Washington, D.C.: JPRS, 1974), I, p. 149. By autumn 1958 Mao would observe that his favored model, Xushui, was not alone in "tying up, beating, shouting at, and disputing with company commanders. Therefore each and every one is afraid of debates, which they have turned into struggle meetings, into some kind of punishment." MacFarquhar, Cheek, and Wu, eds., *Secret Speeches of Chairman Mao*, p. 460. Given the pressures for speed and leaping, it is not surprising that lagging behind was a far more serious crime than beating or cursing.

25   Hebei sheng di ming bangongshi, ed., *Hebei sheng qu yan ge zhi* (Shijiazhuang: Hebei kexue jishu chuban she, 1985), p. 326.

26   *HBRB*, September 17, October 23, 1977; *DSSCT*, p. 4.

27   Wei-yi Ma's *Bibliography of Chinese Language Materials on the People's Communes* (Ann Arbor, Mich.: Center for Chinese Studies, 1982), contains no mention of Wugong.

28   *RMRB*, November 2, 1958.

29   *HKDYZ* (1963), p. 355.

30   Mark Selden, *The People's Republic of China* (New York: Monthly Review Press, 1978), p. 80.

31   MacFarquhar, *Origins of the Cultural Revolution*, II, p. 114.

32   *SCMP* (1958), 1877, September 9, 1959.

33   *SCMP* (1958) 1863, pp. 33–34; *Dagong bao*, January 7, 1958; *Extracts from China Mainland Magazines* 140 (1958), pp. 421–46.

34   Dorothy Solinger, *Chinese Business under Socialism* (Berkeley: University of California Press, 1983), pp. 101–7, 196–98, 276. Mao may have begun to doubt the efficacy of eliminating trade and money. In November 1958 he observed that "without a development of the commodity economy, no wages can be paid. A professor visiting the Xushui University found that the monthly wage paid [there] was 15 yuan, and that wasn't even enough to pay for two packs of Qianmen brand cigarettes a day—can you call that superiority [of the socialist system]?" MacFarquhar, Cheek, and Wu, eds., *Secret Speeches of Chairman Mao*, p. 446.

35   Hebei Provincial Government Work Report, JPRS-1877-N (1958).

36   *Zhongguo nong bao*, no. 21 (1958), p. 3.

37   Walker, *Food Grain Procurement*, pp. 133, 136–37. In 1958 Hebei cut back sharply in

area sown to coarse grains and increased the area sown to rice by 600,000 hectares and sweet potatoes by 1,089,000 hectares.

38   Walker, *Food Grain Procurement*, pp. 136–37.
39   ZZYS, pp. 278, 279, 337, 345.
40   Union Research Institute, *The Case of P'eng Teh-huai* (Hong Kong: Union Research Institute, 1968), pp. 393–95, 400. Parris Chang, *Power and Policy in China* (University Park: Pennsylvania State University Press, 1978), pp. 110–21.
41   Hu, ed., *Shehuizhuyi geming*, p. 188.
42   *RMRB*, October 20, 1959.
43   Walker, *Food Grain Procurement*, pp. 146–50.
44   MacFarquhar, *Origins of the Cultural Revolution*, II, p. 126.
45   Walker, *Food Grain Procurement*, pp. 130, 132, 150, 152.
46   Hu, ed., *Shehuizhuyi geming*, p. 190.
47   *Hongqi*, July 16, 1958, translated in *Survey of China Mainland Magazines*, 138, pp. 5–17.
48   Amnesty International, *China: Violations of Human Rights* (London: Amnesty International Publications, 1984), pp. 50–51.
49   *DSSCT*, p. 99.
50   *WGRM*, p. 97.
51   *DSSCT*, p. 184. For general material on beating children, see Margery Wolf, *Revolution Postponed: Rural North China, 1900–1942* (Stanford: Stanford University Press, 1985), chap. 5.
52   *JDSJ*, p. 225.
53   "Jingji gongzuo bixu zhangwo jingji fazhan guilu," in *Dangqian wo guo jingji ruogan wenti* (Beijing: Renmin chuban she, 1980), pp. 7–9.
54   *GMRB*, January 17, 1983, in JPRS 82 (1983), p. 46.
55   "Comment on Liu Shaoqi's Visit to Hunan," *SCMM-supplement* 25, June 29, 1968, p. 13.
56   *WGRM*, p. 102.
57   For a graphic introduction to Great Leap–period rural life in Henan, see the short story by Liu Qingbang, "The Good Luck Bun," in *Roses and Thorns*, ed. Perry Link (Berkeley: University of California Press, 1984), pp. 83–101.
58   Ma Hong and Sun Shangqing, *China's Economic Structure* (Beijing, 1981), translated in JPRS CEA-84-064, p. 151.
59   Cf. MacFarquhar, *Origins of the Cultural Revolution*, II, p. 322.
60   Cf. Roy Medvedev, *The October Revolution* (1979; New York: Columbia University Press, 1985), pp. xxv, xxvi.
61   An inhabitant of a Xinyang village reported at that time, "I just came back from our native village. . . . Everyone in my family has starved to death . . . only my aunt remains. Her son died too. . . . How can she go on living? . . . In the middle of one night, a pig so starved that it was nothing but skin and bones rushed into her courtyard. She shut the door at once. Then she beat the hunger dazed pig to death. She skinned the pig during the night and buried it. She got up in the middle of the night, dug up the pig and cooked a piece of it to eat. She did not give any of it to her five-year-old son to eat for fear that he would talk about it. Once they found out, those who were still alive in the village would come rushing in and threaten to kill her. They

would beat her to bring out the pig. She looked at her son crying that he was hungry! Mama, I'm hungry. Mama! This went on until he died." "Bai Hua Speaks His Mind in Hong Kong," *Dongzhang,* nos. 45 and 46 (December 1987, January 1988), translated in JPRS-CAR-88-009, March 4, 1988, p. 9.

62   Basil Ashton et al., "Famine in China, 1958–61," *Population and Development Review* 10:4 (December 1984), pp. 613–45; John Aird, "The Preliminary Results of China's 1982 Census," *China Quarterly,* no. 96 (December 1983), pp. 613–40. In the 1980s the Chinese press gave "more than twenty million" as the death toll.

63   "The Secret of the Underground Palace in Tianjin," *Wei Dong,* April 2, 1967. This Red Guard newspaper was published in Tianjin.

10   The State of the Revolution

1   *GMRB,* January 17, 1983, in JPRS 82 (1983), p. 46.

2   *RMRB,* December 7, 1963.

3   Hu Hua, ed., *Zhongguo shehuizhuyi geming he jianshe shi jiangyi* (Beijing: Zhongguo renmin daxue chuban she, 1985), pp. 197, 203.

4   Jiang Boying et al., *Deng Zihui zhuan* (Shanghai: Shanghai renmin chuban she, 1986), p. 343.

5   During Mao's Cultural Revolution this story of Geng Changsuo's early opposition to "capitalistic" reformers won Geng political points. We spoke to Boss Geng in 1984 when the fundamentalist line was in official disrepute. Then in his eighties, with the reform line ascendant, he still insistently, even pugnaciously, embraced this account of his opposition to the new economic policies at the Beijing Hotel conference.

6   The reconstruction of grain statistics by Kenneth Walker produces generally higher output figures for 1952–58. *Food Grain Procurement and Consumption in China* (Cambridge: Cambridge University Press, 1984), pp. 136, 150.

7   Hu, ed., *Shehuizhuyi geming,* p. 205; ZZYS, pp. 293, 295, 296.

8   Jiang Boying et al., "Deng Zihui," in Hu Hua, ed., *Zhong gong dang shi renwu zhuan* (Hanchang: Jiangxi renmin chuban she, 1983), VII, p. 374.

9   Yue Daiyun describes the system of special stores available for leading intellectuals who ranked toward the lower end of the hierarchy. Yue Daiyun and Carolyn Wakeman, *To the Storm: The Odyssey of a Revolutionary Chinese Woman* (Berkeley: University of California Press, 1985), pp. 94–95. The system is also described in Lowell Dittmer, *China's Continuous Revolution* (Berkeley: University of California Press, 1989), pp. 58–61.

Conclusion

1   For a recent scholarly effort to grapple with the issue of totalitarianism in China, see Tang Tsou, *The Cultural Revolution and Post-Mao Reforms* (Chicago: University of Chicago Press, 1986).

2   For contrasting approaches to these alternative Leninist paths, see Dorothy Solinger, ed., *Three Visions of Chinese Socialism* (Boulder, Colo.: Westview Press, 1984), and Alec Nove, *The Economics of Feasible Socialism* (London: George Allen and Unwin, 1983).

3   Andrew Nathan, "A Factionalism Model for CCP Politics," *China Quarterly*, no. 53 (1973); Tsou, *Cultural Revolution and Post-Mao Reforms*, chap. 3.

4   On cultural continuity, see Richard Madsen, *Morality and Power in a Chinese Village* (Berkeley: University of California Press, 1984), and Margery Wolf, *Revolution Postponed: Rural North China, 1900–1942* (Stanford: Stanford University Press, 1985).

5   Prasenjit Duara, *Culture, Power, and the State: Rural North China, 1900–1942* (Stanford: Stanford University Press, 1988).

6   The debate is represented in the conflicting approaches to revolution of George Rudé and E. P. Thompson, on the crowd side, and Gustave Le Bon and Sigmund Freud, on the mob side. Cf. Rudé, *The Crowd in the French Revolution* (Oxford: Clarendon Press, 1959), and *Gustave Le Bon: The Man and His Works* (Indianapolis: Liberty Press, 1979).

7   For a historical approach that also shows how different situations and ecological environments can lead to different popular responses, see Elizabeth Perry, *Rebels and Revolutionaries in North China, 1845–1945* (Stanford: Stanford University Press, 1980).

8   Similar vengefulness has been described in other socialist systems. "This reduction to the lowest common denominator brought out in peoples' souls the worst and lowest instincts and reactions. . . . The rebellious slave does free himself for a moment but his main desire is revenge, which is rarely constructive. The rebellious slave will at best look for a better tsar." Adam Michnik, *Letters from Prison* (Berkeley: University of California Press, 1985), pp. 45, 51.

9   James Scott, *The Moral Economy of the Peasant* (New Haven: Yale University Press, 1976); Samuel Popkin, *The Rational Peasant* (Berkeley: University of California Press, 1979).

10   For scholarly work highlighting regional diversity, see Steven J. Levine, *Anvil of Victory: The Communist Revolution in Manchuria, 1945–1948* (New York: Columbia University Press, 1987). As with Levine's book, regional studies stop or start around the establishment of the People's Republic. See, for example, Yung-fa Chen, *Making Revolution: The Communist Movement in Eastern and Central China, 1937–1945* (Berkeley: University of California Press, 1986).

11   Kang Chao, *Man and Land in Chinese History: An Economic Analysis* (Stanford: Stanford University Press, 1986), p. 103.

12   *RMRB*, February 26, 1985, p. 6.

13   Jean-Luc Domenach, *Aux origines du Grand Bond en Avant* (Paris: Presses de la Fondation Nationale des Sciences Politique, 1982).

14   The many works on famine of economist Amartya Sen show that political factors, not crop failures, are decisive. See, for example, "How Is India Doing?" in *Social and Economic Development in India: A Reassessment*, ed. Dilip Basu and Richard Sisson (New Delhi: Sage, 1986), pp. 28–42, and *Poverty and Famines: An Essay on Entitlement and Deprivation* (Oxford: Oxford University Press, 1981).

15   Robert Conquest, *Harvest of Sorrow* (Oxford: Oxford University Press, 1986).

16   Lowell Dittmer, *China's Continuous Revolution* (Berkeley: University of California Press, 1989), calls China's Leninist state neofeudal (pp. 58, 79, 245). Kenneth Jowett, *The Leninist Response to National Dependency* (Berkeley: University of California Institute of International Studies, 1978), was the first systematic approach to this

traditionalist reality. Andrew Walder, *Communist Neo-Traditionalism: Work and Authority in Chinese Industry* (Berkeley: University of California Press, 1986), has creatively applied this traditionalist approach to a study of Chinese factories. The metaphor of feudalism to analyze China's socialist-state reality was applied as early as 1957 by student leader Lin Xiling. See Dennis Doolin, ed., *Communist China: The Politics of Student Opposition* (Stanford: Hoover Institution, 1964). Tsou, *Cultural Revolution and Post-Mao Reforms,* chap. 5, analyzes what he terms feudal totalitarianism.

17   Lu Xun, *Wild Grass* (Beijing: Foreign Languages Press, 1974), p. 33.

INDEX

Agrarian Reform Law, 93, 94, 97
Agriculture, xiv–xv, xxi, xxiii, 4; collectiv
  ization, xvii–xviii, xxi, 54, 122–24,
  134, 140, 148, 154–55, 169–70, 183,
  185–252, 277–79, 281; deep plowing
  campaign, 228–29; early *1950s*, 115–
  32, 136–59, 188; early to mid-
  twentieth century, 9, 12–14, 15–19,
  24, 41–43, 52, 53, 54–58, 61–79, 82;
  land-pooling group, 54–58, 61–79;
  late *1950s*–early *1960s*, 214–66; mechanization of, 140, 142, 157–58, 160,
  166–71, 226; mid-eighteenth century,
  1–5, 8; mid-*1950s*, 160–84, 185–213,
  278–79; mutual-aid teams, 122–24,
  137, 138, 143, 146, 172, 183, 186;
  and *1956* flood, 198–203; *1956–57* reforms, 203–6; *1960–61* reforms, 252–
  66; post-Japanese war, 80, 91–92, 93,
  112–13; Soviet model, 54–55, 56, 69,
  113, 123, 130–32, 137, 140–43, 158,
  164, 165–85, 193, 203, 222, 281,
  282; transition from cooperation to
  collectivization, 185–91; Wugong cooperative, 54–58, 61–79, 83, 90–91,
  94–109, 112, 115–84. *See also* Collectivization; Communes; Cooperation;
  Irrigation; *specific crops*
Ai Qing, 106
Alcohol, 13, 114, 128
Anguo, 8, 47–48, 49, 72, 217
Anhui province, 243, 254
Animals, 3, 8–9, 12, 52, 60, 62, 65, 70,
  75, 97, 102, 107, 141, 144, 146, 162,
  171, 172, 184, 189, 191, 204, 228,
  231, 232, 234, 242, 252
Anping county, xiv, 11, 30, 182
Anti-Americanism, xx, 140–41

Anti-Japanese war, xxii, 27, 29–51, 52,
  54, 57, 62, 65, 72, 80, 82, 85, 112,
  274. *See also* Resistance, anti-Japanese
Antimarket policies, xxii, xxiii, 126–29,
  134, 153–55, 159, 169, 171, 175–76,
  202, 203, 210, 229, 230, 248, 253,
  256, 260, 262, 266, 270, 271, 278
Anti-rightist movement (*1957–58*), 209–
  13, 215, 222, 230, 273, 280, 284
Arson, 151
Asian-Pacific Theater (World War II), 52,
  57
Association, 26, 27, 36, 39, 82, 270

Bai Qingcai, 14–15
Baoding, xiv, 13, 16, 30, 38, 47, 72, 112,
  113, 116, 123, 124, 128, 130, 134,
  139–40, 148, 171, 199, 214, 215,
  217–18, 247, 249
Baoding prefecture, 158, 171, 185, 217–
  18, 232
Baotou, 220
Beijing, xiv, xvi, 8, 9, 16, 19, 30, 72, 105,
  111, 112, 113, 118–19, 120, 122,
  128, 139, 148, 157, 178, 179, 203,
  216, 217, 223, 231, 244, 246, 248
Beijing Screenwriters Institute, 133–34
Bethune, Norman, 47
Black markets, 128, 174, 175, 201, 207–
  8, 217, 242
Bo Yibo, 122, 123
"Boundless Earth," 177–78
Boxer Rebellion, 9, 277
Brigades, 224
Buddhism, 7, 14, 20, 234, 235, 238
Burial mounds, transfer of, 235–37

Cannibalism, 5

HN 733.5 .F75 1991
Chinese village, socialist
state / Edward Friedman